Advanced Game Design

Advanced Game Design

A Systems Approach

Michael Sellers

♦♦ Addison-Wesley

Boston • Columbus • Indianapolis • New York • San Francisco
Amsterdam • Cape Town • Dubai • London • Madrid • Milan
Munich • Paris • Montreal • Toronto • Delhi • Mexico City
São Paulo • Sidney • Hong Kong • Seoul • Singapore • Taipei • Tokyo

Dedicated to all those creating and becoming the next generation of game designers.

Contents at a Glance

Contents

ACKNOWLEDGMENTS

Any book is a journey in the writing. I would like to thank all of my family members, friends, and colleagues who have over the years helped me sharpen my thoughts on game design and who urged me, sometimes forcefully, to take this journey. In particular, I'd like to thank Ted Castronova and Jeremy Gibson Bond for their continuous support; my students in the Game Design program at Indiana University for playtesting this book with me; and most of all my wife, Jo Anna, for her unwavering love, support, and inspiration across many years and adventures.

I'd also like to thank Kees Luyendijk for taking on the role of illustrator and early reader for this book, while also being a graduate student! I am grateful, too, to Laura Lewin, Chris Zahn, and the rest of the editing team at Pearson Education for their guidance and support in making this book a reality, and to Daniel Cook and Ellen Guon Beeman for being such generous, thoughtful, and incisive technical reviewers. This book could not have happened without the hard work of each of these individuals.

ABOUT THE AUTHOR

Michael Sellers is Director of the Game Design program and a Professor of Practice at Indiana University in Bloomington, Indiana.

Sellers has worked as a professional game designer since 1994, with a focus on designing social, mobile, and massively multiplayer online games (MMOs). He has started and run three successful game studios and has also worked for notable game developers such as 3DO, Electronic Arts, Kabam, and Rumble Entertainment as a lead designer, executive producer, general manager, and creative director.

His first commercial game was the award-winning *Meridian 59*, the first 3D MMO, released in 1996. He was also the lead designer on *The Sims 2*, *Ultima Online*, *Holiday Village*, *Blastron*, and *Realm of the Mad God*, among other games.

In addition to his work in games, Sellers has conducted and published original research in artificial intelligence. His AI research, partly funded by the U.S. Defense Advanced Research Projects Agency (DARPA), focuses on "social artificial intelligence"—creating agents that behave plausibly in social situations. As part of this effort, Sellers has published groundbreaking work on enabling artificially intelligent agents to learn, form social relationships, and have and express emotions based on a unifying psychological architecture.

Sellers has a BS in cognitive science. In addition to working on games and AI, he has worked as a software engineer, user interface designer, RPG miniatures sculptor, and briefly as a circus roustabout and movie extra.

He has a Bacon number of 2 and hopes someday to have an Erdos number.

INTRODUCTION

"One of the most difficult tasks people can perform, however much others may despise it, is the invention of good games. And it cannot be done by those out of touch with their instinctive values."

—Carl Jung (Van Der Post 1977)

A Combined Approach to Game Design

This book is an unusual guide to game design. In it you will learn deep theory, practice based on game design principles, and tested industry practice. All of these are informed by understanding and applying systems thinking. As you will see, game design and systems thinking complement each other in surprising and informative ways. Combining these together will help you become a better game designer and to see the world in illuminating new ways.

Where This Book Came From

I have been working as a professional game designer since 1994, when my brother and I formed our first company, Archetype Interactive. Long before that, I'd been designing games as a hobby, since I first ran into an old hexes-and-counters game about Assyrian chariot warfare in 1972. In my career in games, I've had the opportunity to lead multiple ground-breaking projects, including *Meridian 59*, the first 3D massively multiplayer online game, *The Sims 2*, and *Dynemotion*, an advanced artificial intelligence package for use in military training and games, as well as many other games, large and small.

Throughout this time, while in school and then working as a software engineer, user interface designer, and then game designer, I have been fascinated by the ideas of systems, emergence, and moving beyond older models of linear, centralized control. Games seem to me to be unique in their ability to allow us to create and interact with systems, to really get to know what systems are and how they operate. If there is real magic in the world, it resides in how systems operate, from how atoms are formed to how fireflies synchronize their flashing and how economies set prices with no one to tell them what to do.

Taking a systems approach to game design isn't easy—it's difficult to understand and express, much less to nail down in a specific design. But I have found that this approach works extremely well for creating living worlds—systems—in which players can immerse themselves. In my experience as a game designer, it has been vital to maintain a childlike sense of awe and wonder side-by-side with a clear-eyed practical knowledge of how products get made. Viewing games as systems, seeing both the whole and the individual parts at the same time, has enabled me to do this. Learning how to articulate and use this combined sense of wonder and practicality in game design and in life is the genesis of this book.

What This Book Is and Isn't About

This book is intended to be a text for advanced game design. It can be used as part of a university-level course or read on its own. This book offers a rigorous, broad, and in-depth examination of game design grounded in the language of systems thinking. It is intended to be foundational in terms of "digging down to the foundations" but not in terms of being an easy, light introductory book. If you're just getting started with game design, this may be an arduous journey. However, if you want to learn a combination of systemic game design theory and industry-tested design practices based on them, this book is for you.

More specifically, this isn't a book focused on level design, puzzle design, modifying existing games, creating animated sprites, crafting dialog trees, or similar topics. Instead, it's mainly focused on creating all those things we informally call systems—combat systems, quest systems, guild systems, trading systems, chat systems, magic systems, and so on—informed by a deeper understanding of what systems actually *are* and what it means to design systemic games.

To get to that deeper understanding, we will peek into many other fields along the way, including astronomy, particle physics, chemistry, psychology, sociology, history, and economics. These may at first seem disconnected from (or even an impediment to!) learning about systems and game design, but in fact being comfortable borrowing from a multitude of disciplines is an important part of being a successful game designer. As a game designer, you will need to learn to cast a wide mental and educational net and to find knowledge and principles in widely varying fields of study that you can use to inform and improve your designs.

This book is also about what it means to be a professional game designer. By reading this book, you'll learn the principles and methods of game design, and you'll also learn what it's like to work in a relentlessly dynamic industry. You'll also learn about being part of effective, diverse creative teams and the process of designing and developing successful games.

Goals of This Book

Reading this book and applying the principles in it will give you a greater appreciation for how systems and games reveal and illuminate each other. Ultimately, the goal is for you to be able to build better games and better game systems, though this goes far beyond a practical, industrial goal.

Games and systems can be seen as lights shining on each other or as mutual lenses, each helping to focus the image of the other. As such, systems and games form two parts of an overall system (see Figure I.1). As you will see, games and systems are intimately intertwined. In the language of systems thinking, they are structurally coupled, forming two parts of an even larger system, much as do a horse and rider or a game and player. The "game+player" system is one you will see often throughout this book.

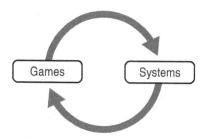

Figure I.1 Games and systems inform each other and together form a larger system

In terms of principles and theory, the goal for this book is to help you come to a greater under-standing of systems and what it means to think in systems. This includes contextual thinking and the ability to see how disparate elements interact to create something entirely new and often surprising. Systems thinking itself is a broad topic, but game design provides a unique viewpoint for understanding it—and vice versa.

On the more practical side, the first goal of this book is to help you learn about analyzing exist-ing game designs within the framework of systems thinking, recognizing, and teasing out the systems hiding in plain sight within them. You will learn how systems within a game interact and whether they work effectively in context: do they create the framework for the kind of experience the designer intended? To answer this, you need to know how to move between different levels of organization in games. As a game designer, you will learn to see the entire game, the systems that make it up, and the individual parts and their relationships. Figure I.2 shows a diagrammatic version of this. You will see more detail about this process throughout the book, both in terms of systems in general and games in particular.

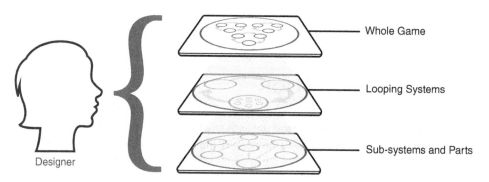

Figure I.2 A game designer is able to shift vision and focus between the whole, the loops, and the parts. Learning to see games and game design this way is a primary purpose of this book

In addition to recognizing games as systems, the next goal of this book is to help you create your own game designs that intentionally and explicitly link the experience you want to create with the underlying structures and processes in the game. Being a successful game designer involves practicing pulling ideas for games out of your head and shaping them into reality that others can experience. This often feels like dragging a game idea kicking and screaming out of the fuzzy shadows where it never has to be fully defined and into the bright, unforgiving light where all its specific parts and behaviors have to be thoroughly catalogued and tested. This is never easy, and it is not a one-time exercise: with each game, you as the designer will interact with the game, the player, and the game+player system in your own interactive loop to bring to life the game experience you want to create. A graphical depiction of this is shown in Figure I.3. You will see this diagram again in Chapter 4, "Interactivity and Fun," and you will see many more systemic looping diagrams like this throughout the book. This figure and the preceding two figures give you the basic idea of this book in just a few pictures.

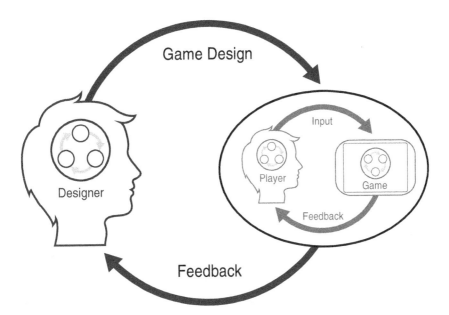

Figure I.3 The designer's loop, showing the system of the designer interacting with the player and the game as a subsystem. See Chapters 4 and 7, "Creating Game Loops," for more details

A big part of defining and designing a game is working as part of a team that develops the design and brings it to life. This next goal is to help you understand the roles and processes involved in game design as part of game development. This knowledge is not idealized theory but is based on decades spent on actual game teams doing the hard work—along with some recent data-driven insights into why some teams and games are successful, while others are not.

To return to the first goal as also the last, the deepest aspiration for me in writing this book is that you will not only be equipped to create intentional, systemic game designs, but that you will generalize this knowledge of systems into your daily life. Systems are all around us, and, as you will see, understanding them is becoming increasingly important.

To clarify all of this, the hypothesis at the core of this book has three parts:

- **Game design is system design.** Games and game design provide a unique perspective on systems thinking. There is no more effective way to truly internalize how to think in systems than to explore systems in games and to design engaging games. Understanding systems enables you to create better games, and creating better games deepens your understanding of systems. They are mutual lenses, each focusing and enhancing the comprehension of the other.

- **A detailed grasp of systemic game design will be informed by—and will itself inform—your ability to think in systems.** Game design today is still more exploration or ad hoc practice than established theory. Having a deeper knowledge of how to design and build games as systems will provide needed grounding in design principles that extend beyond games. These principles will help you create better, more engaging games and will increase your overall understanding of systems thinking. Being familiar with each will help you excel in both.

- **Systems thinking is as important for the 21st century as basic literacy was for the 20th century.** In the early decades of the 20th century, you could get by in many parts of the Western world without knowing how to read and write. As time went on, that ability was more and more assumed, to the point that it became difficult to navigate daily life without being literate.

  In the same way, knowing how to recognize, analyze, and create systems is a crucial skill for the 21st century. Many people get by (for now) without this ability, but as time goes on, systems thinking will be like reading and writing: it will be a way of thinking that's so natural and so central to how you navigate the world that you won't even think about it anymore. Those who continue to think in limited, linear, reductionist terms will be left behind, unable to react effectively to the ever-more-rapid interrelated changes happening in the world around them. You need to be able to see the world as systems and to intentionally use them in your game designs as well. Building this up in your game design skill will help you more and more as our world becomes ever more interconnected and interactive.

How to Read This Book

There are a couple different ways to read this book and gain something from it. The first is to read the chapters in order, focusing first on foundational theory, and then game design principles, and finally the practical elements. Doing this may seem like going the long way around, but it will provide the most effective grounding to support and contextualize the practical aspects of game design. Reading the first theory-heavy portion of the book is like digging the foundation for a tall building: going down instead of up may seem like moving in the wrong direction, but doing so ensures that the whole structure won't topple over later on. In the same way, first gaining a better understanding of systems themselves before applying them to games will help you create better and more successful games later on. (You can then return to the systems portion of the book again and see how much better you understand systems by viewing them through the lens of what you have learned about game design.)

If reading all that theory before getting to the actual game design parts of a game design book seems unnecessary to you, you can bounce back and forth between theory, principles, and practical aspects in the three different parts of the book. I suggest getting a bit of grounding in systems and how they work, but you may then want to go and read some of the chapters on how they are applied in game design and go back and forth. At some point you will hopefully have enough theory to spend more time on the practical side without having missed anything significant. The systems thinking aspects will help support and improve your design efforts, but it is, after all, on the practical side that things actually get done.

A Quick Tour

This book is organized into three parts: Part I, "Foundations," Part II, "Principles," and Part III, "Practice." As mentioned earlier above, each builds on and references the information in the section before it. Part I is the most theoretical, examining systems, games, and interactivity. Part II builds on and applies the foundational elements to designing systems in games and designing games as systems. Finally, Part III talks about what it takes to actually design, build, and test a game in the real world.

This three-part structure forms a loop, with the third practical part informing your understanding of the theory in the first part. In this way, this book forms a system, as shown in Figure I.4. This idea of parts affecting each other to form loops and create a coherent whole is the heart of this book, and one with which you will become more familiar as you read it.

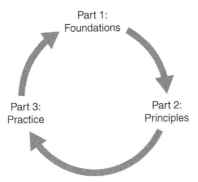

Figure I.4 Foundations, principles, and practice are parts in this book and parts in a larger system of game design

Chapter Overviews

Chapter 1, "Foundations of Systems," is the beginning of Part I. This chapter outlines different ways of seeing the world. It includes a brief history of how systems thinking has evolved over the past few centuries. It also looks at why systems thinking is so important and takes a bit of a strange journey from Theseus' ship down to the heart of the atom (and back) to illustrate just how pervasive, if also often invisible, systems are in the world. That may sound pretty abstract, but it relates directly to a deeper comprehension of systems, game design, and how players experience games in ways you may not expect.

Chapter 2, "Defining Systems," dives into systems themselves in more detail, providing definitions of structures and functions that are used throughout the rest of the book. This is where you first see the hierarchical structure of parts, loops, and wholes that is common to all systems and that you will use in designing systemic games. Through all of this, you become familiar with a diverse array of examples, such as the problems with cobras, the behavior of snowballs and equilibria, how boundaries form between things, and the hard-to-pin-down and sometimes mind-bending nature of emergence. This will lead us into an exploration of meaning and how it arises in the world and (of course) in games. By this time, you will likely start seeing systems everywhere and will be ready to look at games from this point of view.

Chapter 3, "Foundations of Games and Game Design," answers some basic but important questions like What's a game? You will see that sometimes the answers to such questions aren't all that clear-cut, and you will begin to understand the limits of current game design theory. You will also gain a better understanding of how game design has been done in the past and how it has moved from tacit, ad hoc empirical design to explicit, theory-based, systemic design.

Chapter 4, "Interactivity and Fun," takes on the important and slippery topic of interactivity, which will add to both your theoretical and practical game design scaffolding. This includes not only different kinds of interactivity but how the player builds a mental model of the game and how you as the designer interact with the player and the game. In the process, this chapter even attacks the nettlesome question of defining *fun*. As a designer, you need to think about what *fun* means in terms of why you design games as you do.

Chapter 5, "Working as a Systemic Game Designer," opens Part II. Having flown far off into theoretical space in Part I, this section orbits back toward solid ground. Everything you learned about systems in Part I is now applied to game design and creating the same kinds of structures in games as are found in systems generally. As part of this, you will begin to find your strengths as a designer—and those places where you need to seek help from others.

Chapter 6, "Designing the Whole Experience," covers the highest levels of systemic design and the creation of your game concept. This includes the process of doing blue-sky design and capturing your ideas in a single sentence and a brief document.

Chapter 7, "Creating Game Loops," returns to the ideas of systemic loops and applying them to game design. about it discusses the various loops inherent in any game—the game's internal loop, the player's mental loop, the interactive loop between them, and your loop as the designer viewing the game+player system from the outside. This chapter also details some of the common kinds of loops in game systems, as well as tools for designing and documenting them.

Chapter 8, "Defining Game Parts," gets down to the nuts-and-bolts of creating any game system. You have to have a clear and detailed understanding of the parts in any game system, right down to their defining attributes and behaviors—and how to use them to construct the game loops discussed in the Chapter 7.

Chapter 9, "Game Balance Methods," opens Part III. This final section of the book focuses on practical elements of designing and building games, and this is the first of two chapters focused on game balance. This chapter covers different methods, such as designer-based, player-based, analytic, and mathematical modeling that can all be applied to balancing the parts and loops in a game. This chapter also introduces the concepts of transitive and intransitive systems, and how they are each most effectively balanced.

Chapter 10, "Game Balance Practice," is the second half of the game balance discussion. Using the methods discussed in Chapter 9, you learn how to balance systems for effective progression and for economic balance, as well as how to balance your game based on actual player behavior.

Chapter 11, "Working as a Team," zooms out from game design itself to the process of being part of a successful development team. There are definite best practices, shown both quantitatively and as best practices learned over decades of experience, that will help you as a game designer. This chapter also outlines the different roles needed on any development team so that you can better appreciate all the different human parts that make up any game development system.

Chapter 12, "Making Your Game Real," brings together all the foundations, principles, and practical points and adds some of the most important aspects of actually making a game. To develop a game, you have to be able to communicate your ideas effectively. You also have to be able to quickly build prototypes and effectively playtest the game to move it closer to the experience you are trying to create for the player. Understanding these aspects of development as well as the phases that any full game development project goes through will help you not just talk about or design your game but actually build it and see others play it. That is the ultimate goal for any game designer.

Summary

This book presents a combination of foundational theory, systematic principles, and practical process as an approach to game design. By understanding in detail how systems operate, you will learn in this book how to apply principles of systems thinking to make better games. You will also come to see systems at work throughout the world and use your understanding to create similar systems in your game designs. The result will increase your ability to make use of both these principles and industry-tested methods to create games that are systemic, creative, and engaging.

CHAPTER 1

FOUNDATIONS OF SYSTEMS

Having a clear idea of what systems are is vital to building systemic games. In this chapter we dig deep for our foundations by examining different ways of seeing and thinking about the world and reviewing a quick history of systems and systems thinking. This will lead you to a better understanding of the importance of systems thinking in general as well as in game design.

Finally, we go on a strange journey from ships to water to the heart of the atom, all to more clearly understand what systems, things, and games actually are.

Ways of Seeing and Thinking

Most of us rarely think about *how* we think. This is a process called *metacognition*—thinking about thinking—and one that is important for a game designer. You need to be able to think about how players think and about your own thought processes. As a game designer, you must be able to understand the habits and limitations related to how people see and think about the world. While this book isn't primarily about perceptual or cognitive psychology, it does cover some aspects of those areas r.

There are several different ways of thinking that we will discuss. To start, we will look at a cross-cultural test known as the "Michigan Fish Test," after work done by Dr. Richard Nesbitt and Takahiko Masuda with both American and Japanese students (Nisbett 2003).

Take a quick look—no more than a few seconds—at the image in Figure 1.1. What do you see? Look away from the picture for a moment and quickly write down what you saw or close your eyes and say it out loud.

Now go back to the image and compare it to your description. Did you say anything about the snail or the frog? Did you say something about the three big fish, or all five of them? How about the plants and rocks; did you include those in your description? How do you think others from different cultures might describe this scene differently?

Figure 1.1 Nisbett's Michigan Fish Test. (Used with permission)

In Nisbett and Masuda's study, students were shown this picture of an aquarium scene for five seconds and asked to describe what they saw. Most American students described the three big fish, while most Japanese students described a more holistic scene. The students were then shown variations on the original picture. The Americans were quick to recognize the three big fish (or that new ones were in place if the fish had changed), but they often missed the plants, frog, snail, and smaller fish. The Japanese students were more adept at noticing changes in the overall scene, while they more often missed changes to the three biggest fish. In other words, students from these different cultures literally saw and thought about the same image differently.

As a result of this and other studies, Nesbitt found that Americans (and those from the Western tradition of thought in general) tend to be more reductive: they *reduced* the scene to its individual parts, ignoring the relationships between them. By contrast, they found that those from East Asian cultures were more likely to see the aggregate image and to be less focused on the individual pieces.

The Michigan Fish Test highlights the fact that different people have different ways of thinking, and most of us believe that "our" way is the way that *everyone* thinks—which clearly isn't the case. To be able to think effectively in systems and to use them in game design, we need to understand some of the different ways that people think.

Phenomenological Thinking

For millennia, especially in the Western tradition, people had few unifying theories in their thinking. The world was just as it was experienced, with separate, often unpredictable phenomena explained either via mysticism, philosophy, Aristotelian logic, or simple observation.[1] Even in this last case, if the observations resulted in any models that combined different phenomena together, they were made without the requirement of any underlying relationship or driving principle; things simply were as they were.

A major example of this is the geocentric view of the universe, with Earth at the stationary center and the stars, planets, Moon, and Sun all wheeling in orbit around us. This view has been around since at least the ancient Babylonians and survived on a mixture of observation (the heavens do appear to sweep past day and night) and philosophy (of course we are at the center of everything!). Over time, astronomers made elaborate models to account for increasingly precise and sometimes troublesome observations, such as when planets appear to move *backward* in their orbits, which is called *retrograde motion*. We know now that this apparent motion occurs because the faster-moving Earth is passing more slowly orbiting outer planets, but if your model is that everything orbits around the Earth, this is a very difficult observation to explain.

---

1. It is in this sense that the term *phenomenological thinking* is used here, rather than in the sense used by later philosophers such as Kant, Hegel, or Husserl, in terms of the apprehension of the world and the resulting study of consciousness of the world.

The difficulty in accounting for increasingly problematic observations eventually led to more deterministic, logical, and eventually systemic thinking—as you will see. The key point here is that for thousands of years, and in some ways still today, people have approached the world via a mixture of simple observation and reasoning: because the Sun passes overhead each day, it must orbit the Earth; or because it's snowing today, the climate must not be warming; or because our company made money last year, we should reapply the same strategy with more effort. As a way of viewing the world, this leaves an individual with a limited understanding and a great probability of being affected, often dramatically, by underlying systems at work.

Compare, for example, the person who thinks, "Oh, the tide has gone far out very quickly, and I can take this opportunity to search the exposed beach" versus someone who understands the underlying systemic principles and that such a rapid retreat of the water is an indicator of a devastating incoming tsunami. Or the person who thinks, "Wow, mortgages are suddenly really easy to get; I can take this opportunity to get a loan for a much bigger house" versus someone who can see the systems at work that lead to a credit crunch and devastating financial meltdown. Seeing the world as isolated events that are generally unrelated to each other or any deeper systems—phenomenological thinking—is insufficient for us today. Fortunately, we have better tools.

Reductionist Thinking and Newton's Legacy

We will explore Isaac Newton's key role in the rise of systems thinking shortly. For now, it's sufficient to say that he was an important part of the change from limited observational and phenomenological thinking to scientific, model-based, but also reductionist thinking about the world.

The French philosopher René Descartes championed this view in his 1637 masterwork *Discourse on Method* (Descartes 1637/2001). His central idea was that the universe and everything in it could be seen as great machines that could be taken apart—*reduced*—to their component parts to figure out how they work. In this view, any phenomenon, no matter how complex, could in principle be seen as merely the sum of its parts, each part contributing its function to the whole, as, Descartes said, "a clock composed only of wheels and weights can number the hours and measure time more exactly than we with all our skill."

While Newton built on these ideas of a universe that could be discovered and analyzed via reductionism as championed by Descartes and others, he was the first to bring Descartes' idea of the universe as a clockwork mechanism out of the realm of philosophy and into a unified view in mathematics and science.

The Scientific Method

The scientific method, briefly stated, involves two main parts:

- First, observing something, making a hypothesis (informed guess) about what might happen next under certain conditions (based on what's underlying what's observed), and then testing the hypothesis to see if it was correct

- Then doing this over and over with a variety of observations and hypotheses

These hypotheses and observations typically require holding all conditions constant except for one and determining the effect of that changing condition. This is a form of analysis, of breaking something down into simpler bits, where each part or condition is examined in turn. The idea that the universe can be discovered and understood using such a method is one of Descartes' central philosophical tenets and is what separates scientific thinking from earlier phenomenological views of the world.

The second part of the scientific method is to take those accumulated observations and build models out of them to describe the universe (or some very small part of it) based on the combination of observations and verified hypotheses. If constructed well, these models create new questions to answer—more hypotheses that can be tested by new observations. If the model holds up, it gains credibility; if not, it tends to fall by the wayside.[2]

The hypothesis-driven analysis is largely reductionist in nature and has led to the broad application of reductionism and determinism in much of our current thinking. As the reductionist view holds, we tend to believe that we can take any seemingly complex problem and break it down into simpler problems until the solution is obvious. Part of this reductionist thinking is the idea that, like machines, the world operates *deterministically*: what happens once will happen again. Events do not occur randomly, and if we only knew all the relevant conditions, we could predict the future perfectly. This is the view expressed by Albert Einstein in his letters to his friend and colleague Max Born, in their discussions of the then-new theory of quantum mechanics. In these letters Einstein expressed the deterministic view multiple times with comments like "You believe in the God who plays dice, and I in complete law and order in a world which objectively exists" (Einstein, Born, and Born 1971).

In this interpretation of the world, the underlying aspects of the problem, like the universe at large, can be reduced to simpler parts that are entirely deterministic and predictable. As a result, using such analysis, we can find the root cause that determines a problem and apply whatever fix is indicated by the analysis. This kind of thinking has many advantages and benefits. It has given us centuries of scientific advances in every aspect of life and, in general, an improved ability to shape our environment, avoid dangers, and increase benefits from food and shelter to communication and trade across the planet.

In fact, this kind of thinking is used throughout the business and engineering worlds, typically to great effect. In many computer science classes, for example, students are taught to break down a complex problem or set of tasks into pieces that are progressively less complex until

---

2. This is admittedly an idealistic view of how science works. Scientists, being humans, tend to hang on to ideas they like too long and dismiss others too quickly. It has long been said that "the most progress in science is made at funerals," meaning that sometimes the old guard of scientists have to retire or die off so that new ideas can get the attention they deserve. The idea of "paradigm shifts," first popularized by Thomas Kuhn (1962), is central to this understanding of how science actually works. It's important in understanding how ways of thinking change in general, too, but a longer discussion may be a little far afield even for this synoptic game design book!

they arrive at a series of tasks that are easy to understand and implement. Or in working with materials, engineers often employ finite element analysis, in which each part of an object (a structural steel beam, for example) is broken down into discrete parts ("elements") and assigned properties, and then analyses of strength, stress, and so on can be done on the overall object as the sum of the parts. Of course, these analyses are approximations, but they have proved useful in constructing everything from buildings to airplanes and spacecraft.

However, as a society, we often overapply this kind of logical, analytical, deterministic thinking.[3] We aggressively pursue solutions that reduce situations to their simplest, most deterministic elements even if that means ignoring complex interactions and choosing a single solution that leads us into error. For example, we often confuse correlation (two things happening together) with causation, the idea that one of them causes the other. One common way this is put is to say that "since drownings increase as ice cream consumption increases, ice cream must cause drownings." Of course, this ignores a common underlying factor: people go swimming more often and eat more ice cream when it's hot. Ice cream and swimming are merely correlated; one does not cause the other.

There are many fun examples of this kind of thinking ("global temperatures have increased as the number of pirates has decreased; therefore, driving off pirates causes global warming!") but some real-world ones, too. For example, a study published in the prestigious journal *Nature* reported that children under two years of age who slept with a light on developed myopia (nearsightedness) later in life (Quinn et al. 1999). However, other studies (Gwiazda et al. 2000) found no such result but *did* find that myopia is strongly genetically linked (if your parents are near-sighted, you likely will be, too) and that parents with myopia were "more likely to employ night-time lighting aids for their children" (Gwiazda et al. 2000). Despite being professional and skilled scientists, Quinn and colleagues appear to have fallen into the trap of mistaking the correlation of sleeping with a light on and nearsightedness with the idea that one causes the other.

A similar example from the realm of economics was the argument that excessive national debt (above 90% of gross domestic product [GDP]) slowed economic growth and thus led to hardship for people in that country (Reinhart and Rogoff 2010). Other economists later found, however, that the causality was reversed: growth first slowed, and then countries increased their debt load (Krugman 2013). Of course, different economists will wrangle and argue over this for years, in part because they are looking for *root causes*—conditions that cause specific, direct effects—in areas where such clear causes are rare.

In fact, for many situations, there are no simple, logical solutions, and attempting to reduce a complex area to simpler elements via analysis yields only incomplete or misleading results. For example, what Dennett (1995) called "greedy reductionism" can lead to believing that the

---

3. This might be culturally true of Americans more than others. Many years ago, a Norwegian journalist told me that in his view, what makes Americans different from others is that "you believe there is a solution to every problem." At the time, I was baffled by this. My thought was, "As opposed to what?" (Sellers, 2012).

human body is nothing but a bunch of chemicals—mostly oxygen, carbon, and hydrogen—with a total worth by one analysis of about $160 (Berry 2011). Something seems to have been missed here: surely the way those atoms all combine and relate to each other has some effect?

Another famous example of linear, reductionist thinking is illustrated by an anecdote known as the "cobra effect." (The original sources are obscure, leading back to a German book by Horst Siebert [2001].) The story goes that when India was under British rule, the prevalence of venomous cobras was a significant problem—so much so that the government offered to pay for each cobra head brought in. This touched off a wave of cobra hunting with predictable results: the number of cobras bothering and biting people dropped precipitously. This is what the British no doubt intended: a good clean linear result, where if you pay people to bring you cobra heads, they will do so, and the plague will be removed from the land! Except pretty soon government officials noticed that while there were no cobras in evidence anywhere, they were still doing a brisk trade in paying for them. Clearly something else was going on.

Becoming suspicious that it was somehow being had, the government announced it would no longer pay for cobra heads. The results at this point are, in retrospect at least, completely predictable: it turned out that people had figured out that they could make good money *farming* cobras, killing them, and then turning in the snakes' heads for money. When the government stopped these payments, the farmers had no more need for the reptiles—and so they released many more carefully farmed cobras back into the wild than had been out there in the first place!

There are many such examples of unintended consequences, when one result was desired and another one, often dramatically worse, occurred. Occasionally, though, the unintended consequences are positive. Later we will discuss an example of the far-reaching unintended effects of releasing a small number of wolves into the wild in the United States in the 1990s.

To close out this discussion of linear, reductionist, deterministic thinking, we will consider the example of the pendulum (see Figure 1.2). A weight attached to a rod and fixed at the other end will swing with exact predictably. A pendulum is so regular in its motions that you can use one to show how the Earth rotates under it, as discovered by the French physicist Léon Foucault in 1851. This is a good example of the clockwork world seen by Descartes, Newton, and other great minds.

However, if you make a simple change to the dependable pendulum, it changes into something else entirely. If you add a joint in the middle of the rod that the pendulum hangs from and allow that joint to move freely, suddenly the path of the pendulum changes from being entirely predictable to being entirely *un*predictable. The path of the double pendulum is *chaotic*: not random because it stays within known bounds but unpredictable because it is very sensitive to its starting conditions. A very slight change in where you let the double pendulum fall will create enormous changes in the path it traces out. Figure 1.3 shows an example of the wild path traced by a double pendulum (Ioannidis 2008). If you dropped such a double pendulum twice from as close to the same place as you could, its path would be entirely different each time. A tiny difference in its starting condition does not create a tiny difference in its path but instead results in a path that is utterly unlike any it has taken before.

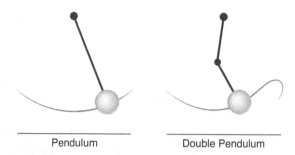

Pendulum   Double Pendulum

Figure 1.2 A pendulum (left) and double pendulum (right)

Figure 1.3 The chaotic, unique, unpredictable path of a double pendulum (Ioannidis 2008)

This kind of behavior is often difficult for us to understand because we see the parts rather than the whole. We can understand how a pendulum operates, more or less, because its parts lead to a direct, seemingly linear effect. Add just a little more variability, as with the addition of a single joint to the double pendulum, and often the behavior changes drastically. We often have a difficult time grasping how such behavior could arise.

This is an echo of the Michigan Fish Test we discussed earlier: we tend to see the fish in the scene, not their surroundings, and we see them as static independent parts. Looking at the double pendulum, we tend to see the two rods and the joints as static pieces, but we do not see how they move or interact together. Or if we do see how the two joints move, if we apply logical, reductionist thinking, we typically fail to understand how such a setup could produce crazy, nonlinear curves like those shown in Figure 1.3. Would we be better off seeing the whole scene together then, as one integrated piece? This leads us to the next kind of thinking: holism.

Holistic Thinking

Holism is the effective opposite of reductionism. Whereas reductionism is about analysis, holism is about synthesis, finding unities, and bringing and viewing seemingly different things together. In its more extreme philosophical forms, the holistic view is that everything is connected to the point that everything is one. As such, holism isn't used as often in daily life, though for many the idea of everything being connected is appealing at an aesthetic or philosophical level.

As with reductionism, there is something to recommend this kind of thinking: by thinking holistically, you don't get lost in the details and are able to watch for significant macro effects and trends that operate at a higher level of organization, such as the group, economy, ecology, and so on. Holism avoids the errors of Dennett's "greedy reductionism," for example, seeing people as whole individuals rather than as a collection of chemicals.

However, depending too much on synthesis and holism can lead to errors just as readily as can leaning too much on reductionism and analysis. If everything is connected, finding any significant cause-and-effect relationships can be difficult. Moreover, it's easy to find false positives, where two completely unrelated phenomena nevertheless *seem* related from a holistic point of view. In addition to the incorrect conclusion that ice cream causes drownings discussed earlier, there are examples such as what Vigen (2015) showed in his many "spurious correlations." For example, Figure 1.4 shows that the age of Miss America and murders by steam, hot vapors, and hot objects tracked *very* closely together for two decades.

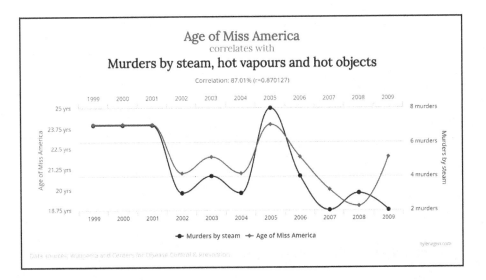

Figure 1.4 One of many spurious correlations (Vigen 2015)

From a holistic point of view, we might be tempted to say that these two effects are correlated if not causative, but this would be a clear error. There may be a hidden underlying factor, but in this case, that seems unlikely. It's far more likely that this is a coincidence of data without any real connection and that a holistic, synthesizing view is misapplied in such a case.

Holism does bring us one other important concept that we will return to multiple times in different ways. This is the idea of *emergence*, of a whole that is "greater than the sum of its parts." This is an ancient idea, apparently first articulated by Aristotle, who said, "In the case of all things which have several parts and in which the totality is not, as it were, a mere heap, but the whole is something beside the parts, there is a cause" (Aristotle 350 BCE). Similarly, in the early days of Gestalt[4] psychology, the psychologist Kurt Koffka famously said that "the whole is *other* than the sum of the parts" (Heider 1977). In Koffka's view, the whole (such as the white triangle shown in Figure 1.5 that we see even though it is not actually there) was not *greater* than the parts, but as Aristotle said, it has an existence of its own separate from the parts that make it up (Wertheimer 1923). This thought was echoed a few years later in holistic evolutionary biology by Jan Christian Smuts (1927), who wrote that "wholes are not mere artificial constructions of thought; they point to something real in the universe....Taking a plant or animal as a type of a whole, we notice...a unity of parts which is so close and intense as to be more than the sum of its parts." This persistent idea that *wholes* are "something real in the universe," that emerge from, yet are independent of, the reductive, analyzed parts that they comprise, is a vital point that we will see again.

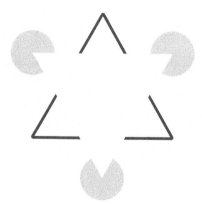

Figure 1.5 A "subjective contour," researched in perceptual and Gestalt psychology. Our minds fill in a shape formed by its surroundings even though the shape itself does not exist

---

4. *Gestalt* is a German word meaning "form" or "shape." This branch of psychology studies the holistic aspects of shapes that we see and complete with our minds even when only part of the shape is visually present.

Systemic Thinking

In between reductionist and holistic thinking is a way of seeing the world that can be called *systemic thinking*. In many ways, this is a sort of "Goldilocks" thinking, in between the too low-level reductionist and too expansive holistic ways of thinking and using methods from both. Systemic thinking takes into account the structural and functional context of a process or an event rather than treating it as a machine to be broken down or an elemental whole. As you will see, learning to think systemically is a vital skill for game designers.

The key aspects of systemic thinking include being able to analytically find and define the parts of a system and, just as importantly, understanding how they exist and work together as a whole in an operational context: how they affect and are affected by other parts of the system. This in turn leads to finding the loops formed by these interactions and how the various parts increase or decrease each other's activation. You will see a lot more about loops later on, but for now, the idea that "thing A affects B, B affects C, and C affects A" defines a systemic loop. This single idea is vital to systems thinking and to systemic game design.

It's also worth noting that describing how loops and systems function together is difficult in part because language is linear: I have to write and you have to read these words in a line, one at a time. This means that the description of a looping system is going to seem odd until you have gotten all the way to the end and looped back to the start, possibly even more than once. Systems are made of loops, and our language doesn't handle loops well.

Let's start off with a simple example of loops by looking at what happens when you heat up an oven. You have a desired temperature you want inside the oven. The gap between that setting and its current temperature increases the amount of heat applied to the oven. As more heat is applied, the temperature rises, and the gap between the current and desired temperatures becomes smaller. Eventually the target temperature is hit, and no further heat is applied (see Figure 1.6). In this way, the oven forms a simple feedback loop: the temperature setting gap affects the amount of heat applied, and the heat applied reduces the gap.

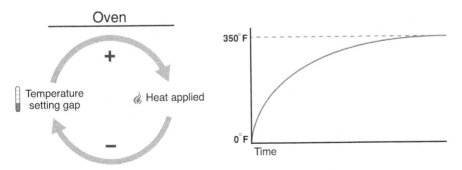

Figure 1.6 Heating up an oven as a feedback loop and the temperature change over time as heat is applied

Figure 1.7 shows a more complex but still classic physical example of a looping structure (and one that is difficult to describe linearly). Unless you know something about engines, by just looking at the picture, you may not be able to see what this does; you're lacking its operational context. The important parts are the two heavy weights (A) on the left side of the diagram, the connecting rods (C, D, E) above them, and the valve (F) on the right.

These parts all interact to form an operational loop as follows (take it one step at a time, following each part of the operation): As the valve (F) on the right opens, it lets in air, which allows an engine (not shown in this diagram) to run faster. This causes the central vertical spindle (B) on the left to spin faster. This in turn causes the weights (A) and the arms they are on to spread out due to their mass and centrifugal force; the momentum from the spindle makes them want to fly outward. As a result, the arms they are connected to (C) pull downward and, in turn, pull the left end of the horizontal lever (D) at the top downward. Because the lever (D) pivots in the middle, this brings its right-hand side up—which pulls up on the rod (E), which brings us back to and closes the throttle valve (F).

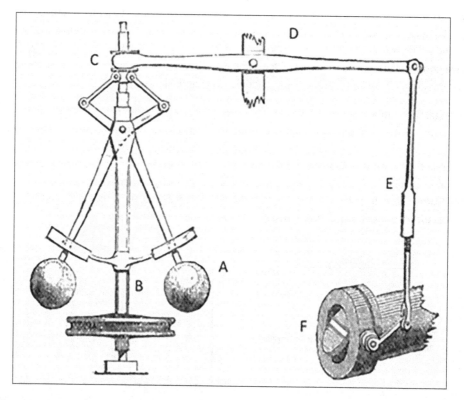

Figure 1.7 A centrifugal governor (Routledge 1881). The only way to understand this assembly is systemically, via its operation and context. It forms a system that is itself a part in a larger system. See the text for the parts associated with each letter shown here

As the valve opens, the engine gets more air and so spins faster. This causes the weights to move out, the horizontal lever tilts, and the valve begins to close, causing the engine to slow down. As it slows down, the weights drop back down, the horizontal lever is pushed up on the left and down on the right, and the valve opens back up, causing the engine to once again run faster.

This loop is what makes the centrifugal governor so effective: it enables the engine to self-regulate, staying within certain bounds, never going too fast or too slow. But to understand this, you have to be able to see the individual parts, their connected behaviors, *and* the overall systemic effect on the engine.

Seeing and thinking through the mechanism this way enables you to build a mental model of the system and to try it out both mentally and physically. Part of an operational, systemic understanding is figuring out which parts interact in what context and which effects of those interactions dominate others. In a straightforward example like the centrifugal governor, all the parts and interactions seem about equally important. But what part does friction play? What if some of the joints are too tight or too loose? Does that have a significant effect on the operation of the engine? It might be, for example, that if there is no looseness, or "play," in these connections that the engine will continually oscillate up and down as the valve opens and closes, causing unwanted wear and tear on the engine and overall uneven performance. Increasing the friction on the weights, so they move up or down more slowly, or increasing a bit of play in the horizontal lever so it doesn't tilt instantly, can be useful if, as in this example, it causes the reaction of the weights and valve to happen more slowly, thereby making the engine run more evenly. Whether the system under consideration is a steam engine governor, an economy, or a fantasy game's magic system, creating the desired loops and effects requires understanding and modeling the system operationally and changing individual parts or their effects on one another to maximum effect.

Systemic thinking requires seeing a system holistically as an organized whole but without losing hold of the analytic grounding of its parts and how they work from the reductionist point of view. Systemic thinking is thus "both-and" not "either-or": it employs the strengths of both reductionist and holistic thinking without falling into the trap of seeing the world via the lens of either one or the other. This "both-and" quality—being able to comprehend the system while maintaining both analytic and synthetic views—can be difficult but becomes easier with practice and with a clearer understanding of what systems are.

Systems of Rabbits and Wolves

Let's look at two more examples of small changes that had broad systemic effects. These may not seem at first glance to have much to do with game design, but the interactions within both examples, seen as systems, are exactly the kind you need to have in mind when designing any complex game.

First, in the mid-19th century, Thomas Austin released 24 rabbits into the wild on his property in southeastern Australia. He is reported to have said that "the introduction of a few rabbits could do little harm and might provide a touch of home, in addition to a spot of hunting" (The State Barrier Fence of Western Australia n.d.). For a few years after their release into the wild, the population of these rabbits remained relatively small and stable, but within a decade, their numbers had exploded. They faced relatively little predation, had ideal burrowing conditions, were able to breed year-round, and may have enjoyed increased hardiness due to hybridization between two types of rabbits released together (Animal Control Technologies n.d.).

The result of this fast invasion by a new species was catastrophic environmental damage to native plants and animals (Cooke 1988). Rabbits in ever-increasing numbers flattened areas of brush, killed small trees by chewing off their outer bark close to the ground, caused widespread erosion, and removed sustenance and areas that other animals needed to live.

A concerted response to this plague of rabbits began in the late 1800s and continues to this day. A wide array of methods—including shooting, trapping, poisoning, fumigating, and over 2,000 miles of fencing—have been attempted, but none with complete success. Wild rabbits, introduced for a bit of sport and "a touch of home," altered the landscape and biosphere of Australia in ways that surely Thomas Austin could not have imagined.

While there are many such ecological disaster stories of unintended consequences, not all are negative. The second example here involves the reintroduction of wolves into Yellowstone National Park in the United States. Wolf packs roamed the Yellowstone area in the late 1800s but were hunted to the point that none were left by the 1920s. Within 10 years, the deer and elk populations in Yellowstone had increased dramatically, and many plants were dying off. By the 1960s, biologists were concerned that the entire ecosystem in the area was out of balance due to the large number of elk in particular, and talk began of bringing back wolves. There was a great deal of opposition from ranchers and others to the idea, as the wolf is a pack-hunting apex predator that, some thought, could wreak entirely new havoc on both the natural ecosystem and ranching herds of cattle and sheep in the area.

After decades of public opinion and legal wrangling, in January 1995 a small initial group of 14 gray wolves was reintroduced to Yellowstone, followed by an additional 52 over the course of the next year. The results were wide-ranging, far beyond what many thought possible. This has now become a classic example of a *trophic cascade*, in which changes to the population of a high-level predator cascade downward through an ecosystem, causing broad and often unexpected effects.

In this case, the wolves fed on the far too numerous elk, as had been expected. But with so many elk and only a few wolves, the predators could not be expected to constrain the elk population on their own. What the wolves did beyond killing and eating some of the elk though was to drive them out of their relaxed life in the valleys and back into the highlands, where they could more readily hide but where life was more difficult. This caused the elk to change their habits: no longer did they come down to the river banks for succulent eating and easy drinking. As a result, they were unable to breed as much or as successfully, which diminished their herds to more sustainable sizes, while still providing enough prey for the wolves.

In the absence of the elk, the trees and grasses in the lower valleys began to spring back. Grasses were no longer being trampled by enormous herds, and George Monbiot (2013) reported that the heights of many trees in the valley floors quintupled in just a few years. This allowed more berries to grow, which in turn supported more bears (who also ate a few of the elk). The flourishing bushes, grasses, and trees allowed for more birds, who through their activity helped spread seeds and grow more trees and bushes.

The increased stability in trees and grasses in turn decreased the erosion that had begun to alarm ecologists as far back as the 1960s. This meant that the riverbanks collapsed less, and the rivers became clearer, enabling more fish to grow. Trees growing by the banks supported more beavers, which in their turn created niches for many more animals via their dam building.

Finally, the reduction in erosion meant that the rivers in Yellowstone Park changed and then stabilized in their courses. Far beyond just eliminating a few elk, as Monbiot notes, the reintroduction of wolves into Yellowstone changed the course of the rivers there. The physical geography of the land itself was altered as part of this wide-ranging trophic cascade.

As incredible an ecological success story as this is, it is also a great example of the kinds of interactions and loops that occur in the natural world and that can be appreciated only by seeing them as systems. Figure 1.8 shows in graphical form the effects of the wolves in Yellowstone. Each arrow with a "−" beside it means that the target was reduced—for example, the wolves reduced the number of deer and elk—while those with a "+" indicate that the target was increased. These have inverse transitive effects as well: for example, because the deer and elk were previously eating (reducing) the trees and grass, having the wolves eat (and reduce the number of) elk in turn reduced the elks' effect on trees and grass, and this flora was now able to come back. By examining this diagram closely, you may be able to better understand the looping systemic effects created by putting a small number of wolves back into Yellowstone and the dramatic consequences this addition had on the whole ecosystem there.

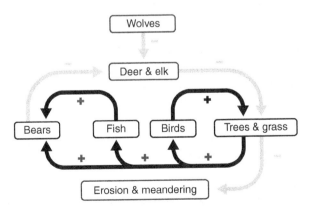

Figure 1.8 The effects of reintroducing wolves into Yellowstone National Park as a systems diagram

A Quick History of Systems Thinking

Now that you know a bit about systems thinking as compared to other ways of seeing the world, this section provides a brief history of how our understanding of systems and the world has evolved.

Plato to Galileo: "A Whole Organized Out of Parts"

The word *system* appears in English essentially unscathed from the ancient Greek *systema*, meaning "standing together," or, more broadly a "whole compounded of several parts," which is very much like our existing definition. For the Greeks at least as far back as Euclid, this definition had several telling variations in meaning, including a single chord formed from several musical tones, a flock or herd, or an organized government (Armson 2011, Liddel and Scott 1940). Each of these variations captures important aspects of systems as we consider them today, all focused around the idea of disparate parts interacting to form a greater whole.

Nevertheless, the Greeks and those who followed them did not apply this *systema* view itself systemically: it took many centuries until this became *the* system of the world—and in some ways it hasn't fully happened even now. Instead, as discussed above, the ancient phenomenological view of the world combined limited observation and overriding philosophy. This provided the people of the time with a geocentric understanding of the universe: as it appeared to any observer, the Sun, Moon, and stars all rotated around the Earth, which sat in the center of it all. This model dates back at least to the ancient Egyptians, and over time people constructed increasingly elaborate models of the solar system and universe to account for new observations, but all in a kind of *ad hoc* way, where there was no unifying principle. Even the idea that there might be some kind of unifying system to the world seems to have borne little consideration beyond the regularities of the seasons and the rising and setting of the stars and planets. *Why* they were as they were was a matter of philosophy, not observation.

This ever-more complicated view of the universe culminated in the model proposed in 1588 by Danish astronomer Tycho Brahe, in which both the Sun and Earth's Moon orbited around the Earth, while the remaining known planets orbited the Sun. This model enabled Brahe to maintain the philosophical purity of the venerable geocentric model while also accounting for a variety of other observations, including Galileo's later 1610 observation via a revolutionary telescope that Venus had phases, just as did the Moon (Thoren 1989). This Tychonic, or "geo-heliocentric," model and those that followed it were effectively the last stand for the philosophical, phenomenological model of the universe.

Nearly a century after Tycho's model of the universe was published, it remained the dominant view. But there were a lot of rumblings, some of which eventually changed how we see the world completely. During this time, Descartes famously created the philosophical foundations for trusting our senses in careful observation and for using mathematics to validate and extend our observations. Galileo then championed the Copernican, or heliocentric, view of the solar system—which put the Sun, not Earth, at the center of things—in a landmark book published in 1632 innocuously called *The Dialogue Concerning the Two Chief World Systems*. (Not incidentally, this was the same book that caused Galileo to be suspected of heresy.) While this work didn't directly address the Tychonic system, it set the stage for another major development that did.

Newton's Legacy: "The System of the World"

In the late 1600s, Isaac Newton, who was familiar with Descartes' work and who had almost certainly read Galileo's book as it so clearly influenced his own, corresponded with Edmund Halley (for whom the famous comet is named) about the calculations of comets and the moons of Jupiter. Halley had kept precise observations of these with his telescope, and Newton used Halley's notes in his mathematical modeling. Based on their correspondence (including an earlier, unpublished paper that we have now only in draft form) and Halley's observational data, Isaac Newton was able to make the final argument in favor of Copernicus and the Sun-centered view of the solar system, and in so doing, he removed geocentrism and Brahe's model from serious consideration of how the world worked (Newton c.1687/1974).

Newton did this as part of publishing his master work, the *Principia Mathematica,* in 1687. (Newton 1687/c.1846). Book III of the *Principia* is called *De Mundi Systemate*, or *The System of the World*—an important volume and title. In this volume, Newton derived his now famous equation describing gravity, based on Halley's meticulous observations of Jupiter's moons. More importantly, he showed that this gravity was the same on Earth and in the heavens. Prior to this there was no assumption, much less an equation to show, that physical mechanisms operated the same on Earth as on Jupiter. There was simply no expectation that physical mechanisms were unified in any way. Newton's equations showed that there were not many systems operating, but one…one gravitation, one organizing principle, one system: *the* system of the world.

It's difficult to overstate the importance of Newton's *Principia* or the change it brought about in how people viewed the world. The idea that the path followed by a ball tossed into the air on Earth can be described by the same equations as the paths of the dimly seen sparks of light that are the distant moons orbiting Jupiter was more than revolutionary. This idea created a new, unified, mechanistic view of the universe. The Sun and the planets were all part of an enormous mechanism that could be fully described mathematically like a giant clockwork.

Newton's work ushered in and was part of the scientific revolution. This was a revolution not only in increased knowledge but in the idea that such knowledge was attainable, that the universe was not capricious but was instead based on steady, definable principles—if only they could be discovered. The world was no longer subject to phenomenological whims and philosophical musings but was bound by strict deterministic logic.

Newton to the 20th Century

Newton's ideas of the universe as a giant clockwork quickly spread from mathematics into physics, chemistry, biology, economics, and, of course, philosophy. But as with anything else, its popularity waxed and waned. Romantic philosophers (so-called because they favored individualism, imagination, and emotion rather than the cool logic and rationalism of the Enlightenment) such as Blake and Goethe critiqued Newton and Descartes. Goethe introduced the idea of "morphology" in describing biological form, with form being determined as "a pattern of relationships within an organized whole" (White 2008), a view that then hearkened back to the ancient Greeks and today is consistent with systems thinking. Nevertheless, this systemic view did not catch on. And, despite the efforts of the Romantics, the general trend until well into the 20th century was toward the acceptance of the world as mechanistic. Along with this came the idea that because Newton had shown that everything could, in principle, be reduced to mathematics, mathematics (or physics, or chemistry) could be used to explain everything.

The Rise of Systems Thinking

In the 20th century, variations on what has become systems thinking appeared in widely diverse areas including biology, psychology, computer science, architecture, and business. While many people have contributed to the overall rise of systems thinking and its allied fields (systems engineering, complexity theory, and so on), we will briefly go over just a few of them here to provide some context and hint at the breadth of ways people have approached systems thinking.

As discussed earlier, psychologists Kurt Koffka, Max Wertheimer, and Wolfgang Kohler created the Gestalt ("form") school of psychology (Wertheimer 1923), identifying the holistic emergent effects that are created when parts come together to create a new whole. Similarly, Jan Smuts explored the Goethe-like idea that "wholes are not mere artificial constructions of thought; they point to something real in the universe.…Taking a plant or animal as a type of a whole, we notice…a unity of parts which is so close and intense as to be more than the sum of its parts" (Smuts 1927). These lines of thinking were essentially proto-systems thinking, though generally without giving in to the individualist and sometimes even anti-scientific ideas of the Romantic philosophers. As in the pre-Newtonian phenomenological view, disparate ideas of systems were not generally applied or seen as being indicative of a systemic universe. The general application of systems would not begin to happen until late in the 20th century; even now we remain on the threshold of this change.

Following Smuts, Karl von Bertalanffy, an Austrian biologist, took a big step toward a broad systemic view of the universe. He wrote what was arguably the first true formulation of systems thinking as a general approach in 1949 when he wrote of these foundations as:

> …models, principles, and laws that apply to generalized systems or their subclasses, irrespective of their particular kind, the nature of their component elements, and the relation or 'forces' between them. (Bertalanffy 1949)

In his 1968 book *General Systems Theory,* Bertalanffy expanded on this greatly, including this introduction to what he saw as both a broad topic and one that was fundamental to all others:

> General systems theory, therefore, is a general science of "wholeness" which up till now was considered a vague, hazy, and semi-metaphysical concept. In elaborate form it would be a logico-mathematical discipline, in itself purely formal but applicable to the various empirical sciences… [including] most diverse fields, such as thermodynamics, biological and medical experimentation, genetics, life insurance statistics, etc. (Bertalnaffy 1968)

While Bertalanffy was never able to see this vision fulfilled, his work was crucial in spreading the principles of systems thinking into many disciplines.

During the mid-20th century, others were active in exploring and winnowing concepts that would lead to broader systems thinking. One notable is Norbert Wiener, who wrote the seminal book *Cybernetics* (1948). This mathematically oriented book led to many advances in computer science, artificial intelligence, and systems thinking. At the same time, its title, focus, and later influence may be indicative of an important divide in thinking about systems. *Cybernetics* comes from the Greek word meaning "governance" or "one who steers or controls."[5] Wiener defined *cybernetics* as the science "of communication and control" (p. 39) and envisioned cybernetics to be about "automata effectively coupled to the external world" with sensors and effectors—inputs and outputs—interacting with an internal "central control system" (p. 42). This idea of centralized control was very much in vogue in the 20th century and has been a difficult one from which to break free. However, as you will see, systems thinking and systemic design both require and enable us to leave behind the limitations of a central controller, enabling instead organized function to emerge from the system itself.

Beginning a few years after Wiener's book was published, John Forrester started work on what would eventually become known as system dynamics—another branch on the tree of systemic thinking. In his 1970 testimony before the Subcommittee on Urban Growth (and later paper on the same topic), Forrester noted that "social systems belong to the class called multi-loop nonlinear feedback systems." (Forrester 1971, p. 3) These, he said, were the province of "the professional field of system dynamics," a new way to understand how social systems worked with better fidelity than ever before. System dynamics is now used primarily in business and some engineering disciplines. The compact model of causal relations makes it much easier to disentangle complex, messy real-world situations. This usage later led to the highly popular book *The Fifth Discipline* (Senge 1990), which introduced many in the business community to the concepts of systems thinking.

While early work in cybernetics maintained a central control mindset, it also led to work in complexity science and complex adaptive systems (CAS), which focuses on the study of

---

5. Wiener's coinage of *cybernetics* is also what led, somewhat mistakenly, to the use of the *cyber*-prefix referring to cutting edge or information technologies that was especially popular in the late 20th century.

simulations of many small, typically simple agents and the complex behaviors that arise from their interactions. This has led to breakthroughs in understanding of evolution and artificial life, as well as organismic, ecological, and social processes. John Holland contributed enormously to this field; his books *Hidden Order* (1995) and *Emergence* (1998) have both greatly increased our current understanding of systems as universal processes.

In parallel with these developments, others such as Christopher Alexander were developing similar ways of thinking—in his case in the field of architecture. As you will see later in this chapter, Alexander's books *A Pattern Language* (1977) and *The Timeless Way of Building* (1979) led to a greater awareness of the importance of patterns, or systems, in many contexts, from physical architecture to software engineering.

Systems Thinking Today

The deep development of systems thinking has continued from the last years of the 20th century to today. A few luminaries of this area include Donella Meadows, Fritjof Capra, Humberto Maturana, and Francisco Varela (together and individually), as well as Niklas Luhmann.

Meadows was an environmentalist writing primarily in the late 20th century. She was highly influential in bringing many people to both a greater sense of environmental awareness and systemic thinking. In particular, her book *Thinking in Systems* (2008) has been the introduction to systems thinking for many people.

Capra is a physicist who turned his sights on systemic and often holistic thinking via popular books. His work thus far is bookended by *The Tao of Physics* (1975), which sought a holistic meeting of science and mysticism, and more recently and more specifically focused on applying systems thinking, the biology text *The Systems View of Life* (2014). In both these and other works (including the 1990 movie *Mindwalk* that he co-wrote), Capra argues for moving from the limitations of the mechanistic Descartian and Newtonian view of science, life, and the universe to a more interconnected, systemic view.

Maturana and Varela came to the world of systems thinking via biology. They are known in particular for coining the term *autopoiesis* and exploring this important concept in detail (1972). Autopoiesis is the process by which living things create themselves. As Maturana and Varela said in their book:

> An autopoietic machine is a machine organized (defined as a unity) as a network of processes of production (transformation and destruction) of components which: (i) through their interactions and transformations continuously regenerate and realize the network of processes (relations) that produced them; and (ii) constitute it (the machine) as a concrete unity in space in which they (the components) exist by specifying the topological domain of its realization as such a network. (p. 78)

This description may be a bit dense, but it calls out important systemic concepts: the whole viewed as a *unity* and the underlying network of processes that support it and actually continually create the machine (or cell or being) in physical space. This concept of a network of processes working together and without centralized control to create a more organized whole is one we will revisit many times.

Finally, Luhmann was a German sociologist writing near the end of the 20th century. While his focus was on systemic models of society, he borrowed and expanded on many of Maturana and Varela's ideas, in particular the idea of social systems as being autopoietic and resulting from communicative interactions between individuals (Luhmann 2002, 2013). In Luhmann's view, communications exist not within a single individual but only between people or, in the terms we use here, as the emergent systemic effect of two or more people communicating, where the individuals are interacting parts within the resulting system. Luhmann's contributions to systems theory, treating it as broadly applicable across disciplines, are still being explored today. This is in some ways a resurgence of Bertalanffy's "general systems theory," a view that lies at the heart of applying systems thinking to game design and using game design to illuminate our understanding of systems.

The history of systems thinking is not finished; it has likely only begun. Despite its rich history and many advances, systems thinking and its associated fields (system dynamics, complex adaptive systems, and so on) remain elusive for many who are not directly involved with them. A few texts have begun to appear, such as Capra's *The Systems View of Life* (2014) at the university level and *Gaming the System* (Teknibas et al. 2014), intended for teachers of younger students; there are also many business-oriented books and websites focused on systems thinking. Nevertheless, many people—even those whose work would seem to require a strong sense of systems thinking—remain uncertain about what systems are and why they should know or care about systems at all.

Systems as the Process of the World

Systems thinking is a vital skill for surviving in the 21st century. As stated earlier, being able to think in terms of systems is as important for this century as being able to read was for the previous one. We need to be able to shift our perspective and recognize the systems at work in the world, such that we can understand or even predict events like the ecological destruction wreaked by a few rabbits or the positive trophic cascade created by a few wolves.

We also need to be able to anticipate and react effectively to changes in the human world. In particular, since the 1980s, our world has become far more interconnected and interactive, which has created a host of new potential problems and opportunities, ranging from the financial crisis of 2008 to increased global trade and international interdependence. Linear, reductionist thinking is insufficient for understanding the processes behind these events and trends and those we will face in the future. Our world can no longer be segmented into neat pieces, nor is any form of linear analysis sufficient for comprehending all that goes on around us.

An Interconnected World

As an example of how our world has changed in the past few decades, looking at how technology has changed since the 1980s gives us a sobering view of how interconnected the world has become and how far it may yet go.

Cisco Systems is the largest manufacturer of computer networking hardware in the world. The company's CEO, John Chambers, described in 2014 how the world had changed—in no small part due to work done at Cisco—since the company's founding in 1984 (Sempercon 2014). He said that in that year, there were about 1,000 computing devices in the world that were connected together through the Internet, mostly at universities and a few technology corporations.[6] In less than a decade, by 1992, that number had jumped to over 1 million interconnected devices. By 2008, there were more than 10 *billion* connected devices—far exceeding the population of Earth. Chambers expects the number of connected computing devices to rise to at least 50 billion by 2020. And yet he noted that today fewer than 1% of all devices that could be connected to the Internet are connected; we are, in other words, still on the early side of the threshold of having an interconnected world.

In a similar vein, in early 2017, Stephen Mollenkopf, the CEO of chip manufacturer Qualcomm, discussed the advent of fifth generation (5G) networking between computing devices. He said this new generation of connective chips "will change society in ways we haven't seen since the introduction of electricity," ushering in an era with "connected cities where everything from the houses to the street lamps talk to each other" (Reilly 2017). That may well be just a lot of marketing hyperbole, but as Mollenkopf (2017) said, the chips will support "a vast diversity of devices with unprecedented scale, speed and complexity." In short, the fast rise in connectivity and interrelatedness shows no sign of slowing.

That's just the hardware. In terms of words, pictures, and other data, Cisco's Chambers noted that the amount of information created *every single day* just by Facebook and Amazon exceeds 20 petabytes (that is, 20,000 terabytes). This is more, every day, than the sum of all human records created from the time of the oldest pyramids to the beginning of the Internet Age, and it is all connected online.

These interconnections can have reverberations far beyond the local scale. For example, your ability to get a loan for a car or house is directly affected by the outlook and fears of bankers and investors in cities around the world. As a specific example of how tightly connected world markets are, in 1993 a fire destroyed the Sumitomo Chemical Plant in Nihama, Japan,

---

6. The Internet was around in 1984, but it was much, much smaller than it is today. I was a university student and programmer at that time. There was no World Wide Web (that would arrive about 10 years later), but we had email, Usenet (a sort of ur-Reddit), and many other services. It was also during this time that game designers began communicating electronically with each other via new services like Genie and CompuServe. At the time, we thought the online experience was amazing and could not possibly conceive of how it would grow over the coming decades.

a factory that made epoxy resin. The result of this one fire was that computer memory chip prices unexpectedly soared from $33 per megabyte to $95 per megabyte (in 1993 US dollars) worldwide in just a few weeks because this plant manufactured 60% of the plastic used to make these chips (Mintz 1993). This one event affected the sales of computer memory for over two years after the fire.

In this world where finances, economies, families, ecologies, and nations are inextricably connected, if we remain ignorant of the systems they form and the effects these systems have, or if we assume that simplistic linear solutions will be sufficient, then we doom ourselves to be driven by the effects of these systems rather than understanding and driving them.

As far back as 1991, the U.S. Department of Education and the Department of Labor recognized the necessity of improving systems thinking at all levels of society. They labeled systems thinking as a "critical 21st century skill," calling it one of "five competencies" needed for workplace preparedness:

> Workers should understand their own work in the context of those around them; they understand how parts and systems are connected, anticipate consequences, and monitor and correct their own performance; they can identify trends and anomalies in system performance, integrate multiple displays of data, and link symbols (e.g., displays on a computer screen) with real phenomena (e.g., machine performance).

> As the world of work has become more complex, all workers have been required to understand their own work in the context of that of others. They must think of discrete tasks as part of a coherent whole. (U.S. Department of Education and U.S. Department of Labor, 1991)

Along these lines, software engineer Edmond Lau cited systems thinking as one of the top five skills any programmer needs to develop (Lau 2016):

> To build and ship code that actually matters, you need to elevate your thinking beyond your code to the level of the entire system:
>
> - How does your code fit in with other parts of the codebase and features other people are building?
> - Have you sufficiently tested your code, and will the quality assurance team (if any) be able to exercise the functionality you've built?
> - What changes need to be made to the production environment for your code to be deployed?
> - Will this new code adversely affect the behavior or performance of any other running systems? Are customers and users who interact with your code behaving as expected?
> - Does your code lead to the desired business impact?
>
> These are hard questions, and answering them well takes effort. But you need a clear mental model of where your code fits into the big picture to know how to direct your time and energy toward the work with the greatest positive impact.

Despite the clear need for improved systems thinking and the benefits of being able to recognize and analyze the systems at work in the world, systems thinking has continued to languish as primarily an academic pursuit or one used narrowly in business. We continue to approach the world as if reductionist, linear, clockwork methods were sufficient to understand and affect it. We are, in effect, still stuck in seeing only the big fish in Nesbitt's test, ignoring the operative context even though we often know better.

Experiencing Systems

Part of the reason we are still seeing only the big fish is that systems are extremely difficult to explain from the outside. Systems are not static, and trying to understand them using a reductionist, analytic, static point of view is doomed to failure.

For example, as first shown by Craig Reynolds (1987), it is possible to define the system of a fully organized flock of birds using only three rules:

1. Each bird tries not to hit any of its neighbors.

2. Each bird tries to go in about the same direction and about the same speed as its neighbors.

3. Each bird tries to get to the center of mass of the birds it can see around it.

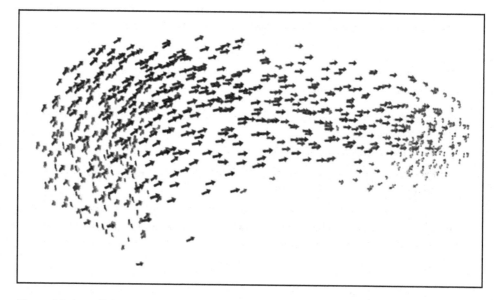

Figure 1.9 An artificial "flock" of arrow-shaped birds (Scheytt 2012)

Following these rules with small artificial birds or similar agents in software generates an entirely believable flock that moves about naturally in flight (see Figure 1.9). But having read those three rules, it is unlikely that you now have a sufficient mental model to create the feedback loops between them from which the flock emerges. Reading these as static rules is not sufficient to create the interactive, interconnected system.

Instead, to recognize and effectively analyze systems requires a systemic view: Systems must be viewed in their operational context—they must, in a word, be *experienced* to be fully comprehended. Experiencing systems, and in particular creating and modifying them, is the only way to understand them and to improve the ability to see the world in terms of systems.

Game Design and Experiencing Systems

The position of this book, perhaps not surprisingly, is that by far the best way to experience systems—to learn to recognize, analyze, modify, and create systems—is by designing and creating games. As you will see in Chapter 3, "Foundations of Games and Game Design," games are unique in several ways that make them ideal for learning about and creating new systems. Among these are the opportunity that games provide for people—especially game designers—to reflect on their own thinking (metacognition, as described earlier) and the mental models they have created as part of the game. This reflection enables people to discern the systems in the game that are otherwise invisible and to recognize similar systems operating in other aspects of their life.

As one example of this, a number of years ago, my wife and I were about to put our house on the market and were discussing how to price it. This brought questions from our children at the dinner table about how the price of a house was determined, whether anyone set a limit on the price, what would happen if you priced it too high or too low, and many similar and understandable questions.

Before too long, one of the children made the crucial connection: "This sounds just like the Auction House in *World of Warcraft*!" In that game, as in many other online games, players can take items they have found in the game and put them up for sale. To sell effectively, the player has to watch the prices for other similar items, not pricing theirs too high or too low. If there were few similar items, they would have to make their best guess and see how well their item sold. All this complex player behavior arises out of the economic system that Blizzard created and that is the underpinning of the Auction House. On that day, the experience with that system generalized to the real world, and it all made sense in terms of selling a real-world rare item (our house) just as it did selling a rare in-game item.

Understanding the World as Systems

With the understanding of the importance of recognizing, analyzing, and creating systems, we still need to more fully understand what systems are and how they operate. But to do this, we need to start from a different and more recognizable place: the world of *things*. This is the world we're used to and probably don't think about much. We're going to change that a bit and come to comprehend systems by first understanding *things*. Once we've done that, we'll come back to seeing how games and systems fit together.

A Strange Systemic Journey

Systems are for us like water for fish: all around us, creating our world, vital to our existence, and difficult to see. Mostly we're not aware that systems exist in our daily lives, though like the fish in water, we're immersed in them all the time.[7]

Theseus' Ship

To start with, there's an old story from Greek legend often told as a paradox. It's the story of Theseus' ship. Theseus, it seems, is a sailor and shipbuilder. He owns a ship that he maintains regularly. Whenever he sees a board or some other part starting to wear out, he removes it and replaces it. Over the years, he eventually replaces every single piece of the ship until none of the original parts remained. Now the question: is the ship he has then still his ship? If every single piece had been replaced, is it the same old ship or an entirely new one? Where does the identity of the thing, the "ship-ness," reside?

To add a further wrinkle (first suggested by English philosopher Thomas Hobbes in 1655), suppose Helen is on the beach near Theseus, watching him closely. Every time Theseus takes off a piece of his ship and tosses it away to be replaced, Helen picks up the old piece (they're still in good shape because Theseus always replaces them early). With these, she builds *another* ship (see Figure 1.10). So one day, Theseus replaces the last old part on his ship with a new one. He steps back to admire his now completely refurbished ship and bumps into Helen. She's just stepped back to admire *her* handiwork too, since she's just added the final part to her ship.

Figure 1.10 Theseus, Helen, and the ships

---

7. This insight was inspired in part by the video "This Is Water," based on the speech by David Foster Wallace (2014).

The question is, which one is Theseus' ship? Does he have two ships or no ship at all, or is one his and one Helen's? What is the essential quality that makes a ship a ship? What is it that gives it its identity as a *ship* and its sense of integrity and wholeness?

This is the kind of paradoxical question that has worried philosophers for millennia; you can think about it for a bit, too. We'll return to Theseus and Helen and the question of the identity of Theseus' ship with a new way to view the question. Before we do, we're going to go on a bit of an odd journey.

We're going to take a new look at *things* and what they actually are. This is a strange journey that will take us down to the very smallest levels of reality and then back up again to our world of things. This will mean first diving down to examine the smallest structures we know of, right down to atoms and even the unfamiliar—but, as we'll see, entirely relevant—world inside the atom. From there we will come back up to the scale of the familiar world and beyond. This may lead to some unexpected conclusions and possibly change how you see the world around you.

Talking about the nature of things this way may seem like the long way around to start talking about systems (much less games), but it's important to understand the literal rather than metaphorical reality of what systems are by first understanding what *things* are. And if you're not a "science person," don't worry; this won't get *too* technical.

Things and Identity
So what makes a thing a *thing*? What is *stuff*? These may seem like simple (or even silly) questions. After all, this seems obvious: things are what you can see or touch; they have mass, heft, and substance. You can pick up a pen, rap your knuckles on a desk, or drink a glass of water. At least macroscopic things seem to be pretty well behaved as *things*. But what's the real structure? What's inside that makes a thing a thing? Moving down in scale to the microscopic world, we understand that this eventually leads us down in scale to molecules and atoms. That's where we'll start.

Let's look at water. As you probably know, it's one of the most common substances there is, made of small molecules containing two hydrogen atoms and one oxygen, often depicted as shown in Figure 1.11. If you stop to think about it, though, those three atoms don't look like what you know as *water*. What is it that enables these hydrogens and oxygens to have the properties of water—to slosh around as a liquid, freeze as clear ice, or form clouds in the sky?

That's a question that will require us to think in systems to answer. We'll come back to it on our way back up in scale. For now let's go even smaller, into the hydrogen atoms that exist as part of every molecule of water.

Hydrogen is the smallest atom. It consists of a single proton surrounded by a single electron. But the electron and proton are so small that the atom is almost entirely empty. Specifically, "almost entirely empty" means the atom is 99.9999999999996% empty. That's not an approximation but a figure chemists and physicists have worked very hard to calculate.

Figure 1.11 A water molecule as commonly depicted: two small hydrogen atoms and one larger oxygen

So a hydrogen atom is almost entirely empty—made of nothing at all. That empty space isn't filled with air but just empty space. With that much emptiness, it's difficult to see how an atom amounts to *anything*. To give that some scale, imagine something tiny—maybe a peppercorn or a BB from an air gun, about 2 mm across, sitting in the middle of a big professional sports stadium, in the middle of a football field. The peppercorn is the proton at the heart of the hydrogen atom, and the stadium is the approximate volume of the hydrogen atom, about 60,000 times the size of the proton. All the rest of the volume around the tiny seed, the size of a sports stadium all around it, is completely empty—no air, no nothing, just emptiness. Together, these form the hydrogen atom. Hydrogen is also by far the most common element in the universe. It makes up about 74% of all elemental matter, and the hydrogen atoms inside you account for about 10% of your body weight.

But how can something that is so close to being completely empty—completely nothing—also be so much of everything? How can it account for so much of the mass of you and other *things*? The electron in the atom contributes only a miniscule amount of its substance (about 0.05% of the hydrogen atom's already tiny mass), so the vast majority of the mass, more than 99%, comes from the tiny proton at its infinitesimal heart.

Now, here is where the story starts to become a little weird. We often see pictures in textbooks that show atoms as little spheres, like in Figure 1.11. Within these spheres the protons and neutrons that make up the atomic nuclei typically appear as even smaller spheres, little hard nuggets of reality at the heart of the atom. It's a convenient view, but one that also leads us completely astray from how reality—*things* and systems—actually work.

Atoms aren't little balls. Electrons don't orbit in clean paths, and there is no defined spherical wrapper around the atom. The nature of an electron in a hydrogen atom is more complex than we need to dig into here, but the fact is that it's more accurate to think of the atom as having a fuzzy, nebulous border region defined by where the electron can be found—insofar as anything that is almost entirely nothing can have a boundary at all!

At the center of the hydrogen atom is its proton. This too is something we often envision as being a hard little sphere, an essential if tiny bit of solid stuff. This is what makes up over 99.95% of the mass of the hydrogen atom, and yet, just like the atom itself, it's not actually anything like a concentrated little lump of anything. In order to really find out what *things* are, we need to continue our journey to dip into the proton at the atom's heart and see what that tells us.

Protons are one of the two main parts of the atomic nucleus, the other (in atoms heavier than simple hydrogen) being the neutron. Together these are responsible for very nearly all of the mass of the atom, and atoms add up to being all the mass and solidity we experience. They are essential to things being *things* as we experience them with substance and heft. While protons and neutrons are essential, they are not fundamental: it turns out that they are made up of even smaller particles called *quarks*. As far as we know, quarks are fundamental particles with no internal structure, and they are in many ways as strange as their name implies.

It's often taught that a proton is made of three quarks.[8] These quarks aren't "inside" the proton; they *are* the proton. That may be a bit confusing, but remember that the proton doesn't have a wrapper or spherical shape hiding quarks inside it. The quarks are simply what the proton *is* when viewed in more detail. This is actually a very important concept that we'll return to in a moment.

Each of the quarks that make up a proton (or neutron) has a little bit of mass, though strangely the amount of mass of all three put together amounts to only about 1% of the total mass we find when we measure the mass of the proton. But if the quarks *are* the proton, how is that possible? Where does the rest of the mass come from?

You saw earlier that we need to discard the convenient idea that atoms or even protons are hard little balls of matter. Atoms are "fuzzy" and made mostly of nothing. Protons can be said to have a size and shape, though they too are best described as fuzzy (or indeterminate within bounds, to be more precise). Just as the atom gets its size and shape from the volume where its electrons may be found, the proton's size and shape come from where its quarks may be found.

The three quarks that make up the proton are tightly bound to each other: they zoom around in a very, very small space (about 0.85×10^{-15} meters, or less than one-millionth of a billionth of a meter) and never get very far from each other. But at this small scale, physics operates differently than we're used to, and even the difference that we see between matter and energy essentially vanishes. (Fortunately, Einstein's succinct equation $E = mc^2$ allows us, and subatomic particles, to convert from one to the other easily.) In addition to the energy of the three bound quarks, in the same very small volume, there are innumerable pairs of quarks and anti-quarks

---

8. In a proton, two of the quarks are labeled as "up" and one as "down." Neutrons are also made of three quarks: two "down" quarks and one "up." Don't be confused by those terms; they don't really refer to directions. If anything, they show that physicists often have a quirky sense of humor when naming things. The name "quark" itself comes from a passage in James Joyce's *Finnegan's Wake*, and was chosen by co-discoverer Murray Gell-Mann (1995) to describe these bizarre subatomic entities.

always popping in and out of existence. These pairs appear and disappear almost instantly, out of nothing and into nothing but nevertheless adding their energy to the proton. This creates a stable but constantly changing environment in a very small space, based on the relationships between these small eruptions of energy.

What this means is that the combination of the kinetic energy of the quarks and their binding relationship to each other (known in physics as the "gluon field") and the momentary but continually fizzing existence of the virtual quark pairs popping in and out around them, altogether create the other 99% of the observed mass of their aggregate whole—the stable-but-always-changing particles that we call protons and neutrons. Strange as it sounds, this is the root of what *things* are. This is what makes up everything around you, everything you've ever seen or touched. Despite our typical experience of solidity and stability, everyday things are actually "less like a table, more like a tornado" as Simler (2014) aptly noted. Understanding things this way will also help us understand more clearly what systems are.

Looking at quarks and the protons they make up, we can see that at their most essential, things (whether atoms or ships) aren't what we typically consider them to be: they aren't in fact well-defined, primly bounded objects that stand on their own, clearly separate from everything else. At the smallest levels of reality, they aren't anything like little nuggets of matter. They're energy, forces, and relationships. As difficult as it may be to understand at first, the networks of relationships that allow protons and everything else to exist are the same kinds that we see as the core elements of game design.

Going back to protons and neutrons for a moment, these exist because of the energetic stable-but-always-changing relationships between quarks. A quark itself is a stable-but-always-changing effect (possibly a wave in the multiple dimensions of space–time, but that's another discussion). Together, three bound quarks and zillions of "virtual" (real but very-short-lived) pairs of quarks are related to each other in space and time in a way that makes up stable-but-always-changing protons and neutrons. The same is true of atomic nuclei (containing protons and neutrons) and electrons: it is by the *relationships* between them that they become stable-but-always-changing atoms.

Metastability and Synergy

This concept of *stable-but-always-changing* is called *metastability*. Something that is metastable exists in a stable form across time (typically) but is nevertheless always changing at a lower level of organization.[9] The outwardly stable proton is actually a teeming swarm of smaller particles at the next lower level of organization. Likewise, the atom is stable in itself but inside is made

---

9. In many branches of science, the groupings of things into metastable structures are called "integrative levels" (Novikoff 1945). In the atomic and subatomic realm, physicists have created what they term "effective field theories" that approximate the variances at the next lower level of organization into a metastable whole at the current level.

from the constantly changing relationships between its nucleus and its electrons. In addition to protons and atoms, there are many other examples of metastable structures, such as a flock of birds, a hurricane, or a stream of water. We will examine more of these shortly.

To continue our climb back up from the subatomic realm, just as an atom is a metastable structure, so too is a molecule. The simple molecule of water we looked at earlier is a *thing* every bit as much as a proton or an atom is a thing. It, too, is metastable, as the atoms within the molecule undergo changes, sharing electrons between them and changing their positions relative to each other.[10]

Just as a hydrogen atom is made up of a proton and an electron, a water molecule is made up of two hydrogens and one oxygen atom. The water molecule doesn't "contain" these, it simply *is* these. And yet, while there's no skin or hard boundary around it, when considering the ways in which water molecules interact with each other, it often makes sense to think of them as being "one level up" in organization from their atoms.

That is, the water molecule exists because of the synergistic relationship between the atoms that constitute it, just as the hydrogen atom exists because of the synergy between the proton and electron, and the proton exists because of the synergy between quarks. The word *synergy* means "working together." It has been used in many contexts in recent decades, especially in business, but was originally brought into modern usage by Buckminster Fuller, who described it as "behavior of whole systems unpredicted by the behavior of their parts taken separately" (Fuller 1975). This is another way of describing metastability, where some new *thing* arises from the combination of parts at a lower level of organization, often resulting in properties not found in the parts themselves. Like the proton and the atom, the molecule at its level of organization possesses the qualities of stability and integrity: it cannot be divided without changing its essential nature.

The idea that systems are metastable things with their own properties and that they contain other, lower-level metastable things within them is one of the key points to understand for both systems thinking and game design. We will see this again when we discuss the phenomenon of emergence.

As things with their own identity, water molecules can be thought of as somewhat lumpy spheres, more like a potato than an orange in shape (as shown in Figure 1.12). This lumpy shape is made from the *relationships* between the constituent oxygen and hydrogen atoms

---

10. Water molecules, while metastable, still act in very odd ways we don't normally consider. A hydrogen atom might jump off to leave an OH^- ion behind and create a new H_3O^+ molecule for a short time, before hopping back or being replaced by another H^+ ion. Water as a bulk substance is itself metastable, even with molecules exchanging hydrogen ions and other shenanigans like this going on at the molecular level.

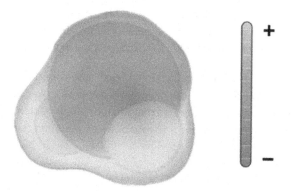

Figure 1.12 The "lumpy sphere" of a water molecule's electrical charge

The relationships between the atoms in a molecule govern the metastability of the molecule and its overall electrical attributes. The quarks inside the proton and neutron determine their respective electrical charges,[11] and the protons and electrons in the hydrogen and oxygen atoms determine the water molecule's overall charge. The oxygen atom partially pulls the electrons off the hydrogen atoms, sort of like stealing the covers from the poor hydrogens. This leaves the protons that make up the nuclei of the hydrogen atom somewhat exposed and gives their lumpy end of the molecule a partial positive charge. In the same way, the other side of the molecule, closest to the oxygen and away from the hydrogens, takes on about 10 times more of a negative electrical charge as the hydrogens' electrons now spend some of their time by the oxygen.

As a result, the water molecule as a whole, as a *thing*, has electrical polarity, with some parts more positive and some parts more negative. Understanding this—and understanding how things are built out of the relationships between components at a lower level of organization—allows us to answer the question of how it is that water molecules become the *water* we recognize. D. H. Lawrence (1972, p. 515) wrote about this in his poem "The Third Thing":

> Water is H_2O, hydrogen two parts, oxygen one, but there is also a third thing, that makes it waterand nobody knows what that is.

This "third thing" is at the heart of this discussion. This is the independently existing whole that Aristotle thought of more than 2,000 years ago, echoed by Smuts and Koffka in their fields in the early 20th century. This "third thing" is vitally important, but it's not a separate

---

11. For the curious: each of the quarks making up the proton and neutron has an electrical charge; the sum of these is where the proton gets its charge, and this is why the neutron is electrically neutral. Since the proton was already given a +1 charge before we knew about quarks, the quarks have to have fractional charges: the two "up" quarks each have a $+\frac{2}{3}$ electrical charge, and the "down" has a $-\frac{1}{3}$. $\frac{2}{3} + \frac{2}{3} - \frac{1}{3} = 1$, which is how these add up to the proton's +1 charge. Similarly, a neutron has two "down" quarks and one up, which equates to $\frac{2}{3} - \frac{1}{3} - \frac{1}{3} = 0$, which is why a neutron is electrically neutral.

element or object: it is the whole that arises out of the *relationships* between the things we already know about from a lower level, creating a new independent thing at a higher level. To quote Lawrence again, saying virtually the same thing in a different context, in his 1915 novel *The Rainbow,* he writes:

> Between two peoples, the love itself is the important thing, and that is neither you nor him. It is a third thing you must create.

This creation of a "third thing" that emerges from the relationship of lower-level components is what makes everything—atoms, water, love, interactivity, games, life—possible. In the case of water, as H_2O molecules form loose but metastable clusters, these groups begin to slide past each other. As this happens, large number of these molecules and clusters begin to take on the properties of fluidity that we recognize as being liquid water—properties not found in the molecules or their atoms but that arise as entirely new from the relationships between the constituent parts.

As we move back up in scale from looking at molecules to looking at things we can see around us, metastable structures are evident all around. Continuing with water as an example—whether in a drop, a stream, or a wave—it creates additional metastable structures at much larger levels of organization. Keep in mind that water molecules are very small. They're many thousands of times bigger than the protons we talked about earlier but still unimaginably small.[12] So anything from a drop of water that hangs on the end of your eyelash to the largest hurricane is one of many metastable structures formed by water.

Going Back to Where We Started

As far as *things* go, that's it: everything you know as a "thing" is made out of the relationships between smaller components within them. Each component is a metastable level of hierarchy of its subparts, all the way down to the fundamental sub-basement of the universe, where quark/anti-quark pairs continually fizz in and out of existence, creating protons and neutrons (and their mass—and your mass) in the process.

Understanding this enables us to go back to where we started. We can now take another look at Theseus and Helen and their ships. Just as a proton, an atom, and a molecule are all metastable structures, so too is a ship: a ship isn't just a bunch of planks of wood; it's the synergistic relationships between those planks, and they exist *in a particular metastable relationship*

---

12. Here's a thought exercise to help you visualize how many molecules of water are in a single drop: imagine the population of Earth, which currently stands at a little over 7 billion people. Now, as hard as that is to do, imagine each and every person on the planet holding *10* copies of Earth, each with its own population of more than 7 billion. Got that? Every person on Earth now has 10 shimmering Earths in front of them, each with its own enormous population. That *total* number of all those people on all those copies of Earth (plus the original!) is about equal to the number of molecules in a single small drop of water. That is, there are about 7.2×10^9 people on Earth. Squaring this is like giving each person a copy of the planet with its own 7.2×10^9 people. Together that's about **5×10^{19}** people. Now give each person on the original Earth 10 copies, not 1, and that's about 5×10^{20}, or just about the number of molecules of water in a drop of water about 3 mm across and weighing 0.015 grams.

to each other. So if Theseus removes a plank and replaces it with a new one, he has changed not only that one physical component but even, more importantly, its relationship to all the other physical components in the ship. He has removed the plank from the system that is the ship, but the ship itself remains (as long as it retains enough components to retain its metastability and function as a ship). For her part, Helen has created a new metastable structure, a new ship, by gradually creating new relationships with old parts. It's important to remember that just as we said earlier that the two hydrogen and one oxygen atoms aren't "inside" the water molecule, the planks aren't "inside" the ship: they are, by virtue of their relationship to each other, what creates the ship as a thing itself.

To return all the way to the world of game design for a moment, this understanding of how *things* come about—and in particular the importance of relationships and interactions in creating new, higher-level systems (and things)—will help us design more systemic and, ultimately, more satisfying games.

Bricks and Houses, Patterns, and Qualities

The philosopher and scientist Henri Poincaré (1901) said that "science is built of facts the way a house is built of bricks; but an accumulation of facts is no more science than a pile of bricks is a house." Recall too Aristotle's statement that "in the case of all things which have several parts and in which the totality is not, as it were, a mere heap, but the whole is something beside the parts, there is a cause." The *cause* he speaks of is the structural and functional relationship between things. In the case of the house described by Poincaré, it is the bricks and their relationships—their position, physicality, and support for each other. This is what separates it from "a mere heap" and creates the organized system we call a house, just as the structural and functional relations between facts that create organized theory and models constitute what we call science. Without these inter-elemental effects that transcend the elements themselves, there is no house, and there is no science.

Complementing this are two more observations, both from architect Christopher Alexander. The first is from his book *A Pattern Language*. This is a book about physical architecture—towns, houses, gardens, and nooks. Beyond that, this book and its principles have greatly influenced generations of software engineers and game designers. Whenever you hear someone talking about a *design pattern*, whether they know it or not, they are referring to the work in this seminal book. Alexander's approach is entirely systemic. Consider the preceding discussion about water molecules, quarks, and ships in this light:

> In short, no pattern is an isolated entity. Each pattern can exist in the world, only to the extent that it is supported by other patterns: the larger patterns in which it is embedded, the patterns of the same size that surround it, and the smaller patterns which are embedded in it.
>
> This is a fundamental view of the world. It says that when you build a thing you cannot merely build that thing in isolation, but must repair the world around it, and within it, so that the larger world at

the one place becomes more coherent, and more whole; and the thing which you make takes its place in the web of nature, as you make it. (Alexander et al. 1977, p. xiii)

Where Alexander says "pattern," we would say "system." The essential overall pattern-of-patterns is that this systemic organization exists in the real world from quarks to hurricanes (and onward to the unimaginably immense structures in the universe); in creating the architecture of homes and kitchens and cities; and even in games as designed experiences.

The second thought is from Alexander's book *The Timeless Way of Building*, a somewhat more philosophical companion to *A Pattern Language*. In this book, Alexander introduces what he calls the "quality without a name" that he believes must be infused in all architecture and indeed in anything designed. This quality includes "oneness," dynamic harmony, balance between forces, and a unity arising out of nested patterns that support and complement each other. Taken together, Alexander asserts that as a unified pattern containing these subpatterns, it cannot be contained in a name. As Alexander says,

> A system has this quality when it is at one with itself; it lacks it when it is divided....This oneness, or the lack of it, is the fundamental quality for anything. Whether it is in a poem, or a man, or a building full of people, or in a forest, or a city, everything that matters stems from it. It embodies everything. Yet still this quality cannot be named. (Alexander 1979, p. 28)

Alexander's "quality without a name" resonates with Aristotle's unnamed "cause" found in an organized system and with Lawrence's "third thing" that makes water wet. It has had no name, perhaps, because naming it also flattens it in our minds, moving our perspective from that of a complex, dynamic pattern-of-patterns to a reductionist view of a stable, inert thing. With the understanding we have now, we can refer to this as the quality of some thing or process being *systemic*. We will define this more precisely in Chapter 2, "Defining Systems."

Onward to Systems

The systemic perspective is crucial: you must learn to see the animated tornado in the apparently motionless table and to see the dynamic processes in our own designs. In game design terms, you must learn to see the totality of the experience, the game as played, while understanding that each player will have a unique experiential path through it. At the same time, as a game designer, you must be able to "zoom in" and specify each individual piece of the game without requiring that this collapses down into a single path through the state-space of the game.

Keeping all this in mind, not giving in to the vagueness of overly holistic thinking nor the linearity of greedy reductionist thinking, you will be able to see the world systemically. By doing so, you will be able to understand and recognize this unnamed, unflattened systemic, synergistic, metastable, emergent quality—and then work to include it in your creative designs.

With this in mind, you are now in a position to examine a more comprehensive definition of what a *system* is and why it's important to be able to recognize, think about, and intentionally use systems in designing games.

Summary

In this chapter you have learned about different ways of viewing the world and about the importance of seeing the world as systems. You have started down the path to understanding systems as networks of interrelated parts that create metastable wholes.

This systems view is vital for understanding how the world works, for seeing mundane things all around you as vibrant systems, and for creating engaging games. With this deeper understanding of how systems make up the world, you are now prepared to define systems more precisely. This will enable you to bring the terminology and comprehension of systems to bear on game design.

CHAPTER 2

DEFINING SYSTEMS

With a foundation in systems thinking, you can now build a more formal and specific definition of what systems *are*. Here we explore how systems are organized and how new things and experiences arise from their disparate parts.

Doing so gives you the foundational concepts and vocabulary needed for analyzing and designing systemic games.

What We Mean by *Systems*

As you have seen, systems are a familiar yet often only vaguely defined concept. By carefully examining what "things" actually are, this amorphous concept becomes clearer. As you saw in Chapter 1, "Foundations of Systems," systems are things, and things are systems. Systems are literally all around us. They make up the physical world we live in and the social world we help create.

It is important to remember, however, that systems (and things, deep down) are dynamic, not static: you cannot understand a system by freezing it in place; you must experience it operating in its context to truly understand it. Because systems embody Alexander's "quality without a name," (Alexander 1979, p.28) it is difficult to define them in a single bumper-sticker-like sentence.[1] Systems have the (perhaps maddening but also magical) quality that they must be understood in terms of their constituent pieces *and* how they all dynamically combine to form something greater—both at the same time. They must be understood in terms of their contextual operations, not as a static snapshot.

In other words, any definition of a system must itself be systemic.

A Brief Definition

In the interest of providing a short definition that does not gloss over too much, a system can be described as follows:

> *A set of parts that together form loops of interaction between them to create a persistent "whole." The whole has its own properties and behaviors belonging to the group but not to any single part within it.*

That's a lot. Throughout this chapter we will break this down (and assemble it back up!) to get closer to a formal definition and detailed explanation. As noted earlier, the linearity of language does become a problem here: you will see references to things that have not yet been explained, and it may take more than one reading (more than one loop!) to construct your own mental model of what a system is.

To start then, here is a list that expands a bit on the statement above. We will examine this in greater detail throughout this chapter:

- Systems are made out of *parts*. Parts have internal *state* and external *boundaries*. They interact with other parts via *behaviors*. Behaviors send information or, more often, *resources* to other parts to affect the internal state of the other parts.

---

1. The closest I have seen is "This sentence is a system." The interactions between letters and words creates emergent organized meaning in a brief statement. Thanks to Michael Chabin for this concise definition.

- Parts interact with other parts via behaviors to create *loops*. Behaviors create local interactions (A to B), while loops create transitive interactions (A to B to C to A).

- Systems are organized into hierarchical integrative *levels* that arise from *emergent* properties based on their looped structures. At each level, the system displays organized state and behavior, synonymous with being a part in larger system at the next level up.

- At each level the system displays *persistence* and *adaptability*. It does not fall apart quickly, being self-reinforcing, and is able to tolerate and adapt to different conditions that exist outside its boundaries.

- Systems exhibit organized, decentralized, but coordinated behaviors. A system creates a unified whole—which is in turn just a part of a larger system.

We will now examine each of those aspects of a system in greater detail.

Defining Parts

Every system is made of and can be broken down into separate parts: the parts could be atoms in a molecule, birds in a flock, units in an army, and so on. Each part is independent of others in that each has its own identity and acts on its own. Specifically, each part is defined by its *state*, *boundaries*, and *behaviors,* as described in the following sections. (You will see these again in game-specific terms in Chapter 8, "Defining Game Parts.")

State

Each part has its own internal *state*. This is made up of a combination of attributes, each of which has a specific value at any point in time. So each bird in a flock has its own speed, direction, mass, health, and so on. The bird's speed and mass are attributes, and each have a value (for these, a number) that is the attribute's current state. The part's state overall is the aggregation of all of its current attribute values. This is static at any point in time but, if the part is affected by others, changes over time.

In the real world, an object's state is not defined by a simple attribute with a value. (People don't really have a specific number of "hit points," for example.) Instead, state emerges from the aggregate states of subsystems at one level of organization lower or finer in detail. (See the section "Hierarchy and Levels of Organization," later in this chapter.) These subsystems are made of parts as well, all interacting together. As you have seen, in the real world we have to go down to quarks before we stop finding subsystems made of smaller parts.

In games, a part's state is often determined by the states of parts within it at a finer level of detail: a forest might not have its own "health" attribute but instead may use the aggregate of the state of every tree defined within it. However, at some point you have to "hit bottom" and create simple parts with attribute/value pairs that are simple, nonsystemic types—integers, strings, and so on. For example, chess pieces have a type (pawn, rook, and so on) and a position on the board as their state. In a computer game, a monster might have 10 hit points and be named Steve.

This degree of specificity provides us with a feasible floor to our designs, enabling them to be implemented. Since the default or starting states of various parts in a game are typically kept in a spreadsheet, we sometimes refer to this level of definition as being "spreadsheet specific." This is an important quality of game design, as you cannot actually build a game until you have hammered out all the vague parts of the design and brought them down to the level of being spreadsheet specific. You will see this again throughout the book, especially in Chapters 8 and 10, "Game Balance Practice."

However, the spreadsheet level of specificity is not an upper limit to how systemic a game design can be. By building systems out of subsystems that contain parts, you can create a more engaging, dynamic "second-order design" (see Chapter 3, "Foundations of Games and Game Design") that does not depend for success on extensive and costly content creation. You should look for opportunities in your designs to group simpler parts together to create greater systemic wholes.

Boundaries

A part's *boundary* is an emergent property (see below for a discussion of *emergence*) defined by the local neighborhood of interaction of subparts within it (see Figure 2.1). Parts that are closely networked together—those with more interactions with each other than with other parts—and in particular those with interactions that create loops, form a local subsystem that creates a new part at a higher level of organization (more on levels below).

The boundary between parts isn't absolute, as some local parts necessarily have interactions with other parts "outside" the boundary as well. As with our discussion of atoms and protons, it is important to remember that generally there is no overt skin or wrapper around a part[2]; its boundary is defined by clusters of closely interconnected subparts that make it up. In effect, the boundary may look well defined from a higher-level perspective, but on closer inspection, it becomes fuzzier and more difficult to say exactly where it lies.

The typical rule for defining something that is "outside" versus "inside" a part is whether it can change the higher-level *system's* behavior. If so, then it's inside the boundary and is part of the system. If something communicates with a part inside a system but cannot by its behavior change the system's overall behavior, then it's considered to be outside the part's or system's boundary.

---

2. In some cases, like that of a cell membrane, there literally is a skin that forms the boundary between inside and outside. Even here, though, there are specialized channels that allow the densely interconnected inside to bring things in or send things out through the boundary.

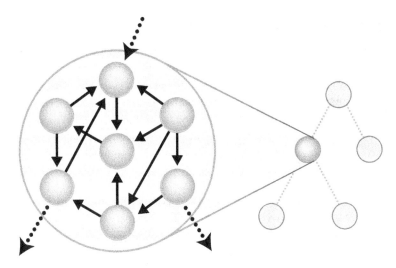

Figure 2.1 A part with its boundary, interconnected subparts, and where it fits in the overall system. Note that the boundary is conceptual, formed by the interconnections between parts, not a separate part on its own

As a practical matter, the boundary and the organization it provides is a form of modularity that may be emergent or enforced when creating parts and systems, as in software. Using a boundary can make the parts of a system more comprehensible and reusable, and it also removes the temptation to rely on various forms of centralized control. This is the same idea behind the idea of "small pieces loosely joined" that Weinberger (2002) used to describe the decentralized World Wide Web: each web page is a part in the overall system. None controls the entire thing, and if one or another goes away, the rest continues to function.

Behaviors

Parts affect each other via their *behaviors*. Each part has something that it does—most often some resource it creates, changes, or destroys in the system. These behaviors may be simple or complex, and they typically affect other parts by communicating some resource or value change to them. A given part may affect itself via its behaviors as well, such as by a monster in a game healing its own wounds over time or an account adding to its own balance via compound interest calculations.

An important concept related to behaviors is that a part may perturb or affect another part with its behavior, but each part determines its own changes to its internal state as well as any behavioral response. In object-oriented programming terms, each part *encapsulates* its state, meaning that no other part can "reach in" and change it. Each part determines on its own what behavioral messages it will pay attention to and be affected by. So one part may by its behavior send a message to another, but it is up to that second part to determine its own response: it may ignore the message or use it to change its internal state, based on its own internal rules.

Sources, Stocks, and Sinks

In discussing parts, the language of systems thinking often talks about different types of parts, such as *sources*, *stocks*, and *sinks*. The behaviors by which they interact are often shown as *connectors*, the most common type of which is a *flow* between two parts. What flows between parts may be messages or other forms of information but is often a *resource* of one type or another. (Note that while these names and the symbols for them have been used widely in systems thinking, science, and engineering, today there remains no canonical form for them. We will use common names and symbols here, but they are intended to be utilitarian, not prescriptive.)

A *source* is any part that increases another part's state. One of the simplest examples of this is a faucet that fills a bathtub with water (see Figure 2.2). In the real world, the water comes from somewhere, but in games (and in systems thinking in general), we often assume that a source represents an inexhaustible supply of some resource, such as water.

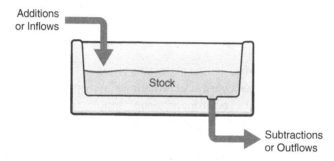

Figure 2.2 Source, stock, and sink, along with inflow, storage, and outflow of the resource

Using the bathtub example, an amount of water (the resource) flows from the source and into the stock. The state inside the part that represents the source specifies the rate at which it creates new units of its resource. So a source might have an internal variable with a value of 2, meaning that it creates 2 units of water per unit time (e.g., per second). The source's behavior is what passes this water along; this is often called a *flow*. The source doesn't keep any water itself; it just generates some amount and passes it along if it can.

The *resource* represents the numeric amount of something (in this example, water) that flows from one part to another, as from the source to the stock. Generally speaking, anything that is countable, storable, or exchangeable qualifies as a resource, even if it is not strictly physical. Health as represented by hit points in a role-playing game may be a resource, as may the provinces an empire controls. We will discuss resources again in Chapter 7, "Creating Game Loops," and Chapter 8.

The *stock* is where the resource created by the source flows to. It is the bathtub in this example. You can also think of this in terms of a store having items "in stock" or how many fish are in a "stock pond." Stocks accumulate things; for example, bathtubs accumulate water, and bank accounts accumulate money. For any stock, its state is described as an amount (of some resource) at a particular time. So a bathtub might contain 10 units of water, and a bank account might contain $100. Those amounts may change over time, but at any given time, you can check the stock's state, and it will tell you how much of its resource it contains. Stocks may also have a limit past which they will accept no more. Your bank account probably doesn't have an upper limit, but you can only put so much water into your bathtub before no more will go in!

The *sink*, then, is the drain: it is the outflow from the stock. Just as the stock's state is "how much" of a resource it contains right now, its behavior is to send some amount of the resource onward per unit time. In this way, it functions very much like the source, with the key difference being that if the stock is empty, it cannot pass anything along, whereas the source is typically assumed to always be able to generate its resource.

While it might seem odd to talk about "faucets" and "drains" in systems, these are key elements, particularly for games. At some point, you have to draw the bounds around what you are designing and leave aside considerations from outside it. For example, if you are creating a system model for a factory, you might assume that water and electricity would flow in from an external (and unbounded) source rather than also taking on the modeling of the power plant and water distribution. In games in particular, as with making a part's state "spreadsheet specific" by creating its details in nonsystemic terms, you typically need to specify a variety of sources and sinks, faucets and drains, in terms of how they affect the game.

For example, in the early days of massively multiplayer online games (MMOs), the economic systems in these games were referred to as "faucet/drain" economies. Figure 2.3 is adapted from a diagram describing the economy in the game *Ultima Online* and shows how this was diagrammed in a way that highlights sources, stocks, flows, resources, and drains.

In this system model, there is an unbounded faucet (actually more than one) at the top left, representing an unbounded source of various "virtual resources," including goods supplied by non-player characters (NPCs), monsters that pop out of nowhere, and gold that NPCs pay to players. These resources flow through various stocks and mostly drain out of the economy via the connecting flows leading to the lower right.

In this diagram, resources are shown being kept in various stocks (the gray dish-like boxes), but the grouping shown here is more diagrammatic than actual. For example, a player might "manufacture" goods and keep them in inventory (box 6), but their inventory is separate from that of any other player. These stocks are also typically not limited in how much they can store, and outflow through the drain is not guaranteed: Simpson (n.d.) relates a well-known story of a player who kept over 10,000 manufactured (virtual) shirts in his house in the game. This caused real problems for the game economy as it meant that each object (each shirt, for example) had to be tracked and accounted for at all times.

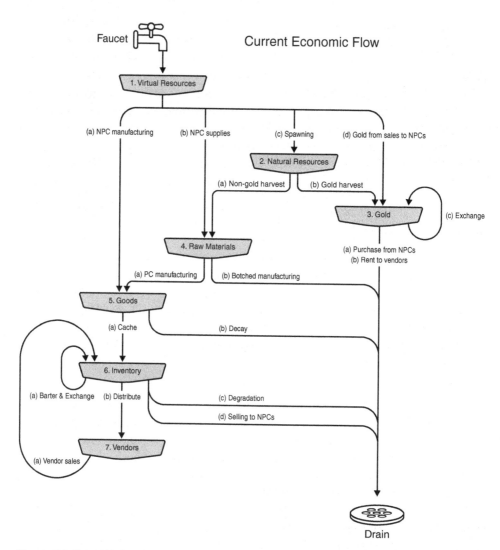

Figure 2.3 Faucet/drain economy adapted from *Ultima Online*. Each gray box is a *stock*, with *flows* between them. These start at a never-ending faucet and end at a never-filling drain

A similar issue that arises from this sort of economic system is rampant inflation. Note that "gold" (one of the primary resources and the monetary currency in the game) is created *ex nihilo* from the unbounded faucet-source. Every time a player in the game kills a monster or sells an item to an NPC vendor, new gold is created and added to the economy. This gold might flow back out of the economy via the manufacture of goods or other means, but a great deal of it remains in the economy. As the amount of available gold grows, each individual unit of it becomes reduced in value to the players—the definition of economic inflation. While the solutions to this problem are typically complex, even the issue itself is difficult to understand without a sufficiently systemic view of the economy. You will see more about economies as game systems and their issues (including inflation) again in Chapter 7.

Converters and Deciders

In addition to sources, stocks, and sinks, there are other specialized kinds of parts that we often encounter when diagramming systems. Two of them are *converters* and *deciders*. Figure 2.4 shows a system diagram that incorporates these, as well as a source and a sink.

In this system, some resource flows from a *source* to a *converter* process and then to a *sink*. That in itself is not very remarkable (and it's not really even a system), but it is an abstraction to help keep this diagram clear. As part of the process, there is also a measurement: is the process going too fast or two slow? This is where it becomes systemic, as these connections create a loop back to the source. By means of the measuring *decider* parts, the converter process is kept within the required bounds.

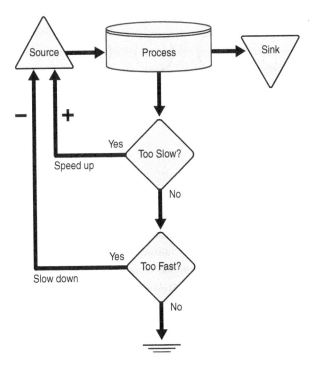

Figure 2.4 An abstract system diagram including a source, a converter, a sink, and two deciders

Careful readers may note that this diagram is essentially the same as the more detailed drawing of a centrifugal governor in Figure 1.7: the engine is the source, and it provides power to some process (such as converting heat to rotational motion), and the sink is the exhaust. The engine goes faster or slower, making the weights move up or down with the centrifugal force. The weights act as a mechanical decider, keeping the engine within bounds.

Complicated Versus Complex

Parts that connect to form systems always do so in ways that form loops. As you will see here, looping systems become *complex*. Nonlooping collections may create *complicated* processes, but ultimately they do not create complex systems. This has significant consequences for systems design overall and for game design in particular.

Simple Collections and Complicated Processes

If you have a bunch of parts that don't really have any connections in that they have no behaviors that affect each other's state, then they form a simple *collection* and not a system: a heap of bricks (as Poincaré said) or a bowl of fruit is a collection.[3] The items in these collections have no significant connections or interactions between them, and so they remain isolated. Parts have to have significant, state-changing connections based on their behaviors to create a system.

Figure 2.5 A complicated process of linearly interconnected parts

A complicated process is one with multiple parts and many interactions. However, these parts are connected sequentially and affect each other only linearly, one after another (see Figure 2.5). A process like this is often predictable and repeatable, and you know what happens after each step. However, because there are no loops to create feedback, the process does not form a system.

One example of a complicated assemblage is the simple pendulum we encountered earlier (refer to Figure 1.2). The weight of the pendulum and the length of the rod it hangs from interact to create a highly predictable (if sometimes complicated) path. But there are no significant feedback loops to make this into a complex system.

Similarly, many assembly-line processes are complicated: there's a lot involved in putting together a car on an assembly line, but it's not going to vary a whole lot from car to car of the same type. Sending a rocket to the Moon is even more complicated: there's a lot going on and no one would say it's easy, but the different phases of the process don't have disproportionate

---

3. This is mostly true. Fruits in a bowl actually do interact on a long enough time scale as they ripen and spoil, but for most purposes, we can look at each piece of fruit as a separate thing that doesn't interact with the other fruits around it.

effects on each other. Once you get through launch and boost, those stages aren't going to have unpredictable effects on later phases, such as lunar orbital insertion. More importantly, what happens in the lunar landing phase has no effect on the initial launch phase. And because the connections are linear, once you have sent a rocket to the Moon, there's little variance in doing so a second time (at least until parts do interact and things go wrong, which is when the process veers into complex territory).

In game design terms, games that present the player with sequential levels are more complicated than complex: typically what happens on Level 10 has no effect on the state or gameplay on Level 2. Once a player has played through a level, they may never play it again (and if they do, it will not have changed even though they have been there before). This sequential rather than systemic game design requires the designer to create more content, as once the player has been through part of the game, its future gameplay value is sharply reduced.

The key concept here is that in a complicated process, there are interactions between parts, but these are essentially linear or random: there are no feedback loops in the process. One result of this is that when something unexpected happens in a complicated process, it's either entirely random or, more often, it's possible to trace the problem from the effect back to a single cause and fix or replace the specific part that caused it. Therefore, this kind of process is typically amenable to linear, reductionist thinking in looking back from one part to the previous one to find a root cause.

Complex Systems

When parts affect each other in ways that connect together to form a loop, things become a lot more interesting. In a case like this, parts still interact with each other, but now they do so such that the actions of one part cycle around and come back again so that a part's behavior inevitably comes back to alter its future state and behavior (see Figure 2.6). These loops are what create a complex system.

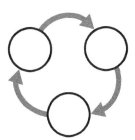

Figure 2.6 A highly simplified complex feedback loop. Each part in the system directly or indirectly affects the others

Just as the simple pendulum is an example of a complicated assemblage, the double pendulum (refer to Figure 1.2) is a relatively simple example of a complex system. The parts of the double pendulum—the mass of the weight, the location of the joint, and the position in space of the weight, the joint, and the pivot from which it all hangs, all interact and feedback on each other. This is why the path the double pendulum takes is so sensitive to its initial conditions: as it moves, the position and force on each part change, each part feeding back on the others (and thus itself), creating wildly divergent paths from similar starting locations.

There are many examples of complex systems across every part of our existence, including the human body, the global economy, a romance, hurricanes, termite mounds, and, of course, many games. Even Figure I.1 at the start of this book shows an abstract view of the complex system that this book is about.

Each of these systems has the qualities of having multiple, independent parts that have their own internal state and affect each other via their behavior in ways that form feedback loops. They also, as you will see here, remain adaptive and robust to external changes over time and create organized behavior and emergent properties.

The way in which parts form loops means that each part affects its own future state and behavior. Part A affects B, which affects C, which then affects A again. These behavioral effects take some amount of time, so "future A" will be in a different state from "current A" after one cycle through the loop and having been affected by C. This looping connection has dramatic consequences. It means that, despite the reductionist view of the universe (as championed by Descartes and Newton), complex systems cannot easily be broken down to be turned into merely complicated ones: "unwinding the loop" destroys its essential nature by breaking the final connection (for example, from C back to A).

We will return to this point as it relates to nonlinearity and the whole being other, or greater, than the sum of its parts—as understood by those from Aristotle to the psychologist Koffka and the ecologist Smuts, and as referred to by Lawrence as the "third thing" in his poem about water and Alexander as the "quality without a name." This connection between complicated and complex, between reductive parts and how they can create emergent wholes, is vital for understanding and creating systems.

Loops

Complex systems contain parts that have behaviors, and these behaviors connect the parts in ways that form *loops*. These loops are in many ways the most important structures in systems and in games. Recognizing them and building them effectively is key to working in systems.

At their most basic, loops may either be constructive or destructive. In systems thinking, they are typically called *reinforcing* or *balancing* loops (sometimes *positive feedback* or *negative feedback* loops). Reinforcing loops increase the effects of each part's behavior in the loop, while balancing loops decrease them. Both are important, but in almost all cases, if a system does not have at least one primary reinforcing loop, it will soon diminish and cease to exist: if the loop extinguishes the behaviors of the parts within it, they will soon cease their function and have no connection to each other at all. (The exceptions are when stable loops are made by each part preventing another from acting, as in a wall held up by opposing buttresses, either of which would topple the wall if not for the other.)

Loops exist as the interactions between parts. Each part has a behavior that affects another and that is shown by the arrows in the loop, as in Figure 2.7. In the examples shown here, the text portions (for example, "Account balance" and "Properties owned") are examples of stocks, as described earlier: this is where some amount or value is held. The arrows indicate an effect on the amount in stock, as enacted by a part's behavior: if an arrow has a + beside it, then the more there is of the first stock, the more is added to the second. If there is a − beside an arrow, then an increased amount in the first stock *reduces* the amount in the second.

Reinforcing and Balancing Loops

Reinforcing loops involve two or more parts where each enhances or increases the amount of some resource in stock of the next, which increases its behavioral output. These loops can be found in a lot of situations in life and in a lot of games. Two common examples are shown in Figure 2.7. In a bank account, the account balance increases the interest earned—and the interest earn then increases the account balance. That is, the more money-resource you have in stock (the account balance), the more this amount is increased due to interest. Similarly, in the game *Monopoly*, the more cash you have (your stock of cash as a resource), the more properties you can buy. Properties are also resources, and the more of this resource you have, the more cash-resource you gain.

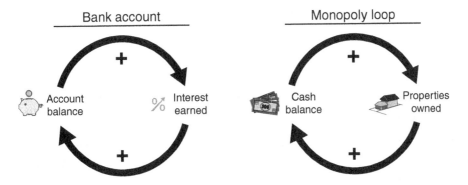

Figure 2.7 Reinforcing loops in a bank account and in *Monopoly*

In general, reinforcing loops increase the value or activity of the parts involved. In a game, they tend to reward winners, magnify early success in a game, and destabilize the gameplay. They can lead to runaway win conditions if one player is able to capitalize even a little bit better on a reinforcing loop in the game. Because of this property, these loops are sometimes called "snowball" loops (like a snowball that grows larger and larger as it rolls downhill) or "the rich get richer" loops. You will see these conditions again in Chapter 7, with a more detailed discussion of how reinforcing loops in games can go awry.

Balancing loops are the opposite of reinforcing loops: each part reduces the value and thus the activity of the next part in the loop. Two simple examples of balancing loops are shown in Figure 2.8. The first is an abstract depiction of an oven thermostat. Based on the temperature set for the oven, there is a gap between its current temperature and this setting. The larger that gap, the more heat is applied. The gap acts as a resource in stock that is slowly draining down. As more heat is applied, the gap becomes smaller (the resource is reduced), causing the amount of heat being applied to become smaller as well.

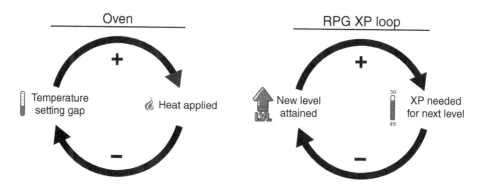

Figure 2.8 Balancing loops in an oven and a role-playing game

The diagram on the right in Figure 2.8 shows a common scheme for how experience points (XP) are handled in a role-playing game (RPG). On gaining a new level, the XP needed for the next level increases (often dramatically) over the number needed to attain the current one. This has the effect of reducing the speed with which the character will gain another level.

Balancing loops are used to maintain or restore equilibrium, or parity, between parts in a loop. In games, they tend to be more forgiving to players who are behind, stabilizing and thus prolonging the game, preventing early winners from permanently pulling ahead. A classic example of this is the "blue shell" (officially called a "spiny shell") in the game *Mario Kart*. This item is a power-up randomly made available in the game to anyone except the person in first place. Once fired, it moves forward and can hit anyone who does not get out of the way, but it only specifically targets the racer in first place. Upon hitting, it flips the player's cart over, slowing them down. In this way, it acts as a powerful balancing factor, providing those behind the opportunity to catch up.

Combined, Linear, and Nonlinear Effects

Every system has both reinforcing and balancing loops. To return to the centrifugal governor (refer to Figures 1.7 and 2.4), you can see that it uses both kinds of loops: if the engine is going too slow, the reduced spin causes the weights to drop and the valve to open, increasing the engine's speed (a reinforcing loop). But if the engine is going too fast, the weights rise, the valve closes, and the engine's activity is reduced (a balancing loop).

In the case of the centrifugal governor, the output results may be *linear*: that is, the weights rise and fall in direct proportion to the engine's speed. Relationships like this are easy to understand. Most systems, however, have outputs with a *nonlinear* relationship to the inputs or underlying changes, and this makes their behavior far more interesting.

For example, suppose you have two populations of animals, one predator and one prey: lynxes and hares. Both will try to reproduce and increase their own population, and of course lynxes will hunt and eat the hares. (The lynxes probably also have their own predators, but we will represent them only abstractly in this model.)

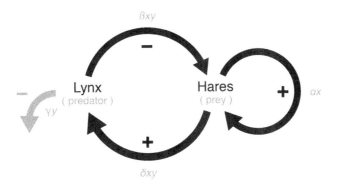

Figure 2.9 Lynxes and hares in a typical predator–prey relationship

You might imagine that the lynxes and hares form a balancing loop, as shown in the big loop in Figure 2.9. For now don't worry about the Greek letters shown there; just focus on the loops. The hares reproduce, increasing (reinforcing) their number, as shown in the little loop on the right. However, the lynxes eat the hares, which reduces (balances) their population. As a result, when the hare population goes down, the lynxes have a harder time surviving because there's less to eat. What emerges from this complex relationship is not just a linear balancing act but a nonlinear oscillating graph, as shown in Figure 2.10. This graph shows time moving to the right, with the number of predators and prey rising and falling over time. The lines show how the numbers of predators and prey (lynxes and hares) change as a result of their mutual and overall balancing relationship to each other. The predators are never as numerous as their prey, and their rise and fall is consistently offset in time from that of the prey: once the hares start to disappear, the lynxes have a more difficult time reproducing (or surviving), and so their numbers start to dwindle. As that happens, the hares have an easier time surviving, and so their numbers begin to grow again. This makes it easier for the lynxes to survive and have offspring, who then eat more of the hares, starting the cycle all over again.

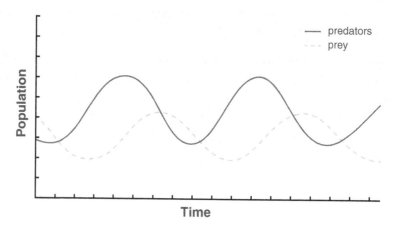

Figure 2.10 Lynx and hare model of population data over time (Iberg 2015)

The nonlinearity that emerges from this system is important to understand. We often (naively) expect that a quantity that is rising now will continue to rise indefinitely: if things are going well today, they will continue to go well tomorrow. This ignores any underlying nonlinear effects, as any mathematical or systemic modeling will show. If you think about the relationships between the parts of the system, the reason for the nonlinear and oscillating relationship becomes clear: whenever a predator kills a prey animal, it is removing from the prey population not just the animal it has killed but all of the potential offspring it might have had. This has a magnifying effect over time. Thus, the relationship between the two is not merely additive but multiplicative. Stepping through this may help make that last point clear:

- When a lynx kills a hare, it reduces the hare population by one.
- But the future hare population also loses the offspring that this hare would have had.
- And the next generation of hares isn't down by one but by one *multiplied* by the number of offspring that one would have had.
- The following generation is down by the number of offspring each of *those* hares would have had…and on and on.
- The overall result is that killing one hare has a magnified, multiplicative relationship with the future hare population.
- Finally, since the lynx population needs the hares to survive, when there are few hares, the lynxes have a hard time surviving, which allows the hares to bounce back a bit.

By looking at the system of the lynxes and the hares, you can see that their relationship isn't merely linear or additive. There's more than the sum of each at work. Another way of saying this, from a systemic level is, as Smuts (1927) said, the result of interactions like this at an individual level creates a nonlinear whole that is "more than the sum of its parts."

However, nonlinear output from a system is not necessarily periodic and oscillating like this population data; all sorts of results are possible. You have already seen one example of this in the unpredictable behavior of the path traced by a double pendulum (refer to Figure 1.3). The behavior of a few stable parts (the weight and two rods connected by joints) is completely nonlinear and chaotic.

Mathematical Modeling of Nonlinear Effects

To be more precise about the multiplicative relationship between predator and prey, we can look to what have long been known as predator–prey, or Lotka–Volterra, equations (Lotka 1910, Volterra 1926), as shown in Figure 2.11. These equations look a lot more daunting than they are—and we don't typically use them in game design or even in general systemic representations of relationships like those between predator and prey. Nevertheless, it's useful to understand how these equations work and how to approach the same kind of problem from a systems point of view.

$$\frac{dx}{dt} = \alpha x - \beta xy$$

$$\frac{dy}{dt} = \delta xy - \gamma y$$

x = number of prey

y = number of predators

$\alpha, \beta, \gamma, \delta$ = parameters

t = time

Figure 2.11 Lotka–Volterra, or predator–prey, equations

What both the equation in Figure 2.11 and the causal loop diagram in Figure 2.9 show is that prey increase at a rate of αx— that is, the number of prey, x, multiplied by how fast they have offspring, designated by α (alpha, used here as a variable). Another way of saying this is that every living prey animal x is assumed in this model to give rise to α offspring in the next generation. These prey animals die at a rate given by βxy, where y is how many predators there are, and β (beta) is a parameter that states how often a meeting of x and y, prey and predator, results in a prey animal dying. This equals the left side of the first equation, which expresses the "change over time" in x, the number of prey animals (dx/dt is used in calculus to mean "a very small change in x over a very small period of time," with d indicating an amount of change or time that is as close to zero as possible and t representing time).

So, to state that whole first equation again, the change in the number of hares (prey animals) at any given time is based on the number of hares times their birth rate, minus the number of hares eaten by lynxes, which is given by the number of lynxes, the number of hares, and the rate at which a lynx gets a hare.

The equation for the predators is similar, but here we abstract out their reasons for dying. So the number of lynxes (predators, y) at any given time is based on how much food they have and their birth rate (δxy) and the rate at which they die off (γy), where δ (the lowercase Greek letter delta) is the modifier for how efficiently they can essentially turn food into little lynxes, and γ (gamma) is the modifier for how quickly each one dies off.

To show that this kind of nonlinear model is reflected in the real world, Figure 2.12 shows a depiction of data of actual lynx–hare population oscillations collected in the late 19th and early 20th centuries (MacLulich 1937). This data is messier than the model above, of course, because there are other dependencies not used in our abstract system: food sources for the prey animals, other animals preying on either predator or prey, weather effects, and so on. The nonlinear oscillations in the populations are nevertheless apparent.

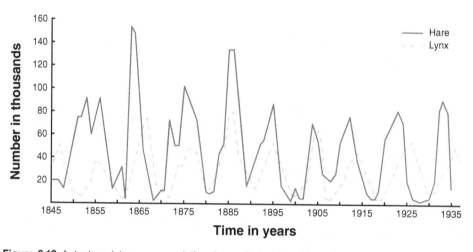

Figure 2.12 Actual predator–prey population data, adapted from MacLulich (1937)

Mathematical Versus Systemic Modeling

The Lotka–Volterra equations used in the preceding section create a concise mathematical model for a set of systemic effects. They demonstrate well the nonlinearities that emerge from the predator–prey relationship, and they do so in a way that those who are familiar with such mathematical modeling can find not only succinct but even beautiful. Such a set of mathematical statements does not, however, inform our understanding of the inner workings of the system itself. It treats the parts of the system, the individual hares and lynxes, as abstracted aggregate symbols rather than as entities interacting with each other via their behaviors.

It may be worth taking a moment to discuss what is meant by a *model* in this context. Both the systemic and mathematical representations above provide abstract approximations of real-world processes. As shown in Figure 2.12, the real-world relationship between lynxes and hares is messier than the inexact illustrations provided by either the systems diagram and its graph or the mathematical equations. In games, as in most other systems you create, you are making a model of some part of the world. No model is ever really completely accurate, just as a model ship is never quite like an actual full-size ship. The models we make are nevertheless useful, as they allow us to improve our understanding of a larger-scale, more detailed process—and, in our case, to make games. We'll talk more about the internal model of games in Chapters 3 and 7.

In the mathematical model shown in the equations in Figure 2.11, the parameters like the birth, predation, and death rates—α, δ, β, and γ above—are controls you can tweak to change the overall behavior. In games, these parameters are often informally called "knobs," with the designer's action being that of turning a knob up or down to change a particular response. In a mathematical model, these knobs are essentially on the outside of a black box: they affect the internal workings via the equations given, but their actions may not be at all obvious to the observer.

In systemic design, these parameters are more typically implemented via lower-level interactions of the internal state of the predator and prey rather than as high-level parametric knobs. For example, in a systemic model, the lynxes and hares likely have their own internal states and behaviors that determine their effective birth rate (α and δ in the equations above), and the attack strength of the lynxes versus the defense value of the hares will together determine what is shown in the above equations as the aggregated predation (β) parameter. Such a systemic view can make for more comprehensible and nuanced models that are less opaque from the designer's point of view. It is important to construct your systems such that nonlinear results like these emerge from them at higher levels. Nevertheless, at some point, as a designer, you will need to decide the lowest level of detail for your system and implement appropriate parameters there (including random values) to represent even lower-level behavior.

Chaos and Randomness

In discussing mathematical and systemic models in the context of looping systems, we should also touch on the differences between *chaos* and *randomness*. You will see another detailed discussion of probability and randomness in Chapter 9, "Game Balance Methods."

Random Effects

A system that is random is unpredictable, at least within a range; for example, a system with a random state between 1 and 10 may be at any value within that range. That is, whenever a value for an attribute on a part is called for, rather than simply assigning it a single number, say 5, you randomly determine what the number is within its range. In the simplest case, if the range is 1 to 10, then each number in that range has the same chance—1/10, or 10%—of appearing any time the next value is determined. Since the attribute's state is random, you can't tell what its value will be in the future based on what it is now.

In games, systems like this are useful as a way to simulate the action of low-level systems we are not actually modeling: rather than have the output of a system always be the same, we can enable it to vary randomly across its prescribed range. This provides variability to the higher-level system of which this is just one part so that the result here is not predictable and boring. A common example of this in games is how much damage is dealt by an attack. While a multitude of factors may be taken into account (the weapon used, the user's skill, the type of attack, any armor or other defenses, and so on), at some point a variable amount of damage, random within a specified range, takes the place of simulating 1,000 more factors that in themselves are too difficult, time-consuming, or negligible to simulate on their own.

Chaotic Effects

In the real world, we encounter chaotic systems far more often than we experience random ones: like the double pendulum discussed earlier, these are systems that are deterministic, meaning that in principle, if you know the complete state of the system at some point in time, you can predict its future behavior. However, these systems are also highly susceptible to minute changes in conditions. So starting a double pendulum or another chaotic system from two positions that are different by a tiny amount will result in two paths that are not just a little different but completely different from each other.

But of course things are not always this simple. A system that is chaotic but deterministic and not random is not amenable to reductionist, "clockwork" analysis, as discussed earlier. Systemic, nonlinear effects often make it impossible to analyze a system by taking it apart; such a system must be analyzed as a whole system, either by representing its subparts, their relationships, and the effects that come from these interactions, or by use of mathematical modeling like the Lotka–Volterra equations discussed earlier.

Moreover, chaotic systems sometimes display what looks like nonchaotic behavior. This is particularly evident when a chaotic system can behave nonlinearly *with itself*; such events are often known as "resonance events." Resonance events happen when a large number of small, chaotic events combine in a reinforcing loop to create a nonlinear result with an enormous effect on the system itself. This can be seen in the ways that wind or even people walking across a bridge cause it to sway, sometimes disastrously.

Collapsing Bridges

The Tacoma Narrows Bridge in Washington State famously self-destructed in 1940 after being buffeted by wind. While the wind alone couldn't have caused the bridge to collapse, it did push on the bridge, causing it to sway—just a little at first. As the wind pushed on the bridge, the length of the main span caused it to sway with a particular frequency. This swaying then increased how much the bridge caught the wind, further increasing the intensity of its motion.

The bridge and the wind quickly became joined in a chaotic system with a dominant reinforcing loop that had violent and disastrous results (Eldridge 1940). See Figure 2.13.

In a similar case, authorities in London in the late 1800s posted signs on the Albert Bridge that read, "Officers in command of troops are requested to break step when passing over this bridge" after other similar bridges collapsed due to the resonance created by many stamping feet. Each footfall in itself was small compared to the strength of a bridge, but together they created enough of a reinforcing loop that the soldiers' steps could lead to a tragic, nonlinear resonant result (Cookson 2006).

Figure 2.13 The catastrophic collapse of the Tacoma Narrows Bridge and a reinforcing loop diagram of this event. Eventually the bridge's motion was so violent that it broke out of the loop with the destruction of the bridge

Fireflies

A far less destructive example of a chaotic system that achieves a kind of nonlinear resonance can be found in some fireflies. These little bugs provide a wonderful light show in the evenings in many parts of the world, as each one emits a flash of light to try to attract a mate. However, in some parts of Southeast Asia and the Smoky Mountains of the southern United States, entire populations of fireflies will blink at the same time, all synchronized together (NPS.gov 2017).

They do this on their own, without any firefly conductor telling them when to flash, by means of a simple mechanism: whenever one firefly sees another nearby light up, it hurries up to flash a little sooner than it would have otherwise. With this simple mechanism, the whole system moves from chaos to resonance.

Each firefly here is a part in a system, with a behavior of flashing its abdomen light. When another firefly (another part in the system) sees this behavior, it alters its own internal state to flash sooner than it might otherwise—which of course is seen by other fireflies. The result is that in a short period of time, more and more fireflies are flashing at the same time, until they are all flashing in unison. The system is chaotic in that it is highly sensitive to its starting conditions, and there's no way to tell exactly when any firefly will light up. However, because of their one form of local interaction, the entire population of fireflies soon begins to resonate: first in small patches, then in big waves, then all together, as each bug slightly adjusts its next flash time based on what it's seeing.

Similar resonance effects can be found in nerve cells in the mammalian heart, in the brain, and in many other parts of nature. They are excellent examples of nonlinear effects that create resonant, synchronized order out of distributed actions of parts in a system.

Examples of Loop Structures

There are many examples of systemic loops that illustrate how these structures create various (often nonlinear) effects. We discuss a few of them here.

One general class is often called "fixes that fail" and is exemplified by the "cobra effect" (Siebert 2001) discussed in Chapter 1. In that situation, the problem was "too many cobras!" and the solution was "reward for cobras," as shown in Figure 2.14. This forms a nice balancing loop: as people take the reward for turning in cobra heads, there are fewer cobras around (and fewer to breed the next generation), so the severity of the problem diminishes.

Figure 2.14 The balancing loop for "too many cobras"

However, there is another outer loop here, as shown in Figure 2.15. This is often called an *unintended consequences* loop, as it creates a reinforcing loop that is hidden for a little while and brings back the original problem (or another, related condition) with a vengeance. Notably, in this loop there is a delay, signified by the two hash marks (\\) on one arc, meaning that this outer loop happens more slowly than the inner loop. The result in the end is typically that the problem is worse than when it started—plus a great deal of time and energy have been spent on an illusory "solution."

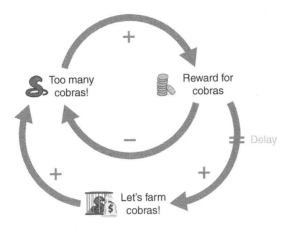

Figure 2.15 The outer reinforcing loop showing fixes that fail

There are many examples of this structure in real life: you need to save money, so you don't maintain your car regularly. This works for a little while, until that delayed outer loop catches up with you, and now you need to spend more money to fix a major failure that could have been prevented at a lower cost. Or, a division at a company is in trouble, so a new manager institutes a bunch of quick fixes. Revenue starts to rise, things look great, and the manager who "saved the day" is promoted. However, soon the long-term unintended consequences (the metaphorical "farmed cobras") begin to become apparent. The person who replaced the promoted manager begins to scramble, but the situation is now far worse than it was before, and they end up being blamed not only for the poor performance but for messing up the terrific situation provided by the previous manager (who may now be their boss). A short-term view that ignores the underlying systemic causes and effects often leads to this kind of fix-that-fails.[4]

In a game context, a player in a strategy game who builds a huge army quickly may actually find themselves at a disadvantage to another player who instead invested some of their resources in researching how to make better troops. The first player took the fast route but ignored the deficit built up by not thinking longer term; their "fix" failed to take into account the value of troops that were more effective individually but that took longer to make. The second player avoided the quick fix (having a large army) by investing their resources with a longer-term view. This choice between "build fast now" and "invest for the future" is an example of a looping structure called an *engine* that you will see again in Chapter 7.

---

4. I am sorry to say that this is a pattern I have observed many times in the software industry.

Limits to Growth—And the Crashes That Can Follow

Another example of a loop structure, and one that shows nonlinear results well, is the class that shows *limits to growth* (see Figure 2.16). This name comes originally from a book of the same title (Meadows et al. 1972) that was intended as a forward-looking commentary on the overall world system and whether its growth could be maintained through the 21st century. (The authors were not optimistic.) Beyond this particular usage, the pattern overall is worth examining and understanding.

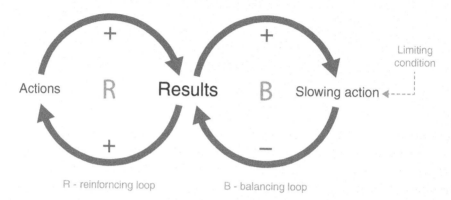

Figure 2.16 Two interlocked loops that illustrate limits to growth

We often assume that given some result, doing more of what led to it will give us a result that continues to increase linearly. We often hear statements like "if our business continues to grow at this rate..." or "if the population continues to grow at this rate" that contain the implicit assumption that things will continue in the future as they have been in the past. This is almost never the case. The reason is that for every accelerating condition fed by a reinforcing loop—increased sales, crop yield, or number of units built—there is a separate balancing loop fed by a limiting condition. This condition is typically some resource that is necessary for and diminished by increasing growth (new customers available as a market becomes saturated, a mineral in the soil taken up and not replenished, ability to pay for units, and so on).

The overall nonlinear result is a curve that rises slowly, then quickly, and then more slowly until it levels off again. A typical example of this is depicted in Figure 2.17, which shows how yields of wheat production have leveled off since the late 1990s (Bruins 2009). The factors contributing to this slowdown in growth are no doubt complex in a global situation like this one, involving physical, economic, and political resources, but the overall effect is the same: if someone predicted the future based on a linear extrapolation from data in the 1970s or 1980s, they would have been sorely disappointed a decade later.

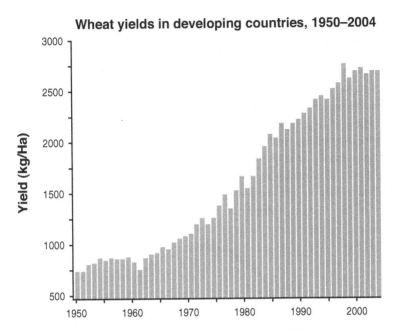

Figure 2.17 The limits to growth of wheat yields. Note that increased yields accelerate quickly and then slow down, flattening in a classic S curve rather than remaining linear

Even some seemingly simple and potentially unending reinforcing loops have limits to their growth—and, as with the unintended consequences of fixes that fail, these limits sometimes appear abruptly. A classic version of this is evident in the stock market crash of 1929. In the years prior to the crash, the economy was booming, and stock prices seemed to only go one way: up. For an investor, buying something today that you could turn around and sell tomorrow for a profit seemed like an easy bet. As a result, many investors bought stocks on credit. As long as the cost of the credit was less than the profit they would make when they sold, it was, as the saying goes, "easy money." A form of stock purchasing called "buying on the margin" made this even easier for investors. In buying this way, an investor only had to keep a cash reserve of 10% to 20% of the total stock they were buying, with the assumption that they could always sell some stock (at a profit) to cover any costs from buying a different stock. This meant, in effect, that if you deposited $100 into a stock brokerage account, you could buy as much as $1,000 worth of stock. Since stock prices were continually rising, the belief was that you could always sell and still make a profit. Lots of people became wealthy this way, which enticed even more people to flood into the market.

Of course, there is always some limit to growth. In 1929, the first sign of trouble came with some companies reporting disappointing performance in March, which caused the market to dip and gave investors pause about their behavior. However, the market rebounded by the summer, which had the ironic effect of making people even *more* certain that the values of their shares would continue to rise without limit. Then, in October 1929, with stock prices at incredibly high values, several companies reported poor performance. This made some investors think that, while things were still going well economically, perhaps the time had come to cash in and get out of the market. Since so many had invested on the margin, they had to cover their prior purchases, which meant they had to sell more stock to do so. As stock prices began to fall late in October, investors had to sell more and more shares to cover their previous purchases, and a new reinforcing, snowballing loop came into effect (see Figure 2.18). The previous "irrational exuberance"[5] exhibited by investors now turned to panic, and they all tried to salvage what they could by selling as fast as they could. With everyone trying to sell and few buying, prices fell even further, and the reinforcing loop—in this case, one driving prices downward—accelerated quickly. By the end of the year, over 90% of the value and accumulated wealth from the stock market rise had been wiped out, ushering in the global Great Depression.

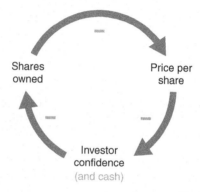

Figure 2.18 The reinforcing loop that drove the stock market crash of 1929. As investors lost capital and confidence in the market, they sold shares. This caused the price per share to drop, which further eroded investor confidence. Note that while all the effects are negative, this is a reinforcing loop, not a balancing loop—one that is sometimes known as a vicious cycle

Unfortunately, a similar example can be seen in the financial situation in 2017. According to Turner (2016), subprime lending is on the rise, as it was prior to the financial crash of 2008. This time, however, the lending is in credit cards and things like cars rather than mortgages. "Subprime" means that the loans are risky, an acknowledgement that many will not be paid back just because those borrowing won't have the money to do so. To cover this risk, borrowers pay more in interest for the loans. The more risky loans that are made, the more defaults—borrowers not being able to pay back the loans—there are (see Figure 2.19). In addition, this is happening against an economic backdrop in which there has for several decades (unalleviated by the crash of 2008) been an increase in concentration of money among the very wealthiest in U.S. and global society. This means that there are a few who want to make a further profit

---

5. A phrase used by Federal Reserve Chair Alan Greenspan (1996) to describe a similar situation in the markets of his day.

on their (already increasing) wealth, and there are many more who need to borrow that money even at a high cost. Basing his analysis of figures from UBS Bank, Turner characterizes the situation this way:

> As the pool of wealth becomes more concentrated, the greater the asymmetry between the haves, who typically want to invest and get a return on their money, and the have nots, who are typically borrowers. That pushes down the creditworthiness of the average borrower. Add in a low-interest-rate environment, where investors are searching for yield, and you have a problem. (Turner 2016)

Figure 2.19 Investors search for profits to offset losses from investment defaults. What is the limit to this growth?

That is, the more concentrated the wealth is, the more difficult it is for those holding that money to find ways to increase it via investment because so many others have less money and are increasingly risky as investments. This difficulty pushes investors to look further and further afield for ways to make a profit and to become increasingly willing to take on higher-risk investments. Those higher-risk investments will increase the rate of loan defaults, which reinforces the investor's need to show a profit, thus driving their search into riskier and riskier territory (refer to Figure 2.19). What's worse is that there is another component to this loop, as shown in Figure 2.20: for those on the borrowing side (the "have nots"), their need to make purchases (including necessities like food and rent) drives them to take out more loans and increase their debt. Sometimes people feel forced to take out very high-cost loans to cover *other* loans they already have, but this just leaves them further in debt. Between additional interest, fees, and in some cases not being able to repay these debts, the loop becomes reinforcing, with those same people needing more loans for further purchases.

Neither of these reinforcing loops is sustainable; both have strong limits to their growth as the cost of borrowing increases and the ability to pay decreases. Unlike in 1929, as of this writing, we do not yet know the end of this financial story. Hopefully, if we can recognize and analyze systemic effects like this around us, we can prevent the worst of the crashes that may follow.

Apart from these grim examples of limits to growth, we will see the effects of this same principle along with others in uneven competition in games when we discuss the use of loops in game design in Chapter 7.

Figure 2.20 Borrowers seek to get ahead of debt. What is the limit to *this* growth?

The Tragedy of the Commons

Another well-known issue best understood from a systemic point of view is known as the tragedy of the commons. This ancient problem, described originally in modern times by Lloyd (1833), still occurs in many forms today. Lloyd described the situation in which individuals acting on their own, and with no ill intent, nevertheless manage to destroy a shared resource—and thus their own future gains. As shown in Figure 2.21, each actor has their own reinforcing loop: they takes some action and gains some positive result. This could be anything, but the original description was of grazing animals in an area open to all in a village—known as the "commons." By grazing cattle or sheep there, an individual increased the value of their herd. As the commons was available to anyone, any farmer who grazed more cattle there would benefit more and so had an incentive to do so. However, the grass eaten by the cattle was a shared resource. Therefore, if too many people tried to graze too many cattle there, soon the grass would be depleted, and no one would be able to use it.

In systemic terms, the use of the shared resource forms an outer balancing loop not unlike that seen in the unintentional consequences in fixes that fail. Certainly in the tragedy of the commons no single individual intends to make the resource fail for everyone, and it is often the case that no one has used so much of it that they feel at all responsible. As another example, dropping a single piece of litter on the street doesn't seem to add much to the unsightliness of the community, and puffing out a bit of smoke doesn't seem to add much to overall pollution. But when taken together with everyone else's actions, the loss of environmental beauty or air quality can be significant and obvious—even if no one feels responsible. This is another example of how looking for reductionist root causes can lead you astray: just because too much grass has been eaten from the commons, or there is too much trash on the ground or pollution in the air does not mean there is a single villain responsible. Systemic responsibility often equates to distributed, decentralized responsibility. Recognizing that and how individual actions can create unintended consequences is an important aspect of systems thinking.

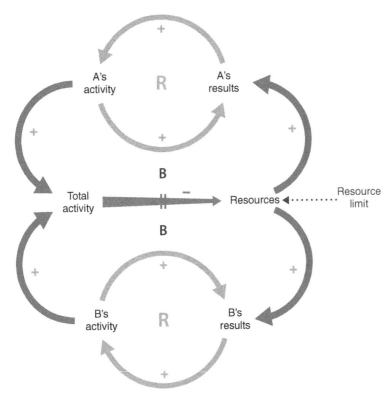

Figure 2.21 The tragedy of the commons. Individuals act in their own best short-term interest, but in so doing they deplete a common resource and reduce long-term gains for themselves and others

In games, systemic conditions like the tragedy of the commons can be seen whenever there is a limited resource that multiple people want to use, especially if they want to maximize their use of it. The resource may be physical in the game, like a gold mine or animals that can be used for food, or it can be anything with a limited availability and dwindling value with use. In a game with a working ecology, for example, if the players each kill a few rabbits for food, but in so doing cause the rabbit population to crash, this puts them into a tragedy of the commons situation. (Moreover, if the rabbits are food for lynxes, and the lynxes also keep some other kind of pest at bay, losing the rabbits means losing the lynxes, which can lead to other consequences for the players.)

Trophic Cascades

For a more positive example, we can also look back to the example of the trophic cascade created by reintroducing wolves into Yellowstone National Park (see Figure 2.22). This is a complex series of reinforcing and balancing loops: the wolves reduced (balanced) the number of elk and deer, and their reduced numbers *reduced* the balancing effect they were having on trees. Thus, in effect, the wolves were in a reinforcing relationship with the trees, and thus (transitively) with the bears, fish, birds, and so on.

Many systemic loops you will find and create will be even more complex and potentially confusing than this one. As long as you can remember to look for the stocks and resources (number of wolves, number of elk, and so on) and figure out the behavioral relationships between them (the arrows that make the loop), you will be able to disentangle even highly systemic, highly complex situations.

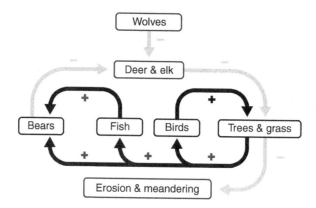

Figure 2.22 The trophic cascade resulting from reintroducing wolves into Yellowstone as a system diagram of reinforcing and balancing loops

Emergence

When reinforcing and balancing loops in a complex system are themselves in a dynamic balance, they create a metastable, organized systemic behavior. That is, every part in the system is changing, influencing and being influenced in their behavior, and yet the overall structure remains stable (at least for a time). This metastability creates a set of organized behaviors not found in any of the individual parts. For example, the action of each bird traveling together creates a metastable flock, just as the action of each atom bound together creates a metastable molecule. Similarly, the populations of fireflies discussed above create an emergent effect when they all flash at the same time. The effect is metastable and persistent, creating a surprising, often breathtaking visual property not found in (or directed by) any single firefly.

This overall metastability is an *emergent* effect, one that arises from the action of multiple parts. Emergent effects create new properties that are qualitatively different from any of the individual parts and do not result from a simple sum of the parts themselves. Such metastability also enables other emergent effects to arise from the actions of all the parts in the system.

As another example, in a school of fish, each part (each individual fish) has internal state such as mass, velocity, and direction. The overall weight of a school of such fish is not an emergent property, as it is just the sum of the weights of all the fish in the school. However, the *shape* of the school may well be emergent, as when they form a closely packed school called a baitball to get away from predators (see Figure 2.23) (Waters 2010). While each fish has its own shape, that shape does not itself determine the shape of the group of fish. Instead, each fish's position, velocity, and direction contributes to (but does not itself determine) the shape of the school.

Figure 2.23 Fish forming a closely packed baitball to evade a predator. The shape is a natural emergent effect (Photo by Steve Dunleavy)

The shape of the school cannot be found in any one fish, nor is any fish responsible for determining the shape of the school; there is no central controlling fish calling out shapes the fish should create together, like a marching band. Recognizing that there is no "fish in charge," no "central control system" (as Wiener said in his 1948 book *Cybernetics*) is an important aspect of truly grasping emergence and systemic functioning. It may be an artifact of our centralized culture (an aspect that has many positive effects), but in some cases even scientists have a difficult time seeing past it. As one example, Wilensky and Resnick (1999) pointed out that at least as late as the 1980s, scientists assumed that certain kinds of molds that aggregate themselves together must have had "founder" or "pacemaker" cells to start and guide the process. These molds start as single-cell organisms and end as large groups that even differentiate into organ-like structures. Is it possible this could happen without some kind of central control? For many years, this wasn't even a question that scientists asked. They had to first learn to see the distributed system and the organized behavior arising out of it without any central controller whatsoever.

When a metastable structure resulting from multiple interactions of the parts within it is

- not determined by any one part within it,
- not based on the linear sum of the attributes of its parts,
- more easily described in terms of the aggregation ("a spherical school of fish") than in terms of the individual parts and relationships (a tedious recounting of each fish's position, velocity, and direction),

then a new *thing* with its own properties has emerged. As discussed in Chapter 1, a water molecule has electrical polarity that is simpler to describe in terms of the "lumpy sphere" as a unified metastable structure (that is, as a thing on its own) than in terms of the contributing atoms—just as each atom has an electrical character that is easier to describe on its own than by referring to the protons and electrons or by diving still further down to the quarks with their fractional electrical charges inside the atom's nucleus.

There is no clear demarcation for emergence, just as there is no wrapper around a proton or an atom, but the unification of the constituent parts and relationships into new properties held by the whole thing is the telltale sign of emergence, of identity and integrity—and systems.

Upward and Downward Causality

In a system with emergent properties, the interactions of individual parts within the system cause the emergence. This is what is known as *upward causality*: a new behavior or property emerges from the distributed actions of lower-level structures. An example of this is in a stock market, where each individual person is making decisions to buy and sell. The aggregate behavior of these individuals can cause new effects to occur: for example, many decisions to buy by individuals can cause a rise in the overall market (as measured by its indexes of activity, volume of trades, and so on) that changes the character and behavior of the market, just as fish all trying to escape a predator change the shape of their school.

Similarly, the aggregate—the stock market as a thing, or the school of fish—can exhibit *downward causality* on the parts within it. When individuals in a stock market all begin to sell rapidly, the market itself goes into a crash—and this crashing affects the decisions of those in the market to sell more, thus creating a downward spiral. This is why stock market bubbles and crashes and similar phenomena seem to be so extreme and so irrational: the individuals within them are causing (upward) the behavior of the market, and the market is reciprocally causing (downward) the future behavior of the individuals. When many individuals buy, a bubble forms (out of their "irrational exuberance"); when a few begin to sell, they can quickly form a reinforcing loop that affects the behavior of others who also start to sell, and the market quickly crashes.

This downward causality helps explain otherwise baffling realities of how systems behave. It also highlights why reductionist thinking is insufficient to explain how complex systems work. By taking apart a complex system, you can reveal the upward causality—how the parts come together to create the whole. But such a reductionist approach will not yield the contextual downward causality that occurs only when the entire system is in operation and as a result affects its lower-level parts.

Hierarchy and Levels of Organization

Several times thus far, phrases like "levels of organization" have appeared here without definition. We have talked about these levels and upward and downward causation without really defining what these terms mean. As with emergence, *levels of organization* can be a difficult concept to articulate, though you may already have an intuitive idea about what this is.

The fundamental idea is, again, that a functioning metastable system creates a new thing. This thing's properties (its state, boundaries, and behaviors) are typically emergent from the mutual, looping interactions of the parts within it. Once such a new thing has emerged as the conglomeration of underlying parts, we describe it as being at a "higher level" of organization. This is easily recognized in the precedence from quark to proton to atom to molecule and on upward to planet and solar system, galaxy, and further on still. At each level of metastability, new recognizable, persistent things emerge. Likewise, as we dive down from our everyday world to the level of the molecule, atom, proton, and quark, we are able to recognize "lower level" systems. Each contains and emerges from the systems within it, and each (with those at the same level) creates the system at the next higher level.

As Alexander et al. (1977) were quoted earlier as saying, "Each pattern [or system] can exist in the world, only to the extent that it is supported by other patterns: the larger patterns in which it is embedded, the patterns of the same size that surround it, and the smaller patterns which are embedded in it." Every system is a part of another higher-level system, interacts with those around it, and contains lower-level systems within it. (See Figure 2.24 for an abstracted version of this.) As mentioned earlier, in the real world, these levels go down at least to the level of quarks—and we have no idea where the highest integrative level of organization is. In games, fortunately, we are able to choose our levels of organization and abstraction, though as you will see, there are rewards for taking the difficult road to making them deeper rather than shallower.

Like boundaries, these levels are not absolute or externally defined. They are an emergent property, whereby the state, behaviors, and loops of one set of parts work together to create new discernible properties. In this way, the system at one level becomes a part of a system at a higher level of organization.

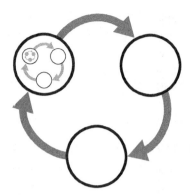

Figure 2.24 A highly simplified depiction of a hierarchical complex feedback loop. Each part in the loop at each level is itself a subsystem made up of interacting parts at a lower level

At each level, the system also displays *persistence* and *adaptability*. The property of persistence can be thought of as a boundary through time. That is, systems that persist are self-reinforcing within their own boundaries across time. A key part of this persistence is that the system is able to adapt, at least to some degree, to new signals or inputs from a changing environment. In living systems, this persistence and adaptability is called *homeostasis*—the ability to maintain internal conditions (within the organism's boundary) within a narrow range despite significant changes outside.

Structural Coupling

This hierarchical organization—parts within parts—is another hallmark of organized systems. It also leads to what Maturana (1975) called *structural coupling*. This is what occurs when "recurrent interactions [lead] to the structural congruence between two (or more) systems" (Maturana and Varela 1987). These systems are parts within a higher-level system that interact closely together. Each benefits from molding itself to the other in one way or another. In so doing, they alter each other and create a new, tightly integrated higher-level system. Examples of this include a horse and rider, car and driver, and many co-evolutionary relationships, as when an insect and flower over time affect each other as part of their mutual relationship.

A game and player also form a structurally coupled relationship. If the game is systemically designed, it will have defined a sufficiently broad and diverse state-space (a consequence of its "second-order" design, as described in Chapter 3) that it can adapt to the player as the player adapts to it. As you will read in Chapter 4, "Interactivity and Fun," this structural coupling is important for building engagement and fun in a game: the close mutual interactions between a game and player can make it difficult to break out of the interconnecting loops.

Systemic Depth and Elegance

Having discussed emergence, hierarchy, and levels of organization, we can now turn to what are otherwise difficult areas to define and discuss: the concepts of *depth* and *elegance* in systems and in games in particular.

A system can be said to have *depth* when its parts exist at multiple levels of organization—when they are themselves subsystems composed of lower-level parts interacting together. When considering such systems, you can think of them as unified things at each level and then change your perspective to go up or down a level, just as you did in our journey down to quarks and up to drops of water. These changes in perspective may at times become dizzying, but there is something so universally compelling about this experience that we often see it as harmonious and beautiful. This is why the quality of self-similarity seen in fractals, where each part resembles the whole but in miniature (see Figure 2.25), is so captivating: it is the visual manifestation of systemic depth.

Figure 2.25 Romanesco broccoli, one of many examples in nature and simulation of fractal self-similarity and systemic depth (Photo by Jacopo Werther)

Whether in real-world systems or in games, it can be difficult to build a mental model of systems-within-systems. Once you are able to construct a model that parallels this hierarchy, it is fascinating to comprehend the system from different perspectives at different levels, looking up and down the organizational hierarchy in your mind. The same is true in various forms of art, literature, and so on, where a thoughtful compliment is to say that something "works on so many levels." This is both an acknowledgement and a reflection of our own internal model-building process, as well as our fascination in seeing a system from different perspectives.

Games with Depth

Designing game systems that each contain subsystems with their own subspaces that can be explored by the player provides multiple benefits. The depth is itself attractive, if for no other reason than it enables players to build multilevel systemic mental models: the player is rewarded for learning each new subsystem over time, much like opening a present to find another present inside. In addition, a game with depth in its systems creates enormous variability for the player to explore as gameplay, since the designer has set up a wide space for the game using systemic design rather than creating a narrow path of custom content that never changes.

In some cases, deep games may have few rules. The spare but systemic design enables players to more quickly grasp the structure and see it from multiple levels of perspective—though this is still cognitively taxing for most of us!

A prime example of this is the ancient game *Go*, shown in Figure 2.26. The game has fascinated people for thousands of years with its simplicity, depth, and subtlety. *Go* consists only of a square board, typically marked by 19x19 intersecting lines, and a collection of black and white pieces, each color played by one player. Players take turns placing a stone of their color on an empty spot on the board. Each player attempts to surround and capture the other player's pieces. The game ends when the board is filled or both players have passed in succession, and the player with the most territory on the board wins. With that very brief description, you have all the state, boundaries, and behavior of the system: you know enough to play the game and see its many levels of emergence. There is of course a great deal more to the game—lives have been spent and books written on comprehending the game's decision-space more fully—but that is how deep, emergent games work.

Such games are often described as "easy to learn, difficult to master" (known as Bushnell's Law, after Atari founder Nolan Bushnell [Bogost 2009]). Such games present the player with only a few states and rules to start, each of which opens up into hierarchical subsystems to reveal more detailed inner workings as the player learns the game. The depth of the internal systems and their multiple perspective requires great skill to comprehend.

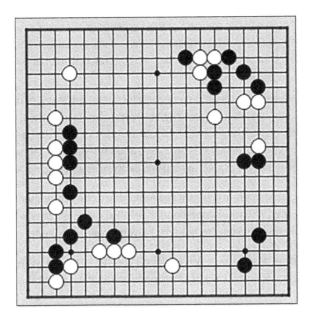

Figure 2.26 A game of *Go* in progress (Noda 2008)

Finally, *elegance* is the quality we see in games where several characteristics of the game and the gameplay experience are brought together:

- There is a metastable rather than static uniformity to the entire system that is cognitively and emotionally satisfying. The game changes each time it is played but retains an overarching familiarity in the experience it provides. The player is able to continue to find satisfaction in exploring the ever-changing gameplay space through repeat plays without feeling that the theme or the overall experience itself changes.

- The high-level systems are simply defined but have great hierarchical depth. As a result, the player is able to gradually discover this depth, building a mental model of the game along the way. This multilevel organization gives rise to complex behaviors and gameplay that further inform the player and reveal the game's systems and theme.

- The deep systems exhibit a degree of symmetry or self-similarity: each lower-level system reflects the overall structure of the system of which it is a part (as shown in loop form in Figure 2.24 and in plant form in the broccoli in Figure 2.25). The subsystems need not be exactly the same as those above them, as long as they are similar enough that higher-level systems provide scaffolding for learning more detailed ones. This creates an unobtrusive, highly contextual aide to the player's ability to easily increase comprehension and build a mental model of the game. As players explore the game more deeply, they have the positive feeling that they almost already know what they are seeing for the first time.

- There are few "loose ends" in the form of rules exceptions or special cases. Such exceptions ruin the mental symmetry of the self-similar hierarchical systems and increase the player's mental load—requiring the player to focus on remembering rules and *how* to play the game rather than just playing it.

- Finally, as players have thoroughly learned the hierarchical systems of the game to the point that they can reflect on them (an instance of metacognition), they are able to perceive and appreciate the qualities of depth and symmetry in the game's dynamic structures. At this point, the game is enjoyable and satisfying not only while it's being played but even when the players are musing on its rules and systems.

Elegance of this degree is rarely attained. It requires a masterful comprehension of the game systems by the designer, who must apprehend them all at once, as if they were laid out, while at the same time seeing them in linear form as the players experience them.

While this level of game design mastery is a difficult apex to attain, we will revisit emergence, depth, and elegance as desirable targets of systemic design throughout this book.

Wholes

Systems form greater *wholes* out of constituent, interacting parts. The whole is itself a part in the next-highest level of systemic organization.

When designing a game, the ultimate whole that emerges is not just the game itself. Instead, it is the system that is composed of the game and the player. This *game+player* system is the game designer's true goal; the game itself is just the means to get there. The game as experienced by the player and the player acting within the game create the overall system. When we discuss the systemic architecture in terms of designing a game in Chapter 3 and Chapter 6, "Designing the Whole Experience," we will return to this thought. You will look then at the importance of interactivity, depth, and systemic elegance in enabling the player to create a truly meaningful experience.

Summary

In keeping with the hierarchical nature of systems, having gone through all the parts and interactions within a system, we can now return to the initial description given at the start of the chapter.

A *system* is the integrated whole that arises out of independent, interacting parts. Those parts have their own internal state, boundaries, and behaviors by which they mutually affect each other. This whole persists over time, adapts to external conditions, and has its own coordinated behaviors that emerge from the interactions of its parts. The system both contains lower-level systems within it and is itself part of a higher-level system.

Note that while the definition given at the start of the chapter is similar to this one, the first was more bottom-up, starting with parts and going to systems, while this one is more top-down, starting with the systems first. These two views are equivalent. It is important to be able to switch perspectives on systems in this way—both as part of comprehending and "thinking in systems" and as part of the process of game design. Game designers have a particular need to be able to see their games bottom-up, top-down, or anything in between. This is a particular challenge that is best met by understanding games as systems and game design as system design.

Postscript: Thinking About Things

To return briefly to the philosophical discussion of things, identity, and "thingness," you can now consider the earlier discussion in light of the extended definition of systems and see where this takes you. You should now be able to see atoms and molecules as both systems with internal structure and as unified things. This also means that you can understand more fully systems as things that we might not otherwise see in that light.

For example, our brains are systems, and it appears that our minds emerge as unified things from their functioning. It may be that our understanding of how new *things* arise from relationships provides the answer to the contemplation of the deceptively simple ancient Buddhist "Diamond Sutra" koan: "Out of nowhere the mind comes forth" (Seong 2000). As with D. H. Lawrence's poetic musing about water, it turns out there is no "third thing," no identifiable single place from which water becomes wet, or from which the mind comes—but these are also not from "nowhere." Like flocks of birds, the fractal patterns in plants, hurricanes, or enormous structures built by unguided termites, complex systems like the mind emerge from the innumerable relationships between the constituent parts to become something more than—and entirely different from—these underlying components.

So too do corporations and cultures arise from their component parts. No one at my university was there 100 years ago, and no one who is there today is likely to be there in another 100 years: and yet the university itself, as a thing, has persisted and adapted; it was there and continues on beyond any of us as individuals. It is a metastable system with its own very real identity. The same is true of a family, a conversation, or an economy. Some may persist longer than others, but each is the result of a process of emergence, of the complex interactions and relationships between lower-level parts creating new properties not found in them.

This leads to a conclusion that we have touched on already. It's one that initially sounds at best metaphorical yet which is now supported by the examination of systems that we have made: atoms, ships, flocks, cultures, universities, and even marriages, friendships, conversations, minds, and tornadoes…. These are all not only systems; they are, in every sense that matters, *things*. To look at just two examples, there are metastable structures that emerge over time from the relationship I have with my spouse and that many thousands of us have with our universities that are in every way identical to properties of persistence, identity, and integrity—the *thingness*—we observed from the interactions of virtual quarks in forming protons, protons and electrons in forming atoms, hydrogen and oxygen in forming water. Recall that at its root, even what we think of as solid matter is itself elusive in its nature. A marriage may not have mass or shape, but it is nonetheless a real, non-metaphorical *thing* every bit as much as a desk, a computer, or a drop of water.

The truly curious aspect of this is that, stuck as we are being where we are in the systemic organizational hierarchy in which we are all parts, we often have such difficulty perceiving the emergent properties of the systems, the things, of which we are part: our culture, economy, company, or family—much less the emergence in a biome, in our planet's biosphere, or in the unimaginably vast cosmological structures we now know exist. We seem, at least for now, to be poor at recognizing and accounting for systemic effects, even though these are for us like water for fish. Hopefully, this is not a limitation of our species but a skill we can learn. A systemic view of games and game design can help us create more engaging, effective games; hopefully in so doing we also come to a deeper, fuller understanding of the systems that are all around us as well.

CHAPTER 3

FOUNDATIONS OF GAMES AND GAME DESIGN

This chapter provides some definitions of *game*, according to philosophers and designers. These definitions are then used to describe the structural, functional, architectural, and thematic elements of games in systems terms. This systemic view acts as a foundation for game design in later chapters.

Having examined this foundation of games, we look briefly at the development of game design from its hobbyist beginnings to current more theoretically informed approaches.

What's a Game?

In some ways, defining *game* seems like explaining a joke: you can do it, but you risk losing the essence of it in doing so. Nevertheless, because the topic is game design, you do need to know what is meant by the word *game*. Fortunately, many people have offered up wide-ranging definitions of *game* for decades. To provide some grounding for the discussion that follows, this section provides a brief examination of these definitions.

Huizinga

In what has become one of the foundational pillars of academic game study, Dutch historian Johan Huizinga examined the role of play as a key component of culture in his 1938 book (translated to English in 1955) *Homo Ludens*, or *Playing Man* (as differentiated from *Homo sapiens*, "wise man") (Huizinga 1955). In his view, play and games are "absorbing" but "not serious," taking place "outside of ordinary life" (p. 13). In addition, play has "no material interest, and no profit can be gained by it" (p. 13). Finally, play takes place "within its own proper boundaries of time and space according to fixed rules and in an orderly manner" (p. 13).

Huizinga is probably best known for calling out that play takes place in a separate space: "the arena, the card-table, the magic circle, the temple, the stage, the screen…" (p. 10). This has been condensed in recent times to the idea of the *magic circle:* whether a game has anything to do with magic or not, it takes place in a separate space and time set aside for it, "within which special rules obtain" (p. 10). This may be a table around which players replay the Cold War, as in *Twilight Struggle*; an imaginary universe where my little spaceship is outrunning the Rebellion, as in *FTL*; or anything in between. If the activity is absorbing but not consequential in terms of everyday life, if it has its own rules and takes place in its own separate space, then from Huizinga's point of view, it is a game, and its activity is play. As you will see in Chapter 4, on interactivity and what it means for a game to be "fun," this quality of a game being inconsequential turns out to be, perhaps paradoxically, extremely important.

Caillois

Building on Huizinga's work, French philosopher and writer Roger Caillois (pronounced "kai-wah") wrote *Man, Play, and Games*[1] (Caillois and Barash 1961). Caillois agreed with Huizinga about some of the definitional aspects of games, including the following:

- They are separate from regular reality and thus involve some amount of imagined reality.

- They are not profitable or obligatory, meaning that no one *has* to play a game.

---

1. In French, *Les Jeux et les Hommes*, loosely "Games/Play and Men," highlighting that in that language and in Caillois' view, *game* and *play* are essentially synonymous (*jeu*). One does not occur without the other.

- They are governed by rules internal to the game.
- They are affected by uncertainty so that the course of the game depends on the players' choices.

Caillois went on to specify four types of games for which he is now known within game design circles:

- **Agon:** Games of competition where there is typically a single winner. The word in ancient Greek refers to contests and can be found in the English *antagonist*.
- **Alea:** Games of chance, where dice or other randomizers rather than the players' strategy or choices predominate in determining the course of the game. The word is Latin, meaning "risk" or "uncertainty." Originally, it came from the word for "knuckle bone," because these bones were used as early dice.
- **Mimicry:** Role-playing, where the player mimics real life by taking on another role, such as "pirate, Nero, or Hamlet" (Caillois and Barash 1961, 130).
- **Ilinx:** Play where your physical perception is changed, as for example by spinning around and around. *Ilinx* is Greek for "whirlpool," thus evoking vertigo and similar feelings achieved through such play.

In addition, Caillois specified a range of play from games with structured rules (*ludus*—a Latin word for sport-like games involving training and rules and also the word used for schools) to unstructured and spontaneous play (*paidia*—"child's play" or "amusement" in Greek). Games and play of the types listed above may be anywhere along the *ludus–paidia* spectrum.

These in-depth thoughts on games and play continue to inform game designers and discussions of the nature of games. In addition to these, several definitions from contemporary game designers are worth noting and referencing later in exploring games as systems.

Crawford, Meier, Costikyan, and Others

Chris Crawford, one of the earliest modern game designers, also wrote about game design as an art (1984). He wrote, "What are the fundamental elements common to these games? I perceive four common factors: representation, interaction, conflict, and safety." (p. 7) He explained this sentence at length, first echoing Huizinga and Caillois in saying that a game "is a closed formal system that subjectively represents a subset of reality." (p. 7) It has "explicit rules," which form a system where "parts interact with each other, often in complex ways," (p. 7) which is the focus of this book. Games possess interactivity that "allows the player to create his own story by making choices" (p. 9) and provide the player with goals along with obstacles and conflict to "prevent him from easily achieving his goal" (p. 12). Finally, Crawford noted that a game must be "an artifice for providing the psychological experiences of conflict and danger while excluding their physical realizations" (p. 12). In other words, games take place in Huizinga's "magic circle"—a nonconsequential space with its own rules set apart for the purpose of playing the game. Along these lines, the American educator John Dewey made said that all play necessarily retains "an attitude of freedom from subordination to an end imposed by external necessity" (Dewey 1934, p. 279). When games become too connected to an "external necessity," they cease to be experienced as play.

Veteran game designer Sid Meier has said that "games are a series of interesting choices" (Rollings and Morris 2000, p. 38). That's a pithy definition that seems to assume a lot: many things in life involve "a series of interesting choices," such as education and relationships, but these are not typically considered games (perhaps due to their consequential nature). Nevertheless, Meier's definition is a useful one, as it highlights the necessity of meaningful, informed player choices as a key difference between games and other forms of media (Alexander 2012).

Another thoughtful and prolific game designer, Greg Costikyan (1994), has provided this definition: "A game is a form of art in which participants, termed players, make decisions in order to manage resources through game tokens in the pursuit of a goal." In the same article, Costikyan noted what a game is *not* as a way to arrive at his definition: a game is not a puzzle because puzzles are static, and games are interactive. It's not a toy because toys are interactive without having directed goals, while games are interactive and have goals. It's not a story because stories are linear, while games are inherently nonlinear. Games are unlike other art forms because those "play to a passive audience. Games require active participation."

More recently, game designer and author Jane McGonigal supplied this definition: "all games share four defining traits: a goal, rules, a feedback system, and voluntary participation." (McGonigal 2011, p. 21) McGonigal didn't specifically bring out interactivity as others have, but her inclusion of "a feedback system" speaks to that key point. (There is more detail about feedback and interactivity in Chapter 4, "Interactivity and Fun.") Along similar lines, game designers Katie Salen and Eric Zimmerman provided this formal definition: "A game is a system in which players engage in an artificial conflict, defined by rules, that results in a quantifiable outcome" (Salen and Zimmerman 2003, p. 80).

Game Frameworks

In addition to the definitions just presented, several well-known frameworks for understanding games and game design have sprung up in recent years.

The MDA Framework

The first and possibly best-known of the game frameworks is the Mechanics-Dynamics-Aesthetics (MDA) framework (Hunicke et al. 2004). These terms have specific meanings in this framework, as defined in the original paper:

- *Mechanics* describes the particular components of the game, at the level of data representation and algorithms.

- *Dynamics* describes the run-time behavior of the mechanics acting on player inputs and each other's outputs over time.
- *Aesthetics* describes the desirable emotional responses evoked in the players when they interact with the game system.

A key point of this framework is that players typically understand a game from its aesthetics first, then the game's dynamics, and finally its mechanics. The MDA framework posits that in contrast to players, game designers see their games first via their mechanics, then the dynamics, and finally the aesthetics. Part of the point of the model is to try to get designers to think of aesthetics rather than mechanics first. In practice, however, different game designers work from any of these as a starting point, depending on their own style and the design constraints they face.

Another important point inherent in the MDA model is that only a game's mechanics are wholly in the designer's direct control. The designer uses the mechanics to set the stage for the game's dynamics but does not create the dynamics directly. This points toward a systemic understanding of the designer's task in specifying the parts to create loops to enable the desired whole (discussed in more detail later in this chapter).

Apart from the linear view of how players and designers approach games, and despite being a strong example of early game design theory, as other designers have noted, the terms *mechanics*, *dynamics*, and *aesthetics* are themselves problematic. *Mechanics* is a term often used by game designers to refer to commonly recurring "chunks" of gameplay (Lantz 2015) and what Polanksy (2015) called "ludic devices," such as the 52-card deck, turn order, jump, and double-jump. This definition is itself hazy, with some designers referring to only the most specific actions (for example, play a card, left-click to jump) as mechanics and others including more complex aggregations of actions, such as balancing loop effects like the blue shell in *Mario Kart* (Totilo 2011). The difference here is one of "chunk size" and thus may be somewhat elastic. In the MDA framework, however, mechanics include some but not all of these; mechanics include game pieces and rules but not how they combine. This is a useful distinction, but unfortunately, using the term *mechanics* in this way collides with preexisting usage.

Similarly, MDA uses *aesthetics* as a term of art intended to take into account the player's entire game experience, but unfortunately, the word already has strong meaning related to *visual* aesthetics. Confusion between these two is common and, unfortunately, often results in driving a focus among game developers on a game's visual "look and feel" rather than on the player's overall experience with it.

Despite these difficulties—or at least keeping them in mind—MDA is a useful advance in game design theory that helps set the stage for a more systemic understanding of games and game design.

The FBS and SBF Frameworks

Similar to the MDA framework is an earlier model known as the Function-Behavior-Structure (FBS) ontology (Gero 1990). FBS is not typically used by (or even known to) most game designers, so we don't spend a lot of time on it here. It does, however, provide something of a bridge between MDA's three-layer structure to a more systemic understanding of game design and how design as a generic activity is considered outside the realm of games.

This framework has a similar three-part structure to MDA, albeit inverted with the highest or most user-facing part first and the most technical last:

- **Function:** An object's purpose or teleology—why it was designed and created. The function is always the result of intentional design.

- **Behavior:** An object's attributes and domain-specific actions that are derived from its structure and allow it to achieve its function. The behavior may change over time in order to fulfill the object's designed function.

- **Structure:** An object's physicality, the physical parts and relationships that make it up. The structure does not change, though it may allow the behavior of the object to change. Examples of this include anything that can be expressed in topology, geometry, or material.

FBS originally came from the field of artificial intelligence as a way of representing design-oriented knowledge and the process of design in general. The teleological aspect is one that is often important in various kinds of physical object design but not one that is a major topic in game design. Today this framework is all but unknown in game design, though it and many variants (Dinar et al. 2012) are widely used in other areas of design and design research. Like MDA, the FBS model is not overtly systemic, but it provides useful pointers toward a systemic understanding of game design (and design in general).

A later general design modeling language inverted FBS to be *SBF* (Structure-Behavior-Function) and added important design/programming language and systemic components (Goel et al. 2009). Whereas FBS is top-down, SBF is a more bottom-up framework. SBF is a hierarchical description of both designed objects and the design process represented in the form of a modeling language that starts with the individual components and their actions—the parts and behaviors in the system—works up through behavioral states and transitions, and defines functional schemas in terms of those behaviors. At each level of the SBF representation is a component that incorporates structural, behavioral, and functional aspects, down to the base level of integers and other fundamental representations.

While FBS and SBF are not themselves game design or game description frameworks—or particularly applicable to game design—they provide a useful bridge from MDA and similar popular frameworks to a more systemic view of games and game design.

Other Frameworks

Various designers and authors have constructed many other frameworks to help articulate what game designers do when they create games and how they go about doing so. Some of these have proved useful to game designers despite being ad hoc and nonsystemic. That is, they are more of an accumulation of rules of thumb based in praxis (informed by practice) than systemic theory; they are helpful descriptive tools rather than maps of the territory to be covered. If other frameworks or tools help you create better games, use them! The systemic approach used here complements and includes others, but this does not mean other approaches are not useful.

Summing Up Game Definitions

Bringing together the ideas, definitions, and frameworks discussed so far, we can highlight some of the elements that are common:

- A game is an experience that takes place in its own context, separated from the rest of life (the "magic circle").
- Games have their own rules (whether formal, as *ludus*, or tacit and dynamic, as *paidia*).
- Games require voluntary, non-obligatory interaction and participation (not simply observation).
- They provide players with interesting, meaningful goals, choices, and conflict.
- A game ends with some form of recognizable outcome. As Juul (2003) put it, a component is "valorization of the outcome"—that is, the idea that some outcomes are considered better than others, typically codified in the game's formal rules.
- Games as a product of a design process have specific parts that are implemented in some form of technology (whether digital or physical); loops formed by the behavioral interactions of those parts; and experiential (dynamic, dramatic) wholes in the game as played when interacting with the player.

There are, of course, arguments and exceptions about each of these points. If you are playing *Poker* with friends for real money, is that truly a separate context, as Huizinga and Caillois said, or does this just point out that the magic circle is porous, having multiple points of contact with the real world? Do all games *require* conflict? Must every game have an end? Many massively multiplayer online games (MMOs) have as one of their central tenets that the game world continues even after any player stops playing. It may be then that these characteristics are typical but not necessarily prescriptive.

To that point, the philosopher Ludwig Wittgenstein (1958) wrote about the search for defining characteristics that are shared by all games. In his comments, he dissuaded the reader from trying to find one definition that covers all games. He discouraged the thought that "there must be something common, or they would not be called 'games.'" Instead, he noted that in looking for a definition, "you will not see something that is common to all, but similarities, relationships, and a whole series of them at that....The result of this examination is [that] we see a complicated network of similarities overlapping and criss-crossing" (Segment 66).

Wittgenstein's "network of similarities" recalls Aristotle's "cause" that acts as an organizing principle to keep things from being "a mere heap," D. H. Lawrence's "third thing" that makes water wet, and Alexander's "quality without a name," discussed in Chapter 1, "Foundations of Systems," and Chapter 2, "Defining Systems." Rather than seeking hard-and-fast defining characteristics or building up ad hoc frameworks, the pervasive importance of these relationships, the "network of similarities," is a big hint about the systemic understanding of games—and everything else.

A Systemic Model of Games

Taking the above definitions into account along with an understanding of systems enables the creation of a new and more informative model of games as systems. The model presented here is intended to be descriptive, not prescriptive: this model represents elements of Wittgenstein's "complicated network of similarities" among all games rather than limits beyond which no game designer can go. This framework is systemic in its structure, clarifying the practice of game design by helping you create a well-defined mental model of games in general and of particular games you want to create.

Designers often have trouble finding where to get started with a design or not getting lost in the fog of an idea that they want to articulate. This systemic model provides important structural and organizational guides that allow you as a designer to focus on the game you're trying to design. Think of this as scaffolding for constructing games, not as a straitjacket that keeps you from designing what you want to create.

Systemic Organization of Games

Starting at the highest level, the game as played is a system that has two primary subsystems: the game itself and the player (or multiple players), as shown in Figure 3.1. (It should be no surprise that this bears a striking resemblance to figures you have seen before in this book.)

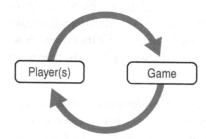

Figure 3.1 Players and games are subsystems of the overall game+player, or game-as-played, system

This chapter explores in detail three levels of components within the game subsystem and how they map to a systemic view of games:

- **Parts:** Fundamental and structural components.
- **Loops:** Functional elements enabled by the structure and built from parts.
- **Whole:** Aspects of architecture and theme arising from the functional elements, the loops.

The player as a subsystem of the game is only briefly covered in this chapter; you will see more details in Chapter 4.

In systems terms, the common structural components are the game system's parts, each with its own internal state and behavior, as described in Chapter 2. The functional elements of the game are created by the interconnected effects of these parts' behaviors and how they come together to construct game loops. Finally, the architectural and thematic elements are different sides of the whole that emerge from the systemic looping interactions of the parts.

The overall purpose and action of the game is its gameplay. This is communicated to the player as an emergent effect of the structural, functional, architectural, and thematic elements. The forms that this communication takes are examined in detail in Chapter 4.

The Player as Part of a Larger System

The player is the companion to the game: without the player, the game itself still exists, but gameplay, the playful experience, exists only when game and player come together (thus the "game+player" terminology used here).

Games may of course be designed for a single player, two or a small group of players, or even many thousands of players at the same time. Traditionally, most games have been designed for multiple players; it is only with the advent of computers-as-players that "single-player games" (meaning a single human interacting with the digital game) have become popular.

Players typically have some sort of representative and identity within a game. This may be an explicit persona, often called an *avatar*, which defines the physical and functional attributes that the player can use in the game. Or the player may be represented by an aggregate avatar, such as a pirate ship, including its captain, crew, and guns; or by nothing visible at all, being the "invisible hand" directing a small village or great empire.

You will see more about the subsystems within the player portion of the game+player system in more detail in Chapter 4. For now, the key points are as follows:

- Both the player and the game are parts within a larger system.
- Without a human player, the game has no utility or purpose; it is not really a game outside the played experience.

- The player is represented within the game as part of its model of reality, just as the player constructs a mental model of the game as part of play. (Recall from the discussion in Chapter 2 that a model is necessarily more abstract than the "real thing." This is true of both player and game as they model each other.) This co-representational relationship enables the interactive relationship between game and player and the creation of the playful experience.

Structural Parts of a Game

Like any other system, each game has its own particular parts. These are representational *tokens* and *rules* that operate on them. In later chapters, you will see these as specific elements within individual games. For now, consider them as structures that are common to games—the parts in the game as a system—that are expressed differently in every game.

Tokens

Every game has representative objects that denote the different aspects of the game state. These tokens are not typically meaningful in themselves; they are figurative and representational, being part of the structure of the game but not, for example, functional parts of any world-simulation done by the game's internal model.

Tokens are used to communicate current state and changes in state from the game to the player and vice versa by their accepted meaning within the context of the game. These tokens may be any of the following:

- Highly conceptual in their representation, such as the black and white pieces in *Go*
- Semi-representational, such as the medieval royalty pieces depicted in *Chess*
- Detailed in their correspondence to recognizable real-world objects, as with the comprehensive specifications of weapons and armor in many role-playing games

Tokens are to some degree necessarily figurative in their representation, as no game fully represents the world. A map that has full fidelity at a 1:1 scale is of no use, and a game that attempts full verisimilitude leaves the magic circle and ceases to be a game.

Game tokens define the "nouns" in the game—that is, all the objects that can be manipulated as part of play—and include the following:

- The player's representation, as discussed above
- Independent units (as in *Go*, *Chess*, and war games) that act on their own or that the player uses as part of the gameplay
- The world in which the game takes place, including any divisions that have their own state (from black and white squares in *Chess* to complex terrain and geography in digital strategy games)

- Any resources to be used in the game, such as money in *Monopoly* or wheat, sheep, and wood in *Settlers of Catan*
- Nonmaterial objects in the game, including the concept of a player's turn (the order and frequency with which players may act in the game), what constitutes a hand of cards, how many items a player may carry, how many dice a player gets to roll, and so on

In short, anything in the game that has state and behavior is one of its tokens, and everything that maintains state and has behavior in the game must be represented by a token or as an aggregate of other tokens.

While game tokens are necessarily symbolic, they are also highly precise in their state and behavior. A *Chess* piece always has a specific location—it exists in one and only one square on the board—and has entirely specified ways it can move or attack. Along with rules, game tokens are the precise specification needed for any game. They each have definitive state and behaviors at all times. This is as true for the player's and world's representation as for any other objects in the game. Can the player fly in the game? Leap over mountain ranges? Are there mountain ranges in the game world? Each such concept the designer wants to include must first be specified in detail and contained in the game's tokens and rules, a process you will see in detail in Chapter 8, "Defining Game Parts."

Rules

Whereas game tokens are symbolic objects within the game, rules are process specifications. They are understood cognitively by players and are expressed in code in computer games. Rules determine how a game operates by specifying the behaviors of the tokens.

Specifying Acceptable In-Game Actions

Rules help create the playful space wherein players act differently. It is generally not socially acceptable to lie, steal, or kill, but in a game, such behaviors may be entirely acceptable and even necessary. For example, in the popular tabletop game *The Resistance*, players have to lie flat-out to others about being a spy and betraying the cause. Similarly, in games like *EVE Online*, while stealing from other players isn't required, it is entirely allowed as part of the play of the game and has created some stunning schemes between rival player factions.

Another part of "acting differently" in play is the acceptance that players do not always act in the most efficient way possible; for example, in *Chess* one player does not simply reach out and grab the other's king and declare themselves the winner, as that's "against the rules." Similarly, in card games players do not routinely rifle through the deck to find the cards they want, even though that would be more efficient than just using the ones they were randomly dealt. The experience of play arises from our voluntary participation in the separate space in which some otherwise unacceptable actions are possible and not all possible actions are acceptable.

Specifying How the Game World Works

What are often loosely called the rules of a game are the specifications for how the game is to be played; they are the conditions by which the game universe operates. If the players and tokens are the nouns, rules are the verbs: how the player and the game pieces are able to behave and affect each other as part of play. This relationship between the tokens and rules, the nouns and verbs, is a fundamental part of understanding how the system of a game is built out of its parts.

Rules define the allowable states at any given moment in the game, how those states may change over time, and how the players progress through the game. They describe how different parts of the game relate to and affect each other. They also detail the obstacles players must surmount in the game, how conflicts are resolved, and potential endings players may reach (particularly those defined by the game as "winning" or "losing").

The physical structure of the world is specified by rules: this includes how the player moves through the world and even the shape of the world itself. The game world may be a grid, like a chessboard, or it may be a sphere, or something else entirely. The rules may even specify the topology of a world that would be impossible in reality, such as the mind-bending Escher-like worlds in the games *Monument Valley* and *Antichamber*.

Rules include stipulations involving not just the physical in-game world but the structure and behavior of the game pieces. This includes conventions for how many cards a player may keep in their hand or how many workers each player possesses at the beginning of the game. Rules may also address universal circumstances, such as "a player may fall an infinite distance and still take no damage on landing." Or even "gravity will change direction every 30 seconds."

Preserving Player Agency

Rules enable different player paths—goals, strategies, and styles of play—to emerge. The rules must not overly restrict the player's ability to decide their own course, known as *player agency*. If the player's actions are overly constrained, their decision-space of the game collapses to a small number of choices or even a single path. When this happens, the player is reduced from participant to observer, thereby removing one of the essential qualities that makes a game a game.

Part of the game designer's challenge in creating rules as part of the structure of a game is to make as few rules as possible to create a well-defined game-space; the game world and everything in it must be specified by the game rules. If there are not enough rules, the game is ambiguous, and a player is unable to construct or navigate a mental model of it. If there are too many rules, the player's agency is overly constrained, and their engagement with the game evaporates.

Avoiding Exceptions to Rules

Rules that are arbitrary or create situational exceptions quickly tax the player's ability to keep an accurate model of the game in mind and make the game more difficult to learn and enjoy. This is the opposite of the concept of elegance in games discussed in Chapter 2.

For example, many board games use six-sided dice to determine the result of combat. Say that rolling all sixes is generally a "good result" except in a few cases, it's actually a bad result; this creates a situation where the very same combination of token and rules (dice and how they are rolled) has varying definitions. This increases the amount the player has to learn and remember without increasing their engagement or the possible actions they can take. The same can happen in digital games when controller or key bindings to carry out various actions are assigned arbitrarily: left-click once with a mouse to jump, for example, but clicking twice to do something completely different, like drop everything you're carrying. Because the two mouse-related actions are cognitively and physically similar, their results in the game should also be similar. When arbitrary rules or rules with lots of exceptions are used in a game, it becomes more difficult to learn, and the player's engagement suffers. (You will see more about player engagement and mental load in this in Chapter 4.)

Structural Elements and Game Mechanics

The term *game mechanics* has been used in many different ways by game designers and in design frameworks (Sicart 2008). Grounding this term within systemic design, *game mechanics* can be thought of as semantically viable (that is, meaningful) combinations of tokens and rules. They can be thought of as the combinations of tokens and rules, much as meaningful phrases or short sentences can be constructed by combining nouns and verbs. Mechanics are typically simple, such as "when you pass Go, collect $200." Those that are more complex are typically combinations of multiple simpler mechanics, just as a complex sentence is a combination of several phrases.

The point here is not to create a precise definition for *game mechanics* but to ground such phrases in systemic terms. Tokens and rules can combine in many ways, and so mechanics may take many forms.

Games and Metagames

The separate space of the magic circle is defined by the game's structural elements—its tokens and rules. With a few exceptions, tokens have no meaning, and rules do not operate outside the play of the game. For example, how many properties you own in one play of *Monopoly* does not affect how many you have in the next game. There are occasional exceptions that players may mutually agree to, such as "I went first last time, so you go first this time" that bridge the operation of rules between games. Other exceptions to this have begun to be known as "legacy" games, where the actions or events of one game affect the conditions or rules the next time it's played. These illustrate both how important the structural parts of a game are and how they can be creatively superseded to create new and more enjoyable play experiences.

This application of tokens or rules across games is called *metagaming*. In transcending the rules of a single game, the players traverse the barrier of the magic circle, bringing aspects of the game into the real world and vice versa. Some metagame rules are considered "house rules," such as winning money when you land on Free Parking in *Monopoly*. Others might be special benefits for inexperienced players. In some cases, metagaming refers more to a player's actions than to the game itself. For example, tit-for-tat actions referring to an out-of-game situation between players ("you didn't help me in our last game, so I won't help you now") are not specifically forbidden by the game but may be considered poor behavior by other players whose own metagame response may be to not play again with a person who behaves this way.

Incidentally, "tit-for-tat" metagaming leads into what is known as *repeated games* in game theory. (Strangely, game theory as such has little to do with game design; it's more closely related to economics, but there are points of commonality.) Repeated games include those where the metagame is effectively part of the game; for example, if you know you're going to play *Rock-Paper-Scissors* multiple times, this knowledge can help you, as players' behavior in such games is not as random as it might seem. There are predictive mathematical models for how to play repeated games based on the economic payout—how often you are likely to win, given a particular strategy. In cases like this, the metagame becomes subsumed into the game; the magic circle is maintained across iterations of the underlying game.

Functional Aspects of a Game

In addition to examining the structural elements common to games, it's important to understand how those parts come together to create the game's functional organization. As tokens and rules are the parts and behaviors—the nouns and verbs—of the game system, the functional elements are the looped assemblies that arise out of those parts. By analogy to the structures being phrases made of nouns and verbs, the functional elements are the meaningful concepts that can be constructed out of them. This is how the game comes to life and becomes an operational system with which the player can interact.

Functional aspects of a game include any construct around which a player forms goals or any dynamic portions of a mental model. For example, economies rise out of the ebb and flow of resources represented as tokens in the game that interact via rules. Similarly, players work with functional aggregations of the game's parts when they build heroic characters in role-playing games or vast empires in strategic ones. There is no way to make an exhaustive list of all possible functional components, but, briefly, anything within a game that completes or supports the statement "in this game, the player is a…" (pirate, pilot, florist, emperor, and so on) or that is a significant part of a player completing a goal is clearly one of the functional aspects of the game.

These are also typically the types of concepts game designers spend a lot of their time thinking about. While all concepts in a game need to be reduced to tokens and rules, game designers spend a lot of time creating the game itself by organizing those parts into functional, operational subsystems that work to support the desired experience.

Creating the Possibilities for Play

It is important to understand that by their nature, the particular economies, characters, empires, and other similar functional constructs created are not static; they change over time as part of play. Nor are they coded directly into the structure of the game—but their *possibilities* are. That is, the structural tokens and rules set up the conditions and possibilities for an economy, a character, or an empire without determining the exact characteristics of how these appear in a given game.

As a result, the game must be designed to provide a space for these changing functional structures to emerge. It must define a model of the world built from its internal structures that provides scaffolding for these to grow and change throughout play. As discussed in Chapter 4, this model must correspond with and support the player's understanding of the game world in their mental model; it must provide for opposition, meaningful decisions, and player goals to develop as part of play. Enabling these and, as a result, the construction of an effective mental model is a significant part of creating engagement and the playful experience.

Functional Elements as Machines

While the functional components of a game are part of the game as a system, people often refer to these complex looped combinations of parts as "the game systems." If the structural elements are "static," then these, by virtue of their looping interactions, are seen as "dynamic" in the general sense (of changing over time) and, to a large degree, in the sense used in the MDA framework.

In a similar way, game designer Geoff Ellenor described his concept for this part of a game as "a machine that does X" (Ellenor 2014), meaning, for example, "I want a machine that makes weather in my game" or "I want the player to receive an email from the mission-giver whenever a mission is completed." In Ellenor's thinking, these "machines" are nested—simpler ones inside more complex ones—rather than being built as big monolithic machines. This is an excellent description for the functional aspects of a game, with complex, long-lasting systemic "machines" built hierarchically out of simpler ones, all the way down to structural tokens and rules.

The functional or dynamic parts of a game—the "machine" in Ellenor's terms—consist of the game's internal model of reality and the space it creates for the player to act within. This "space" for gameplay provides for meaningful decisions made by the player to chart a course through the space and, thus, for the emergence of player goals and a player's mental model of the game. This is all based on the idea of second-order design and on the inclusion of uncertainty in the game's representation. Each of these is explored in detail here.

The Game's Internal Model of Reality

Every game has its own *internal model* of reality. This arises from the interactions of the game's tokens and rules, as created by the game designer, and is explored and experienced by the player. Koster (2004) said that games "are abstracted and iconic" and "exclude distracting extra details [of] messy reality" (p. 36). That is, games are not isomorphic with reality but, like all other designed systems, are themselves models of something more complex.

In many ways, each game is its own pocket universe with its own governing laws. This little universe may be abstract, such as that defined by the tokens and rules of *Chess* or *Go*, or highly detailed and with a high degree of verisimilitude, as in strategy or role-playing games that create a simulacrum of the real world. In either case, the structural and functional elements also create what Costikyan (1994) called the game's *endogenous meaning*. This is the meaning that players attach to tokens and rules within the game. The tokens and rules are meaningful solely because they have some function in the game. Costikyan uses the example of *Monopoly* money: $1,000 in this currency is meaningless outside of the game but has significant meaning inside it, potentially making the difference between winning and losing.

It is important to note that no matter how "realistic" a game's model of reality, it will never be as complex or inscrutable as actual reality. Even if it were possible to create a game with this degree of detail and complexity, doing so would work against the nature of the game as a locus of a playful experience. Part of having the player enjoy the game is their ability to build an effective mental model of the simplified version of reality it presents. If the game's model of reality is so complex, variable, or unpredictable that the player cannot build an effective mental model, it might be an interesting simulation to build, but it will not be a fun game to play. Sometimes game designers mistake creating a "hyper-realistic world" or a super-complex system for creating a compelling game. The two aren't the same, and pouring on more realism or complexity does not inherently make for a better game.

Creation of the Game World as a Space for Play

In talking about the internal model of reality of games, Salen and Zimmerman (2003) pointed out that game design is *second-order design*. This has a couple of different but related meanings. First, the game's design as expressed in its tokens and rules creates the specification for a state-space, not a single path. That is, the internal reality of the game must be one the player can explore and traverse (as allowed by the game's rules) along multiple paths, not just a single one that the designer has in mind. If there is only one path allowed by the design, then in effect the game has become a single narrative like a book or a movie. In such a case, the player is put into a passive role with no decisions or meaningful interactivity, and the experience of play evaporates. (There is a detailed definition of *interactive* in Chapter 4, but for now the common fuzzy sense of that word is good enough.) Defining the tokens and rules to allow the player to take multiple different paths through the game enables a player to have different experiences when playing and replaying the game and also to have experiences that vary from those of other players. Each time a player takes a single path, based on their actions in the game, they know that there are many paths they *could* have taken, even if not all are equally preferable.

Contrast this with a movie or book in which the path the viewer or reader must take has already been determined. You as the viewer or reader cannot affect the course of the events of the story; you are a viewer, not a participant, and have no choices you can make in how the story unfolds. This highlights the well-known (and still unresolved) tension between traditional stories and games: stories follow a single scripted path that does not change on repeat encounters,[2] whereas games provide a space with many possible paths that can provide different experiences. The game designer's job is not to create a single path—a first-order design for the experience that will be the same for all players—as that will quickly become boring rather than engaging as a participatory experience. Instead, the game designer must use the tokens and rules of the game to create a many-dimensional space through which the players define for themselves their particular experiences.

The second but related meaning of *second-order design* is that designing the tokens and rules to form dynamic systems (and the space for an experience) is an example of enabling emergence in ways that are unique to games. As mentioned in the discussion of the MDA framework, the game's mechanics—its tokens and rules—are directly designed; but its dynamics—its functional aspects—arise out of the tokens and rules during the play of the game. The game's systems do not provide a single, predefined path but instead create an entire explorable play-space, as described above.

The player's experience emerges from their interaction with the designed space—arising from it but not being mappable back to any single part of the design or the simple sum of its parts. Often the player's experience unfolds in ways the designer could not have predicted. If the space is sufficiently large and the player has enough autonomy in the game, that experience may be wholly unique and emergent. (You will see more about second-order design and emergence in Chapter 8 and elsewhere in this book.)

The Curious Case of Systemic Cat Deaths in Dwarf Fortress

The kind of emergent gameplay just described is at the heart of making systemic games. It can take innumerable forms, but here is one particular, possibly extreme, example of systemic interactions in a game creating an emergent situation. *Dwarf Fortress* is possibly the most systemic game yet made. The game depicts the growth and hazards encountered by a group of dwarves creating (with the player's guidance) their underground empire. *Dwarf Fortress* is entirely procedural, meaning that the world and all that happens in it are defined as a second-order design, not handcrafted to depict a particular place or set of events. (The game also consists of almost nothing but ASCII graphics and is generally regarded as one of the most difficult video games to learn to play. This is an issue separate from its systematicity; it may well be that players strive to learn to play the game because its systemic nature makes it so compelling despite these obstacles.)

In late 2015, one player began noticing an epidemic of cats dying in the game (Master 2015). Cats aren't a major aspect of the game but are part of the lush world it presents to the player. The cat deaths were unrelated to any combat or similar circumstances. After investigating,

---

2. Some may cite "choose your own adventure" books as an exception. These provide limited choice where the reader can decide which course to follow, enabling the story to unfold in different ways. These books in fact originated as "an RPG [role-playing game] in book form" in the late 1970s (*History of CYOA* n.d.) and are representative of many hybrids on the narrative-game spectrum.

the player discovered that the cats were often dizzy (a "syndrome" that can be attached to a creature in the game) just before they died, and disturbingly "their death always leave [sic] a pool of vomit with them"—another systemic in-game effect. At first, the player thought there was a bug in the game where tavern keepers would serve cats alcohol if the animals were located in a tavern (as they often were). In actuality, the cause was even stranger: the cats frequented taverns to hunt mice and rats—this is what was programmed in as part of the cats' behavior, without regard to any significant in-game effects it might have. The dwarves drinking in the tavern would often splash their wine on the floor, some of which would get on the cats. Since cats have a "self-cleaning" behavior, they would in effect *drink* the alcohol that had splashed onto them, and then shortly thereafter become drunk, dizzy, and, due to their very low body weight, often die.

This entire situation is the result of multiple interacting systems. No designer working on this ever said, "Make sure cats can be splashed by wine and die from alcohol poisoning." There are many systems in the game, including those for drinking alcohol (important to the dwarves in the game), for wine being spattered on things (in great detail: the game logs show entries for a cat in a tavern with "dwarven wine spatter fourth left rear toe," for example), for ensuring that the size of the drinker increases or decreases the alcohol's effect, and for animals to have the ability to clean themselves (only cats and red pandas have this ability in the game) and thus ingest alcohol, among others.

All of these systems interact together as functional parts in a higher-level system to create a large play-space that includes the effect of the poor cats dying of alcohol poisoning. This wasn't preplanned but emerged as an element of gameplay for a curious player. This is just one, albeit extreme, example of emergent systemic gameplay and, thus, of the second-order design of the game world.

Uncertainty and Randomness in the Game World

A common functional element of game worlds is uncertainty, typically achieved through some form of *randomness*. This takes many forms, from familiar dice rolls and cards dealt from a deck to sophisticated random number generators used in digital games (more on these in Chapter 9, "Game Balance Methods"). Not all games use randomness as a functional component, but all present the player or players with some degree of uncertainty. Some ancient games, such as *Chess* and *Go*, have no random action built into their rules; the uncertainty in these games comes from each player not knowing the actions of the other in advance. Most games today, however, have some amount of randomness as part of their rules. This is often seen as a balancing factor to the skill the players may have developed in navigating the game world.

In short, the more deterministic the game world is, the more it can be known in advance. The more it is known, the more the game-space collapses to a single path, robbing the player of the ability to make any decisions about how to traverse the space. A prime example of this can be seen in the elaborate, dance-like, but also entirely deterministic openings memorized and used by skilled *Chess* players. That game becomes interesting as players manage to use existing functional "chunks" of information (combinations of pieces on the board—in effect, subsystems defined by the mutual relationships between pieces and their locations) in novel ways. As you will see later in this chapter, the ability for players to make meaningful decisions is crucial to creating engaging gameplay.

The Player's Mental Model

The game defines a play-space, a world for players to explore. Corresponding to this, the player creates their own internal *mental model* of the world as they play. While the player's mental model is not part of the game per se, the functional aspects of the game must come together to support its creation within the player. As you will see in Chapter 4, the formation of this mental model is a vital part of the player being engaged by the game and ultimately of their experience of having fun. For now it's enough say that the player builds their model of the game world by interacting with the tokens and rules and, via them, the functional elements presented by the game.

The more easily this model is to build within the player's mind, and the more consistent the player's understanding is of the world-model defined by the game designer, the more engaging the game will be. Conversely, if the player has a difficult time discerning the rules underlying the model of the game, or if those rules appear incomplete or inconsistent, the game will often fail to be engaging, or will at least demand more time and cognitive resources from the player (and in so doing will limit the game's audience to only those willing to take the time and devote the resources needed to learn it).

Saying that a player's mental model must be easily constructed does not mean that the game or the mental model must be simple. The mental model required for a game like *Tic-Tac-Toe* is simple because the game has few tokens and rules—but it is also a game that players tire of quickly, as they can easily see the game's outcomes: there is no randomness in the game, no systemic depth, and few opportunities for players to create significant uncertainty for each other. The mental model for a complex game like *Go* or a modern strategy game like *Stellaris* can take a great deal of time and effort to build. However, the systemic quality of such games means that there are few inconsistencies to incorporate along the way. As a result, players are rewarded with increased capability as their mental model grows in completeness, which encourages further exploration of the game's model—a highly effective reinforcing loop.

Meaningful Decisions

As the player constructs a mental model of the game world (building on what they learn of its tokens and rules), they interact with it and exercise their understanding, trying out various courses of action. To do this, the player must be able to make *meaningful decisions*. As stated above, being able to make meaningful decisions requires uncertainty in the player's mental model and typically in the game's world model as well; without that, there is no decision for the player to make. Some games create the uncertainty wholly between players, with no hidden or random elements in the game's representation. Most, however, include some hidden informa-tion the player does not yet know or that cannot yet be known because it is to be determined randomly and is not knowable in advance.[3]

No Choices, Ineffectual Choices, and Choices That Lead to Change

If a game presents a player with no decisions to make, the player is forced into a passive rather than interactive role. They cannot explore but can only follow a single path, and so the experience of play collapses. (This can still be enjoyable, as when watching a movie or reading a book, but in those cases, all the decisions have been made, and there is no experience of play.) Similarly, if the game provides illusory choices—decisions that have no effect on the player or the world, such as choosing between two doors that are then seen to lead to the same place—these quickly become equivalent to no choice at all. Since there is no effect from choosing one option or another, the decision becomes arbitrary and thus as if it didn't exist.

The game must instead provide the player with opportunities to make meaningful decisions: choices that affect the player's state or the state of the world in discernable ways and that either create or block the opportunity for further exploration and decisions along a particular path.

Ultimately, what constitutes a "meaningful" decision may vary with each player. However, if the player believes the outcome of a decision will either bring her closer to a desired end or push her further from it, the decision carries meaning. This is for now a cursory description of mean-ing within the context of a game but one that will be filled out in the discussion of player goals and thematic elements below and different forms of interactivity in Chapter 4.

Opposition and Conflict

Games require opposition, and almost all games contain some form of overt conflict. If there were no opposition in a game, a player would be able to achieve their desired outcome without any significant effort. Being able to pick up your opponent's king in *Chess* as your first move and say "I win" or being able to have all the money and power you want in a strategy game quickly drains the game of any engagement or fun. Thus, for players to be able to exercise their mental model of the game, to make meaningful decisions to achieve their goals, in addition to uncertainty, there must be forces in the game that obstruct their progress.

The types of opposition found in games fall into a few categories:

- **The rules:** A large part of the opposition that players face in a game comes from the rules themselves. For example, in *Chess* the rules do not allow for simply swooping in and grabbing the other player's king. Most games limit the player's actions by the rules, using the tokens in the game. These may be articulated as limitations on movement, on

---

3. Random determination includes both wholly random results, where, for example, a number can take any value between 1 and 100 with equal probability, and weighted results, where some numbers are more probable than others, such as in a statistical normal or bell curve distribution. See Chapter 9 for more on this.

resource-based actions, or on factors within the world (for example, terrain that the rules deem impossible to the player). Such rules should feel during play like a natural part of the game world rather than something forced into it to create a limitation. The more arbitrary a rule feels to players, the more they will think about how to play the game rather than just playing it, and the less engaged they will be.

- **Active opponents:** In addition to the rules and the world, many games provide agents who actively oppose the player's actions. Loosely, these can be termed "monsters"— anything that opposes the player and has some degree of agency in its actions—though this includes everything from anonymous goblins attempting to block the player-character's path to a finely crafted nemesis spinning elaborate plans to ensure the player's downfall in the game.

- **Other players:** Players may have roles defined by the game's functional elements that put them in opposition to each other. In any game where players compete with each other, whether directly (for "who wins") or indirectly (for example, for who has the higher score), players may act as obstacles in each other's way. Many games are built on the idea of two or more players trying to balance achieving their own desired outcomes while thwarting others.

- **The players themselves:** Balancing different desired outcomes shows how the player may be their own opposition. If a player has a limited amount of resources, they form their own economy, where they cannot apply resources to all the things they would like. The player may have to make a decision, for example, about whether to spend in-game resources on building troops now or on upgrading barracks to build more powerful troops later. This kind of trade-off is common and presents the player with meaningful decisions based on the fact that they cannot do everything at the same time.

Player Goals

Decisions that a player makes are typically made within the context of the player's goals within the game. If a player has no goal, no destination in the state-space of the game, then no choice is better than any other, and so there is no intent, meaning, or engagement. As such, goals are the guiding stars by which players choose their course through the game. Without goals, the player simply drifts, a condition as contrary to engagement and the playful experience as the passivity arising from not being able to make any decisions at all.

Players thus desire goals within the game. Often, their ultimate in-game goals have to do with a measurable or valorous end (that is, "winning"). Such goals are often supplied by the game designer as part of its functional elements as a quantification of the game's objectives. These are called *explicit goals*. When someone asks, "What is the object of the game?" or "How do I win?" they are asking about the game's explicit goals.

Most games have explicit goals that either cover the entire play of the game ("win conditions") or that at least help the player learn the basics of the game and begin building a mental model. In games where these are not the only possible goals the player can have, they can be seen as "training wheels." After a player has a sufficiently detailed mental model of the world, in some games they are then set free to create their own *implicit goals* that drive their actions and decisions. Even within the context of explicit goals provided by the game ("finish this level"), players may create their own goals simply for their own amusement ("I'm going to finish this level without killing any monsters").

Implicit and explicit goals can be combined, such as when there are game-provided optional achievements or badges that are ends in themselves (such as a "pacifist" tag for completing a level without killing anything). Such achievements may incentivize players to begin creating their own implicit goals. Doing so increases the player's engagement and the probability that they will continue playing the game.

On the other hand, games that have only explicit goals tend to have lower longevity and replay value because the player's potential set of goals is circumscribed by the game itself. This is consistent with the idea that as the game's design reduces the possible actions the player can take, the state-space is narrowed, the player's set of goals becomes smaller, their ability to make meaningful decisions is decreased, and their overall sense of engagement is either fleeting (until they see through the illusion of agency created by the game) or reduced. The game may still be enjoyable in the same way that a book or movie is, but without the same sense of agency and meaning that players can derive from creating their own goals and charting their own path through the game's world.

Types of Goals

Chapter 4 explores different types of interactivity, but it is worth foreshadowing that exploration here in terms of different types of player goals. These types of goals all arise out of the endogenous meaning created by the functional elements of the game and from the mental model the player creates. If the game has no internal meaning, or if the player cannot create a viable mental model of it, then the player cannot form goals about the game. In that case, they are reduced to wandering aimlessly in the game (around the game world and/or its play-space), which quickly becomes boring.

Player goals may be thought of as varying in several dimensions, including duration and frequency: how long does a goal take to complete and how frequently does the player attempt it? Player goals also correspond to different kinds of psychological motivations, as you will see in Chapter 4. Both explicit and implicit goals may be any of the following:

- **Instant:** Actions the player wants to accomplish immediately by effectively making a time-based action. Examples include jumping or grabbing a rope at just the right time or using fast reactions to block an opponent's shot.

- **Short term:** Near-term goals such as solving a puzzle, killing a monster, using a particular tactic, gaining a level, and so on. These goals are cognitive in nature, requiring planning and attention, but without a long time horizon. They typically include multiple instant goals that are satisfied along the way to completing an overall goal.

■ **Long term:** Strategic, cognitive goals that encompass what the player wants to achieve in the game—for example, taking out a strong opponent, gaining a complete set of items, building up a particular skill tree, creating an empire. These goals require a great deal of focus and planning and are the backbone of a player's long-term engagement with the game. Long-term goals contain multiple short-term ones, which in turn contain instant ones. The systemic hierarchy of these goals should be evident and is often a point of satisfaction to a player. (Again, see Chapter 4 for a more in-depth discussion of goals.)

■ **Social:** Goals the player has that primarily involve their relationships with other players within the game. These goals can easily spill over into relationships outside of the game, too, illustrating the porousness of the magic circle. However, these goals are primarily those having to do with inclusion, status, cooperation, direct competition, and so on. Given the time it can take to form and adjust social relationships, these goals often contain multiple immediate, short-term, and even long-term goals.

■ **Emotional:** Game designers often don't think explicitly about a player's emotional goals, though it should be one of the first things you consider in game design. Achieving an emotional resolution is key to many games (*Gone Home*, *Road Not Taken*, *Undertale*, and so on). While the players themselves may not consciously consider satisfying an emotional goal the way they do a more cognitive short- or long-term planning goal, these are even more important to enjoyment of the game.

Each of these dynamic and operational functional components—the game's model of reality that creates a space for play, opposition, and decisions—enables the player to build a mental model of the game and interact with it, creating goals that are vital to their engagement. The player's experience via these interactions and goals leads us to the highest level of the systemic description of games.

Architecture and Thematic Elements

At a systemic level above its functional aspects, at the level of the whole experience, each game has both architectural and thematic sides. These emerge from the underlying functional interactions between the structural parts. In systemic terms, the architecture and theme are two faces of the same whole: the architectural elements are more inward (developer) focused, and the thematic ones are more outward (player) focused. Game designers must be constantly aware of both architecture and theme and how they link to each other and emerge from the more fundamental structural and functional aspects of the game to create effective gameplay.

Architectural aspects of a game are high-level constructions—built on structural and functional components—that support the player-facing themes of the game. The architectural elements include the following:

■ The game's balance of content and systems

■ The mechanical, technical components of the game's narrative structure

- The organization of the game's user interface—what is often called "user experience" development and is the more technical side of how the player interacts with the game
- The technological platform used (whether this is a board game or a digital game)

The game's *thematic* elements are all the elements that arise out of its structure and function to create the overall player experience. If the game's theme is about finding love, achieving great power, or conquering the world, this must be conveyed by the thematic elements with the support of the game's design architecture. The thematic components include the following:

- The way in which the game's content and systems support the creation of player interactivity and goals—in particular autotelic goals (described below)
- The content of the game narrative, if any
- The appearance and feel of the game's user interface—what is often called its "juiciness," for the simple enjoyment derived from viewing and operating it separate from the player's reasons for doing so

Architectural and thematic elements work together to enable the game's interactions with the player and the player's goals within the game. These will be discussed here as the final part of the systemic model of the game's structure.

Content and Systems

A game's content and systems are key aspects of its architecture and theme. In terms of architectural organization, there is an essential difference between groups of parts that are complicated and those that are complex (as discussed in Chapter 2). Those that are complicated have sequential interactions, where Part 1 affects Part 2, which affects Part 3 (refer to Figure 2.5). These connections form no feedback loops; Part 3 does not loop around to affect Part 1 again. In complex systems, parts *do* form loops that feedback on themselves, a hallmark of systems in general (refer to Figure 2.6).

Games can be separated into those that are mainly based on content versus those based primarily on systems. To be clear, all games have some amount of content and systems; the question is which of these a game design primarily depends on for the gameplay.

Content-Driven Games

Many games are based on *content* rather than systems. In terms of game development, content includes any locations, objects, and events that the designers must develop and assemble to create the gameplay they want to see. All games have *some* content, but some games rely on specific configurations of content to create the game. This includes games that are primarily level or mission based, where the designers have laid out exactly the placement and timing of objects and obstacles the player will encounter.

In such games, the play is primarily linear, as the player progresses along a path laid out by the game designer, experiencing—and consuming—the content created for players. The player's primary goals are explicitly defined by the game, the forms of opposition they face are clear along the path, and their decisions are predetermined (both in opportunity and outcome possibilities) by the designer. Once a player has completed a level, or the entire game, they may replay it again, but the essential experience will not differ significantly: they may create implicit goals (for example, "beat my previous fastest time"), but the overall gameplay and experience do not change. Another way of saying all of this is that content-driven games show little emergence; in fact, designers often work hard to prevent emergent results, as they are inherently unpredictable and thus untestable and risk creating a poor gameplay experience.

Designers can add more gameplay to content-driven games by creating a new level or other objects, but the game is fundamentally content-limited because it is so directly authored by the designers. The creation of content itself becomes a bottleneck for the developers, as players can consume new content faster than the developers can create it, and adding new content becomes an increasingly expensive proposition. This is sometimes known as the "content treadmill" in game development. Being on this treadmill makes for a more predictable development process (an important factor to game development companies), if at the cost of needing huge development teams to create all the content needed—and the risk of not being seen as being sufficiently innovative by players.

In extreme cases, when new content does not add to or change the underlying tokens and rules (the parts, states, and behaviors possible in the game), players quickly realize that there is little novel in the new content and become bored with the game. When a player realizes that a game fits exactly with an existing mental model, at first this can be comfortingly familiar; but as soon as they realize that there is nothing new to be learned and no new mastery to be attained, they become bored and stop playing the game. This has been the case with games that have been "reskinned" from other games, where only the context and art style changed (for example, from medieval to science fiction or steampunk) but the underlying gameplay remained the same. Game development companies that have tried this have learned that players are enthusiastic at first but then burn out of the game quickly as there is nothing new to be learned or experienced.

Systemic Games

In contrast to content-driven games, *systemic* games use complex interactions (that is, feedback loops) between parts to create the game world, opposition, decisions, and goals. In such games, the designer does not have to author the specifics of the player's experience. The designer doesn't create a path (or a small set of branches) for the player to follow but sets up the conditions that will guide the player in creating their own path—one of a large number in a vast game-space that could exist, as described in the discussion of second-order design. This path typically changes each time the game is played, keeping the game feeling fresh and engaging even after many replays.

Game designer Daniel Cook wrote an excellent description of the difference between taking a content-driven versus systemic approach to designing his company's air-combat game *Steambirds: Survival* on his blog, *Lostgarden*:

> When the game wasn't engaging, we added new systems such as having downed planes drop powerups. A more traditional approach might be to manually create more detailed scenarios with surprise plot points where a pack of planes pop out of a hidden cloud when you collide with a pre-determined trigger. However, by instead focusing on new general systems, we created an entire universe of fascinating tactical possibilities. Do you head for the heal powerup or do you turn to face the Dart at 6 o'clock? That's a meaningful decision driven by systems, not a cheap authored thrill. (Cook 2010)

Even when a systemic game sets an overarching explicit goal for the player (for example, *Civilization*'s "conquer the world" or *FTL*'s "destroy the rebel mothership"), the player makes his own decisions and thereby creates one of innumerable routes to this goal. The game systems provide ample uncertainty and different potential combinations to ensure that the game-space does not collapse into a single optimal strategic path through it. Of course, this is not *entirely* random but is itself systemic in nature. For example, while a systemic game may create a new physical landscape each time it's played, a game constructed with effective subsystems might place cacti at random locations in a hot desert but would not make polar bears appear there.

Balancing Content and Systems

Even in highly systemic games, game developers still need to create supporting content, and the game design will often define an overarching set of explicit goals. Likewise, in a content-driven game, there are many subsystems at work (economy, combat, and so on), but they exist within a primarily linear/complicated context rather than a systemic/complex one. Thus, content and systems are not exclusive but represent balance points for game design.

The focus in this book is on designing systemic games while making use of linear aspects of play when appropriate. The fundamental idea is that games are becoming more systemic over time—more complex rather than just more complicated—and creating systemic games leads to more engaging, enjoyable, replayable games overall.

The Autotelic Experience

An *autotelic experience* is an experience that has a purpose in itself rather than being dependent on some external goal or necessity. When a player creates their own implicit goals from their own motivations and is able to take actions in the game whose results have intrinsic value to the player, then their goals and actions are autotelic.

As discussed earlier, the experience of playing a game is necessarily separate, nonconsequential, and voluntary, but it must also be satisfying in and of itself; remember what Dewey said—that the play of the game must not be subordinate to some other end, or it loses the essential nature of play. This is the point on which many "gamification" efforts often run aground: you can make something look like a game, but if the player's experience is not seen as valuable simply for the experience itself, it quickly becomes subordinated "to an end imposed by external necessity" (Dewey 1934) and thus becomes something other than play.

Explicit goals in a game help the player learn the game and create their own mental model of it. Eventually, however, leading the player by the nose with one explicit goal after another becomes what many call "the grind"—one mission or quest after another but none that the player finds inherently valuable. Each mission or quest is done for an explicit, external reward. For many players, this can become more like a job than play. This approach also tends to rely more on creating expensive, ephemeral content rather than evergreen systems for the game.

In contrast to these extrinsic, explicit goals, many games—in particular those that players return to over and over for years (*Chess, Go, Civilization*, and so on)—enable the players to create their own intrinsic, implicit goals. Early on, a player may be given predefined objectives to complete, but eventually, as the player constructs a sufficiently advanced mental model of the game, these give way to implicit, autotelic goals created by the player for their own enjoyment. This autotelic play is based on and supported by the thematic, systemic elements in the game and is inevitably more engaging, enjoyable, and meaningful to the player.

Narrative

A brief working definition of *narrative* is a recounting of one or more individuals living through a series of connected events in a way that becomes meaningful to the reader or viewer. Both the events and the individuals living through them are important. A series of events alone is not a story, nor is a recounting of time passing for someone during which nothing noteworthy happens. Most games have elements of narrative in them; only the most abstract seem to be wholly free of any sort of connected series of events that carry meaning.

Narrative is important in that it bridges both architecture and theme: it has an inward, developer-focused side in terms of how the story is put together out of the underlying functional elements, and it has a player-facing thematic side in how it sets the stage for the players and informs them of what the game is about.

In a game, the narrative or story may be the focus of the player's experience, or it may be only the game's premise. Whether or not there is additional story in the gameplay, the premise informs the player as to why the world is the way it is when they encounter it, and the narrative typically gives them an idea of what their goals are in the game (for example, right a wrong, kill a dragon, discover a secret). In this way, the story behind or within the game helps the player situate themselves and begin creating their mental model of the game's world. In the same way, narrative elements may be used during the game as rewards, further informing the player about the world (for example, using narrative cut-scenes or similar expository/revelatory story).

Games with a story built in as the backbone of the player's ongoing experience are called *story-driven* games. In these, the player takes on the role of a particular character, making choices to work through various crisis points in the story and to an eventual end. On the architectural side, such games tend to be more content driven than systemic. (Although games where the story arises from underlying systems are also possible, few examples exist.) In story-based games, the player's opposition, goals, and decision points are defined by the designer, and rarely does the player have the opportunity to alter them. Thematically, such games have to balance driving the story in a particular direction (and thus narrowing the play-space potentially down to a single unalterable path) against giving the player the ability to make their own decisions. The more directive the game is, the fewer decisions the player makes, and the more passive their role becomes. But if the game does not direct the player's course, they may miss the story (and its expensive content) altogether, and the game may not effectively communicate its theme.

Story-based games can be immensely enjoyable but tend not to have a lot of replay value. In some cases, the player has sufficient options that exploring other parts of the game-space provides for more replay experiences. The game *Knights of the Old Republic* is an example of this; in this game, players decide to build a character as a "light side" or "dark side" Jedi and experience the built-in story differently depending on those choices. Even here, though, there are only a couple of possible endings. Such narrative construction typically leads to a narrowing of paths, if for no other reason than building the content for multiple endings is simply too expensive.

A systemic game can have a premise that sets the player going in a particular direction but then leaves later events up to them. In such games, the possible forms of opposition are set by the designer, but the player's choices (and potential randomness in the design) determine how and when the player confronts them. In these situations, the player has a great deal of latitude in decision making and setting their own goals. *Terraria*, for example, provides a bare-bones premise for the procedurally generated world, and once play begins, the player may determine almost entirely their course in the game. Likewise, in classic systemic games like *Sid Meier's Pirates*, the player inhabits essentially the same world each time, having a basic narrative set up for how they became a pirate. Once play begins, they can literally chart their own course, following optional story-related goals they may pursue if they choose. In these games, the narrative is not written but is experienced by the player nonetheless.

Theme, Experience, and Meaning

A game's *theme* is built from and yet supersedes its tokens and rules and its functional elements. The theme is what the game is about and relates to the type of experience the game designer wishes to provide for the players. The game may be about being a heroic adventurer, a skulking thief, a skilled gem merchant, or great empire builder; finding true love; surviving a betrayal; or any other imaginable experience.

The theme is the player-facing side of the game as a whole. It provides overall scaffolding and direction for the player, acting as the context for the player's mental model, decisions, and goals. The player has to interpret the game's tokens and rules in light of the theme in order to create a mental model, make meaningful decisions, and set effective goals. If the player is able to do so—if the structural, functional, architectural, and thematic elements of the game combine effectively together as a system—then the game and the player together create meaning. This meaning is ultimately the result of the overall player+game system, the effect of the combination of these two subsystems via play.

This does not mean that the theme needs to be particularly deep or profound. It only needs to be consistent with the structural and functional elements in the game and help propel the player forward. Even in the most systemic, non-story games, it is important for the game designer to keep in mind the experience they are trying to create and the architectural elements needed to embody it. Nearly all successful games—even the most "open world" ones—have a directed experience and theme, though sometimes it can be a bit thin. For example, in *Minecraft* the overarching theme is one of open-ended exploration and crafting new objects. That's not thematically deep, but it is sufficient for many players to begin building a mental model of the game and mastering the world; anything more would just get in their way.

However, when game designers include just the barest of story premises or don't connect the theme to the game's architecture, gameplay suffers. The game *No Man's Sky* allows the player to explore all over an almost endless number of planets, for example—but as the game neither provides explicit goals nor allows players to create many of their own implicit goals, the almost entirely themeless experience ultimately falls flat. The model of the world is technically deep but not in a way that supports a deep mental model or coherent theme. The lack of meaningful decision points and intrinsic player goals comes from the lack of theme (downward causality in the design) and prevents an emergent theme from arising (upward causality).

Similarly, the board game *Splendor* is visually beautiful and has mechanics that are cognitively attractive. However, the theme (being a gem merchant) is only tenuously connected to the gameplay as expressed in the game's highly abstract tokens and rules. As such, those who are not enamored of the game's mechanics in and of themselves often find that the game does not hold their attention. The game design doesn't provide a sufficient connection between the game's architecture and its theme, and so players may have difficulty creating an internal sense of meaning from the experience.

As game designers learn more about systemic design and how to embody story and theme in systemic games, more of them will make games with broad and deep play-spaces, within which players can explore many different sides of the game's theme. These games may often be coupled with strong narratives that avoid either overly directing players into a few different options or leaving them stranded in a thematically barren and uninteresting play-space.

The Evolution of Game Design

Having developed an extensive definition of games, our discussion turns briefly to the development of game design itself to understand how it has changed over the past several decades.

Games have been part of the human experience for millennia. The oldest known game, *Senet*, was invented more than 5,000 years ago in ancient Egypt (Piccione 1980). Our oldest records of this game show it as already having elaborate tokens and rules, indicating that it had been known and developed long before. Games have remained a pastime in cultures around the world since then. However, it wasn't until the technological revolution of the late 20th century that game design became a recognized activity of its own rather than being a side effect of the ad hoc creation of games.

It's difficult to say when game design started as a field rather than as a collective hobby practiced sporadically by a small group of designers. However, it's safe to say that it has been around as a known area of practice since at least the early 1980s. Chris Crawford's book *The Art of Computer Game Design* was published in 1984 and has been cited as the first serious examination of game design as a field of its own (Wolf and Perron 2003). Crawford would go on to publish the *Journal of Computer Game Design* (1987–1996) and organize the first Computer Game Developer's Conference in his living room in 1988 (Crawford 2010)—a conference that is now thoroughly professional and attracts tens of thousands of people each year.

There were game designers prior to Crawford's book, of course, but there was little in the way of an acknowledged shared craft of game design before the advent of both early computer/video games and detailed paper simulation and role-playing games in the late 1970s and early 1980s. During the 1980s and 1990s, up until the early 2000s, most people who became game designers more or less fell into it: they wandered in from fields like theater, anthropology, psychology, or computer science—when they came from a field at all; many were just avid players who tried their hand at game design and found they had a talent for it. Then as now, for many people game design has primarily been a hobby, and now and again a few figure out that maybe they can turn it into a career.

Since the early 2000s, game design as an educational field has gained ground. Nevertheless, for many years, at least up until 2010 or so, most game design degrees were generally seen in the games industry as not creating strong, professional designers. Not only did the large majority of universities offering these degrees not know what they should be teaching (few of those teaching these courses were themselves professional game designers), even game designers had a difficult time articulating what went into the occupation of being a game designer.

As a result, game design remains a difficult area to teach because it's still forming. Most senior game designers even now have learned most of their craft by the age-old apprenticeship method: you make a game and see what works or doesn't. If you're lucky, you get a job where you can shadow a more senior game designer and learn from them. And, even with improved game design curricula today, the number-one way people learn game design is by *doing it*. There is still no substitute for going through the process of designing, developing, testing, and launching a game.

Toward Game Design Theory

Game designers are now well into a movement beyond apprenticeship and simple praxis. There has been an explosion in the number and types of both digital (computer-based) and analog (table-top or board) games that are being made. One of the benefits of this is that just since 2010 or so, actual game design theory has begun to accumulate in more articulate, generally applicable ways. (As noted earlier, *game design theory* is not the same as and has little to do with *game theory*. The latter is the province of mathematics and economics, having to do with highly constrained decision making in abstract situations, and rarely has any relevance to or effect on game design.)

There is a long way to go yet, and no doubt a lot more game design theory will be added in the field in coming years. Game design as a field is, however, at the point where anyone wishing to learn game design can speed their education by incorporating principles, theories, and frame-works along with examples and exercises into their design work.

It is easier than ever today to design and build your own games. Game designers have available a wealth of free or low-cost technologies, tools, and distribution methods that were unimagi-nable just a decade ago. The combination of tools and well-tested principles and frameworks will make you a much more successful game designer much faster.

Summary

In this chapter, you have examined games in detail, first from the views of various philosophers and game designers and then in systemic terms, as applied systems thinking. You have seen that the following:

- Games take place in a separate, nonconsequential context (the "magic circle") expressed by their own tokens and rules.
- Playing a game is necessarily voluntary and requires participation, not just observation.
- Games provide players with a defined world, meaningful decisions, opposition, interaction, and different types of goals.

This chapter also provides a detailed examination of games in systemic terms, focusing on the following:

- **Structures:** The game's parts—its tokens and rules that are the "nouns and verbs" of any game
- **Functional elements:** The looping operational components created as "phrases" from the nouns and verbs that enable the game's world model as a second-order creation and, thus, the player's mental model along with meaningful decisions and goals
- **Architectural and thematic constructions:** The whole of the game experience; its balance of content and systems, narrative, and the overall experience of play

Understanding games in terms of their structures, functional aspects, and the combination of architecture and theme is the first application of systems thinking discussed in Chapter 2.

This chapter has set the stage for the next topic, a detailed exploration of the other part of the overall system that is the game as played: player interactivity, engagement, and fun. With these foundations in place, you will be ready to begin applying these concepts and learn more about the details of the process of game design.

CHAPTER 4

INTERACTIVITY AND FUN

Games must be interactive and fun; if they aren't, they don't get played. But what do the words *interactive* and *fun* really mean? A fuller and more detailed understanding of these concepts is crucial to effective game design.

In this chapter we construct a systemic understanding of interactivity, along with what goes on in the player's mind as part of interacting with and becoming engaged by a game. With this understanding, we are able to define in systemic, practical terms how interactivity and engagement create fun and how we can build them into games.

The Player's Part of the Game as a System

In Chapter 3, "Foundations of Games and Game Design," we defined games and the overall game+player system. As noted there, the playful experience exists only when both the game and the player come together, each as part of a larger system (see Figure 4.1). The game creates its own internal system with structural, functional, and thematic elements—the parts, loops, and whole that define the game.

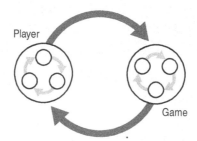

Figure 4.1 Players and games are subsystems that together create the overall game+player system. In this abstract view of the multilevel, hierarchical game+player system, each has its own structural (parts), functional (loops), and thematic (whole) elements

In this chapter we examine how the player and game create the larger game+player system via the emergent process of interactivity. Understanding interactivity enables us to go "one level down" into the internal aspects of the player subsystem—the player's mental model—and see how it is constructed as part of the experience of play.

The player's mental model corresponds to the game's internal model, discussed in Chapter 3. To build this mental model, the player and the game each act in ways that affect the other, as discussed in detail in this chapter. Through these mutual effects, the player carries out his intentions to test and affect the game's internal state. The game in turn changes its state and progressively reveals its internal parts and loops. As discussed in Chapter 2, "Defining Systems," complex systems are created with such mutual looping effects. As you will see here, this mutual looping cycle is the core concept behind interactivity, gameplay, engagement, and fun.

A Systemic Approach to Interactivity

The word *interactivity* is used throughout the games industry and in many related fields. We often treat this word as having to do with what happens when the player taps on a button or clicks on an icon in a game, but it is much deeper than that. Interactivity is central to the experience of playing a game and, more than ever before, common to the human experience. While interactivity has been cited as what differentiates games from other forms of media

(Grodal 2000), our world is far more interactive today than in the past as a result of increasing interconnections geographically and technologically. Recall from Chapter 1, "Foundations of Systems," the shift we have seen from only about 1,000 connected computing devices in 1984 to a number approaching 50 billion today, each enabling both technological and human-to-human connectivity. This is an unprecedented change in human history. And yet, despite the magnitude of this change and the ubiquity of interactivity in our lives, and despite many discussions of the topic in the fields of communications, human–computer interaction (HCI), and game design, we still lack a clear, practical definition of this core concept.

According to *Webster's*, *interactive* means "mutually or reciprocally active." This concise definition gets to the heart of what it means for something or someone to be interactive: there are two or more agents acting in relation to each other, mutually or reciprocally affecting each other by their actions. This simple definition was expanded on by Rafaeli (1988) to include the idea of two or more agents in a series of communication exchanges, where any given message is contextually related to earlier ones. This communication may be between two individuals face-to-face; in a conversation mediated by technology (for example, over the telephone); or between agents who may or may not be human, as in a human interacting with a computer game. By contrast, some authors have in the past argued that interactivity is resident only within the individual (Newhagen 2004), in the technology or medium used for communication (Sundar 2004), or even solely in human-to-human communications, on the assumption that only "the human has potential for transcending his or her programming" and that "the machine makes judgements or decisions only on the basis of its program" (Bretz 1983, 139) and is therefore somehow not truly interactive.

In game design, Chris Crawford's definition of *interactivity* reflects that of Rafaeli, cited above. Crawford characterized interactivity as "a cyclic process between two or more active agents in which each agent alternatively listens, thinks, and speaks—a conversation of sorts" (1984, 28). This turns out to be a highly useful way of looking at interactivity, and one that we will generalize here. In particular, Crawford's definition calls out the cyclic nature of any interaction, where different parts (actors) affect each other by their behavior. It begins to sound very much as if any interaction forms a system and thus can benefit from a systemic view, including parts, loops, and wholes.

Parts: Interactivity Structures

The structural parts of any interactive system are two or more actors or agents; this is true in games and any other interactive setting. In designing games, we assume that there is at least one human involved in the interactivity loop. It's possible (and often desirable) to have multiple computer-driven players in a game but only if there is also at least one human there. A game "playing itself" without human involvement can be useful for testing, but otherwise it misses out on the essential, meaningful aspect of the experience of a game as played, one that requires a human participant.

Each part in a system (here the player(s) and the game) has its own state, boundaries, and behaviors. Each part in an interactive system uses its behaviors to affect, but not wholly determine, the internal state of the others. In-game actors have an internal state such as health, wealth, inventory, speed, and so on, as well as behaviors such as talking, attacking, evading, and so on. Each agent uses its behaviors, based on its internal state, to affect others and is in turn affected by their behaviors.

Internal State

As systems in themselves, the internal states of the player and a game are necessarily complex. The human player's internal state is ultimately the totality of their current mental and emotional processing. As far as their interactions with the game are concerned, the player's internal state is their mental model of the game.[1] This includes their understanding of the following:

- Current in-game variables, such as health, wealth, country population, inventory, or whatever is relevant in the game context for their understanding
- The game state, particularly how their understanding has changed based on feedback provided from their most recent actions
- The immediate, short-term, and long-term goals within the game, including their predictions of what will happen in the game based on their actions
- The effects of past decisions and what they have learned about the game as a result of them

We will spend much of this chapter focused on these elements and the player's overall psychological state; it is, after all, for humans that we make games.

The game's internal state is the working embodiment of the game design as described in Chapter 3 and as explored in more detail throughout the rest of this book. It includes not only game-related variables and rules but also the overall event loop that determines the game's processing, when it accepts input from the player, and so on. In this chapter we treat the game's internal state as more abstract so as to focus on the interactions with the player.

Behaviors

Actions in a game are whatever the game designers enable them to be; players and non-player characters (or other actors) may talk, fly, attack, or carry out any number of other actions. These behaviors are necessarily enabled and mediated by the game, occurring as they do only within the game's context. If, for example, a game disables an ability (as by means of a "cooldown"

---

1. More broadly, each of us carries a mental model of every interaction we have, whether with a game, another person, or even ourselves. Here we focus on the mental models we form as part of playing a game.

timer after use), an actor cannot use that behavior until it becomes available again. Both extraordinary abilities and limitations are part of existing within the context, the magic circle, of the game environment.

Player Behaviors and Cognitive Load

A player's in-game behaviors begin as mental goals, part of the player's mental model of the game and intent within it. These behaviors must at some point become physical: the player must move a piece on the board, click on an icon, and so on. The transition from mental to physical marks the boundary from mental model to behavior.

In taking action in a game, a player typically provides input via a device, such as by tapping on a keyboard, moving or actuating (for example, clicking) a mouse or another controller, or providing a gesture (for example, tap or swipe) on a control that is sensitive to touch. In some cases, even moving their gaze to a certain part of a computer screen is a valid behavior recognized by the game.

Planning for and taking an action in a game requires intent on the player's part. Some of their limited cognitive resources have to be devoted to what they want to do, and some to the actions needed to accomplish their goal in the context of the game. The fewer cognitive resources that are needed to perform an action, the less active thought it requires, and the more natural and immediate it feels to the player.

The general term for taking up cognitive resources is *cognitive load* (Sweller 1988). The more things you are thinking about and attending to at any moment, the greater your cognitive load. Reducing how much the player needs to think about *how* to play the game reduces their cognitive load and allows them to focus instead on what they are trying to do. This ultimately increases engagement and fun. (More on this later in this chapter.)

In HCI literature, the cognitive load induced by having to think about *how* to do something is known as the combination of *articulatory* and *semantic distance* (Norman and Draper 1986). The more cognitively direct an action is—pointing with a finger being more direct than using a mouse cursor, which in turn is more direct than typing in (x,y) coordinates—the shorter the articulatory distance and the fewer cognitive resources are needed to complete it.

The semantic distance of an action is reduced when the game provides ample, timely feedback to the player and presents an easily interpreted result of an action. The more closely the feedback matches the player's understanding and intent, the fewer cognitive resources are needed to evaluate it. In a game, seeing an icon of a sword has a shorter semantic distance than seeing the letter *w* (indicating *weapon*) or the word *sword*. Seeing an animation of a building gradually being constructed is more easily evaluated than assessing a completion bar in the user interface, which is in turn more easily evaluated than seeing a text display such as "563/989 bricks placed."

The combination of these two "distances" adds to or reduces the player's cognitive load—the mental resources they must devote to understanding the game. The shorter these distances, the less the player has to actively think about the game, and the more cognitive resources they have left over to devote to the playful context within the world of the game.

Similarly in terms of game rules, the less the player has to remember about how to play the game—the fewer special cases there are in the rules—the more they can concentrate on the game itself and the shorter the semantic distance between their intent and their actions in the game. Recall the discussion of elegance in games in Chapter 2: a game such as *Go* has so few rules that the semantic distance is virtually zero, and the player is able to devote the entirety of their cognition to mentally inhabiting the game-space.

Game Behaviors and Feedback

A game's behavior must provide feedback to the player about its state. This is how the player learns how the game works and builds a mental model of it. In modern digital games, this feedback is most typically communicated via graphics (images, text, animations) and sound. This lets the player know in a timely fashion that the game's state has changed, so that they can update their mental model of the game.

While the feedback provided must be perceptible to the player—a color they cannot see or a sound they cannot hear are the same as providing no feedback at all—the game's behavior does not have to provide *complete* information about its state. This incompleteness allows for hidden state (for example, cards the game holds that the player can't see) that is a key ingredient to many game designs. Koster (2012) referred to this as the "black box" part of the game—the part that must be inferred by the player as they build a mental model of the game and that provides a great deal of the gameplay experience. Similarly, Ellenor (2014) referred to the internal game systems as "a machine that does X," meaning that the heart of the game—its internal systems—are a machine that the player discerns only through its behaviors.

It is important for you as a game designer to remember that all that the player knows about the game comes through the game's behaviors and feedback in response to the player's actions. You may want to assume that the player comes to the game with some knowledge— for example, how to operate a mouse or touch screen, how to roll dice. You must be very careful with these assumptions, though, to avoid putting the player in a position of not being able to play the game because of some missing knowledge that the game isn't going to provide.

As a player learns a game, there will be parts the player believes they know and understand well; their mental model is solid there. The more they can use this information to extend their understanding into new areas, the more easily they will learn the game. In addition, the more certain they are of some areas, the more able they will be to make predictions about areas where they are not certain or where the game is withholding some of its state information. This is where a lot of the gameplay resides, as the player tries different actions with predicted outcomes and builds their mental model based on whether those predictions were accurate.

Making Intentional Choices

It is important that an actor, whether human or computer, be able to choose its behaviors rather than fire them off at random. The choice of behavior must be based either on internal state and logic, or, in the case of a human player, on their ability to consciously choose their next action. The player must understand which actions accomplish the following goals:

- Are valid in the current context

- Have the information they need to make a choice

- Will help them accomplish their goals based on predicted outcome

- Can be decided on and selected in an appropriate amount of time

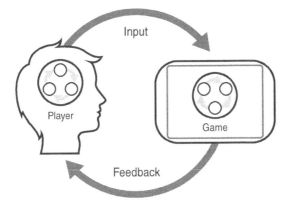

Figure 4.2 Players provide input to a game, and the games provides feedback to the player, forming a generalized interactive loop. Note that the player and the game both have internal loops as well

Interactive Game Loops

In systemic terms, the player's and the game's behaviors are the result of their internal state. Based on their state, each selects actions to take, which then affect and perturb the other's state. This drives new behavioral responses in return. The player provides *input* to the game via their behaviors, which changes the game's state. The game processes this and provides *feedback* responses that are input for the player, changing their internal state (see Figure 4.2). This creates a reciprocating loop that is the essence of interactivity. This give-and-take between the player and the game is often referred to as the game's *core loop*, a term we will define more precisely later in this chapter and revisit in Chapter 7, "Creating Game Loops."

We discussed different types of systemic loops (for example, reinforcing and balancing loops) in Chapter 2. All systems have interactive loops; the parts interact and form loops that create systems. In this case, we are focused more on interactions between the player and the game as subsystems of an overall system. We will examine these game+player interactive loops in this chapter (for brevity's sake, we call them simply "interactive loops"), and then see them again in more detail from the game's side in Chapter 7. The earlier discussion of systemic loops (see Chapter 2) and here of a systemic view of interactivity provide a foundation for more detailed design discussions later on.

There is one other form of loop that is worth mentioning here: the *designer's loop* (see Figure 4.3). You first saw this type of loop in the introduction to this book, and it is a single image that shows what this book is really about—you as a game designer working with the player and the game and the experience you are trying to create. You will see descriptions of this again in more detail in the coming chapters.

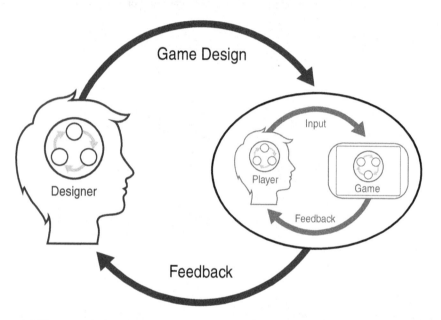

Figure 4.3 The game designer's loop enables a designer to iteratively design and test a design

Thus far you have seen at least brief discussions of the player's internal mental loop, the game's loop inside itself, and the interactive loop between the player and game. This fourth loop is unlike the others, in that it is not directly related to the play of the game but is central to its design. In creating a game, the designer must interact with the game+player system from outside that system. The game designer supplies input in the form of game design ideas and prototypes and receives feedback on what works and what doesn't. This is a brief embodiment of the overall game design process, which is itself an interactive system based on the looping interactions of its parts.

The Whole Experience

The whole of the game+player system arises as an emergent effect of the interactive loops between the player and game. As noted earlier, Crawford (1984) has described interactivity in games as being like a conversation, a view also discussed by Luhmann (1997). The "conversational" nature of interactivity is a more colloquial way of describing the whole of the interactive system: each participant has their own complex internal state, and each affects the others with their behaviors selected based on their current state.

This whole is the game as experienced by the player and is where the meaning of the game arises. Whatever the game *means* to the player—its theme, lessons, morals, and whatever stays with the player long after the game is done—comes from the totality of all the player's interactions with it. This meaning is an emergent effect of the interactive system, not resident in just the player or the game alone. As Newhagen (2004) put it, "Meaning is generated when the outputs from [subsystems] interact, and higher order symbols holistically emerge at the next level" (p. 399). It is those symbols that form the basis of the player's mental model as the result of the interactions in the game.

Understanding interactivity as a system that includes the interplay between the player and the game sets us up for a greater understanding of the psychological experiences of engagement and fun.

Mental Models, Arousal, and Engagement

Having defined interactivity in systemic terms, we now turn to study the player's side of the interactive loop in more detail. This involves a close look at how someone playing a game builds understanding—a *mental model*—of the game using various forms of interactivity. A wide range of neurological, perceptual, cognitive, emotional, and cultural interactive effects all come together to create a layered dynamic experience and psychological model of the game being played. In studying these, we will see that the totality of this experience of playful engagement is what we know in many different forms as "fun."

The player's mental model of a game is their reflection of the game's internal model, which is defined by game designers and embodied in the game (as described in Chapter 3 and detailed in Chapters 6, "Designing the Whole Experience," through 8, "Defining Game Parts"). The player has to get to know the game's world by interacting with it. By playing the game, the player learns important game concepts. These are perceived as worthwhile and attainable by the player, who tests their understanding based on their actions. If the feedback provided by the game is positive (the player "did something right"), they feel a sense of accomplishment, and those concepts are added to their mental model. The player now knows more and has greater abilities in the game than before. Otherwise, they may feel set back, have to reconsider, and correct their model. The player's mental model thus arises out of a combination of their attention, plans, goals, and emotions that are all part of the creation of the game+player system. As noted in Chapter 3, this same cycle is related to the player making what they believe to be meaningful goals and thus to having their actions in the game imbued with a sense of personal meaning.

While playing a game, the player cycles through their primary interaction loops many times. If in so doing they are unable to construct a coherent model of the game that matches what the game designer has created, or if the interactions involved in doing so are tedious, boring, or overwhelming, they will stop playing the game. (In psychological terms, this is known as *behavior extinction*; in games, it's often referred to as *burnout*.) As such, it is the game designer's job to build the game to attract the player's attention and then hold their interest in it over time.

Contained in the player's mental model is their understanding of a game as a multilevel system: the parts, loops, and whole in the game's systems and subsystems. This includes any overt systems, such as economic, ecological, or combat systems, and also the ability to navigate the game's spaces, whether geographical or logical. For example, if a player in *World of Warcraft* knows the best way to get from Ashenvale to Stormwind, they have an effective mental model of this game's world (potentially as good as their mental model of their home town). Similarly, if someone playing *The Witcher 3* knows how to navigate the game's highly detailed and often confusing skill tree (and why, for example, you would choose the Muscle Memory skill over, say, Lightning Reflexes), then they have been successful in building a mental model of that system. The mental model is the sum of the player's knowledge of the game world, along with their ability to use its systems and anticipate the effects of their actions in the game. It allows the player to form valid intentions, predict the effects of their actions in the game, avoid or over-come obstacles the game may throw in their way, and ultimately achieve their desired goals within the context of the game.

Bushnell's Law, an aphorism attributed to Atari founder Nolan Bushnell, said that a game should be "easy to learn and difficult to master" (Bogost 2009). In terms of the mental model, this means it should be easy for the player to construct and validate a model, being free of ambigui-ties and exceptions that may trip up the player. The game must present its basic information and interactions in ways that are clear and familiar to a new player and in ways that encourage them to explore further and learn more, adding to their knowledge and model of the game.

A game that is well designed rewards a player with an ample mental space to explore that emerges from the game: the player may play the game over and over, revisiting their mental model often, and yet not feel that they have mastered the game quickly, if at all. Once the player has seen all the game's content, if the behaviors and interactions between those parts are also fully explored, then there is nothing left to learn, and there are no new experiences to be had, so the game loses its ability to engage the player. Once again, the game of *Go* provides an archetypal example of a game that fulfils Bushnell's Law: the game has only a few rules and is easy to learn. It may, however, take a lifetime to master, as even dedicated players reevaluate and reassemble parts of their mental model as they continually expand their understanding of its systemic depth.

Interactive Loops: Building the Player's Mental Model

Figure 4.4 shows the high-level features of what happens in the loop between the player and the game in a more detailed version of the interactive loop shown in Figure 4.2. The very beginning of this loop involves the player forming the intent to start the game and then acting to do so. The game begins by offering some initial form of attractive feedback and a *call to action* to urge the player on (starting with the splash screen and introduction). The call to action, sometimes called a *hook*, impels the player to start or continue playing the game. This is similar to but not quite the same an *affordance*, a term that comes from user interface design. An *affordance* is a visual or otherwise perceivable clue about how something operates. As Norman (1988) wrote, "Plates are for pushing. Knobs are for turning. Slots are for inserting things into. Balls are for throwing or bouncing. When affordances are taken advantage of, the user knows what to do just by looking: no picture, label, or instruction needed." The call to action must include affordances so that how the player is to perform the next necessary action is truly obvious. In addition, it must also provide the player with some motivation to perform the next action. The call to action is metaphorically not merely a cup with a handle that says "I can be picked up" but is an attractive mug filled with tasty warm cocoa that makes you want to pick it up and cradle it in your hands on a cold day. The game must from the start draw the player in and then keep their attention and engagement, as discussed in this chapter.

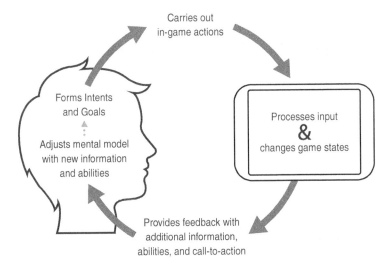

Figure 4.4 A more detailed look at the interactive loop between player and game

In responding to the call to action to begin the interactive loop, the player takes in visual, auditory, and symbolic information from the game, adds it to (or later adjusts) their mental model, and uses the new information gained to monitor existing goals and create new ones within the context of the game. These goals result in actions carried out by the player in the game, which change the game's state (along with the game independently changing its state based on its design and internal model).

The game then provides new feedback to the player that gives more information or abilities (more things that they can do in the game). In so doing, the game encourages the player to continue building their mental model by keeping the loop going with more opportunities and calls to action. If this process retains the player's interest, they gradually build up their mental model of the game as their understanding of it (and typically their abilities in it) increases.

This process of getting and keeping the player's attention is what keeps the player interested in and engaged with the game. To understand this more fully, we must first look at the mechanisms of arousal and attention and several different kinds of psychological engagement. This will then lead us to a discussion of the experience of "flow" and how all these factors contribute to the playful experience of fun.

Arousal and Attention

For a game to be played, the player must be interested and (in psychological terms) *aroused*— that is, alert and watchful and ready to participate. If the player is disinterested or bored, or on the other hand overwhelmed or anxious, they won't be willing or able to devote the energy needed to participate in and engage with the game.

For example, if someone begins to play a game but can't see any usable controls or make sense of what's being displayed, they will soon become bored and stop playing. Recall that no one *has* to play a game, and it is the game designer's responsibility to make the game appear interesting enough to attract and hold the player's attention. In the same way, if there is so much going on in the game (visually in particular) that the player can't figure out what they should be doing or even where to start, then their attention will become overwhelmed, and they will stop playing.

Arousal and Performance

The relationship between psychological arousal and performance was first explored in the early days of psychology by Yerkes and Dodson (1908). It is important for game designers to understand what is now known as the "Yerkes-Dodson Law." Yerkes and Dodson discovered that as an individual's arousal increases, their performance on a task also increases—up to a point. If the individual's arousal is too low, they are bored and doesn't perform well. But above some level, as the individual's arousal increases (as a reaction to additional stimuli or stress), they become increasingly anxious and unable to focus on tasks at hand, and their performance decreases.

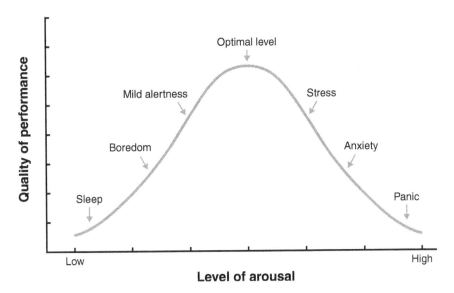

Figure 4.5 An idealized version of the Yerkes-Dodson curve. At low levels of arousal, performance is poor. As arousal increases, performance improves up to some point, beyond which it degrades again

There are variations on this. For example, performance tends not to drop off on simple tasks even at high levels of arousal; with more complex tasks, we each reach our optimum point sooner. Likewise, the more skilled you are or the more you have practiced a task, the higher levels of arousal you can maintain without losing performance. This is the so-called "expert effect," where, for example, a highly skilled car driver, airplane pilot, surgeon, or programmer can stay calm and perform under circumstances that would have a less-practiced individual completely panicked and unable to perform at all.

An idealized version of the Yerkes-Dodson curve is shown in Figure 4.5. As you can see, if an individual is not sufficiently alert, they will not be attentive to a task and will not perform well. At or just past the top of the curve, the player is performing well and may be feeling mildly but not unpleasantly stressed. This is where learning takes place and skill improves as the player surfs the edge of the curve of optimal performance. However, if they slip down the right side of the curve, there is too much going on and too much perceptual input or cognitive load. When this happens, the individual's arousal is too high, and they experience stress, anxiety, and eventually panic, with an accompanying reduction in performance.

Somewhere in the middle of this curve, where the individual is alert and attentive to the tasks at hand, able to discount or ignore extraneous events and inputs, and performing well (and generally aware they are performing well), then they can be said to be psychologically *engaged*.

Engagement

Psychological *engagement* is an important component of interactivity and gameplay; in many ways, it is what we are seeking to provide the player when we design games. This word is commonly used in describing various experiences ("player engagement" is often a measure of commercial success in games) but usually without any clear definition. As with other concepts referred to in game design and discussed here, linking this concept to its psychological roots will help you gain a clearer understanding of what the term actually means and how to use it effectively.

Engagement is a description of an individual's internal state and how they respond to the world and others around them (Gambetti and Graffigna 2010). Schaufeli et al. (2002) characterized psychological engagement as an ongoing cognitive and emotional state typified by a combination of "vigor, dedication, and absorption," where

> vigor is characterized by high levels of energy and mental resilience while working, the willingness to invest effort in one's work, and persistence even in the face of difficulties. Dedication is characterized by a sense of significance, enthusiasm, inspiration, pride, and challenge [and] absorption is characterized by being fully concentrated and deeply engrossed in one's work, whereby time passes quickly and one has difficulties with detaching oneself from work. (pp. 74–75)

These are exactly the qualities that we typically see in players who describe a satisfying experience with a game. As the player focuses on and interacts with the game, their mental model grows and continues to match the game's internal model. As a result, they are able to interact successfully with it: their goals (either provided by the game or created by them) enable them to try out hypotheses on which they act and receive satisfying feedback, and the cycle continues.

When someone is actively engaged by such an activity—one that is pleasurable, voluntary, separate, and nonconsequential (referring again to the "magic circle")—then we often say they are "having fun." We typically call such activities "play" or "games." From the point of view of the game designer (and player!), a game that enables such a positive experience is a success. We will explore engagement and fun in greater detail in the remainder of this chapter.

Becoming and Staying Engaged

Given the importance of engagement in games, how do we define in practical terms the experience of engagement, where does interactivity fit in, and how do these lead to something we can define as "fun" in a way that helps us create better games?

We can look at engagement first from a neurochemical point of view, in terms of psychological motivations, and then from additional layers of experience: action/feedback, cognitive, social, emotional, and cultural. We will look at each of these in turn, building up the model of engagement, interactivity, and fun.

Neurochemical Engagement

Ultimately when we create game experiences, we are attempting to create experiences the human brain will find attractive and relevant, that will hold the player's attention, and that will provide a sense of pleasure or positivity. While we should not try to pin engagement or fun too closely to chemicals sloshing around in our brains, understanding how these contribute to arousal helps us also understand how and why players become attracted to and continue to play our games.

One of the primary ways our brains tell us that an action or a situation is worth repeating is by helping us *feel good* (a subjective but common experience). This happens in particular when certain chemicals are released in our brains. While there is a lot going on in our cortical circuitry as well, these chemicals serve as broadcast signals in the brain that say, basically, "whatever is going on right now is good—do more of that!" However, there is more than one kind of situation that merits a broad "do more of that!" signal, and so we have multiple primary reward neurochemicals. Not surprisingly, it turns out that these map well to fun, engaging experiences. Here are some of the main neurochemicals that have been identified as being associated with different kinds of engaging experiences:

- **Dopamine:** Often called "the reward chemical," dopamine contributes to alertness and arousal, helping you to be attentive and motivated to act. In particular, dopamine gives us a positive feeling in situations that are novel (but not too unusual), that require exploration, or that represent a goal that has been reached. If you have ever felt pleasure just by seeing points going up in a game, that's dopamine at work. Notable too is that if a reward is expected and not attained, the amount of dopamine released is reduced, causing the behavior or situation to be viewed as less positive and pleasurable in the future (Nieoullon 2002). This highlights an important aspect of dopamine-related engagement, habituation: we value new rewards more than we value existing, expected ones. As we gradually get used to existing situations, they become less novel and less rewarding, and we become less vigorous in our dedication to them, ultimately becoming bored as we seek new rewards. Providing players with new rewards and new ways to remain engaged is often a large part of game design.

- **Serotonin:** Serotonin is dopamine's balancing partner. Whereas dopamine is about being alert, seeking novelty, and expecting of reward, serotonin is about feeling secure and having a sense of accomplishment. Whereas dopamine leads to impulsiveness and looking for something new, serotonin urges you to keep plugging along with what you already know. The positive feelings you get from situations in which you gain a feeling of security (in psychological terms, "harm avoidance"), assure or gain social status, complete an achievement, or gain a skill are all due to the release of serotonin in your brain (Raleigh et al. 1991). The sense of satisfaction a player feels when leveling up is in part due to serotonin. It's notable also that many games celebrate such accomplishments with specific visual and sound effects ("Ding!" has long been known as the auditory cue that someone has just leveled up in many MMOs). The conditioning effect of associating a particular noise or visual effect with the feeling of leveling up should not be underestimated.

- **Oxytocin and vasopressin:** These two neurochemicals are important in social bonding and support. They have a number of functions, ranging from enhancing sexual arousal to encouraging learning, but they are particularly important in forming social bonds ranging from friend/stranger reactions to falling in love (Olff et al. 2013, Walum et al. 2008). Oxytocin is often called the "cuddle hormone" because of its release in sexual or other intimate encounters that results in stronger social bonds.[2] Vasopressin performs similar functions, particularly in men. Each of these help us feel good for being socially engaged—being part of a couple, family, team, or community.

- **Norepinephrine and endorphins:** These two neurochemicals relate to concentration, attention, energy, and engagement. They are often referred to as "stress hormones." Norepinephrine (typically called noradrenaline in the UK) helps regulate arousal, especially in short-term vigilance, preparing the brain to quickly react to stimuli that may require a fight-or-flight response. It also helps with very fast learning in such situations. Endorphins act differently, muting feelings of pain and giving us the feeling of having additional energy, especially after strenuous physical activity. These neurochemicals are less directly related to engagement than the others, particularly in the case of generally sedentary games. They appear, however, to aid in alertness and concentration of attention, especially in stressful situations.

This neurochemical view provides an important window into the different aspects of engagement. As noted earlier, we are engaged with something when we have become dedicated to and absorbed in it and vigorously spend time and energy on it. It becomes our focus, and other things tend to drop out of our attention. The internal, subjective feeling of this sense of engagement, based on our neurochemistry, is that we experience feeling the following ways:

- Alert, seeking novelty or expecting a reward
- Secure in a reward or established in our place in a social hierarchy
- Connected to others via shared social bonds
- Vigilant in the face of stress
- That we are successfully "pushing through" in the presence of exertion

Not all of these are felt at the same time or all the time. Manipulating these feelings effectively is part of maintaining engagement in an activity. This is why, for example, a difficult level in a game or a climactic sequence in a book or movie is followed by a quieter, easier moment where

---

2. Oxytocin is released post-sex but also due to mutual gaze in humans. In fact, it's possible to fall in love with someone by talking openly for half an hour and then gazing into each other's eyes for several minutes (Kellerman et al. 1989). Oxytocin is even released due to mutual gaze in both humans and dogs but not between humans and other animals (Nagasawa et al. 2015). So, beyond understanding a little more about social engagement, how is this helpful to you as a game designer? There's no way to tell. But being on the lookout for wide-ranging information like this is an important part of the game designer mindset. Blame it on dopamine.

the player or viewer can catch their breath—that is, reduce their vigilance, rest mentally and physically, and consolidate feelings of accomplishment and social connection.

When such engagement takes place within a consequential (for example, work-related) context, it is often perceived as a fulfilling activity. When it takes place in a separate, voluntary, nonconsequential space (such as within the "magic circle" of a game), it is often perceived as *fun*.

Moving Beyond the Brain

We are more than our brain chemicals, of course, and our attention and overall arousal are as well. As we move from the purely chemical and neural levels of interaction, we can loosely classify subsequent types of engagement as being increasingly psychological rather than physiological. These are under increasing individual control—in psychological terms, moving from reflexive to executive to reflective attention—and in addition operate on longer and longer time scales.

It is important for a game designer to be aware of aspects of player psychology, including the player's motivations. Different motivations are discussed in more detail in Chapter 6, as this is a major consideration when choosing the target audience for a game. Regardless of the mix of motivations your players have, the different forms of interactivity described here apply.

Note that the types of engagement and interactivity outlined here correspond to the types of player goals discussed in Chapter 3. Each type of interactive loop provides the player an opportunity to form an intention, whether an instant in-the-moment physical response to a sensation or a long-term goal with fruition sometime in the future.

Interactive Loops

The concept of interactive loops has already been mentioned—and here we are again referring specifically to the loops of interaction between a player and a game. These loops go from very fast and using few cognitive (much less reflective) resources to taking place on much longer time scales and being far more reflective. Each of the interactive loops shown in Figure 4.6 is the same type of loop shown in Figure 4.4. Each operates on a different time scale and requires different internal resources. In each kind of loop, the player creates an intention and then carries out an action, causing the game state to change and the game to provide feedback, setting up the next iteration of the loop. The only differences between these kinds of interaction loops are the amount of mental (or computing) resources required, the time scale on which they take place, and the experience that the player has as a result. Note also that these loops are often happening at the same time: many fast action/feedback loops occur within a strategic long-term cognitive loop, and several of them may happen during a social or emotional interactive loop. You will see this point again later in this chapter, in our discussion of the time scale of combined interaction loops.

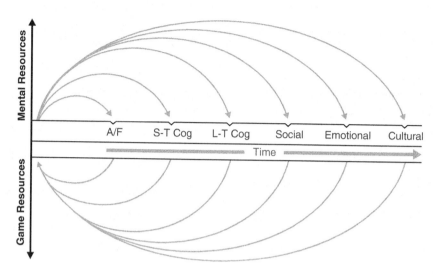

Figure 4.6 Diagrammatic view of different types of interactive loops. Time scales range from subsecond to weeks or longer. Longer loops also typically require more mental or game (computing) resources. These loops often occur at the same time, nested one within another, as described in the text

The following kinds of interactive loops are discussed in detail here and used throughout the rest of the book, listed here from fastest/least cognitive to slowest/most reflective:

- Action/feedback
- Short-term cognitive
- Long-term cognitive
- Social
- Emotional
- Cultural

Action/Feedback Interactivity

In terms of psychological interactivity, the fastest and in many ways most basic form relies primarily on physical action from the player to the game and sensory-based feedback from the game to the player, with little opportunity for thought in between. The interactive gameplay at this level—the loop from action to feedback—happens quickly, on the order of less than a second to at most two or three seconds.

For games that are primarily driven by actions and feedback that need to appear instantaneous to the player, performance is perceived to be essentially instant if there is less than 100 milliseconds between the player's action and the game's feedback. To maintain any feeling of real instant connection, the time lag can be no more than about 250 milliseconds, or one-quarter of a second (Card et al. 1983). Beyond that timeframe, players will not associate feedback with a preceding action unless the feedback is symbolically related to an aspect of a longer-term, more cognitive mental model, and even then it will feel sluggish and delayed.

Present-Tense Action and Reflexive Attention

A player's fast actions and reactions are the first half of the action/feedback interactive loop. This can be described as the player's "present tense." What is the player doing right now? If the player's answer to this question is in the present tense, using verbs like walking, running, shooting, jumping, and so on, then their mental model is primarily taken up with what is happening in the moment, and the action/feedback loop is a large part of their engagement with the game. If, however, the player tends to describe what they are doing in terms of future goals or intentions ("I am completing this quest" or "I am building up this army so I can help my friend attack that citadel"), then while the action/feedback interactions remain important, they exist as part of a longer cognitive, emotional, or social loop (described later in this chapter).

On the feedback side, this is the realm of *reflexive attention*, also known as exogenous attention, or attention controlled by external events rather than the player's conscious intent (Mayer et al. 2004). Our brains are built to be on alert for new stimuli that may be important. This includes the sudden appearance of threats, of course, but also appears to be why our eyes are drawn to bright, colorful, fast-appearing objects, especially those in our peripheral vision (Yantis and Jonides 1990). Many games from *Whack-a-Mole* to advanced first-person shooters make use of this mechanism for their primary form of gameplay, and many players report a feeling of excitement and positive tension while playing such games (Yee 2016b). Games that make abundant use of fast, colorful, animated, noisy feedback are often referred to as being "juicy," as a way of referring to this pleasant multi-modal onslaught of sensory input (Gabler et al. 2005, Juul and Begy 2016). Because the attentional aspect of games with their primary interactivity at this level is so reflexive, the gameplay isn't particularly thoughtful, but it doesn't need to be: as long as this "juicy" loop is maintained, the player remains alert, focused, and ready for whatever may pop up and learns to react quickly as well. This fast loop gives rise to what Steve Swink (2009) called "game feel…the tactile, kinesthetic sense of manipulating a virtual object. It's the sensation of control in a game." Interacting with game objects this way is immediately pleasurable for its own sake.

The Stress and Reward of Fast Action

Many fast-paced games require the player to respond quickly and accurately to (typically visual) stimuli. Doing so stresses the human perceptual and motor system, as described by Fitts' Law (Fitts and Peterson 1964), which states that the time required to move to a specified target varies inversely with the size of the target: we are able to point (using a finger or mouse pointer, for example) to an area within a large target quickly and easily. As the target becomes smaller, and especially if its placement is not known beforehand, our ability to move to it takes longer. The successful completion of such a reflexive attentional task feels good; it releases dopamine and norepinephrine in our brains, encouraging us to go one more time. This kind of fast motion also carries with it a bit of Caillois' *ilinx* play, even if it is only in the player's fingertips on a mouse: the feeling of moving quickly, precisely, and well is part of what makes it enjoyable.

Many simple digital games are little more than action/feedback loops like this. Many early arcade games were deterministic in their play, meaning that the in-game opponents moved and acted exactly the same way every time the game was played; *Pac-Man* is a prime example, as the "ghosts" moved the same way every time the game was played. This determinism meant that the player had to learn a particular unchanging pattern of responses to play successfully. After sufficient practice, this required rote responses in a very tight action/feedback loop but no significant cognition. Executing these patterns accurately enough via procedural memory (sometimes called "muscle memory," learned via repetition) enabled the player to continue playing until the speed of the game exceeded their ability to respond.

More recently, games known as *endless runners*, like the classic *Temple Run*, present a situation where the player is continually hurtling forward and is required to reflexively attend and quickly perceive which direction to go and which obstacles to hit or avoid, at a faster and faster pace. As the game proceeds, the action/feedback loop becomes shorter and shorter in duration and the game speeds up. The game is exciting and enjoyable until it goes too fast and becomes essentially unplayable.

There is an inherent call to action that results from this unplayability, though—we often experience it as the "just one more try" phenomenon. If the player is in a short, focused loop, with his brain ready for that next achievement, the desire to try one more time to see if he can do a little better, get a little further, can be very strong. (This is a form of outer-loop or metagame to the main game.) The player's mental model improves as they learn the game, but in this case primarily at a more perceptual and action-oriented rather than cognitive level via repetition-based motor learning. When the game goes too fast for the player's motor-based skill level, it necessarily comes to an end…unless the player wants to try just one more time.

Even games with other forms of cognitive gameplay layered on top of the action/feedback loops often make significant use of our neurological and low-level perceptual architecture by requiring that players move, tap, or click at just the right time to move in-game units around or make their in-game avatar run, jump, shoot, duck, and so on within tight tolerances. Or, even if the gameplay does not require fast reactions, the feedback provided by many games is juicy as described above: colorful, animated, and using pleasing, exciting sounds and music as feedback to the player, engaging their perceptual systems as arousal and reward mechanisms.

One of the most vibrant examples of this in recent years is the game *Peggle*. The gameplay relies on a combination of fine-tuned physical input and some short-term cognition (as discussed later in this chapter), but where it really shines is in how it provides enormously effective perceptual feedback, particularly as rewards for successful play. The game display overall is colorful and attractive (catching the player's attention), but during key moments of play, it exhibits some of the most over-the-top (in a good way) examples of visual and auditory feedback in games today. The gameplay consists of shooting a small ball to take out various pegs on the game board. At a climactic moment, as the ball flies toward a particular designated peg, the camera zooms in, the ball's flight goes to slow motion, there's a dramatic drumroll—and then, as the ball hits the peg, there's a sudden and triumphant bloom of multicolored fireworks, the glowing words EXTREME FEVER, a swelling chorus of *Ode to Joy*, kaleidoscopic spectral trails, more fireworks with falling brightly colored stars, an enormous brilliant rainbow racing across the screen, and finally a rapidly ascending score displayed in huge numbers.

All this effectively engages perceptual and neurochemical systems as masterful examples of positive reinforcement for correct input and thus keeps the player aroused and engaged.

Moment-to-Moment Gameplay

Action/feedback interactivity is an important consideration in design for most games, even those that rely primarily on other forms of interactivity loops. This is often described as *moment-to-moment gameplay*. One of the key questions a game designer must answer is "What is the player doing in *every moment* that they are playing?" This is related to the "present tense" nature of action/feedback interactivity discussed above. What feedback is the game providing, how does it help them build a mental model, and what actions can they take based on that?

Games that do not provide regular, timely feedback and opportunities for player action risk allowing the player to become bored and disengaged unless they have other forms of interactive gameplay to hold their interest. While not all games make use of a fast-paced action/feedback interaction loop, all do at some level provide output for the player to perceive and methods of input for the player to change the game state. It is this moment-to-moment interactivity loop that acts as a sort of carrier wave for the other forms of interaction that follow.

Cognitive Interactivity

Moving away from the player's neurology and into their psychology, and as a first step away from the often fast-paced action/feedback loop, we can look at *short-term* and *long-term cognitive* interaction loops. These loops can be thought of in terms of puzzles (short term) and goals (long term) or, in military terms often used in games, tactics and strategy. Both involve a high level of endogenous, or *executive, attention*—informally known as thinking focused on planning upcoming actions.

Short- and long-term here are relative and flexible: a quick puzzle requiring a small amount of planning might last only a few seconds (for example finding the right spot for a number in an easy *Sudoku* game), while strategic planning might require minutes to hours of dedicated, focused cognition. The key component here is the inclusion of rational thought and cognition. The player is not merely reacting to circumstances as in action/feedback interaction; they are planning their next moves, creating their goals, and then eventually providing input to the game to carry these out.

An important aspect of cognitive interactivity is overt, conscious learning. Each form of interactivity involves some amount of learning: action/feedback interactions create learning by physical and subcognitive (not really conscious) repetition, and players learn to adjust their behavior in social interactions as well. But with cognitive interactivity, classical increase in skills and knowledge—what is sometimes broadly termed *mastery*—is a major component and benefit. Players who do crossword puzzles or *Sudoku* increase their skill and, thus, their ability to play more difficult versions of the same puzzles. Similarly, many tabletop and digital games have a sufficient cognitive interactions that with increased exposure and building a better mental model, players are able to perform better at the game. This increase in learning and mastery is a major motivation for many players (learning a new skill releases dopamine in the brain, among other things), especially those who are intent on striving and achievement as personal motivations. (Player motivations are discussed further in Chapter 6.)

Creating Cognitive Interaction

To create cognitive interactive loops, a game has to present the player with goals they can plan on and accomplish. These goals should be simple at first (kill this monster, construct this building, move to this point), but over time—as the player builds their mental model—they become more complicated (more steps) and more complex (more looping, more building on results of past actions). These more complex, longer-term plans require more executive attention. They also require that the player be able to predict the outcome of their actions, both short and long term, based on what they have learned about how the game world works.

The game has to have sufficient depth in its internal model to support (and help the player build) similar depth in their mental model. If the game's systems don't have their own hierarchical depth, the player has little ability to form their own deep goals and little reason to do so. Thus in a content-driven game where the player proceeds from level to level, the player has to do little in the way of anything more than short-term thinking; there's no significant long-term goal planning or other cognitive interaction. Some games make up for this by including long-term activities such as character customization (for example, skill trees) that the player considers in parallel with their more linear, level-driven gameplay. This gives the player different paths and alternatives to think about, but once these are exhausted, the player is left without additional options.

By contrast, in a systemic game where the player has the ability to plan ahead and choose different paths based on both short- and long-term utility—for example, where to build a castle for maximum defensive value and for placement of a future market—the solutions are as varied as the game systems allow. The play-space remains broad and explorable by the player, making for better, longer engagement.

Blending Types of Interaction

Cognitive interactivity rarely, if ever, stands alone. The games that are the most thoughtful and free of reliance on action/feedback interactivity are some of the oldest games, such as *Chess* and *Go*. However, even these games do not escape the lowest level of interaction completely. *Go* consists of nothing but black stones and white stones on a grid—about as austere as a game can be in terms of physical input and sensory feedback—but even here players manipulate the stones as they play the game and may speak of a beautiful game despite its apparent visual severity.

As players manipulate the stones on the *Go* board, they are using multiple levels of interaction deeply ingrained in their mental model: even before playing the game, they know how to pick up, hold, and deposit stones, and while doing so, they are thinking both in terms of short-term tactics and long-term strategy for the game. As a player advances in skill, some of the lower-level tactical cognition becomes chunked together into systemic hierarchies. At this point, much of the player's knowledge of the game is essentially tacit, with many moves requiring as little thought as required to pick up a stone from the cup. This leaves the player free to devote more of their cognitive resources to their longer-term strategies. As they chunk more and more tactical aspects of the game together, their mental model becomes deeper and deeper, more and more hierarchical, paralleled by their deepening appreciation for the game.

Far more common than the almost pure cognitive interaction of *Go* are games that combine a rich sensory experience with short-term puzzle-oriented cognition (for example, *Candy Crush*) and often long-term cognition. Many strategic games come with lush, juicy visuals that are not operative in terms of the gameplay but add to the enjoyable experience of playing the game despite their lack of utilitarian value.

Short-term cognitive interaction loops can also be an important part of the player's moment-to-moment experience in the game, especially when the player is completing a series of quick, short-term goals in the pursuit of longer-term ones. For example, a player in a fantasy role-playing game might report that they are clicking the mouse (action/feedback interaction) so their character will attack a monster (short-term cognitive) so that they can level up (long-term cognitive) and eventually join a preferred guild (social interaction— discussed next).

Social Interactivity

Closely related in many ways to both cognitive and emotional interaction is social interactivity. This too involves planning and executive attention on the player's part, though it also begins to introduce a reflective, emotional component in that it involves what players often experience as emotional responses—inclusion, exclusion, status, esteem, and so on—due to their out-of-game motivations. The difference is that these are experiences we have only in a social context, something that is important for us as humans. While there are neurochemical underpinnings (as with the action of serotonin and oxytocin in the brain), social interactivity and engagement typically take even longer to come to fruition than does cognitive engagement. While a conversation with another person may be brief, it often takes many such interactions over a period of hours, days, or even weeks to resolve a social interaction input and response loop.

It is possible to have a positive social experience relatively quickly, but coming to a real feeling of inclusion and community can take a long time.

Like long-term cognitive strategic interaction, social interactivity is a powerful motivator for most people. Some single-player games manage to make social interactivity an important part of the game, even though there is no other actual person in the game. One recent example of this is *Firewatch*, in which the player plays the part of a forest fire lookout. A significant amount of the game is spent in dialog with another character, Delilah, talking over a walkie-talkie. While the player and Delilah never meet, the social interactivity that develops their relationship—which can take different turns, depending on the player's social choices in dialog—evolves into a driving part of the game.

Game-Mediated Social Interaction

Many online games, especially massively multiplayer online games (MMOs) in which players inhabit a virtual world together, owe their success to how they have enabled players to interact socially, whether helping or fighting each other. In multiplayer games, the game (and its internal model) mediates between players: each player interacts with the others by interacting with the world. If my character swings a sword at your character, or if my trader offers to sell some pelts to your shopkeeper, we as players are interacting via the game world. In this case, each player has their own interaction loop with the game, and the effects of one player's actions change not only the game world but, by extension, other players, their mental models, and subsequent interactions. The only case in which the game is not mediating between players is when they are actually socializing in conversation via text or voice chat. This level of social interaction has its own loops, now between individuals, and is aided by the game-mediated loops of gameplay.

While the content in these games—exploring the world, engaging in combat, and so on—is attractive, it is the social aspect of these games that keeps players coming back. People want to have the experience of feeling like part of a group and often want the experience of seeing groups that they can identify as "other" (though this appears to be less a motivator than inclusion and in-group identity). Online games containing many thousands of people provide the social interactivity loops to feed this desire. In my own experience running MMOs, players have commonly said that even after they felt like they had seen and done all there was to do in the game (a content-driven rather than systemic approach), they stayed around for the feeling of community and social interaction.

Techniques for Encouraging Social Interactivity

Social interactivity in the context of a game happens primarily when players find that they need each other or that they benefit from interacting with each other within the game. There are a number of common in-game mechanisms for encouraging players to interact socially beyond just chatting. Some important mechanisms for doing this that are explored here are providing *social referents, competition, grouping, complementary roles,* and *social reciprocity.*

Social Referents

One of the simplest methods to encourage social interactivity is simply to include one or more objects with which multiple players can interact together. This is a lesson taken from the online graphical chat rooms of the 1990s, where just the ability to chat together in a 3D space quickly lost any sense of engagement. "Playful" objects in the game world act as a catalyst to social interaction that players find meaningful. Such objects are known formally as external social referents: something that two or more players can refer to and interact with in a social manner. The simplest example of this is probably a ball. In real life or in a digital game (with in-game physics), if you give some people a ball, they have a foundation on which to build social interactions; preventing an impromptu game of some sort is almost impossible. Thus, providing objects within a game world that invite interactions from multiple players is an excellent way to seed social interactivity.

Competition

Competition is a common aspect of many extremely popular games, where players face off against each other, either singly or in groups, to see who can best the other, and often to take some prize. Having winners and losers, especially if they are ranked by score and/or on a leaderboard, is an attractive incentive for many to play a game. Some genres of games, like first-person shooters and MOBAs (multiplayer online battle arenas), are based wholly on competitive play and now boast entire leagues of professional players. (Note that the existence of teams in these games creates a powerful in-group/out-group effect, enhancing the social interactivity.) Competition is a strong out-of-game motivator for many players. At the same time, it is also highly demotivating for some players, and is the type of motivation that fades fastest with age (Yee 2016a).

Grouping

Giving players ways to group together helps build social interaction, a sense of inclusion, and shared identity. This is the basis for almost all sense of community that players have in a game. Most games make groups formal game structures that go by names like alliances, guilds, parties, and corporations. One player starts the group and typically administers it, including who is allowed to be a member, what in-group privileges different players have (for example, access to shared resources), and, in some cases, to whom the originating player can pass leadership. Other games leave it up to the players to form ad hoc or long-term groups. For example, in the online MMO *Realm of the Mad God*, any time players are near each other, they both gain experience points from anything the other does. This encourages players to play together in a low-friction way, since they don't have to officially "group up"; the game just assumes that if they're near each other, they're helping each other out. At the same time, because this game has no in-game mechanism for forming long-term group structures, the social interactivity remains short term and thus does not encourage longer social engagement. In other games that have formal guilds or alliances that are essentially clubs that players join, the social engagement tends to last much longer, benefiting both the players and the game overall.

Complementary Roles

Complementary roles exist in games where no one player can do everything. These are perhaps most common in role-playing games, where player characters fall into roles like tanks (damage absorption), DPS ("damage per second"—dealing damage over time, typically from a distance), and support (healing and enhancing—"buffing"—other players). This combination of abilities sets players up to interact socially within the game to help each other out. In so doing, the players achieve some goal that none of them could have achieved on their own. Using complementary roles in a game also subsumes a great deal of neurochemical engagement involving dopamine, serotonin, and oxytocin as well as action/feedback and short-term cognition. As a result, it is an extremely powerful mechanism for continued engagement in a game.

Social Reciprocity

Social reciprocity is a form of gameplay that builds on our shared human desire to show our involvement with a group by reflecting back—reciprocating—good deeds done to help us. Many of the top-grossing mobile games, such as *Game of War: Fire Age*, have been immensely successful in large part because of this kind social interactivity. For example, *Game of War* makes it easy for players to help another player in their alliance (the player's team and social group in the game) build or repair buildings faster. When you see that other players have helped you toward your goal, it's common to have a desire to reciprocate by helping them out in turn. This helps all the players in the alliance both individually and as a group, and it is a powerful form of signaling social inclusion.

Game of War also supports players giving each other gifts and, notably, provides gifts to others in an alliance when one member makes a significant purchase. This sets up another form of interactive social reciprocity: if a player receives a gift made possible by someone else's purchase in the game, that player is far more likely to want to do the same—which helps her alliance's strength, increases the social bonds, and, not incidentally, provides the game more revenue. To put a number on the value of this kind of engagement, *Game of War's* actual gameplay—building strongholds and armies and sending them out to fight—is not remarkably different from the gameplay of many other games, and it has been criticized as being mundane or worse. Nevertheless, while the game is free to play, it has also made many millions of dollars, grossing nearly $2 million in micro-transactions *per day* for months on end (*Game of War—Fire Age* 2017).

Not-so-Social Interactions

Many so-called "social games" are anything but social: highly successful social games like *Farmville* involve almost no social interaction at all. Players can visit other players' farms and help them out (clean up weeds and so on), but this is all asynchronous: the players never see each other or interact; they may as well be ghosts inhabiting parallel dimensions. While this may appear to be social, it does not satisfy any out-of-game or in-game socially related motivations for the players. Players may get some feelings of pride from having others see their work on their own farms (or castles, cities, and so on in other games), but this is a pale, thin comparison to the feelings they get from actual social interactions in a game.

Emotional Interactivity

Moving from executive to *reflective attention* (still, strictly speaking, endogenous to the individual, if not to their cognition), we come to emotional interaction and engagement. This is a staple of other non-interactive forms of media, such as books and movies, and yet with a few exceptions remains largely unexplored in games. To be more precise, many games have explored the emotional terrain around anger, fear, tension, surprise, achievement, and delight—those related to what Damasio (2003) and Ekman (1992) call *basic*, or *primary*, *emotions*. These are emotions that are more biological than cognitive, arise quickly and without control from the player's internal agency, and are more reflexive and exogenous than reflective and endogenous.

Only in recent years have game designers begun to intentionally explore games that go beyond these primary emotions to provide the experience of—and the ability to interact on the basis of—more nuanced emotions, such as dread, guilt, loss, longing, fulfillment, love, complicity, gratitude, or honor. These are delicate experiences to create in an interactive setting and typically take longer to arise and reflect on than action/feedback or strictly cognitive interactions—often on the order of many minutes or hours. In some cases, the effects of emotional interactivity can remain for far longer as players reflect on their decisions and feelings made in a game.

In a book, the author has complete control over what the characters say and do. As readers, we may applaud their actions, be repulsed, see them feel betrayed, redeemed, and so on, but all the while we are being taken on a prespecified journey by the author—one that we cannot interact with to change. By contrast, in a game, we have interactive loops. If we feel shame as part of the game, we may act to change our circumstances to avoid or resolve those feelings. If we feel love or tenderness as part of the game, we may be surprised when the game (or nonhuman actors within it) does not act in ways to support that experience.

Games such as *Papers, Please* explore both ethical and often wrenching emotional situations in which the player must decide (and sometimes choose to act on) the fate of other characters. The player plays the part of an immigration officer in a dystopian country who must decide who to let in or not, often with personal and emotional consequences. In a similarly unhappy vein, games like *This War of Mine* and *The Grizzled* provide an emotionally raw look at the effects of war on civilians in a modern setting (*This War of Mine*) and warfighters in World War I (*The Grizzled*). Players must make desperate decisions and trade-offs where there are no clear right answers and where doing the seemingly right thing may have emotionally devastating long-term consequences.

Other games, such as *Journey*, have provided players with a sense of awe and wonder in an interactive setting. Many role-playing games have explored themes of romance—love gained, lost, and satisfyingly regained—such as in the classic interactive romantic arc of *Knights of the Old Republic*. Even tabletop games like the recent (2016) *Burgle Bros* and *Fugitive* are exploring emotions as part of gameplay: *Burgle Bros* ingeniously creates the cooperative feeling of a crime caper that continually teeters on the edge of disaster, while *Fugitive* builds a tense but engaging "catch me if you can"/"they're about to get away" feeling of a criminal fleeing a pursuing marshal. In each of these games, the emotions are a key part of the game, something with which the player interacts, and which thus drive their decisions and their overall experience of the game. The emotions aren't simply an after effect or "bolted on" in an insincere way.

Constructing Emotional Interactivity

While there are more and more examples of games that elicit emotions in their players, how to include emotions in gameplay is still far from a solved problem. In fact, the understanding of emotions in general is an active area of research, with lots of competing models and theories. In game design, too, there are multiple insightful models of emotions in games, including those from Lazzaro (2004), Bura (2008), and Cook (2011a), among others.

Like so much else in game design theory, while these are often based on long experience, lots of thought, and in some cases even some player data, there are no well-grounded, comprehensive theories or models of emotions and how to create them in games that are widely accepted—if only because the basic science around emotions is still in flux. To complicate matters further, many of those who have written about creating emotions in games do so almost exclusively from the point of view of game narrative—treating a game like a novel or movie. Doing so pinches the play-space down to a single path that the designer requires the player to navigate without significant agency and with predefined points to show emotional situations.

While there are techniques that will help you create emotional interactivity in games, you will have to experiment with them for your game and the emotions you are trying to elicit in the players. Before you can create emotional interactivity in a game, you need to consider what sorts of emotions you want as part of the gameplay experience.

Models of Emotion

Without going into the neurological and psychological definitions of emotions too much, one useful and common model of emotions (and one of the few that has been tested cross-culturally [Russell et al. 1989]) is one that divides emotions along two axes: negative to positive (unpleasant to pleasant, often called *valence*) along the horizontal axis, and low-energy to high-energy (often called *arousal*) along the vertical axis. This creates four quadrants: high-energy and happy; low-energy and happy; low-energy and unhappy; and high-energy and unhappy. Though not the intent of the model, it's interesting that these quadrants correspond to the medieval humors of sanguine, phlegmatic, melancholy, and choleric, respectively (see Figure 4.7). Within these quadrants, it's possible to place a wide variety of emotions, from the obvious ones like anger, joy, fear, and contentment to more nuanced ones like greed, jealousy, compassion, delight, and resignation (Sellers 2013).

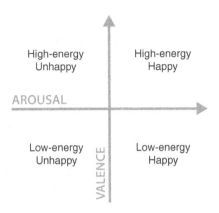

Figure 4.7 The two-axis model of emotions. This leads to models including Russell's circumplex (Russell 1980) and Sellers' multilayered circumplex (Sellers 2013)

This at least gives you a rough guide to start thinking about different emotions you might want to include in a game. To build them into emotional interactions, you can consider emotions to be companions to player motivations: our emotions are in effect how we feel about what we want (or, in the case of negative-valenced emotions, what we don't want).

One way to consider these motivations is in terms of the psychologist Abraham Maslow's hierarchy of needs (Maslow 1968). These range from the "lowest" and most immediate motivations to the "highest" and longest-term ones, as shown in Table 4.1. (These time scales correspond with the time scale of the interactive loops described here.)

Table 4.1   Maslovian Motivations and Related Emotions

Maslow's Level	Example Motivations	Examples of Emotions
Contribution (*self-actualization*)	Looking beyond yourself, leading and serving a group	Compassion, unity, wrath, awe, joy, despair, resignation, humility
Skill and attainment (*skill-esteem*)	Skill, professional value, accomplishment	Victory, honor, guilt, courage, fulfillment, pride, remorse, pity
Social (*belonging*)	Friends, family, inclusion, group membership, identity	Sympathy, shame, jealously, friendship, hatred, contempt, acceptance
Security and objects (*safety*)	Acquisition, preparation, shelter, protection	Delight, hope, envy, disappointed, playful, settled, unstable
Physical (*physiological*)	Food, water, human contact, novelty, avoiding pain or harm	Attraction, pleasure, disgust, anger, fear, surprise, fatigue

This table is meant to be a guide, not a complete list. The idea here is that as you identify the kinds of emotions that you want to be part of the gameplay experience, you can consider what sort of motivations they relate to and then figure out how to create situations and systems that support those motivations in your game. Alternatively, if you look at your game and see what kinds of in-game motivations are most common, you will be able to predict what kinds of emotions the players are likely to experience. (Note that these in-game motivations are often different from the player's own out-of-game motivations. For more on this, see Chapter 6.)

For example, if your game is about a character who is constantly in peril against waves of undead, the emotional engagement your player will have will arise out of motivations for immediate physical needs and safety, resulting in feelings like fear, disgust, surprise, and possibly hope or disappointment. Based on this, your game is unlikely to engender experiences of friendship, compassion, or revenge—though you might get those if you include a social component (for example, someone else to be saved)—or feelings of victory or courage if the player experiences skill-related motivations. To move beyond the primary emotions (anger, fear, pleasure, and so on) to the more subtle ones, you need to provide the player with situations that create matching motivations.

Context

The first technique for creating emotional interactivity is to create the context—that is, create the atmosphere for how you want the players to feel as they play. This helps the players, as they will be more amenable to feeling fear, victory, hope, mystery, and so on if you have already set the stage. You can do this by carefully creating the game's presentation: the colors, lighting, camera angles, music, and setting. A game set in an amusement park will feel very different if it takes place on a sunny day with bright shiny colors on the attractions and viewed from looking down from above than if it takes place in a thunderstorm in the middle of the night, with dimly viewed shapes in low lighting and few colors, with camera angles looking up from the ground. Just by creating the mood this way, you tell the players a lot about the kind of experience they can expect and prime them for the emotions you want them to feel as part of gameplay.

Situation and Goals

Beyond the context, to create potential emotional experiences, you as the designer have to provide motivation-related goals for the players that are meaningful to them, as described above. This is often some object or situation that they want to attain, keep, or prevent. Creating an opportunity where a player can, by choice, work to attain something corresponding to the different Maslovian motivational levels (that is, a physical attribute, desired object, social status, skill, or group reward) opens up the emotions corresponding to each of those levels. Similarly, by putting at risk the player's life, possessions, friends, esteem, or group, you can quickly engender the emotions that correspond to such threats—and in each case the attainment or avoidance of the potential end has resulting emotions as well (victory, disappointment, loneliness, inclusion, and so on).

The player must truly care about the goals you set up, at least within the context of the game. The kinds of emotions they feel about this will correspond to the kind of situation they face, and the magnitude will match the importance they have ascribed to the situation. It is important here to remember the magic circle: the motivations and emotions occur in the game and may have little correspondence to the player's own motivations for actually playing the game. For example, a player may not want their city to be destroyed in your game, but if it happens their emotions will mostly remain in the circle with the rest of the game. However, the more real the game has become to them, the more those emotions will leak out into the rest of their lives. Just as when a beloved character in a book or movie dies, even though their life was entirely fictional, this can have strong emotional effects outside the time players spend within the magic circle of the fictional world.

The Challenge

In terms of game design, the challenge with emotional interactivity is to construct systems that create situations in which the player has the kind of motivation-related and thus emotional experience that you want—but without narrowing the game down to a single path that the player must tread and where you as the designer resort to set pieces that require a linear story. As always, the more you can focus on creating systems out of which the player's motivations and emotions emerge due to their interaction with the game rather than creating specific content that the player has no choice but to experience, the more effective and more robust the gameplay experience will be.

That said, the reason we see more non-interactive cut-scenes showing a preset "emotional moment" to the player rather than letting them discover this emotion via systemic gameplay is because the cut-scenes or single-path content are still more reliable. If you see your role as that of an author delivering a particular emotion at a particular place in your story, this makes sense. If, on the other hand, you see your role as that of setting up the conditions for your player to find in-game motivations by interacting with elements in the game and experiencing emotions as a result, then you may have less emotional precision, but you will generate a more interactive, and thus more personal, authentic experience for the player.

Cautions

Creating emotional interactivity is not easy, quick, or even always predictable. Sometimes players miss an opportunity or do not invest meaning in a goal, and so they miss the motivation and thus the emotion intended. In other cases, they may react even more strongly than you anticipated (see more on this in the next section "Cultural Interactivity," later in this chapter). And in some cases, players may experience different motivations and thus different emotions than you anticipate, which changes how they experience your game overall.

In addition, it takes time to construct the systems and situations for emotional engagement, and it takes time for players to perceive, invest motivationally in, and resolve the emotions they feel as a result of gameplay. In some cases, it may take hours or longer—days or even weeks— for players to work through a full emotional cycle. In general, the higher the motivation and resulting emotion is on Maslow's hierarchy, the longer it will take to engender and resolve, but also the longer it will stay with the player.

As game designers, we clearly still have a lot to learn about using emotions as interactive loops, but this is also clearly a fertile area to explore to create more engaging games.

Cultural Interactivity

At the far end of reflective attention are the very long-term conversations we have about our cultural values and our individual place in our culture. This includes looking back at history to see who we have been as peoples and where we have come from as individuals, as well as looking at our current cultural context. Using games, we can reflect on what our past and current values may actually be compared to what we would like them to be. These conversations may take years to complete, as cultures wrestle with questions of identity, membership, rights, prosperity, and on and on. Games do not tend to last that long, but they can nevertheless capture some of these currents and conversations in an interactive format that enables and benefits from the player's reflections of lifetime-spanning issues.

There are not many games providing this kind of long-baseline cultural engagement, but there are a few. One notable example is *Train* by Brenda Romero. In this seemingly simple game, players load small yellow pegs onto train cars and try to move them to their destinations. Each player's destination is not known at the start of the game but becomes revealed later on. Through this and other gameplay mechanics, the game reveals its true nature: the little yellow pegs are people—Jews—and the players are trying to get their trains to take them to concentration camps in Nazi Germany.

It is difficult to overstate the emotional, social, and cultural impact that this revelatory game has on those who play it—and even those who watch others play it. Many people recoil in disgust as they discover the true nature of the game (which, it should be noted, is telegraphed in subtle ways, such as the bed of broken glass lying under the clear game board, reminiscent of the *Kristallnacht*, or the Night of Broken Glass persecution of German Jews in 1938). Some people have broken down in tears as they have realized that just by playing, they have been complicit in a simulation of such a great horror. Some refuse to leave the game until they manage to get every last peg out of every train car. Some try to subvert the game's goals once they realize what they are playing; others look nauseated, or as if they have touched something toxic.

As an interactive and engaging, if ultimately repulsive, experience, *Train* shows how games can be a vehicle for cultural interactivity. Players are able to inhabit their history and culture and interact with the culture via the game systems created as the model for the culture. In this case, players are not only reenacting the horrors of the Holocaust, they are confronting an issue relevant at any time: since the rules purposefully contain procedural gaps where the players must decide how to proceed, they become complicit in creating the game, not just playing. Nor do the rules reveal the end of the game. As a result, the question the players must confront based on their own actions is one of how far any of us will blindly "follow the rules" without asking "to what end?" This is a prime example of a game creating a conversation and adding to an ongoing loop of cultural interactivity.

This sort of interaction is possible in games in ways that would be impossible in any other medium. By being able to interact with and experience significant cultural conversations, players are able to reflect on the cultural directions presented in the game: do you follow authority, follow the rules, always? While the mechanisms used to ask such questions are built on and similar to those used for cognitive, social, and emotional interactivity, it is the long-arc context of exploring cultural conversations that sets this type of interactivity apart.

By means of this form of interactivity, players are also able to blur the lines of the magic circle surrounding the game. As players continue the conversation about the game outside its play (for example, is it morally right to play *Train*, once you know what it is?), they also continue the overarching cultural conversation about the issues presented.

Players are also able to help create cultural interactivity by other extra-game means, such as fandom activities, cosplay, game forums, and thoughtful criticism. Some players have, for example, been introduced to the various sides of the problematic philosophy of Objectivism via the game *Bioshock*, which has in turn spawned many cultural interactions with other players. These activities and conversations are not accidental or incidental: they are a larger interactive loop designed within the game and spun off from it to continue even after the actual gameplay is completed. This is a nascent area of game design but one that deserves more attention.

Flow in Interactive Loops

Any discussion of interactivity and engagement would be incomplete without addressing the theory of *flow* first articulated by Mihaly Csikszentmihalyi (1990). This is colloquially described as the feeling of being "in the zone" or "in the flow."

Recall that engagement is characterized by being alert and attentive to the task at hand, being able to ignore extraneous input, and generally performing well (along with the non-intrusive awareness of performing well). Flow has many of the same characteristics: when a person is in a flow state, they are engaged in a challenging activity with some uncertainty (not a rote, memorized task), they have understandable goals, and are getting clear feedback. Their attention is focused but not stressed. They may lose track of time, but as with the description of engagement, they generally do not lose the awareness that they are performing well. In this state, the individual is absorbed in their work and not self-conscious about it; they may describe feeling that they "are one" with the work. (This sort of language is often difficult to avoid when describing flow.) Ultimately, the task being performed becomes meaningful in and of itself. It may begin with clear utilitarian goals, but at some point maintaining the performative flow state becomes a meaningful goal itself.

Flow is often described as having a "channel." This is a useful way to visualize the player's state of engagement and flow. As shown in Figure 4.8, the flow state begins with interest if there is a small challenge commensurate with a beginner's skill; if neither challenge nor skill are present, the individual experiences apathy and is no longer engaged. Flow increases as both the task's challenge and the individual's skill increase. If the challenge increases just a little more than the individual is comfortable with, they become aroused; then, if the increase in challenge continues, the individual becomes stressed and anxious, as they fall off the right side of the Yerkes-Dodson curve (refer to Figure 4.5). However, if their skill is too high for the current challenge, they becomes relaxed at first and then soon bored. As the individual cycles between arousal and relaxation (as shown abstractly by the sinusoidal line), they remain in the Goldilocks zone of the flow channel: they are engaged, learning, building their mental model of the task at hand, and performing well. They become psychologically immersed—still aroused and attentive to their task but generally ignoring extraneous stimuli—and may lose track of time.

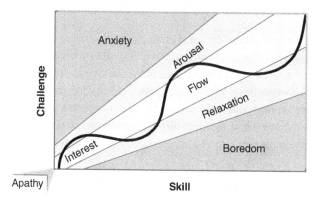

Figure 4.8 A visualization of the flow state as it occurs between the feelings of anxiety and boredom, as both challenge and skill increase

One other feature of the flow channel is that it inherently captures the individual's desire to progress—to learn more and take on new challenges. In any engaging task (and thus in any successful game), the individual experiences the neurochemical rewards described above as the result of the various kinds of interactivity: interactions and accomplishments feel pleasurable ultimately because of the release of dopamine, serotonin, and potentially oxytocin and endorphins. However, they soon get used to these feelings, a process known as habituation, and what was delightful earlier is no longer sufficient to create the same feelings. In any tasks involving attention, interaction, and goals, this natural habituation drives the individual forward to learn more and face greater challenges. This aroused learning is where the individual is "surfing" just at the top-right of the Yerkes-Dodson curve, and right at the top edge of the flow channel. They may fall back toward relaxation without breaking out of flow as part of the stacking of interaction cycles of various durations (see below).

Aside from presenting a clear and helpful model of human engagement, the conceptual value of flow is how it highlights an experience becoming its own end. This is the autotelic experience discussed by Csikszentmihalyi and in Chapter 3 of this book. The player begins by using the types of interactivity provided by the game, including goals set out for them expressed in short-term and long-term cognitive interactions. If the playful flow experience lasts, however, at some point the player has progressed enough in skill and challenge and begins setting their own goals. At this point, they exist in the upper-right part of the flow channel depicted in Figure 4.8; they are not driven forward by external forces for greater challenge or skill but remain engaged based on goals and interactions that they create and drive themselves. Not every game provides for autotelic goals—or needs to. Many players are able to enter a flow state in games with relatively simple action/feedback and short-term cognitive interaction loops—*Tetris*, match-three games, and so on Those that do provide internal models that are deep enough to support a mental model sufficient for players to create their own autotelic goals are also those that are typically played the longest and, ultimately, loved the most.

A Time-Scale View of Interactive Loops

The various forms of interactivity and engagement that we have discussed—neurochemical, action/feedback, cognitive, social, emotional, and cultural—vary from reflexive to executive to reflective in their attentional aspect. They also range from very fast to very slow: less than one second for a complete loop to hours, days, or longer for a complete reflective interaction (refer to Figure 4.6).

These loops also stack on top of each other, each working at different time scales, to provide a more fully engaging interactive experience. In a typical game, multiple interactive loops are operating at the same time, working together to create a more engaging experience overall. Those loops that are faster are also typically perceived as being less deeply meaningful; a fast-paced shooter can be highly engaging, but it's not a vehicle for deep considered thought. It takes the longer-term reflective social, emotional, and cultural interactivity to really begin to create depth of meaning in a game.

For example, in a light and casual match-three game, the player is primarily using action/feedback and short-term cognitive loops along with a longer recurring short-term cognitive loop as they solve puzzles. The game's design does not lend itself to long-term strategic thinking, much less having any emotional, social, or cultural interaction or serious meaning. In an online war game, the players are still involved in action/feedback interactive loops, but they also focus (over longer periods of time) on tactical, strategic, and social interactions.

The result is that games that use primarily faster forms of interactivity are experienced as "lighter"—easier to pick up and put down and of less lasting value to the player. Those that use primarily longer, "heavier" forms of interactivity (long-term cognitive, social, emotional, or cultural) are games that remain engaging for longer periods of time and to which players may remain loyal for years. This is evident in the market for mobile games today, where games with fast, shallow gameplay dominate the market, and where only 38% percent of players are still playing a game one month after starting—and the rest having moved on (Dmytryshyn 2014).

This notion of stacking different kinds of gameplay with different time horizons has been noted by other game designers in the past. Jaime Griesemer, lead game designer on *Halo 2* and *Halo 3*, is noted for what has been called the idea of "30 seconds of fun" in *Halo* (Kietzmann 2011).

This was part of a longer interview comment in which Griesemer said that "the secret to Halo's combat" was that "you have a 3-second loop inside of a 30-second loop inside of a 3-minute loop that is always different, so you get a unique experience every time." Different kinds of interactivity are happening at each scale, even in a fast-paced action game. The shorter cycles are more focused on moment-to-moment things like "where to stand, when to shoot, when to dive away from a grenade," while the longer ones are more tactically (and thus cognitively) focused. By stacking these interaction loops, building engagement at every scale, and varying the experience that each provides, the game designers were able to provide a truly engaging and memorable set of gameplay experiences.

Core Loops

Game designers often speak of a game's *core loops*, loosely defined as "what the player does most of the time" or "what the player is doing at any given time." We can make this definition more exacting, based on the understanding of the different interactive loops discussed here. As with any of these engagement loops, and as shown at a high level in Figure 4.4, the game's core loop or loops carry out the cycle shown in Figure 4.9. The player forms an intent and carries out an action, providing input to the game, as discussed above. This causes a change to the game's internal state, and the game provides feedback to the player as to the success or other effects of their actions. Typically this feedback also provides the player with information about their progression in the game or another reward or another form of call to action to keep the player engaged with the game. The new abilities afforded by their progression or reward encourage the player to form a new goal or intent, and the cycle begins again.

Figure 4.9 An abstract diagram of a core loop. This is mapped onto the player's primary actions in the game. See more detailed descriptions in Chapter 7

As we have seen in discussing interactive loops, this cycle can take place at many different levels of attention and over different lengths of time. A game's core loops are determined by the game's design and, in particular, by what form of interaction is the most significant for player engagement. This almost always includes the low-level action/feedback loop, as this is where the player and the game truly interface: the player performs an action like pressing a key, moving a mouse, or tapping a screen, and the game responds with feedback in acknowledgment.

This action/feedback loop may not be the most significant loop in the game+player system, however. The game design determines which types of interaction demand the player's primary focus, and those then form the core loops. Moving around in the game may be the primary point (often along with jumping, shooting, and so on), or it may be only a means to an end. If the player is mainly focused on constructing buildings, discovering technologies, administering an empire, or building relationships, those forms of interaction will create the core loops for the game. (You will see more on this topic in Chapter 7.)

Cycles of Engagement

Stacking different interaction loops with different durations creates natural cycles of times of high and low arousal. This is important for engagement and learning, as it enables the player to experience times of challenge and tension and then relaxation and consolidation. It also prevents attentional fatigue, where the players simply cannot keep up with everything that is being thrown at them, and their engagement and performance suffer.

One way to think of this is like stacking waves with different frequencies. Action/feedback interactivity loops have the shortest duration and thus the shortest "wavelength" and highest frequency. These interactive loops continue as long as play continues. Each of the other types of interactivity have progressively longer wavelengths and so create longer cycles (see Figure 4.10). As a result, action/feedback loops go on throughout the game like small waves in the ocean on top of large ocean rollers, while periods of tension and release are created by effectively stacking short-term cognitive, long-term cognitive, and potentially social, emotional, and cultural loops within the game.

These stacked cycles also create periods of "rhythm and ritual," as described by game designer Chelsea Howe (2017), that provide signals to the players of the passing of time within the game. These cycles may help indicate the availability of new content (for example, daily quests or rewards), natural starting and stopping places in a game session, times to battle or repair, the rising or releasing of tension in dramatic arcs within the game, or phases like in-game social and celebratory rhythms (whether seasons or just leveling up).

Action / Feedback

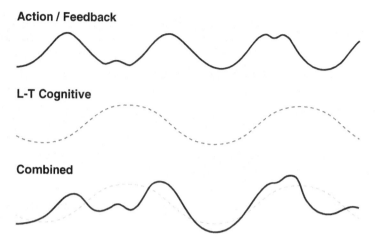

L-T Cognitive

Combined

Figure 4.10 Stacking different "wavelengths" of interaction to create high- and low-tension moments in a game

Narrative and Interactive Engagement

As discussed in Chapter 3, narrative is an important component of many games. It acts as a vehicle for the player's interactions in the game, setting the context and often providing goals for the player to pursue. It is not, however, interactive.

Cook (2012) noted that game narrative forms arcs instead of loops. The game provides feedback to the player, whether in the form of text, NPC-driven dialog, a cut-scene, or something else that provides "a payload of pre-processed information" to the player. These "payloads" can be highly effective at delivering targeted information to the player, but they do not allow for interactivity. As a result, player engagement is limited. In watching a movie (or a cut-scene in a game), an individual may become engrossed in the situation and characters, but within the narrative they have choices to make or actions to take; they have no opportunity for vigorous action or resilience. The player is reduced to being a passive viewer for the duration of the narration.

Many games use non-interactive narrative as bookends to interactive sessions: a game may introduce a mission to the player via narration, allow the player to play out the mission, and then narrate the end-state after it's complete. This can be an effective way to build a seemingly interactive narrative even though the player has limited opportunities for making real decisions or interacting in ways that have long-term consequences. The risk with this format is that the player comes to understand that the beginning and end are preset, and none of the decisions they make in between (for example, in a mission) really matter. This can drain the meaning from any decisions the player makes and create instead a sense of futility that degrades engagement. At a former company, we called this the *"Gilligan's Island* problem," after the TV show where no matter what they did, the characters always ended up stuck back on their island at the end of each episode. This is a convenient way for the writers to ensure that the characters are back to their starting point, but it significantly limits any growth or change in the characters and the narrative overall.

Chaining interactive looped elements together with non-interactive narrative arcs can create an engaging overall experience, but this also suffers from a lack of replayability: once the player has traversed the narrative, he has little reason to revisit it. However, in games that use narrative more sparingly as a context and scaffolding for creating interactive systemic play, the non-interactive arcs can help the player create a mental model of the game more quickly and thus springboard them into the interactively looping parts of the game.

Mental Load and the Interactivity Budget

As the player interacts with a game using different types of loops, they provide input and get feedback on different time scales with different amounts of reflexive, executive, and reflective attentional processing involved. However, there are limits to how much of this any person can do at any given time. Our attentional and overall mental resources are limited. There are only so many enemies a player can track simultaneously, only so many explosions or conversations or parts to a puzzle that the human mind can keep track of before becoming overwhelmed and having performance and engagement suffer. These limits are known as *cognitive load*, as discussed earlier in this chapter. Generally speaking, this is the amount of attention and mental work that an individual can perform without stress or reduced performance (Sweller 1988). Because we are here including attentional, perceptual, cognitive, emotional, social, and cultural aspects in the player's interactions with a game, we lump these all under the somewhat broader *mental load*.

One consequence of having limited mental resources and putting the player under mental load while playing a game is that the player cannot attend to everything a game might potentially throw at them. What takes precedence?

It appears that interactions relying on reflexive, involuntary, exogenous attention get first priority, followed by tasks requiring executive attention, followed last of all by those needing reflective resources. Another way to look at this is that the fast drives out the slow: if a player has to dodge fast-moving obstacles or be aware of objects appearing in their peripheral vision, their abilities to think strategically or even tactically are going to be suppressed, much less their ability to reflect on their emotional situation. This makes evolutionary sense and is consistent with experience: when a more urgent interaction is present, it demands our attention. This is true whether the task is shooting an incoming missile or finding an address on an unfamiliar street; in either case, other interactions that are slower, less demanding, and/or require more reflective internal resources are shoved aside. There are exceptions, as, for example, when someone is concentrating so hard on a problem—using executive attention and control—that they miss clear environmental signals. Nevertheless, it appears that in designing games to help build player engagement and their mental model, we need to take into account their mental load and the degree to which they will attend to different forms of interaction.

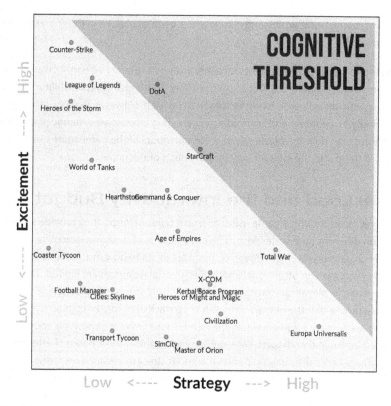

Figure 4.11 Quantic Foundry's diagram of "excitement" versus "strategy" games, showing a clear cognitive threshold past which players cannot operate effectively

Some additional evidence for this idea comes from the work of Quantic Foundry, which has surveyed almost 300,000 game players to build models of their motivation and behavior. One of Quantic Foundry's visualizations of this data (see Figure 4.11) shows how players have categorized games as being low to high in "excitement" (fast-paced gameplay with lots of action, surprises, and thrills) versus games rated low to high in "strategy" (slower games involving thinking ahead and making complex decisions). In the upper-left corner (high excitement/low strategy) are games like *Counter Strike* and *League of Legends*, while in the lower-right corner (low excitement/high strategy) are games like *Europa Universalis*. The former games rely primarily on fast action and short-term planning (that is, action/feedback and short-term cognitive interactivity), while the latter require far more long-term cognition, with only a small amount of action/feedback interactivity to keep the player's attention from wandering as they create generation-spanning, empire-building plans. Most notable of all is the emptiness of the upper-right corner: there are no games that players rate highly on both excitement *and* strategy. Such a game would require too much of the players, creating too much mental load and thus overwhelming any possibility of engagement.

Moreover, the games further along either axis are generally considered more "hardcore"—requiring more mental resources to learn the game and construct a more detailed mental model—while those in the lower-left corner are seen as being more "casual," or what Quantic Foundry calls "easy fun" (see Figure 4.12). The gameplay genre may differ across games in each band, but the relative difficulty of learning and succeeding in the game, consistent with the relative amount of mental resources required to play each, remains roughly the same.

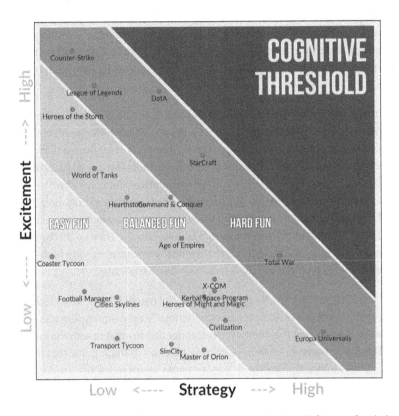

Figure 4.12 Quantic Foundry's cognitive threshold diagram, showing bands for easy fun, balanced fun, and hard fun

The Interactivity Budget

Understanding that different kinds of gameplay and interactivity each add to the player's mental load highlights the idea of the *interactivity budget*. If a player is willing to dedicate himself and his mental resources to a game, he might be interested in a game further along either of the axes shown in Figures 4.11 and 4.12—or perhaps a game that provides a great deal of emotional interaction (for example, *Gone Home* or *Papers, Please*). If a player wants a less taxing experience, he might opt for a game with less interactivity requirements overall; for example, *Candy Crush* and other matching games require only a small amount of short-term cognitive interaction, along with a bit of satisfying (and usually not high-pressure) action/feedback interactivity and juiciness. While a game has to have enough interactivity to remain engaging, those with lower attentional requirements are seen as being more "casual," allowing the player to become as absorbed in the game as he likes without having to construct a complex mental model, which enables the player to drop in or out of the game as he pleases.

More generally, a game design must respect the player's interactivity budget for the kind of experience the game designer wants to create. This includes understanding that the shorter-duration interactivity loops (those that also depend on reflexive attention for building engagement) appear to take from the player's mental resources first. Action/feedback can overwhelm short-term cognitive, which can take up the resources for long-term cognitive, and so on.

This means that if you are interested in developing a high-action game with lots of action/feedback and short-term cognitive interaction, the player will not have the mental resources for a lot of long-term cognitive, emotional, or social interaction. It is possible to include these, as long as you don't require them at the same time as the more fast-paced parts of the game. Many role-playing games intersperse the long-term cognitive interactivity involved in character customization between more tactical, short-term bouts of questing and fighting. Similarly, games like *League of Legends* create greater overall engagement by including social interactivity along with their action/feedback and short-term cognitive loops. They do this by separating it from the main gameplay: the game is played essentially in segments, with high-intensity sessions interspersed with more socially interactive time in the lobby.

In the same way, designs for more long-term, thoughtful games have to avoid too much in the way of high action/feedback or short-term cognitive interaction requirements, as otherwise these would rob the player of the mental resources needed to engage with the longer-duration interactive loops. For example, *Stellaris* is a galaxy-spanning strategic game that focuses on long-term cognitive interaction and gives the player the time needed to consider the many options in building a huge empire. The game is pretty to look at, having high attentional value without requiring the player to interact in a time-pressured action/feedback way. Battles between spaceships do happen, but they are not directed by the player: the player can zoom in to see a battle if they want (and they are dramatic to watch) but they don't have to expend any attentional or interactive effort to run the battle themselves.

Along similar lines, if a game is designed to have a high degree of emotional impact, such as *Papers, Please* or *Train*, it helps the player retain the mental energy and engagement focus to interact with the emotional interactivity loops by not having the game also require that they devote a lot to action/feedback, short-term cognitive, or long-term cognitive interactions. That's not to say that those loops aren't present at all, but that they aren't as emphasized as they would be if the game were not designed primarily to create emotional engagement. Both of these games feature deceptively simple, austere presentations, enabling the player to focus on their emotional impact. The entire setup for *Train* is shown in Figure 4.13.

Figure 4.13 The simple if haunting presentation of the game *Train* (Photo courtesy of Brenda Romero)

The exact nature of the interactivity budget is still a topic for research. We don't yet know how to measure degrees of excitement (action/feedback and short-term cognitive) versus strategic (long-term cognitive) or other forms of engagement, other than by surveying users, as Quantic Foundry has done. Nor do we know for a given player how much sensory feedback is required to maintain attention and engagement or how this is affected by the presence of longer-cycle interactive loops. Experience has shown the reality of these types of interactive loops and their overall relationships, but their application is still a matter for practice and future exploration.

Recognizing, Defining, and Creating "Fun"

As noted earlier in this chapter, *interactivity* is lacking a general consensus definition. *Fun* is, if anything, even more ill-defined. It appears to be dependent on a wide variety of factors, including context and individual preferences. What one person finds fun another may find tedious or overwhelming, and the same activity may be fun for someone in some contexts and boring or distressing for them in another. Caillois and Barash (1961) attempted to capture different kinds of play and different kinds of fun with *agon, alea, ilinx*, and mimicry forms of play. Koster (2004) said that "fun is just another word for learning." Others have proposed 8 (Hunicke et al. 2004), 14 (Garneau 2001), or as many as 21 (Winter 2010) separate kinds of fun! Undaunted by this variety of possible definitions, we will consider here how we can use our understanding of interactivity and engagement to build a comprehensive and usable theory of fun.

Characteristics of Fun

Before beginning to define what fun is and how it relates to games and play, it is useful to review the types of experiences that are often related as being fun and the common characteristics they possess. Most of these are qualities we have encountered already in examining what games are and how people interact with them.

In the most general terms, fun experiences are synonymous with pleasant or emotionally positive ones that have more than a quick duration and that an individual would generally want to repeat. Schaufeli and colleagues (2002) said that in part, the experience of fun is a "pervasive affective-cognitive state" that lasts longer than just a jolt of pleasure and that involves both emotions and cognition.

Fun activities and contexts are entirely voluntary and typically nonconsequential. These attributes fit with the idea of the magic circle: what happens within the circle is free of the weight of any greater importance, and no one is compelled to participate. When the ability to opt out of an otherwise agreeable activity is taken away, so is the feeling of fun.

Fun experiences are attractive—they aren't to be avoided, nor are they merely informative, with no emotional content. They carry a positive rather than negative or neutral emotional valence. That said, even at this general level, there are wrinkles for what can seem like human inconsistency: sometimes an experience that on the surface appears sad or frightening (such as a dramatic movie or haunted house) may still be experienced as fun—if it is also voluntary and nonconsequential. Knowing that you are not truly in danger or that a tragedy has not truly struck leaves you free to enjoy the wash of emotions (from the release of adrenaline on up) as a fun experience.

Within this large scope, there are many different kinds of fun experiences. Some are thrilling to the senses, whether capturing reflexive attention, as with fireworks, or the sense of vertigo referred to in *ilinx*, or they stimulate the release of neurotransmitters such as dopamine, sero-tonin, oxytocin, and endorphins, as discussed earlier. Others provide a sense of material reward, social inclusion, achievement, or even completeness (as with the satisfaction of set completion).

The experience of fun may include learning, but this is not a necessary component; sometimes performing a well-learned skill or simply participating in a physical or group activity is delightful and fun. Nor is the presence or absence of rationality required for fun. Puzzles requiring considerable mental work may nevertheless yield a fun feeling of clever victory, and other experiences that are either entirely sensory based or that are driven by emotions rather than cognition may be experienced as fun.

Fun is also characterized by feelings of satisfaction and a sort of sense of balance: if a situation or an activity is too boring or too stressful (subjectively to the individual), too chaotic or too arbitrary, then it is no longer fun. Fun and flow, as discussed earlier, appear to be deeply related.

Defining Fun

From the foregoing and from the discussion of interactivity and engagement, we can see that there is no one simple definition of *fun* that fits all situations. It is also apparent, however, that while fun comes in many forms, there is some regularity to the forms. Definitional aspects of fun fit well with the types of engagement discussed earlier in this chapter and with the structural, functional, and thematic elements of games discussed in Chapter 3.

First and foremost, fun must be voluntary, and fun activities are typically nonconsequential. If participation is compelled (whether through coercion, addiction, or some other loss of agency), any fun in an activity vanishes. Likewise, in most cases, if there is a potential consequence attached, particularly one that may result in some form of real loss, the fun is gone. Of course, many people gamble with money and consider it to be fun—but that is a voluntary act of risk-taking; it is the risk and the potential for reward (along with the dopamine release accompanying that anticipation) that keeps this in the realm of fun.

Fun induces positive feelings; it is not emotionally neutral. It may arise in sensory or physical contexts, including stimuli such as sight, sound, taste, touch, and movement. Examples of these feelings include the pure—and voluntary—vertiginous feeling of *ilinx* or the roller coaster or the sensory delight of a light show or musical performance.

Fun can, of course, be experienced in cognitive pursuits from simple puzzles to long-range strategies, as long as they remain voluntary and (at least mostly) nonconsequential. This is also where the fun experienced in learning comes into play: constructing a mental model to better understand a situation, even if the context is a "serious" one, may often be experienced as fun. Not all learning is necessarily fun (especially rote learning or learning while under too much stress), and not all fun requires learning, but in terms of the cognitive aspects of fun, learning is an important feature of the landscape.

Certainly many social and emotional activities are experienced as being fun. These may be structured and combined with other aspects of fun, such as a dance (social and physical) or party games (social and cognitive), or they may be more unstructured (watching or participating in a lively conversation). These at least bump against the potential for cultural activities to be fun—those that help us understand our place in our community and culture, if they remain in a voluntary and nonconsequential context. This helps explain how museums can be seen as fun, at least for some.

Another important element of fun that crosses all of these is that it must remain within the subjectively set bounds of the interactivity budget discussed earlier. At various times, an individual may feel up for a challenge, while at other times simpler, less taxing pursuits are more desirable. This amount in the budget changes from person to person and time to time, but the concept of the budget—of how much mental (or physical) effort an individual is willing to expend—remains consistent. Again, this translates back to the discussion on flow: if an activity is too boring or too stressful for a particular individual at a given time, it is not experienced as fun; the individual is outside the flow channel at least at that moment.

Putting these all together, we can say that fun is a complex human experience that incorporates activities and contexts that have these attributes:

- Being voluntary and (typically) nonconsequential
- Having positive emotional valence (sometimes hidden under a negative surface experience) and some duration rather than just a "jolt" of pleasure
- Possessing elements of one or more of sensory, cognitive, social, emotional, and cultural engagement
- Fitting into an individual's current level of desire for interactivity—their interactivity budget—which may vary from person to person and time to time

As an attempt to boil this down, it can be said that while not all engaging experiences are fun, all fun experiences are engaging. They maintain a positive, attractive, engaging aspect across multiple different forms and time scales—to whatever degree of interaction an individual finds enjoyable in the moment.

Operationally—in terms of designing games—what this means is that to be successful, a game needs to be:

- A voluntary activity that the player chooses to engage in on their own
- Perceptually attractive, with an obvious call to action to start the interactive loops
- Interactively engaging in one or more of the ways described in this chapter—providing opportunities for player decisions in a broad play-space and inviting the player's "vigor, dedication, and absorption" (Schaufeli et al. 2002)
- Not overly taxing of the player's mental capacities or interactivity budget

You cannot simply "design in" any of these qualities and then check them off. They are necessarily the emergent result of the whole experience created by your design. As a designer, with everything you do, you need to consider several questions: Are you adding to these qualities or detracting from them? Does the game design provide sufficient opportunities for engagement, including meaningful decisions of some sort? Does it do so in a way that does not overwhelm the player's mental budget? You need to ask yourself these questions multiple times as you are designing, building, and testing a game.

Do Games Have to Be Fun?

Games are systems designed to be interactive and engaging. Because many engaging activities are also fun—voluntary, nonconsequential, attractive, positively valenced, and interactive—we often assume that games naturally fall into this categorization. And most do.

This is not strictly necessary, though. As the example of games like *Train* show, it is entirely possible to use the attractive, interactive, and engaging nature of games in a somewhat subversive way to lead players to experiences that are valuable but that they would never have sought out.

In a workshop on positive and negative affect in gameplay, Birk and colleagues (2015) wrote:

> Most of the time games make us happy, but sometimes they are frustrating or make us feel sad. They allow us to experience pleasure, success and joy, but they can also yield feelings of frustration, failure, or sorrow as a result of darker themes. In games, we can experience the full range of emotions—both positive and negative.

They go on to point out that many games are built on hugely frustrating experiences (for example, *Super Meat Boy*, *Dark Souls*, *Dwarf Fortress*) or those with difficult, often negative emotional contexts (for example, *The Last of Us*, *That Dragon Cancer*). Nevertheless, these games stay well within the terms discussed in this chapter in that they are engaging, voluntary experiences with (as in the examples here) sufficient attention paid to their emotional interactivity that even if they are not necessarily fun, they remain enormously engaging and compelling.

Revisiting Depth and Elegance

Within the context of interactivity, engagement, and fun, we can revisit the notions of depth and elegance in games introduced in Chapter 2. You may recall that systemic depth comes from having a hierarchy of systems within systems, where the part at one level is the whole system for one level down in organization, and the system is just a part in a higher-level organization. When there are enough levels to a game's design that the player can traverse up and down these levels as part of their mental model, finding ways to interact with the system at each level, this adds significantly to the overall engagement and even a sense of captivating cognitive wonder—a combination of rational and emotional engagement also found in (non-interactive) fractals and dynamic self-similar systemic structures.

In the same way, elegance is the quality a game possesses when its systems are not only deep, but generally free from exceptions, special cases, or other irregularities in the systemic structure that ruin its symmetry and metastable regularity. Games with this quality fall squarely into Bushnell's Law in that they are easy to learn and difficult to master, as the player is able to relatively easily construct a mental model with only a few interactions, reusing structures learned in one area when approaching another, thus easing the learning process—but without collapsing the play-space into a narrow path.

When games require that the player keep in mind rules with exceptions or two different systems that operate in contradictory fashions, this allocation of mental resources reduces the player's interaction budget and thus their engagement. The player has to work harder to get to the point where they have understood the game's internal model in their mind; it is more difficult to get to the point where they can worry less about how to play the game and simply enjoy playing it. The easier this is—the fewer rules and especially the fewer exceptions the game has, while maintaining a large space for play (aided by having many levels of organization on which the player can interact with it)—the more elegant and ultimately engaging and enjoyable the game will be.

Summary

This chapter provides the final part of the foundations needed for approaching game design. You have seen how the systems thinking approach introduced earlier clarifies the otherwise muddy issue of interactivity that is so crucial to designing games. This systemic understanding of interactivity sets the stage for discussing how the player builds a mental model as a companion to the game's internal model, aided by the various types of interactive loops that occur between the player and the game they are playing. These in turn illuminates the experience of engagement in many forms.

With this basis, you have seen how it is possible to define the seemingly simple but highly elusive concept of fun. The somewhat paradoxical conclusion in this chapter is that while most games are fun experiences, they do not have to be—as long as they remain highly interactive and engaging.

Starting in the next chapter, we begin building upward from this foundation by applying this understanding of systems thinking, game structure, interactivity, and the player's mental model in the process of designing games.

PART II

PRINCIPLES

CHAPTER 5

WORKING AS A SYSTEMIC GAME DESIGNER

In this chapter, we move from the foundational theory to the practice of designing games. Here we look at different aspects of the game design process and how to get started in each as a systemic game designer.

This is an overview that will be supplemented by Chapters 6, 7, and 8, where we go into more depth on designing the game as a unified whole, then its loops, and finally its parts.

How Do You Even Start?

Lots of people want to design games. They dream about it and talk about it but somehow never manage to actually get started. This is common, and most people who say they have a burning desire to design games never actually do it. Few manage to gather their courage and begin the journey of wading into the dark waters of game design. Rarer still are those who emerge on the far side, dragging their game kicking and screaming from the inchoate sea of design ideas. (That may seem like an overwrought metaphor, but when you complete your first game, you may no longer think so.)

One of the first questions people commonly ask when contemplating doing game design as more than a hobby, more than a "wouldn't it be cool if" activity, is along the lines of "How do I even start?" Designing a game can seems like an impossible problem with no easy handles, no obvious way in. The sheer complexity and impenetrability of the problem can make it seem like the best you can do is leap in with both feet and hope for the best. That is, in fact, what generations of game designers up to now have done. At some point, those of us who have been designing games for decades just sort of made that first leap. For many the first few attempts are utter failures. Rovio went through 51 attempts before hitting it big with *Angry Birds*—and even this attempt looked like a flop at first (Cheshire 2011).

Failure itself isn't a bad thing; anytime you try something new (which is most of the time in game design), you are going to fail a lot. However, you can reduce the amount and duration of failure by approaching game design systemically. Seeing a game as a system (containing other systems) is a good way to crack the problem of where to start in the otherwise overwhelming process.

From Wholes to Parts or Parts to Wholes

One key to knowing how to start is figuring out whether to begin with the parts, the loops, or the whole of your design. Opinions run high on this question. Many designers are firmly in one camp or another, and what they do works for them. Some designers will declare that any game design must start with "the nouns and verbs"—that is, the parts that will form the systems—while others begin with a more intuitive feeling of the kind of experience they want to create. Occasionally some will even start with Ellenor's (2014) idea of "a machine that does x" and then work out what parts make it go and what sort of gameplay experience emerges from it. Differences of opinion on the "right" way to approach game design can make for miscommunication and talking past each other.[1]

---

1. I had this experience while working with Will Wright of SimCity fame. He is firmly a "nouns and verbs" kind of guy, while I often approach designs from a more holistic-experiential point of view. It took a while before we were able to understand each other's perspectives.

Despite strong opinions from some designers, there is no single "right" way to approach game design. Our systemic view should make this clear: in designing a game, you need to get to the point where you have fully defined the parts, the loops, and the whole of your design. As a game designer, you need to be able to move up and down the organizational levels with ease, shifting your focus between the parts, the loops, and the whole as needed. As a result, you can start the design process with whichever of these makes the most sense and bounce between them as needed.

Know Your Strengths, Work to Your Weaknesses

When you begin thinking about making a game, where do your thoughts lead you? Do you think about things like having a game where players are sharks or superheroes, or where each is a kite in the sky? Or are you more likely to approach a game as a simulation or modeling problem? If it's a game about a little one-celled organism, do you start by listing all the parts of the cell? Or do you maybe start thinking about a game where the player is the manager of a remote trading post by jotting down how buying and selling would work?

Every game designer has their strengths; everyone has their "home place" where they start— and then retreat to when making the design becomes difficult. You need to find out where your game design home is and then work out ways to not give in to the temptation to stay there; you also need to figure out how to work with others who approach game design differently from you.

The *doing* of game design is the best way to figure out which parts of the process come most naturally to you. Still, it is worth considering where you think it should start and working from there.

Storytellers

Game designers who tend to start with the whole experience often paint an evocative picture of the player's journey through a game: how the player feels, what they encounter, and what sort of changes they go through. Game designers like these can sometimes seem like expert storytellers. They're able to give you the grand sweep of the world…but they can run into trouble. Games aren't stories. "Telling" a game like a story can be a satisfying first pass at building the world that the players inhabit, but ultimately the game has to be much more than that.

A storyteller needs to hang on to their talent for painting a mental picture of the experience of a world but not get stuck there. If you are a storyteller, you need to build your talents for creating working systems that have their own tokens, rules, and dynamic elements. You likely have the thematic part in hand, but you need to support it with the structure of the underlying game—and work with others who can help you do so.

Inventors

Many game designers are enamored of inventing complex mechanisms—things like clocks with lots of gears, marble-run sculptures, and so on. These can be mesmerizing displays of systems in action. Similarly, sometimes game designers come up with ideas for new kinds of ecological or economic mechanisms and spend time playing with them. For example, the early prototypes for the game *Spore* included lots of different simulation mechanisms, including one that (with a bit of help from the player) simulated the formation of a star system from an interstellar cloud of gas and dust.

But as fascinating as these inventions can be, they aren't games. As with telling a story about a game, designers will sometimes build a mechanism that scratches the "watch it go" itch, only to realize that they left out the need for a human player. The designer may toss the player a few scraps of things to do, but it's clear that the mechanism or simulation remains in the spotlight. If you are an inventor, you can do a lot to build fascinating dynamic systems—but don't forget that games must have human involvement as an integral part of the system and that players need to have long-term goals and reasons to play the game (the whole of the game), or it will be uninteresting to them.

Toymakers

Finally, some game designers are first and foremost toymakers. They love to make little pieces or mechanisms that don't really *do* anything but are still attractive and engaging, at least for a minute or so. Or they might be among those with highly specific domain knowledge—things like the climbing rate and ammunition capacity for a Sopwith Camel or the relative merits of different sorts of swords in medieval (or at least fantasy) combat, or the types of coral on a typical reef—or may just love digging in to find this kind of information.

Many game designers who start with the "nouns and verbs" of their design fit into the toymaker category. Maybe you want to make a game about cells in the immune system attacking invading viruses, and so you start with what you know (or anything you can find) about how a T-cell works. What the player does and why this is engaging or fun are questions that you may not think about right away or that you may have difficulty finding answers for. Having the ability to ground your design in specific parts and behaviors—tokens and rules, nouns and verbs—helps you create prototypes quickly. However, to make it into a game, you need to find ways to build interactive systems and find some goals for the player to pursue and experience.

Working Together to Find the Fun

The good news about these different views of game design is that once you find your starting point as a designer, you can extend your abilities into the other areas. Any one of these is great as a starting point, as long as you don't end there, too. The better news is that you can also find others who have different game design talents and work with them. It can be difficult and even frustrating for game designers with different design styles to work together, but the result is almost always far better and more engaging for the player as a result.

No matter which part of the game design process you prefer, you will need to extend yourself into the other areas and learn to listen to and work with those who see the game design process differently from you. A lot of game design comes down to being able to communicate your ideas, hear other people's ideas, and generally work together with those who have strengths that are different from yours. Understanding game design as systemic design helps illuminate these different views on games as systems and on game designers as system designers. That understanding should help you refine your skills and look for others who complement them.

A large part of *doing* game design is in the oft-repeated phrase "find the fun." You may start with a cool toy, an intriguing mechanisms, or a compelling experience—the parts, loops, and whole of a game—but you will need all three elements plus engaging interactivity to build a fun game. To do that, you need to apply your knowledge of systems to creating game systems and games *as* systems.

Designing Systemic Games

As a way to approach designing games as systems, we can look at the properties of effective systems in games and how they affect the process of game design.

Qualities of Game Systems

Achterman (2011) has provided helpful guidelines for building game systems. In his view, five qualities are the hallmarks of effective game systems:

- **Comprehensible:** As a designer, you have to understand your game as a system and the systems within it. Of course, your players have to be able to comprehend it, too. This is why both design documentation (for you) and presenting the game in such a way that players can build a mental model of it are so important.

- **Consistent:** Achterman points out the importance of having "rules and content [that] function the same in all areas of your game." It can be tempting to add an exception or a special case to fix a problem, but doing so tends to decrease the resilience of the system (which sets up the game for later problems) and makes it more difficult to learn. (This is similar to the discussion in Chapter 3, "Foundations of Games and Game Design," on elegance.)

- **Predictable:** Game systems should have predictable outputs for given inputs. While making games predictable helps players build mental models of the games, it can also be somewhat at odds with designing systems for emergence. Being predictable should not be taken as meaning that game systems should be obviously or boringly mechanistic. However, neither should your systems produce wildly different results for similar inputs, much less become brittle and break down due to unforeseen circumstances. You should at least be able to know that you have accounted for any edge cases that might hurt a player's experience or provide them with a gap in the system to exploit to their advantage.

- **Extensible:** Building games systemically typically makes them highly extensible. Rather than depend on custom-created content "set pieces" (e.g., expensive hand-created levels), as much as possible you should create game systems such that content can be reused in new ways or created procedurally. You want to create parts and loops that can be used in multiple ways, not a single-use arc that makes for a complicated rather than complex set of relationships. While in a loop the parts affect each other cyclically, as veteran game designer Daniel Cook said, "An arc is a broken loop that you exit immediately" (Cook 2012). Designing in terms of loops rather than arcs also makes it easier to take a system and add it to a new game or put it in a new context, where it acts as a part in a new larger system. For example, you may decide that you want to add a whole new class of buildings for players to construct; if you have a general "building construction" system in the game, this is much easier to do than if you have to hand-craft another one. By designing game systems carefully, with only the needed parts and sufficient loops between them, you will be able to extend the systems internally or extend their use externally far more easily than if you rely on more static content or fractured, separated systems in the game.

- **Elegant:** As discussed in earlier chapters, elegance is often a hallmark of systems. This quality sums up the ones above. It goes beyond but is related to the quality of consistency discussed above. The following are some examples of elegance:

  - Creating a diverse space for players to explore based on only a few rules (Again, *Go* is the archetypal example of this.)

  - Having systemic rules with few exceptions that are easy to learn, where both predictable and emergent behaviors are possible

  - Enabling the system to be used within multiple contexts or to have new parts added within it

Tabletop and Digital Games

This book uses examples from both tabletop games—also called analog games, board games, physical games, and so on—and digital games—those played on a computer, console, tablet, or phone. From a game design point of view, there is a great deal of commonality between these types of games, no matter their genre or other differentiating attributes.

There is a great deal to be learned from studying tabletop games, even if you never plan to design one. Designing for situations in which the only "computing power" is in the players' heads and where all interaction must happen using tokens the players can physically manipulate presents a significant challenge. It constrains what you as a designer can do to bring a game concept to life and highlights the relationships between the game's tokens and rules, loops, and overall experience. Digital games can hide a lot of game-designer laziness behind flashy graphics and narrative cut-scenes; tabletop games do not have that luxury.

In speaking to university theatre students, actor Terrence Mann said, "Movies make you famous, television will make you rich; but theatre will make you good" (Gilbert 2017). There is an analogy here to game design (not that any particular type of game design will necessarily make you rich or famous): designing tabletop games has the same sort of relationship to designing digital games that acting in theatre does to acting in movies. Like theatre, tabletop games are closer to the audience; you as a game designer can hide less, and must hone your craft in designing for this environment.

This is not to say that all game designers must design board or tabletop games, though it is good practice. But if at times you wonder why so many board games are used as examples when "modern" games are typically played on computer, this is the reason. Tabletop games have undergone every bit as much of a renaissance in the early 21st century as have digital games. As a systemic game designer, you can learn from both, and you may well find that designing tabletop games challenges your skills in ways that designing for games run on the computer does not.

The Process of Designing Games as Systems

Stepping down a bit from the abstract qualities we hope to find in game systems, we can look at the overall design process common to systemic game design (whether tabletop or digital).

This is necessarily an iterative process between designing the parts, the loops, and the whole. At first, this process may be iterative in your head, on a whiteboard, and on scraps of paper and then in documents and spreadsheets. Once the game begins to take shape, the iterative cycle of prototyping and playtesting discussed briefly below (and in more detail in Chapter 12, "Making Your Game Real") becomes important: it is far better to prototype fast and playtest early than to hope the idea you have in your head will spring forth fully formed like Athena from Zeus's skull. (They never do.) This process is the game designer's loop shown in Figure 5.1 (which is the same as Figure 4.3).

As stated earlier, it is possible to begin at any point in the systemic structure: with parts, loops, or the whole experience—as long as, having started with one, you move to the others so that they mutually support each other. With that reminder, for convenience here we will start with the whole, the architectural and thematic elements, and then move to the functional looping aspects, and finally move to the parts.

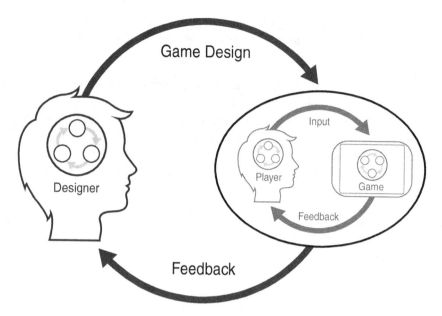

Figure 5.1 The game designer's loop enables you to iteratively design and test your designs

The Whole Experience: Thematic Architecture

As discussed in Chapter 3, the high-level design of a game has to do with the player's overall experience. We can separate this into architectural and thematic elements—the technical aspects of the *user experience* (how the game looks and feels) and the more ethereal, sometimes tacit qualities that define *what the game is about*. Understanding the whole of the game answers the question What is the point of the game (or a system within the game)?

As one example, in a recent conversation, Jason VandenBerghe, creative director on the game *For Honor*, said, "I believe that combat is an art form. The game sprung from that belief" (personal communication, December 2016). His desire was for the player to experience hand-to-hand combat as a lethal, dance-like form of art. While that desire is not enough on its own to support the game design, it is a compelling vision, a star to guide the game's developers and from which all the interactions and details of the game eventually arise.

Many times, game designers or entire development teams will launch themselves into the game development process without stopping to entirely clarify what the "whole experience" is that they want in their game. Questions of theme and vision seem frivolous; the team wants to get to making the game! However, as you will see in Chapter 11, "Working as a Team," having a shared, coherent vision of the game your team is making is the single most important indicator of success.

There are multiple aspects of any overarching vision, as discussed in the following sections. These aspects represent and point to more detailed elements that have to be articulated to get an idea of what the game will be.

The Game's World and History

To begin with, what is the world, and what is the player's point of view within it? You may be thinking of a gritty, cold-hearted world of spies and double-dealing—but is the player a spy working their way up in this world? A spy-master overseeing and pulling the strings on a sometimes wayward team of spies? Or possibly an old spy coming out of retirement for one last vengeful mission? Each of these paints a different picture and will take your game design in a different direction.

To fill in the world somewhat, what are the major events in its history—those that are applicable to the players? If you're a storyteller, you may have to resist the urge to write 100 pages of world lore. If you have the time and money, and especially the experience to know what's useful and what's not, then you can indulge yourself in this; you will likely add important details to the game world that make it come to life all the more vividly. But if you have any time or budget constraints, or if you're just starting out, you should avoid the siren song of diving too deeply into the backstory. You need to know what the world is and what it's about, but to start with, you can do this in a page or two of text. You shouldn't write any more than you need to support the rest of the design. Later, as the game is beginning to come together, you can flesh out the deep, tragic history of the city where the streets hold a million secrets.

Narrative, Progression, and Key Moments

The game world's history is its past. Its present and future are contained in the game narrative. Does your game have a predefined story the player has to work within? Are there larger events happening around the player that grow out of the large-scale history but that leave room for the player to make their own decisions? Or is the game's history a jumping-off point for the player, where what's past is prologue, and there is little in the way of continuing narrative to guide the player's actions?

Understanding your game's world and (some) of its history will also help you begin to define major events that happen in the game, the player's goals and progression through it, and "key moments"—short moments or stories that you can tell that help communicate meaningful, climactic points for the player.

Art, Monetization, and Other Whole-Experience Concerns

There are a variety of questions to work through at the level of the whole-game experience: Will the game's art style be 2D or 3D? Painterly, cel-shaded, or super-realistic? How does your choice reflect the game's heart and theme to the player? Closely aligned with this is the way the player interacts with the game—the user interface and user experience, often referred to as UI/UX. Even monetization design—how your game makes money—is something you have to consider at this stage.

In Chapter 6 we will look in more detail at the process of designing and documenting the gameplay experience as a whole. For now, keep in mind that it doesn't matter so much whether you start with a high-level, blue-sky creative vision that you then support with underlying loops and parts or whether you arrive here after first nailing down those dynamic and specific aspects; either way, you will iterate back and forth between them as you refine your ideas. What matters is that before you begin developing your game—before you assure yourself that you know what the game *is*—you have this theme and vision, the whole of the player's experience, clearly articulated and shared by your team.

Systemic Loops and Creating a Space for Play

Chapters 3 and 4, "Interactivity and Fun," discuss the game's loops: the game's dynamic model of its world, the player's mental model of the game, and the interactions that happen between the player and the game. Designing and building these loops and the structures that support them is the heart of being what is often loosely referred to as a "systems designer." In addition to the overview here, this topic is explored in detail in Chapter 7.

In creating a space for the player to explore and inhabit—rather than a singular path for them to follow through the game—you need to define the game's systems. These systems need to support the theme and desired player experience, and they must work interactively between the game and the player. You need to specify and create (via iterative prototyping and playtesting) the player's core loops, explicit goals, and the way they progress through the game.

Creating systems like this may be the most difficult part of game design: it requires that you envision the system as it uses the game's tokens and rules to create an experience that is hard to see clearly in advance. Of course, you don't have to do this all at once—which is why prototyping and playtesting are so important—but being able to imagine multiple looping systems well enough to record their designs and implement them is nevertheless a daunting task. For example, in many games, the systems controlling resource production, crafting, wealth production, and combat all have their own internal workings, and all interact with each other and the player to create the player's experience. Getting all these to work on their own and contribute to a systemic whole requires skill, patience, and resilience in the face of repeated attempts when something just doesn't quite work.

Balancing Game Systems

Part of making game systems is ensuring that all parts defined by the game are used and balanced against each other and that every system in the game has a clear purpose. If you add a quest system to your game and players ignore it, you need to understand why it isn't contributing to their experience and determine whether to remove it or fix it so that it does. Chapter 9, "Game Balance Methods," and Chapter 10, "Game Balance Practice," go into this process in detail.

The Structural Parts: Tokens, Values, and Rules

It may be that you started the game design process with an idea for a fun looping mechanism or interaction. Or maybe you started with the kind of experience and feeling you want the players to have, and so you're defining the game and interactive loops. Or in some cases you may start with an idea for the building blocks out of which you want to construct your game. In any case, before the game is really a game, you need to situate the game's functional loops into the context of the whole—the game experience—and also create the structural parts of the game's systems.

You first read about the tokens, values, and rules in a game in Chapter 3. You will see them again in detail in Chapter 8. For now, in terms of working as a systemic designer, you should understand that the process of nailing down exactly what is going on in a game—getting past the hand-waving descriptive stage and being able to implement the game—is vital. You don't have a game without it.

This aspect of game design is sometimes called "detailed design," and it is where the game design becomes entirely specific. Does that sword have a weight of 3 or 4? A cost of 10 or 12? How many types of troops, or horses, or flower petals are there in the game, and what differences do these numbers make to the overall gameplay? Tracking and specifying these structural parts of the game has been called the "spreadsheet-specific" part of game design. This is a crucial part of systemic design; it is in many ways how the game becomes real. Such specific design is needed for balancing the different tokenized parts against each other to make the game a cohesive whole rather than allow it to become separate systems that can fly apart.

The issues you need to think about here are how to specify tokens that represent the objects in the game—the player, other people, nations, creatures, spaceships, or whatever the operative units are within your game—and give each of them sufficient attributes, values, and behaviors to define them. One way to think of this is to answer the question What is the smallest number of attributes, states, and behaviors you can use to support the game's systems and provide the overall gameplay experience you want?

Related to this are the issues of how to make obvious to the player what the tokens in the game are, what they do, and how the player can affect them. This in turn feeds into the game's UI/UX—how the board or screen is laid out to present the necessary information about the game to the player. This cannot be specified until you know what the necessary information is. At the same time, approaching this issue by asking what sorts of information you think the player needs to know to play the game can itself help clarify the tokenizing process.

Chapter 8 talks about this process in more detail, including how to create complex objects, game pieces, or tokens by having a small number of general attributes that interact with each other to create their own subsystems within the larger game systems. Chapter 8 also discusses the importance of inter-object behaviors and how to avoid "easy win" or other gameplay-killing tokens in your games.

Revisiting the Systemic Design Process

As a systemic game designer, your loop—the designer's loop—involves cycling between seeing the game as a whole, as systems, or as individuated parts (see Figure 5.2). You need to be able to see them all at the same time and how they affect each other. You also need to be able to dive into any one in detail, depending on what's needed by the game design. It's important that you not focus on any one level to the exclusion of the others; you also don't want to continue to work ineffectively on any one of them. When you find yourself pushing on one level without any real effect, it can often help to switch and work from the point of view of the other levels to help reveal what you need in another. If you can't quite get the experience down, explore the tokens and how they work; see how they inform the experience. Or if you have the experience clearly in mind but can't quite specify the tokens, see what the systems tell you about how those have to work. At the same time, don't let yourself avoid tokenizing your systems, making sure there are interesting interactions, or ensuring a cohesive theme because one or more of these aren't in your comfort zone as a game designer. All of these are necessary for any working game, and all are necessary activities for a systemic game designer.

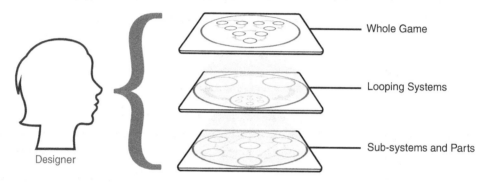

Figure 5.2 As a game designer, you need to be able to see the parts, the loops, and the game's whole experience all at the same time and zoom in on any one of them as needed

Analyzing Games from a Systems View

Working as a game designer doesn't just mean designing your own games; it also means playing and analyzing a lot of other people's games. It's important to be able to understand what makes other games work—or not work in particular areas.

You can follow the same systemic structure for analysis as for design. It involves looking at the whole experience, including how you build your mental model of the game; the game's internal and interactive loops; and the rules and tokens that make those up. By carefully identifying and separating these, you can gain insight into the decisions made by the game's designer and improve your own designs as a result.

When beginning to play a game for the first time, examine how you go about building your own mental model of it: Do you understand the setting and theme? What surprises you about it? What concepts about the game did you find to be important, incomplete, or hard to understand as you learned the game? How might the game have increased your engagement early on?

While playing and after playing, think about the whole of the experience you had. What kind of experience and feelings do you think the game designer was trying to elicit in you as a player? Were there particular aspects of the game that supported or detracted from your experience?

What visual and interactive elements of the game support its theme and the desired player experience? What can you infer about the game designer's intent for the game, based on the art style and interactive aspects?

What specific game systems can you identify in the game? Are there systems that operate independently of the players, or do they all rely on the players doing something first? The board game *Power Grid* is a great example of a (nondigital) game that has systems that operate mostly outside player control. For example, in this game there is a simple but highly effective depiction of supply-and-demand economics: as players buy more of any one kind of fuel, the price for it goes up until its supply is replenished on the next turn (see Figure 5.3).

Figure 5.3 The board game *Power Grid*, showing the track representing prices for the resources coal, oil, trash, and nuclear fuel. As players purchase each and supply decreases, its price rises. Supply is replenished each turn, driving prices lower if the fuel is not used

Continuing with the analysis overview, as a player in a game, how do you progress, and what reinforcing loops can you identify? What balancing loops are there that push back against player advancement or that keep one player who outstrips others early on from simply winning the game?

What are the primary forms of interactivity in the game? How does the game allocate its interactivity budget? Is this a game of strategy and socializing, or one of quick thinking and fast action? Do the ways you as a player interact with the game help establish the game's theme, or do they work against it?

Finally, what are the particular tokens and rules—the atomic parts of the game with their values and behaviors? Do they support the desired gameplay experience or get in its way? Having learned one system in the game, can you transfer how that works to another part of the game, or are there lots of rules to learn, each with its own exceptions—so that you have to spend a lot of time thinking about how to play the game?

Often the art style of a game is expressed in its individual tokens, sometimes in surprising ways. For example, the tabletop game *Splendor* is about building up your business as a gem merchant, starting with individual mines and ending with courting the favor of various nobles. The physical pieces in the game are like poker chips. They represent individual gems, and each has an unusual amount of heft. Their weight subtly adds to the desired experience of the game, even though, like the rest of the art (and most art in games), it is nonfunctional.

As you analyze games by examining their parts, loops, and wholes, you will begin to see commonalities across them, as well as how each is unique. Understanding the similarities and differences will help you improve your own designs—avoiding the mistakes of others, springboarding off their good ideas, and keeping your game design fresh and engaging.

Prototyping and Playtesting

A final important part of working as a systemic game designer is iteratively getting feedback. Game design is necessarily a process of repeatedly testing and refining game design ideas in the service of an overall vision for the game. Game ideas will not make it from your mind to their final form in front of the player without having gone through many changes first. It's common for almost everything about a game except for its single unifying vision to change multiple times during development.

As an example from a related creative field, making movies, Ed Catmull, president of Pixar, has been open about the many gyrations that films at his studios go through. "All of our movies suck at first," he said when speaking to aspiring movie animators. He clarified that statement by adding, "A lot of people don't believe me when I say that. They think I'm being self-effacing or modest, but I don't mean it in that sense. I mean it in the way that the film sucks." He went on to discuss the many story changes that the movie *Up* went through during its development: it started with a story about a kingdom in the sky with two princes who didn't like each other, who fall to earth and end up meeting a giant bird named Kevin. That version went through a huge number of changes. By the time they completed the movie, he said, "All that was left was the bird and the word 'up'" (Lane 2015).

The same sort of thing happens in games. While your game may not change as drastically as a movie like *Up*, you must be prepared for many iterations—many cycles through the creative process. This means you have to be willing to test your ideas over and over again, learning and changing them as you go. And it means you have to be humble enough to change an idea or throw it out if it isn't working. Iterating and "finding the fun" inevitably means throwing away a lot of work—drawings, animations, programming, design documents, and so on. You cannot cling to something you have worked on just because you put a lot of time into it. If you do, you will be settling for an idea that is okay (or mediocre) when with a little more work and polish it could have been great.

To iterate effectively on game designs, you need to make them real. The only way to do this is to make early versions—prototypes—and test them. You may start with drawings on a whiteboard or pieces of paper and coins being pushed around on a table—anything to start actually playing with the idea you have. Most of your prototypes will be varying degrees of ugly or unfinished, converging on the full, finished, and polished product at the end. The point is to take your game design out of the realm of ideas and into real implementations that can be played and tested—and to do so as quickly and often as possible.

Playtesting is how you validate your prototypes—or, more often, how you find out where your game design is broken. Developing a game designer's intuition for what will work or not is important, but even for the most experienced designers, it is never a substitute for testing the gameplay on players who have never seen it before. As Daniel Cook has said, without implementation and playtesting a game design remains an "ineffectual paper fantasy" (Cook, 2011b). You will need to test your design ideas with other people early and often to keep your game on track.

We will return to the topics of prototyping and playtesting often in the following chapters, particularly in Chapter 12. For now, understand that a core aspect of working as a game designer is having the humility and creative flexibility to test and refine your game design ideas based on what others think of them. You will need to make fast, often ugly prototypes, and you will need to test them with potential players repeatedly during design and development. The bright shining idea you have in your head will never survive contact with reality without change—most likely a lot of change.

Summary

This brief chapter provides an overview of what it means to work as a systemic game designer. While getting started on a new game design can be truly daunting, by breaking down the game into its parts, loops, and wholes—not necessarily in that order—you can begin to get a handle on defining the game at each of those levels.

The coming chapters add more detail to the topics discussed here. Chapter 6 examines the whole of the game experience in more detail—how you discover it, document it, and set up for creating the underlying systems. Chapter 7 revisits the game's functional loops, this time using the knowledge of systems thinking and game loops to specify the particular loops for your game. Then Chapter 8 looks again at the game's parts and how to create these "spreadsheet-specific" tokens, values, and rules.

CHAPTER 6

DESIGNING THE WHOLE EXPERIENCE

This chapter looks at how you arrive at the big picture for your game and how you record this high-level vision in a concept document. This document brings together elements from the overall player experience to what makes your game unique, as well as more practical concerns like how you will sell your game and what systems are included in it.

The concept document is a brief overview of the entire design, but it represents the unified whole of your game and will be your touchstone as you develop your game.

What's the Big Idea?

Every game has within it a single big driving idea. This is often called the *concept* or *vision* for the game. It is important that you figure out and clarify your game's vision early in the design process; you need to be able to explain it succinctly to others. If you put this off too long, you will wander around nibbling at one possibility after another without ever finding the heart of your game—and no one else will understand what you are trying to do or why it's worth doing. As you will see in Chapter 11, "Working as a Team," having a clear, compelling, shared vision for your game is the single most important practice that correlates with creating successful games.

Despite being referred to by words like *vision*, the idea for a game doesn't have to be grand and sweeping; in fact, most of the time the smaller and more focused the idea is, the better. The idea behind *Angry Birds* is hardly epic, but the game itself is hugely enjoyable for millions of people. As mentioned in Chapter 5, "Working as a Systemic Game Designer," the far more heroic Ubisoft game *For Honor* has a clear and seemingly simple vision of "combat as dance." While there is a lot more to know about the game, a single evocative phrase like that is incredibly powerful: it helps you communicate the vital, driving idea behind your game quickly and clearly in a way that excites people and encourages them to find out more.

Blue-Sky Design

How do you work out what your game's big idea—its vision—is? In many cases, especially if you are beginning the design of an entirely new game, you may have the opportunity to engage in what's called *ideation*, a fancy way of saying "coming up with and communicating new ideas." A particularly open-ended form of this is referred to as *blue-sky design*—design unfettered by limitations, rules, business realities, or any of the other pesky constraints that can cramp your creative style, where you are flying in the midst of the blue sky, able to go any direction you please. This can be a heady experience, and it's one that many game designers crave, especially early in their careers.

Methods

There are probably as many ways to do blue-sky design as there are game designers. It's possible to do this kind of ideation on your own, in your own head, but it's much more effective to do it with others. Being able to bounce ideas off others and gain from their creativity enhances the whole process and the final game concept.

Most of the time when you're doing blue-sky design, you're with a small team of other designers—which means you're likely to start by sitting in a room with paper and whiteboards all terrifyingly empty, all of you looking at each other…and you have to come up with some big new idea. It's like saying, "Okay, aaaaand be creative—*GO!*"

Brainstorming-ish

Many design teams run blue-sky design like a brainstorming exercise. This is a good place to start, with some careful modifications. As with many other brainstorming techniques, you want to first aim for quantity and not worry about quality: just get the ideas out. You can start with a prompt, or a joke, or anything to help seed ideas. Game designer Ron Gilbert has been quoted as saying that "every good brainstorming session begins with a 15-minute discussion of *Star Trek*" (Todd 2007, 34). The cultural references change over time, but it's important to get everyone mentally loosened up and in a good, fun, engaged, creative frame of mind.

Once you get going, you need to keep the ideas flowing, but with as light a touch as possible: heavy-handed moderation often shuts off the creative flow. You can take turns to make sure everyone is contributing. You can even play it as a game, where the first letter of the idea you say has to be the last letter of the idea of the person who just went. It doesn't really matter, as long as you keep the ideas flowing until you have built up a lot of possible directions.

Getting Past the Easy Ideas

The most important reason it's so important to have a fast flow of ideas and to keep it going is that your initial ideas, more likely than not, will stink. They will be shallow stereotypes and clichés, thin retreads of a game or TV show or movie that you recently encountered. This happens to most designers. These ideas are what's on the surface of your mind, and so they're the easiest thing for your mind to grab out of your bag of creative tricks when you start having to come up with ideas.

You can't really avoid dealing in stereotypes and clichés, but you can and should avoid stopping there. Those first few ideas will be seductive because you thought of them so quickly (proving how clever you are). You may want to stop there, but you need to set that ego-stroking thought aside and keep going. You need to explore and push your own creative boundaries. If you're working with other game designers, you need to see what you can come up with based on what they have said. If this process is working well, you will springboard off each other's ideas and get to places you would never have thought of otherwise.

Twisting Ideas

The second big step is taking an existing idea that's been tossed into the mix and subverting it. For example, suppose the idea that's been stated is that you're a warrior who has to kill the dragon to save the village. Yawn. Not very original. But instead of shutting down the idea and the person who came up with it, twist it: what if you're trying to save the dragon? Why would that be? What if you're trying to convince the villagers to ally with the dragon? What if you, the player, *are* the dragon? In just a few quick steps, you move away from a tired cliché to ideas that are still recognizable but may have more merit and more room to explore.

Another way of handling this is often known as "yes, and…" thinking. This is a common technique in improvisational comedy and other areas where you're trying to collaboratively build on others' ideas. One person lobs an idea into the conversation. Rather than bat it down with a flow-killing "no," another person says something like "yes, and…" followed by their own twist on the first idea. Then someone else does the same to the second person's idea. The process continues as the idea morphs by addition along the way. One of the best parts of this is that no one is trying to hang on to their idea; it's the ideas that are important, not who said them. This is a great way to remove ego from the process and focus on getting to the most viable, innovative ideas.

Curation

There is a limit to idea generation even in blue-sky thinking. In many brainstorming processes, there is the general idea that "no idea is a bad idea" or that you can "yes, and..." any idea enough to make it viable. It's true that you really want to get the idea flow going at first, to run past all the stereotypes and clichés that present themselves so easily, and you also want to get past the insecure, ego-based moment of "but I want *my* idea to win!" But at some point, you need to start turning the nozzle on the firehose and focus more on some ideas than others.

When the team has generated a bunch of ideas—writing them down on pieces of paper, a whiteboard, or similar—take a step back and look at them. It's typically clear which have the most passion and creativity behind them—the ones that get people excited and that the team could keep exploring all day—and which ones are by comparison creative dry wells. The ones that people begin talking about on their own. At the same time, not all of those popular ideas will be ones you can build an entire game on; some will be beyond your means, or require technology that doesn't exist, or just go in a direction that doesn't fit where you want to go overall.

Deciding which ideas to carefully select, enhance, and add to from other ideas is a difficult process that requires a great deal of experience and sound judgment. This type of selection is like a museum director deciding which of many valuable items to exhibit; in curating exhibit, the director is not dismissing some pieces as not being valuable, but not everything can be the center of attention. In the same way, while it's true that anyone can have great ideas, it takes experience to recognize which ones are most worth following, especially when there's a crowd of good ideas jostling for attention.

It typically falls to a senior creative person—in a large organization this might be a creative director, a lead designer, or sometimes an executive producer—to focus the blue-sky team's efforts to just a few ideas that they can dig into more deeply. This can be as simple as circling ideas on a whiteboard and directing the team's efforts toward them or as formal as directing further work on only a few brief written treatments out of many submitted. In any event, this level of idea curation means leaving behind all the other ideas, and that's not easy. It helps to remember that finding the few ideas that are best for the current situation out of all those generated is a key part of focusing the team's creative efforts; you cannot focus on all the ideas. To paraphrase a longer statement by Steve Jobs,[1] it's important to remember that focus is saying "no" to 1,000 good ideas.

---

1. In 1997, Steve Jobs said, "People think focus means saying yes to the thing you've got to focus on. But that's not what it means at all. It means saying no to the hundred other good ideas that there are. You have to pick carefully. I'm actually as proud of the things we haven't done as the things I have done. Innovation is saying 'no' to 1,000 things" (Jobs 1997).

Limits to Blue-Sky Design

Blue-sky design can start out entirely undirected and unfocused, and it can be a way to generate many ideas you would not have otherwise found. As it turns out, however, such unbounded design often leads nowhere—or it leads in many opposing directions, none of which are obvious winners. Presented with the opportunity to design anything they want, many game designers find themselves paralyzed, unable to come up with any coherent design direction at all.

With no limits on creative ideas, many designers find that they return to the conceptual safety of a game a lot like one they already know rather than strike out in entirely new directions. Brainstorming and "yes, and…" can help this process, but only if those involved are able to mentally take the leap into unknown territory. In a similar way, with no limits on time, many designers find that they tinker endlessly with a design and never quite make up their minds and simply finishing the game.

That is not to say that blue-sky design is worthless. With the right people involved, it can be a terrific experience and lead to highly innovative new games. But it's important to understand that this sort of unlimited design space is rarely as desirable as it may seem and often does not result in the amazing new games you might imagine.

Constraints Are Your Friend

Fortunately, opportunities to design truly without limits are rare. You almost certainly have some constraints on your design concept already: you have only so much time or money, you may be limited in what platform you can put the game on, and you are probably limited by your ability to program the game and create the art for it.

An important lesson in designing games is that constraints can help you. These constraints can be limits you set on yourself, or they can come from outside. Typically in professional game development you have real-world limitations of time, money, and technology. You may also have strong limits placed on your ideation in terms of the type of game you're going to make, a licensed property it has to adhere to, and so on. These all limit the amount of blue-sky thinking you can do, but that in no way limits the creativity you can apply within the constraints.

You will also likely want to set limits on your design (if they are not set for you) in terms of the type of gameplay you want, also known as the game's genre, and the overall experience you want for the player. Even in an early blue-sky design session, team members can create their own constraints as a way of setting ground rules for the ideation: "no virtual reality games" or "no games that involve killing." Such constraints necessarily remove immense numbers of ideas from consideration, but as per the Steve Jobs quote mentioned earlier, that's entirely the point.

Cautions

It's important to keep in mind some cautions about the brainstorming or ideation process. While some people celebrate the free-for-all nature of brainstorming, the process has some significant potential downsides that you need to work to avoid.

One of the most common of them is that those who speak up first or most often are often heard the most. The loudest voices can sometimes crowd out important comments or more innovative ideas that are said more quietly. This unfortunately has both personality and gender aspects: males and extroverts who are comfortable taking control of a meeting often end up driving the ideation—even if they don't mean to. Women and those who are just quieter in their personality or who don't feel the need to get up and take control of a meeting can often feel unheard. The group loses potentially important perspectives as a result.

A similar and related issue is groupthink: a common thought is that if everyone in the room agrees on a particular idea or course of action, it *must* be good. But if those in the room represent a narrow range of voices—all male, all fans of a particular genre of games, and so on—then the range of ideas that have been considered may actually be very small (and the group is the least equipped to judge this, as we cannot see our own blind spots). Consider those whom you might bring into ideation sessions to provide broader views: those of different genders, ethnicities, life experiences, interests, and even experience levels. Not every brainstorming session has to fully represent the broad spectrum of humanity, but by making an effort in this area, you will all be more creative. By bringing diverse voices into your ideation *and listening to them*, you can get past shallow, derivative ideas faster and are more likely to get to better ideas as a result.

Another potential problem with brainstorming is the drive to come up with and settle on a game vision or feature idea in a single sitting—taking all day if necessary. This is a poor way to encourage creativity. Many people are not going to be comfortable speaking up in a large group but nevertheless have terrific ideas. Even if everyone does feel comfortable, you're going to drain your creativity quickly if you're all sitting together. Rather than have people try to force their own ideas, when you see the flow of ideas slowing down, take a break. Everyone goes to their own places for an hour or more, taking along some of the ideas (assigned, chosen, or just what's on their mind). Then everyone comes back together later in the day and takes a look at where everyone's thinking has led. You don't need to start over, or necessarily pick up right where you left off. Just give people a chance to percolate the ideas discussed through their minds, and you'll be surprised what new concepts come back.

The Desired Experience

The initial ideation process is designed to help you find and clarify your game's concept and vision. Within this, the single most important question you need to answer is What is the experience you want the player to have? That is, what do you want the player to do, how do you want them to progress, and, most of all, what do you want them to feel?

This can be surprisingly difficult to nail down, especially if you are coming at the design as an inventor or a toymaker. It can even feel like a side issue: you might think that getting the game tokens and rules figured out first is better. You can certainly approach the game design from that direction—but at some point, ideally sooner than later, you will need to grapple with the question of what kind of experience you want players to have in your game. This is not something that will resolve itself well without your focus on it as a game designer. Designing a game without intentionally designing the player's experience makes for a more chaotic mental model that is more difficult to learn and become engaged with.

If you're more of a storyteller-designer you may be able to get to the ethereal, emotional essence of the player experience quickly—but you may need others to help you nail it down to reality. If you have a narrative structure in place, you may already have a good idea of the kind of experience you want the player to have. In that case, though, you need to make sure you are designing a game and not writing a movie. Does the kind of experience you want support second-order design, such that there is a game-space for the player to explore and not just a single story for them to walk through as a spectator?

From these general ideas and directions, we move to more specific aspects of the desired experience that you must decide, including the following:

- Who are your players? What are their motivations?
- What is the game's genre—the type of gameplay most used in the game?
- Combining those two, what is the player's fantasy? What is their role in the game that gives them a reason and space to explore? Are they a hero, a pirate, an emperor, a dung beetle, a young child, or something entirely different?
- What kinds of choices does the player make? How do they progress through the game?
- What sorts of interactivity do you rely on most in the game? How are you spending the player's interactivity budget? Is this mainly a fast reaction game, one that relies on careful planning, or one that is designed first and foremost to evoke an emotional response? What are the visual and sound aesthetics?

These and related items are discussed in more detail later in this chapter.

The Concept Document

It's not enough to come up with the overall concept and desired experience for players in your game; you have to articulate your vision well enough to communicate it clearly to others. It can be tempting to skip this step, especially if you're working on a small team. Going through this process will clarify your thinking, ensure that your team is all working toward the same vision, and help you sell your design to others—new team members, potential funders, game company executives, and so on.

Typically, a game's concept is formalized in a short concept document. This is both an informative and persuasive document: you are trying to convey your idea as quickly and clearly as possible, while also showing why your game idea is worth making. When preparing a design for funding or similar approval, a process known as "pitching," you will often present a structure similar to that found in a concept document (though concept and the pitch documents also differ significantly, based on their audience). (See Chapter 12, "Making Your Game Real," for more details on pitching.) Particular styles differ, and you will likely evolve your own form of concept document. A template for a concept document that follows the material discussed in this chapter is included in the online resources for this book at www.informit.com/title/9780134667607.

The concept document can be created on paper or, more commonly, as an online document or web page. There are significant advantages to maintaining the concept document online: first, it remains current rather than becoming stale and forgotten (a common fate for product documentation). In addition, you can add more details to the design over time in an organized manner and without weighing down the document.

The concept document should always keep a high-level view of the game. As the project progresses, the concept can and should serve as the nexus of all the game's design documentation, becoming the tip of the iceberg. The design overall and the concept document itself may change during development, and it is important to keep the document up to date.

The concept document should remain brief and clear, and it should highlight the vision of the game. The more pictures and diagrams you can use, the better. But in addition to providing brief, high-level conceptual descriptions of the game's art style, the world's history, the player's progression, and so on (all discussed below), the concept document can provide pointers to other, more specific design documents that define those and many other parts of the game in greater detail. This structure enables multiple designers to work on different parts of the game and allows for different documents to be added as the game progresses, all while retaining the concept document as the overarching expression of the design. In the throes of development, having the concept document as a touchstone to the agreed-upon vision of the game and an active organizing principle for the design is invaluable.

There are three main sections to the concept document:

- High-level concept
- Product description
- Detailed design

The information that goes into each of these sections is detailed in the following sections.

Capturing the Concept

The first section of the concept document helps communicate the high-level information about your game quickly and concisely. Typically this section has several subsections:

- Working title
- Concept statement
- Genre(s)
- Target audience
- Unique selling points

Working Title

The working title is simply what you call your game. This should be evocative of the rest of the game and should be a convenient handle to use when speaking of it. Some teams put considerable effort into finding the right title at this stage, going so far as to search out available domain names online, looking at the titles of competitive games, and so on. Other teams go the opposite way, choosing a name that has nothing to do with the gameplay at all (often out of a desire to maintain confidentiality through the use of a codename).

Experience shows that either way works and probably doesn't matter: whatever you call your game early on is not likely to be what it ends up being called as a commercial product. For now, you're better off just finding a name that captures the game as you envision it and is just a convenient temporary name. There will be time to do broad name searches later.

Concept Statement

To show that you truly understand your own game concept and to help others understand it quickly, you need to create and refine your *concept statement*. This is a brief sentence or two that captures all the important aspects of your game and, especially, the player experience. When someone asks, "What is your game about?" this is your answer—and you should have it ready. This is the first impression you make with others about your game. Writing a concept statement may seem easy but is actually difficult to do well. As it is the distillation of your vision for the game, it's worth spending time honing this statement. The concept statement needs to be brief, pithy, and understandable, and it should give someone who hears or reads the statement for the first time an accurate (if not detailed) idea of the main points of your game design, why it's not like the thousands of other games on the market, and why it's fun.

A good way to think about the concept statement for your game is to express it within the confines of a tweet on Twitter: in 140 characters or less, describe everything that is important about your game so that someone who knows nothing about it or you will want to know more. You don't have to worry if you go over that character limit a little, but keeping in mind these guidelines will help you create the statement and choose your words carefully so that you can pack the most punch in your concept statement.

The One Question

Another useful concept closely related to the concept statement is what some game designers call "*The One Question*" (Booth 2011). This isn't, strictly speaking, part of the concept document, but it may appear in or come from your game's concept statement. The idea here is, what *one question* can you use about your game to resolve design questions? For example, if you're making a detailed historical simulation, you might ask about various design features "Is it authentic?" If you're making a game about ninjas, you might ask "Is it stealthy?" This can apply, literally or figuratively, to everything in the game from small features to the user interface.

Jason Booth, game designer on *Guitar Hero* and its successor *Rock Band*, said that the one question about features on *Guitar Hero* was "Does it rock?" If a feature didn't contribute directly to that essential quality of the game, the team left it out. And if they had to decide between two features, they chose the one that rocked more. For example, when choosing between whether players would create their own custom characters or select between premade characters, "Does it rock?" was applied in terms of "Does this make the player feel more like they are the character rocking out?" Creating your own custom look—right down to the eyeliner—is of course a big part of the fantasy of being a rock star.

Booth said that when the team moved on to make *Rock Band*, they had a difficult time settling on the vision because they had all loved working on *Guitar Hero* so much, and yet they "had to reimagine the product in a very different light." As a result, they arrived at the one question "Is it an authentic experience of being in a rock band?" He said, "Once we settled on the one question, a lot of potential arguments over feature directions just went away, because everyone could basically see the dividing line between the two projects" (Booth 2011).

This kind of clarifying question (or statement) can be an enormous help in both getting you to your concise vision and evaluating later ideas and features to see if they belong in the game.

Genre(s)

A game's *genre* is a shorthand way of describing it based on the gameplay conventions used, the types of challenges and choices presented to the player, and often aesthetic, stylistic, or technological aspects of the design. Game genres have no official designations and morph over time or grow subgenres that later split off on their own. A game's genre is thus a heuristic label that typically indicates the kind of interactions that are prevalent in the game: is it a fast-paced action game, a more thoughtful strategic game, an emotion and narrative-driven game, a game where social contact with others is prominent, or some combination of these?

For example, *shooters* are a long-standing subgenre of action games where players typically spend a lot of time shooting things. These games typically rely on fast action using action/feedback and short-term cognitive interactions in a violent, kill-or-be-killed environment—usually actively shooting things as fast as possible. But there are many subtypes of shooters with almost endless qualifiers: a game might be a "2D top-down space shooter" (like *Gratuitous Space Battles*) or a "massively multiplayer bullet-hell co-op shooter" (like *Realm of the Mad God*), among many other possibilities. As a genre matures, there are even games that rethink its tacit assumptions. *Portal* is a good example of this: it's a shooter in that you spend the game shooting things—but unlike just about every other shooter, in *Portal* you don't kill anything, and you use your shooting to solve puzzles rather than just destroy things as fast as possible.

The example of *Portal* highlights an important aspect of discussing your game's genre: while that game is a shooter, it's not like any other shooter, and a lot can get lost in referring to it just by a broad genre. Designers will sometimes toss off a genre name like *shooter* or *strategy* without really considering the ramifications, or even which particular aspects of that genre they are including in their game. Using genre names is helpful but can also lead to lazy design if you're not careful: if you say your game is a strategy game, do you really mean that it has a top-down or isometric camera, or that you command many units, or something else? These are both common features of strategy games, but your game may have little else in common with the rest of the genre.

To be more specific about your design, when you talk about your game's genre, don't just rattle off one or a few labels. Say instead what aspects of a particular genre you mean. For example, you might say, "This game has the multiple-unit control of a strategy game and the fast pace of an action game, and it combines these with the juicy interactions and easy-to-learn aspects of a casual game." Talking about the game this way not only informs others about what you're making but can help you determine whether you're trying to span too many genres at once.

A full list of possible genres would be too extensive—and changes too quickly—to detail here, but the following is a partial and high-level list of common genres:

- **Action:** Action games rely on fast action/feedback loops. They may have story as a backdrop but typically have little in the way of narrative or story as part of the gameplay.

- **Adventure:** These games have many fast action/feedback loop elements but in the context of an overall adventure story that provides the player with longer-term goals as well.

- **Casual:** This is a debated genre because many players of these games play with more than "casual" dedication. Games in this genre are typified by being easy to learn, relying more on a few short-term loops and goals, and tend to have short play sessions. These games rely on action/feedback interactivity loops, but instead of fast-paced adrenaline-fueled action, these games focus on having "juicy" interactions (as described in Chapter 4, "Interactivity and Fun") using bright graphics, clear and easy actions (for example, large colorful buttons), and abundant visual and audio feedback. The "casual" name is also often used to indicate that the game is intended for people who don't consider themselves to be "gamers." While such players may spend hours playing these games, they are typically more interested in gaming as a casual pastime than as a hobby.

- **Idle:** This is a relatively new and often derided genre, yet one that is without question commercially successful and enjoyed by many. In idle games, the player is required to make only a few decisions, and the rest of the time the game effectively "plays itself." While interactivity is not as important in these games as in most others, these games tend to focus on action/feedback—especially in the "clicker" variety, where players simply click as fast as they can as the primary in-game action—along with a small amount of short-term cognitive interaction in solving puzzles and long-term cognitive interactivity in planning strategies. The shallow interactivity is a primary feature of this genre, as the reduced cognitive load relieves the player from having to concentrate on the game. Even with no or minimal player input, the game progresses (often in the player's absence) and provides the player with positive feedback of how much further they have gotten (more money or points accrued, for example) whenever they return. Michael Townsend, creator of *A Dark Room*, an early idle game (with narrative elements), said that his target demographic "was the intersection of People Who Like it When Numbers Go Up and People Who Like Exploring the Unknown" (Alexander 2014). Watching "numbers go up" is a primary attractant in idle games, probably providing a continuous shot of dopamine for the expected reward, at least until that promise fades and the player recognizes that there is no real point to the game besides seeing the numbers go up.

- **MMO:** Short for *massively multiplayer online [game]*, this genre encompasses all those where the player is in a world with many (hundreds or thousands) of other players and where both the player's avatar (typically but not always a single individual) and the world persist even when the player is not actively playing the game. These games have a wide variety of forms of interactivity, with action/feedback interaction being common (for example, in combat, a pervasive feature of these games), along with short- and long-term cognition in planning a character's progression. Social interactivity is extremely important to MMOs, as these games rise and fall on their ability to group and create informal communities within the game.

- **Platformer:** These are games where the player's avatar progresses through the game by jumping from one midair platform to another. The player's main interaction is of the fast action/feedback variety, particularly knowing when and how to jump to keep from falling to an inevitable death. These are a type of action game but are so prevalent that they are often described as their own genre. Platformers go back at least to the video arcades of the 1980s. Their straightforward action/feedback gameplay has remained popular, in part because of how easy it is to pick up, enjoy, and then continue to learn and excel at these games.

- **Rhythm:** These are music-themed games where the gameplay relies on the player's sense of rhythm, musicality, dance, and so on. These games may involve replicating complex dance or musical note sequences, primarily using fast action/feedback interactivity within the context of a song or another rhythmic sequence.

- **Roguelike:** This oddly named genre applies loosely to games that create game maps procedurally. These games typically (but not always) also feature "perma-death," meaning that when you die in the game, you simply lose and must start over. Players expect to die often in these games; the thrill and "deadly precariousness" (Pearson 2013) is part of the appeal. The genre is named for the text game *Rogue*, one of the earliest adventure/role-playing games that created dungeon levels automatically, and in which, when you died, you had to start over. Because the levels were different every time, the game could be played many times without seeming repetitive. Today this designation applies to space exploration, simulation, and other games. These games typically rely on a mixture of action/feedback interactivity (particularly in real-time combat) and long-term cognition for strategically improving the avatar (character, ship, and so on) via skills and equipment in order to meet ever-more-difficult challenges.

- **Role-playing:** In these games, the player takes on a specific role, usually as an individual who pursues heroic adventures. The player may experience the world as a fighter, wizard, pirate, trader, or any of a number of other possible roles, depending on the game. Combat, skill enhancement, and sometimes activities like crafting are mainstays of this genre, relying primarily on action/feedback, short-term cognitive, and long-term cognitive interactions, respectively.

- **Sports and simulation:** These two distinct genres share common underpinnings. Both simulate external or real-world activities with one degree or another of verisimilitude. Games that simulate major sports (football, basketball, golf, and so on) typically use action/feedback, short-term cognition, and long-term cognition interactivity to replicate aspects of the sport as closely as possible. Others primarily rely on short-term and long-term cognition interactions to re-create the experience of running a farm, flying an airplane, or building a city.

- **Strategy:** Much like simulation games, strategy games focus almost exclusively on short- and (especially) long-term interactions to give the player the experience of commanding a large army, running a corporation, or in some other way exercising strategic and tactical planning to achieve a set of goals. While there is action/feedback interactivity as well, that is not the main focus of a strategy game: the game may appear visually unexciting, but this is to serve the goal of using as much of the player's cognitive and interaction budget on long-term cognitive interactivity as possible.

- **Tower defense:** These are related to action and strategy games but have evolved a particular format that is familiar to those who enjoy these games. In tower defense games, the player protects a base or particular objects (such as "life crystals") from waves of opponents. The waves grow larger and more powerful during the game, while the player's defenses—the "towers" in the genre name, though they may take many forms—become more elaborate. In many games, the player is able to construct defenses anywhere in the play area, thus herding the enemies into a particular path of the player's choosing. Typically there is a feedback loop in which the player earns more points/currency for creating new towers or upgrading existing ones based on the number of opponents killed. These games use an effective mix of short- and long-term cognition along with some action/feedback interactivity.

There are, of course, other genres, as well as innumerable combinations of these and other genre designations. For example, there are action-strategy MMO games (such as *World of Tanks*) and probably casual rhythm simulation role-playing games, among many others.

You should be able to find existing games that are similar to yours to help you define its genre. In doing so, beware of designing a game that fits too neatly into a single well-established genre: making a 2D action platformer that is essentially the same as the thousands of other 2D action platformers can make your game less interesting from the outset. This can also lead to lazy design, as you will be less likely to push and find what makes your game truly unique, leaning instead on the genre designation to do the design thinking for you. At the same time, beware of creating genre mashups that are difficult to understand or seem gimmicky. You might really be able to create a bullet-hell narrative-driven strategy shooter, but getting others to understand what that means will be difficult.

Target Audience

As part of defining your game, you need to know who your desired players are. What kinds of players is the game being made for? The description of your target audience includes their psychographics, demographics, and technological/environmental context.

Psychographics and Motivations

One important way to think of your target audience is in terms of their motivations, attitudes, and aspirations. An easy way to get started with this is to describe those who would enjoy your game in terms of other games with similar gameplay: if someone likes "game x," they will also like your game.

A more sophisticated approach is to describe your target audience in terms of their primary motivations related to gameplay. There are many models of player motivations; one of the best—and most based on empirical data—is that created by Quantic Foundry (Matsalla 2016). Based on surveying nearly 300,000 gamers around the world, Quantic Foundry has found six primary motivations:

- **Action:** Destruction and fast-paced, exciting gameplay
- **Social:** Both community and competition (which are not mutually exclusive)
- **Mastery:** Difficult challenges and long-term strategies
- **Achievement:** Completing all missions and becoming powerful
- **Immersion:** Being someone else and experiencing an elaborate story
- **Creativity:** Expressing yourself via crafting and customization, as well as tinkering and exploring

These motivations in turn cluster into three main areas:

- **Action–social:** This includes excitement, competition, and destruction, culminating in a desire to be part of a community.
- **Mastery–achievement:** This includes completion, strategy, and challenge, culminating in the motivation for gaining power.
- **Immersion–creativity:** This includes story, customization, design, and fantasy, culminating in the desire for discovery.

These clusters are shown in Figure 6.1, including the "bridge" motivations for power and discovery that belong in (or reside between) two clusters. According to Quantic Foundry, these clusters can be further abstracted to being thought of as more thoughtful or action-oriented ("cerebral" or "kinetic") and more focused on acting "on the world" or "on other players." This axis is reminiscent of Bartle's player taxonomy model, first suggested in 1996, where he divided up players based on axes of "acting on" versus "interacting with" and "players" versus "world," resulting in quadrants representing achievers (acting on the world), explorers (interacting with the world), socializers (interacting with players), and killers (acting on players) (Bartle 1996). While Bartle's model has not held up to quantitative scrutiny, for many players and game designers, it retains a certain intuitive utility.[2]

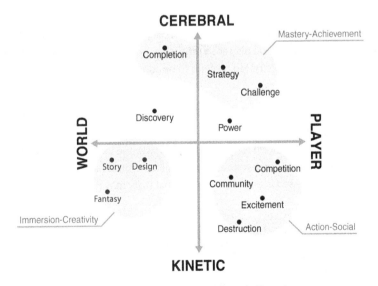

Figure 6.1 The three motivational clusters adapted from Quantic Foundry

_____

2. Recall the aphorism by statistician George Box that "all models are wrong, but some are useful" (Box and Draper 1987).

The clusters shown in Figure 6.1 are present in game populations across cultures and games and correlate with existing research on personality traits as expressed in the widely used Five Factor Model (also known as the "Big 5") (McCrae and John 1992). This model includes five traits that every person has to one degree or another:

- **Neuroticism:** Emotional stability and how much of a tendency an individual has to experience negative emotions

- **Extraversion:** The degree to which an individual seeks the active company of other people and the degree to which they "live out loud" versus being more reserved and reflective

- **Agreeableness:** How friendly and cooperative someone is, versus being antagonistic, untrusting, and aggressive

- **Conscientiousness:** The tendency someone has to being organized, dependable, and having strong self-discipline versus being spontaneous, flexible, or flighty

- **Openness to experience:** How curious and creative someone is, as well as their tolerance for novel experiences, as opposed to pragmatism or having a dogmatic view of the world

Those motivated by action–social motivations tend to be higher on extraversion, or desiring social contact. Players motivated by mastery and achievement tend to be higher on conscientiousness (including ambition and a desire to complete tasks). Finally, those who tend to be motivated by immersion and creativity tend to have high scores for openness to new experiences.

Players tend to choose games that match their own personalities. In the worlds of Quantic Foundry's analysis: "The games we play are a reflection, not an escape, from our own identities. In this sense, people play games not to pretend to be someone they're not, but to become more of who they really are" (Yee 2016b).

By understanding the kind of gameplay you are creating—and, as described in Chapter 4, the kind of interactivity your game provides—you can understand and list the kinds of motivations your players will likely have. Note that, as with the interaction budget, you can use this information to be sure you are not setting up unlikely combinations of motivations: players who want to be immersed in an elegant emotional story may not also want to spend their time blowing stuff up.

Demographics

Along with a psychographic, motivational profile of your players, it is sometimes important to understand their demographics: their age, gender, and context in life. Some game designers create entire persona-stories to describe their players: "Lisa is a divorced woman in her mid-forties with two kids and a career she loves." Describing demographics can be helpful in taking the focus off yourself and your team and putting it on someone else who is not you (and may not share your attitudes and motivations), but it can also be a diversion from considering your player's actual motivations. Unless the number of children players have or the kind of career they have is important to your game, it is best not to spend too much time on details like this.

However, along with psychographics, there are some demographic trends that can be important to consider. For example, the excitement motivation mentioned earlier drops off linearly with age, even becoming an "anti-motivation" in those ages 50 and over. This may help explain why games like *League of Legends* are far more popular with younger gamers than with older ones.

In the same way, the motivation for competition drops off even faster, starting high in the teens and bottoming out by about age 40. During that time, men tend to be more motivated by competition than women, but by about age 45, this difference is gone—that is, it's not a primary motivation for either men or women at that point.

Completion—the desire to finish all the missions or gather all the things—holds pretty steady across ages, and in fact is consistently one of the top three motivations for men and women of any age (Yee 2017).

Environmental Context

Somewhat related to both psychographics and demographics, it can be useful to define your target audience in terms of environmental factors such as the following:

- The technological platform they are likely to play on: dedicated game console, laptop or desktop computer, mobile device, and so on
- The time they have available and potentially environmental factors like "commuters with 10 minutes to spare on the bus" or "dedicated players looking for an immersive all-day experience"
- Their level of technical or game sophistication
- Other factors that may be pertinent to your particular game

Summing Up

In defining your target audience, you should use psychographic, demographic, and environmental and other factors as needed. This is worth serious thought so that your concept of the target audience is clear and doesn't drift over time. Having worked to come up with a clear understanding of your audience, you should be able to create a succinct descriptive statement such as "The target players for this game are those looking for a high-action experience with significant competition supported by some predefined missions (satisfying their desire for completion). These players will typically be interrupt-driven by other factors in life and will appreciate short 10-minute play sessions and an easy learning ramp, combined with the ability to show off their skills and completed missions." Many other descriptions are, of course, possible, based on the particulars of a game design. The point of this is to create a clear but not restricting vision that can help guide your designs and that does not rely on an impossibly broad or overly narrow target audience.

Note that if your answer to the question "Who is your target player?" is "everyone," you have not given enough thought to your game concept or its appeal. No game is universally appealing, and you only make your task more difficult by trying to cast such a wide net. Your concept may have general appeal, but within that there is still an audience in the bull's-eye of your target. Figuring out who your audience is will help you make decisions about your game as you go forward.

Unique Selling Points

The final component of the high-level concept is a short list of *unique selling points* (USPs). In an ever-more-crowded market, it is critical that your game stand out from the rest. You don't need a large number of USPs; having a few (three to five) meaningful brief statements of how your game is uniquely attractive will help you create a higher-quality and more engaging game. Of course, if you are having a difficult time coming up with meaningful USPs, that may well be a sign that you need to rework your overall concept.

One way to think about your game's UPSs is this: no matter how awesome you think your game is, why would someone stop playing a game they already know they like to pick up yours instead? Unfortunately, when starting out, many game designers fall into the trap of believing that because *they* think their game is amazing, everyone else will natural think so, too. Or worse, they think that because it was really difficult to design and build the game, it has to be good, and people will just naturally recognize the passion the team put into it. This never happens. The first step in engaging players is to capture their attention, both visually and in terms of the game's gameplay. Players do not care how much you love the game or how much work you put into it; it has to be interesting and attractive to players.

To make sure your game can catch players' attention, you need to think carefully about what makes your game different and hopefully unique. You can often settle for "fresh"—that is, aspects of your design that may not be entirely new but at least haven't been seen over and over again, and you're presenting them with a new twist. For example, you can probably still make a fun, engaging zombie game—but if you are going to do so, given the huge number of zombie-related games that have been made, there better be something truly unique about it. It might be that a game about rescuing zombies and reverse-infecting them to change them all back might work. But trivial surface changes like "these zombies move fast" or "these zombies are purple" will not make your game stand out.

It's also possible to subvert an existing genre in an entirely new way, as *Portal* did for shooters and *Undertale* did for role-playing games. In cases like this, you take the predominant gameplay tropes from a particular genre—like "in shooters, it's all about destroying things" and change it to be something else, like "but in this game you shoot to navigate and solve puzzles." This is more difficult to do than it is to use some existing aspects of an applicable genre and take the game in new directions—perhaps a narrative game with some action elements, if you can make that work, or an idle game that somehow escapes becoming a soul-numbing click or tap exercise.

In general, though, you want to find the elements of your design that make your game truly different from others. The more new and unique your game is, the more easily you will be able to differentiate it from other games. At the same time, just as with combining genres, the game still has to be recognizable to players; otherwise, they will dismiss it as unintelligible as quickly as they would dismiss it for being too conventional.

The necessity of finding a short list of USPs for your game is another reason taking the time to design the game concept is so important. If you stop with the first idea you think of, it is not likely to be unique in any meaningful way. Thinking about your game concept in terms of USPs can be an effective way to see whether you can articulate what makes it worth spending the time and effort to develop the game. No game is easy to create, and to justify making one, you need something more than "it sounds cool to me."

X-statements

Another way some designers like to think about USPs is with *x-statements*. These have two commonly used definitions that both serve the same purpose. The first is to define what the game's "x-factor" is—what makes it special, different, and uniquely engaging? The answer to this question is typically a short list of USPs.

Alternatively, some designers like to use statements with an "A x B" structure ("A crossed with B"—sometimes said as "A meets B") to create a new, unique game idea out of existing ones. So, for example, you could say "this game is like *The Division* x *Overwatch*" or "*GTA* meets *Undertale*." Matching up two games like that can create whole new, fresh takes on what had seemed like familiar creative territory.

Caveats

While unique selling points are crucial for your design, whether in list or x-statement form, they need to be handled with care. USPs are sometimes used as a crutch for lazy game design. As with x-statements, the thinking goes that if you combine the USPs of other existing games—a few from one game and a few from another—you will create a wonderful hybrid. This almost never works. USPs have to support a coherent game vision, not form a monstrous agglomeration of unrelated points.

In addition, despite the word *selling* in USP, these primarily enable you to more fully and clearly understand and communicate your game design concept. The emphasis needs to remain on the aspects of your game design that make it attractive and engaging in new ways—not on what will make the game sell. These are related, but if you move too quickly to considerations of sales, the design will suffer. It is important to design a good game that will sell, not try to design a game that will sell and that you hope is still good.

Product Description

The high-level concept of the game outlined in the preceding sections needs to be supported by a product-oriented description in the concept document. This description provides an overview of the player's experience in the game and the game systems that support the overall vision. These are typically separated into the following sections:

- Player experience
- Visual and audio style
- Game world fiction
- Monetization
- Technology, tools, and platform
- Scope

It's useful to have pointers (web-based links or at least document references) from the overall concept document to the more specific design documents that focus on particular areas referenced in the concept document. As mentioned earlier in this chapter, the concept document is like the tip of the iceberg, with additional details available in detail design documents via links for those who want them. These documents and their contents are covered in Chapter 7, "Creating Game Loops," and Chapter 8, "Defining Game Parts."

Player Experience

Understanding the experience you want your players to have is a key part of the overall game concept. This should be one of the primary outputs of blue-sky/brainstorming process. In the concept document, the player experience has its own section, usually limited to a few short paragraphs. The information here includes a description of the player's fantasy, key moments as examples of gameplay, and a brief discussion of what the game comes to mean to the player.

What Is the Fantasy?

The concept document makes clear what the player's point of view is in the game and what *fantasy* the game supplies. That is, within the game, is the player a heroic knight, a sneaking thief, a starship captain, a single mother trying to keep her family together, or something else entirely—a small single-celled organism or the disembodied leader of a galactic empire? Each of these provides a different kind of player experience and the realization of a different fantasy.

Typically game fantasies are aspirational: roles or situations the player might like to be in but is unlikely to experience, like being captain, mayor, a brave fighter, or a wise wizard. Occasionally the fantasy is being in a difficult situation and trying to make the best of it—as in *The Last of Us*, for example. And sometimes the fantasy is simply stepping into someone else's shoes: that of a girl investigating what happened at her house in *Gone Home* or that of a family of your own devising in *The Sims*. Each game makes its own magic circle and enables the player to have a novel, separate, nonconsequential experience within the safety of its bounds.

Another useful aspect of the game's fantasy is what Spry Fox game designer Daniel Cook calls the game's *entrance*. The player should understand immediately on starting the game what they are doing and why this is interesting. Cook's recommendation is to use this as a tool to shape your own thinking about how the player begins the game and what they do in it and to validate the concept and the fantasy of the game by talking with potential players. In such a situation, you give a player the game's concept statement and then ask *them* to tell *you* about the game: what do they expect they would do, where would they start, how would it end—and would they find that worthwhile? If the potential player cannot begin to build a mental model of the game that they can relate to you, or if what they say doesn't fit your concept of the game, then you have some significant work to do. On the other hand, if the player immediately understands the fantasy of the game and takes it largely in the same direction your design does, then you are off to a good start. Keep in mind that while this is a useful technique, you should keep it informal and not fall into the trap of trying to have players design the game for you. This is a test of your concept, not a way to get out of doing the hard work of designing the game.

In terms of your own strengths as a designer, it may be that you come to understand the player's point of view and fantasy from the storyteller's vantage point by considering the overall game experience first, or it may emerge from the toymaker's view, by figuring out how to take a set of game mechanics and unify them within an overarching experience. No matter how you come to this point, you must, as part of designing the game's concept and the product vision, create a cohesive description of the player experience. This should also reflect (and be reflected by) the game's overall concept statement and its USPs.

Key Moments

An important and useful way to communicate the player's experience is to tell a few brief anecdotes about *key moments* in the game—when they occur, how they keep the player engaged, and how they make the player feel. (You may get some of these from what the players relate to you about the game's fantasy.) These key moments illustrate the player's experience at different stages of play—when they are first learning, when they have become a regular, and when they have mastered the game—and relate the experience from the points of view of players with different motivations.

To experience these key moments, create a few different player personas that represent archetypal players with different motivations and situations: the experienced player, the hurried player, the uncertain player, and so on. Which personas make sense will depend on the game concept and design. For each, identify situations in the game that represent important events: their first real victory and their first defeat; how the game opens up to them in a new way when they reach level 50 or build their second castle or acquire their first motor scooter;

what happens when they first play with another player online; and so on. As with Cook's entrance-testing method, don't neglect the game opening; many game designers believe that the first 300 seconds—the first 5 minutes in the game—is where the player becomes engaged or not. You probably don't need to map out all 5 minutes of gameplay but find the key moments in there that you believe (and will later test) will engage the player and encourage them to keep going.

Your design documents should tell the story of the key moments in text and rough drawings. These help you more fully understand your game concept from the point of view of different players, and as development continues, they help you remember why you have made some of the design decisions you have—or you can test new options against these personas and key moments.

You may want to create more key moments than you include in the concept document and to point to the additional ones kept in their own separate document. Having a few select moments in the concept document helps the reader understand the game better and provides a pointer for those who want to explore further.

Emotions and Meaning

The sum of the player's experience with your game is how it makes them feel. If your game engenders no emotional response, it will not engage players. This doesn't mean that your game has to tug on players' heartstrings or make them see the world in a whole new way, but you must be able to identify *some* form of emotional component to the game as a whole: the player feels a sense of achievement, of having breathlessly escaped disaster, or even just that (as in many action-puzzle games like *Tetris*) they still died, but they did better than last time (or worse, but they're sure they can do better next time!).

Of course, some games consciously set the player up to feel various more subtle emotions: loss, hope, gratitude, inclusion, revulsion, the list is nearly endless—and as discussed in Chapter 4, we as game designers have barely started exploring it. If your game depends on emotional interactivity in particular, you need to carefully design the player's experience, the key moments, and the systems that support these to enable the emotional ride and response you want the player to experience. This won't just happen; as with anything else in a game, you have to create the space within which the player may, if he chooses, approach the experience you have enabled.

Closely related to the question "What does the player feel while playing?" is the thornier question of meaning. Does your game create any lasting meaning for the player? Consider that even a game like *Monopoly* is rife with meaning: it teaches a particular model of how to get rich and what it means to be successful. What does a shooter compared a game like *This War of Mine* teach about war? What meaning about relationships do games like *Firewatch*, *Gone Home*, or *The Sims* convey?[3]

You can choose to create a game that is light on meaning and is just a fun bit of entertainment. (*Candy Crush* seems to have little in the way of meaning beyond its immediate sensory and puzzle-solving delights; it's certainly not offering commentary on candy consumption.) But you have the opportunity to determine if there is some meaning you want players to derive from your game. This is as worth considering carefully as are your overall concept, USPs, and the rest of the player experience.

Visual and Audio Style

An important part of understanding and explaining the game concept is being able to communicate the look and feel it will embody. In the concept document, it's helpful to describe the intent of the art style and how it supports the overall concept and desired game experience. This can be done qualitatively in words—for example, "the game has a light, airy feel with bright colors that are not too saturated" or "the game's visual tone is pervasively dark and grim, with grays and stark shadows predominating on low-poly scenes"—as long as the words are also accompanied by a few images of concept or reference art.

If original concept images exist, they should be included directly or by reference to an external document. Reference art can also be used. This is a polite term for art from other sources— games, movies, magazines, book covers, and so on—that you will not be using in the game but that is helpful early in the process for defining the look of the game. This kind of usage typically falls under "fair use" of copyrighted material owned by others: you should *never* include anything owned by someone else in your game without explicit permission, but gathering reference art from other sources is perfectly acceptable. In addition to art used in or referenced by the concept document, many projects put together what are known as "mood boards"— large public displays (on a bulletin board or similar) of reference art and concept art so that everyone on the team can get an idea of the tone and mood of the game.

The game's audio, both music and sound effects, is at least as important as the visual aspects. Effective use of sound and music can greatly enhance the player's experience, complementing and unifying the visual art used. While it is difficult to include audio samples in a concept document (though audio links can and should be used in online docs), as with visual art, qualitative language can be used to describe the audio style: "the game's theme music is simple but evocative, played on a single violin or similar" or "the audio in the game has themes

---

3. Will Wright, designer of ground-breaking games like *SimCity* and *The Sims*, said to me in 2001 that part of the original "meaning" of *The Sims* was that time is the only nonrenewable resource we have. We can always get more money, but we can never get more time. In that game, as you purchased more things, there was a greater probability that your Sims would be spending their time fixing something rather than doing anything else—in very real effect, they would become owned by their things rather than the reverse. This is admittedly a subtle message many people did not get, though variations on it did come through to many players.

of electronic distortion throughout, fitting the dark visual tone and creating a foreboding atmosphere." As with visual art, audio reference art can and should be used to give the team (and other stakeholders outside the team) a better understanding of the audio style and the desired overall game experience.

Each of these visual and audio elements should be covered in detail in the game's *style guide*. This guide should not be part of the concept document, but it should be referenced (and ideally pointed to) by this document. The style guide itself may not be completed until close to the time the game enters production (see Chapter 12 for a description of production phases), but it should still be referenced here.

Game World Fiction

It is helpful at the level of the concept document to have a brief description of the game's backstory and the world in which the players finds themselves. This does not mean you should include pages and pages of intricate details of the world, but you should give the reader an idea of the world contemplated by the game design. For example, the game world fiction might be as simple as "The player is an amoeba trying to find its way home" or "the player is a star pilot who has crash-landed on a world where magic works and technology doesn't." A few more sentences to sketch out the game's backstory—what has happened to lead to the point where the game begins—and potentially a map of the game's territory and a brief description of major non-player characters will help enhance the description of the game as a product. These also provide a jumping-off point for more detailed design during development.

Monetization

All commercial games have to make money. It used to be that game designers didn't have to concern themselves with this messy capitalistic reality, but in the days of many business models for selling games, this is no longer the case: the description of your game as a product has to include some thought about how it will make back the money needed to create it, plus a profit.

When defining your game as a product, you need to include a brief definition and discussion of how you will sell the game. Business models for games continue to evolve, but at minimum you will want to consider one (or more) of these methods of monetization:

- **Premium pricing:** This includes games with a single price, paid once when the player acquires the game. This is the venerable and formerly typical model, but it is no guarantee: in today's market, players are strangely reluctant to pay even $1 (in U.S. markets) for a game, much less the $20 or $60 that games used to routinely cost. Outside of games with development and marketing budgets ranging into the tens of millions of dollars, few games that depend on premium pricing become hits that earn back their development costs.

- **Free to play (F2P):** The predominant model for games today, particularly on mobile devices, is the F2P model. These games may be played entirely for free—forever. The player doesn't have to pay anything. However, these games are typically designed to encourage players to make purchases—and some are quite aggressive about it. Some allow players to view an advertisement video instead of making a direct purchase as well. If your game is going to be F2P, you need to think about how you will integrate this with the design from the very beginning; it is not something you can add at the last minute.

- **Limited-play pricing:** A variation on the premium pricing model is allowing a player to play for free up to a point. In some cases, the player can play the first few levels (or similar) and then must buy the full game in order to continue. This used to be a common method of getting people to "try before you buy," but since the advent of F2P, it is less common.

- **Downloadable content (DLC):** Similar to limited-play pricing, some games have additional DLC that can be purchased separately from the game and that enhances the game experience. The question for many developers is whether the DLC they provide could have reasonably been added to the original game or whether the players perceive it as having been held back for additional revenues later.

- **Ad supported:** Some games are free but display ads to players. This model is often attractive to game developers because it lets them give their games away for free but without having to design in F2P features. Unfortunately, the revenue from ads in games is usually paltry at best; this means that unless you have millions of people playing your game regularly, you are unlikely to see significant revenue from this type of monetization model.

There are, of course, other monetization models, including ones that have yet to be invented! You may also be creating a game for a client, or to be funded by a grant, or you may be in some other situation in which monetization isn't a factor in your product design or in the experience of the game. Noting this in the concept document will forestall any questions in the future and help complete the vision for the game.

Technology, Tools, and Platforms

As part of planning your game as a product, you need to specify the technology needed to develop it and make it run. Assuming that you are making a digital rather than analog/tabletop game, you will need a variety of technologies, tools, and platform specifications to develop your game. The following list is not exhaustive but will give you a good starting point for defining the technological needs for your game as a product:

- **Hardware and operating system:** Your game will have to run on a computer (generally speaking, one running Windows or MacOS; Linux is a possibility, of course, but isn't commercially viable as a mainstay). Or you may target smart phones or tablets (iOS or Android operating systems) or rigs requiring virtual reality or augmented/mixed reality hardware. Whatever you decide will have significant consequences for the game's development, so you need to be clear about this from the start.

- **Development tools:** Will you be using a game development environment like Unity or Unreal Engine or something else? Tools can save you a great deal of time and effort, but you have to know how to use them. They also have their own costs and downsides that you should consider as you choose them.

- **Server and networking:** Many games are strictly single player and so don't have any server or networking needs. Still, this is something you should define from the beginning and take into account during development.

- **Monetization and advertising:** If you are going to run ads in your game or support in-game monetization, you need to integrate with ad and payment servers. You may not need to know specifically how you will do this at the concept stage, but you should know whether you plan to make this part of your product.

- **Localization:** Much as with monetization, you should consider from the very start of your development whether your game will be in one language only or whether you plan on offering it in global markets. If you have any plans at all to localize the game for different language markets, you should decide and define this from the start; it is extremely difficult to retrofit localization once development has begun.

You may not know the answers to all these questions during the concept phase of product planning, but you should be able to give answers to most of these—and add the rest to your list of questions to figure out quickly.

Scope

By looking over the concept and product design portions of the concept document, you should begin to get an idea of the *scope* of your game: how many people are needed, how many different skill sets you require, and how long it will take to develop it. The more art and content the game needs, the more systems that have to be created and balanced, and the more items that have to be developed for monetization and localization, the bigger the scope of the project.

In general, you want to limit the scope of any project you are on, *especially* if this is your first game project. Even executive producers on huge hundred-plus-person teams struggle with and try to limit game scope—and if you are limited at all in terms of time or budget, you need to be ruthless in your prioritization and what will be included in the game.

Detailed Design

Whereas the concept and product sections describe high-level plans for the game, the detailed design section forecasts some of the more specific aspects of the game design. These have necessarily not been built yet, so what you say here is predicting the future—and will thus be wrong to some degree. This is nevertheless and important part of understanding what your game is and how you will build it.

Core Loops

We have discussed the idea of *core loops* a few times already, and we will be diving into them in detail in Chapter 7. For your concept document, you should have some idea of the kinds of activities the players will be doing in your game, especially those they will be doing the most, over and over, moment by moment: is it mostly combat, constructing buildings, gathering flower petals, or something else entirely? You should also be able to discuss why this set of core loops is engaging and supports players' objectives and goals in the game.

Objectives and Progression

Closely related to your game's core loops are the players' objectives in the game and how they progress through it. This includes the players' journey from tutorial to mastery and across any spatial extent (for example, traversing a map), if any. It's also useful to sketch the primary progression vectors for the players: do they increase in money, skill, reputation, magical power, provinces owned, crew size, or other dimensions?

To support these progression dimensions, you need to construct immediate, short-term, and long-term goals for players. These must be supported by the rest of the detailed design, particularly the core loops, narrative, and main game systems.

These goals and objectives in turn need to support the player fantasy and the kind of experience you outlined in the concept section: if the game is about being an assassin, raising hedgehogs may be a poor fit for a game objective. Or if the game is about building a vast empire, you need to briefly describe what the player is doing moment-by-moment so that the game remains engaging.

Finally, if the game is set up to support the player's own implicit goals (rather than just explicit ones created by the game itself), note how this is done. If a player can become a master crafter in a game that is primarily about combat, note this as part of the overall potential objectives and progression.

Narrative and Main Systems

If there is a narrative that drives the game, briefly describe it in the concept document. You may want to refer to the world fiction outlined earlier. Whereas the history or backstory is backward-looking, though, the game narrative is about what happens during the game, particularly in terms of events in which the players participate (or that happen to them). This is not the place to develop the entire narrative, but you should refer or point from a brief overview here to a document where the details can be found.

In the same way, and often related to the game's core loops, you should briefly describe the main game systems: physical or magical combat, an economy, ecology, political systems, and so on. Note also which of these the player interacts with directly and which reside solely within the game's model of the world; for example, there may be political machinations happening in the background of the game, but if the player cannot affect them directly, then note that this is the case.

Interactivity

As a more precise part of the visual and audio style for the game, as described above, the concept document should briefly discuss the primary forms of interaction the game will use.

In particular, does the player interact via mouse only, keyboard and mouse, game controller, touch interface, gaze detection, or something else?

A brief comment on how the game spends its interactivity budget is also welcome: is the game mainly about fast-paced (or more casual and juicy) action/feedback, short- or long-term cognition (puzzles, tactics, and strategy), emotional, social, or cultural interactions? Whatever the desired mix of these forms of interaction, how does the game accomplish it visually and with sound? While this is not the place for a detailed user interface description, you should provide some description of the game's primary interaction methods. Also include how these methods support the desired gameplay experience and how these interactions provide sufficient verbs and feedback for the player's actions to affect the game's systems (see Chapters 7 and 8).

At this stage, the entire user interface is not likely to be complete. Nevertheless, in this section provide at least a screen mockup and a list of interactions that are not visible on the screen (typed, gestural, or mouse-based) to round out the understanding of the game's concept and interactivity.

Designing the Game+Player System

The process of coming up with, articulating, and refining your game design concept is a vital step toward developing the game you want to see and have others experience. Ultimately, this is an exercise in designing the system in which both the game and player are parts. By their interactions, they form the larger game+player system. This can happen only if the player continues to play, meaning that the game is comprehensible and enjoyable and that the player's experience is engaging and fun.

At this conceptual stage of design, it is essential to ensure that your overall game idea is clear and consistent. If others cannot understand the vision, it will be muddled to the players as well—if you are even successful at developing it into a game.

Keeping to the Theme

Creating a viable, understandable vision and concept for your game acts as both an important frame and constraint for your game design and as a sort of scaffolding or connective tissue for it. The thematic elements of your game—the "whole" of the game experience—should touch everything in the game. If there is a system or token that doesn't derive meaning from the theme or doesn't support it, then it either needs to be removed or altered to fit the game. Conversely, by making sure your theme is consistent and represented throughout the game, the parts, loops, and whole will all be aligned and unified, all working together to provide the player with the engaging experience needed to form the higher-level game+player system.

Elegance, Depth, and Breadth

Now that you understand the necessity of the game concept and vision, let's revisit the ideas of elegance, depth, and breadth in a game. A game with a clear and consistent vision that is carried all through its systems, tokens, and rules—from the whole to the loops and parts—and that manages to avoid special cases and exceptions in those rules will feel elegant to the player. It will fulfill Bushnell's Law of being easy to learn but difficult to master, as the player will be able to form a viable mental model early on that serves them well, without major adjustments, as they continue to learn and master the game. Learning such a game is subjectively almost effortless, and each aspect learned adds to the player's progression and feeling of mastery, and the player does not have to mentally step out of playing the game to consider how to remember an exception or a seemingly contradictory rule.

How long it takes to truly master a game depends on its systemic depth and feature breadth. If the game has a measure of elegance, it will typically have systems within systems as the mainstay of its design. These will be organized such that early learning is applicable to (rather than undone by) later mastery. Even with a few relatively simple systems in place, the navigable space for play set up by the game design—and thus the complexity of the player's resulting mental model—can be enormous. This space is perceived as great, often unfathomable depth in the game. Players motivated by exploration of the rules and eventual mastery of the game will gladly remain engaged with it as long as they are able to continue expanding their mental model within the mental budget of their cognition, emotion, and interactions.

Many games provide a great deal of breadth by adding more features to the game—more ways to engage with the same content or underlying systems. This is sometimes a substitute for systemic depth, as when a game adds mountains of content to try to keep the player engaged rather than creating systems and depth that do not require so much content creation. In other cases, the scope of the game requires and benefits from a broad palette of features. These might be in the form of multiple character classes the player can try out, vehicles or combat systems to master, or a wide range of resource, economic, political, and combat systems that all interact together. Many "grand strategy" games follow this method.

Broad games may also have systemic depth. The best even retain some amount of elegance, though adding both breadth and depth to a game almost inevitably adds exceptions and special-case rules that increase the difficulty of learning the game. Just the number of features to which the player has to attend increases the difficulty of constructing a mental model. Both of these factors limit the elegance in a big, broad, and deep game. However, players who want that kind of experience aren't necessarily looking for effortless elegance, so this isn't necessarily a failing in the game design; it all depends on the desired experience for the target audience.

Questions to Consider About Your Design Vision

When reviewing your game's concept, there are questions you can consider to help make sure you have a clear and complete understanding sufficient to create a context for the game's loops and parts. The answers to these questions for any game will be different, but considering each for your game will help you clarify your conceptual design. It is helpful to return to these often while developing a game to make sure the design remains where you want it rather than drifting over time.

- What is your concept statement—in just a sentence or two? Does this statement capture all the important elements of your game? Do you have a "One Question" test for features based on the game's concept?

- Who is your game made for? What are the motivations of those in your audience? What other games do those who play your game also enjoy? Are there significant external or environmental factors that affect how someone plays your game (for example, they play during their commute or will need to set aside an entire day for it)?

- What key features or aspects of gameplay set your game apart from all others? Why would one of your target players—someone who already enjoys this kind of game—stop playing an existing one and play yours instead? What will attract players' interest initially, and what about the game design will engage them over time?

- What are the hallmarks of the player's experience of playing your game? How would you characterize this in terms of motivations and emotions?

- Does the experience of the game seem intentional to the player? Is the game a cohesive whole, or is it a poorly matched patchwork of different concepts and systems?

- Do players come to a feeling of mastery, or at least increased competence in playing your game? How do they know they are progressing in their skill with your game?

- How does the art—the visuals and sound—for your game support the game's concept and its gameplay? Does the art set the game apart from others like it?

- What systems in the game directly support the game concept and the player's experience?

- What forms of interactivity does the game use that support the player's experience? Are there extraneous or obscure interactions that tax the player's cognitive resources?

- Does the game *mean* anything to the player? Does the game have a heart—does it engender any emotions in the player? Not all games have to have a deep meaning, but it is useful to consider this—and ask this of players when playtesting, to see if their meaning matches your intended vision.

Summary

This chapter has begun the practical side of systemic game design: creating the concept for the game and conceiving of an intentional, consistent, and clear whole. This includes the process of coming up with your game concept via blue-sky design and then refining that idea into a coherent vision of the game experience you hope to provide to your players.

This process leads to a detailed walk-through of the concept document, with its high concept, product, and detailed design sections. Creating this brief document as a pointer to more detailed aspects of the game design helps bring the whole design together and acts as a unifying influence on it throughout development.

It is not necessary to start with the concept stage and the vision of the whole, but you cannot really design or develop a game without it. Until you understand the framework for what you are building, you will be wandering in your design and development efforts. Many game designers therefore attack the concept first. But if you see yourself more as an inventor or a toymaker than a storyteller, this may not seem like a natural starting place to you. That's okay—just make sure you have gone through the steps in this chapter to create and clarify your vision before you jump into developing your game.

CHAPTER 7

CREATING GAME LOOPS

Systems consisting of looping interactions between parts are the primary means of generating the interactive gameplay experience. In this chapter we revisit loops (first introduced in Chapter 2, "Defining Systems"), including a new look at the four principal loops in game design (introduced in Chapter 4, "Interactivity and Fun").

This chapter also defines the main kind of game system loops and discusses some examples. This is followed by a discussion of the goals, tools, and issues related to systemic game loops and how to create and document your game systems.

More Than the Sum of the Parts

In Chapter 1, "Foundations of Systems," we discussed different kinds of thinking and the idea of a unified whole being other than, or more than, the sum of its parts. This is one of the central notions behind systems thinking and systemic design: that by connecting parts together to form loops, we can create emergent wholes that are not simply the additive compound of the parts but that have entirely new and ultimately engaging properties not found in any of the parts on their own.

In this chapter, we explore in detail how connecting parts together in different ways, via their behaviors, creates the loops that support and in a very real sense create the whole discussed in Chapter 6, "Designing the Whole Experience." In Chapter 8, "Defining Game Parts," we cover how to construct parts to be able to build these loops. This chapter sits in the middle of the systemic design process, much as loops sit between individual parts and the created aggregate whole. As such, while the book is linear, this chapter works together with Chapters 6 and 8 (covering wholes and parts, respectively), much as a system has to loop together to work.

Creating effective loops from interacting parts in order to construct a desired whole experience is often referred to as "systems design" in game development circles. While creating systems intentionally includes far more than just making a combat system or crafting system, it is these kinds of systems that drive the game design and the player's experience. By approaching game design from an intentional, systemic point of view, you can create better systems and more engaging games.

A Brief Review of Loops

Recall from Chapter 2 that collections of parts can be simple, complicated, or complex: those that don't really affect each other are like fruit in a bowl, sitting by one another without significant effects. Those connected linearly form processes that may be complicated (refer to Figure 2.5), but you need interactions between parts that loop back on themselves to make complex systems (refer to Figure 2.6). This characteristic of parts forming loops is what enables the creation of emergent effects and, for our purposes, interesting gameplay.

Reinforcing and Balancing Loops

Looping structures fall into two broad categories: the first is those where the interactions *reinforce* the state of the parts within the loop, such as earning interest on a bank account balance (refer to Figure 2.7)—but also seemingly negative things, like the spread of a disease through a population. That is, reinforcing loops are sometimes called "positive feedback" loops, but it's important to remember that what these loops do is reinforce the quality represented by the state of the parts; this effect may be either positive or negative.

The second kind of loop is the *balancing* loop. In these loops, the effect of one part on another eventually causes all the parts to approach a balance point. A thermostat or an oven is a common example: as the oven heats up due to a temperature gap between its current temperature and the desired setting, less heat has to be applied. Eventually the gap approaches zero, and little or no additional heat needs to be applied (refer to Figure 2.8). Other examples include how predators and prey balance each other in ecologies and how increasing the points needed to gain a new level in many RPGs balances the time it takes to acquire that level.

Most balancing loops, particularly in games, result in dynamic rather than static balance. The mechanical spinning governor shown in Chapter 1 (refer to Figure 1.7) and Chapter 2 (refer to Figure 2.4) is a good physical example of a dynamic balancing loop: as the throttle opens, the engine spins faster, which causes the weights to fly outward, which in turn causes the throttle to close—which causes the engine to spin more slowly, thus causing the weights to fall, which opens the throttle again. As the engine operates, the throttle continues to open and close, and the weights rise and fall, keeping the engine in a dynamic balance within an acceptable range (neither too fast nor too slow).

Using Loops in Game Design

Reinforcing and balancing loops have different kinds of overall effects that can be used in game design. Reinforcing loops reward winners by creating runaway, or "rich get richer," situations. In the game *Monopoly*, having more money lets you buy more property, which leads to your gaining more money. This creates a divergence between players that can be useful but can also destroy the engagement for both winning and losing players: for those winning, as the gap widens, they have to attend less and less carefully to the game to keep winning. For the losers, they have fewer and fewer options that will enable them to win. For both, the gameplay space collapses to the point where the player has fewer decisions to make (fewer choices that will affect the state of the game significantly), the game ceases to be psychologically engaging, and thus it is no longer fun.

Balancing loops decrease the difference between players: they may forgive losers or punish winners, or some combination, in order to keep both in competition. Many games have a turn-taking mechanic whereby when one person or team scores, the other is given an advantage—control of the ball, as in American football and basketball. In *Power Grid*, the player in the best position goes last, creating an ongoing dynamic balancing loop that counteracts the other reinforcing loops of gaining money and buying better power plants and cities in the game.

Parts as Loop Components

As discussed in Chapter 2, parts within loops take on different roles, along with objects passed between them via the parts' behaviors. It is vital that you understand these and how they create functional loops; this is what building game systems is based on.

Resources are, generally speaking, objects passed between parts in a loop. They are in-game tokens, as discussed in Chapter 3, "Foundations of Games and Game Design"—representative objects used in the game as its "nouns." A resource may be gold given to a vendor, money paid for property, mana points used to cast a spell, or water in a bathtub. Generally speaking, anything that is countable in a game is a resource, especially if it is created, destroyed, stored, or exchanged within the game. We will discuss resources in more detail in Chapter 8.

Resources can be *simple* or *complex*. Simple resources like gold, wood, and mana, are in essence elemental and commodified: a gold piece doesn't break down into smaller parts of different types, and one gold piece is as good as another. Complex resources are assembled from the combination of simpler ones and may have different properties (typically assigned by the game rather than being emergent on their own). A sword may be assembled out of simple wood and metal resources, and then the sword can be used, sold, stored, and so on, and it may have different properties from another constructed sword.

It's possible to build up *production chains* of resources, too, such that wood and metal become swords and armor, and adding those to conscripts gives you an army—its own complex resource. Many games that feature crafting (for example, *Terraria* or *Banished*) create a great deal of systemic depth by having long chains of combinations of different resources that enable the creation of increasingly functional and powerful objects.

Currencies are a type of resource often passed between parts in a loop. The key difference between most resources and currencies is that non-currency resources are consumed in any conversion or transaction: you might use wood and metal as resources to create a weapon in a crafting system, but the wood and metal are consumed (or converted) in doing so. A currency resource is exchanged but not consumed: when the player pays gold for a weapon, the gold does not become the weapon; the person from whom the player purchased the weapon presumably uses the gold as currency for some other need of his own. In many game economies, the gold simply vanishes in a sink, as shown in Figure 2.3 and as discussed later in this chapter, but in terms of the simulation, it is assumed to have been spent on something else.

Sources are where resources come from. This might be some specific place or part, like a gold mine being a source for gold, or conceptual, like killing monsters being a source for experience points. In many games, sources create resources *ex nihilo*—out of nothing. While you could model how much gold is contained in the ground and how long it will take to remove it, unless that's the point of your game, it would only add cognitive load to your game without making it more enjoyable.

Stocks are containers for resources.[1] Resources *flow* from their source (or from another stock) to a stock at a certain rate until some limit is reached (refer to Figure 2.2). The stock's state is the

---

1. The use of "stock" may be unfamiliar to some in this context as a container for a resource. This comes from the early days of systems thinking and has persisted in the field. For our purposes, think of a "stock pond" containing fish or a "stock yard" for animals, or even how much stock a store has on its shelves. Some game developers use the term "pool" for this concept.

amount of a resource it contains at any given moment, and its behavior is the rate of flow from it to another part in the system. The resource in the stock might be money in a bank account, hit points on a character, the population of a town, and so on. Some stocks have a maximum limit (like the water in a bathtub), while others don't (like the amount of money you can have in a bank account).

Converters are objects or processes in a game that transform, or convert, one kind of resource into another or into a different sort of object. Note that the original resource vanishes as part of the conversion, while the new resource is created. Converters are a common basic type of verb in a game's structure: how something goes from being one thing to another.

A converter can be as abstract and simple as a magic box that takes lumps of iron in one side and puts out steel (another simple resource) or a sword (a complex resource) on the other. Or, the process might be more complex, with multiple inputs and outputs; to make a sword might require metal, wood, tools, skill, and time—all possible in-game resources—which produce both the sword and waste (slag, heat, and so on). A more detailed conversion process may provide more gameplay (how does the player deal with the buildup of waste around the ironworks?), or it may be an unnecessary detail that only adds to the player's mental load and doesn't provide any real gameplay value. This is something you need to decide as you design the system and the game.

Deciders, or decision points, are representations of logical branches in a system, where a flow may go one way or another, depending on internal logic, the amount of a given resource, or other external conditions. You want to keep the conditions for a decider as local to the part as possible—that is, as close to its level of organization as possible. Sometimes a decision point will depend on conditions at one level higher or lower in the system hierarchy, but greater hierarchical distance than this should be avoided to avoid making the overall system more brittle, as explained later in this chapter.

Sinks are the opposite of sources: resources flow out to them. In some contexts, *sources* are called *faucets*, and *sinks* are called *drains*—but we don't care where the resource (for example, water) comes from as long as it comes out of the faucet. And we don't care where it goes as long as it goes down the drain.[2]

Iconography

As shown in Figure 7.1, the components within a looping system—sources, stocks, converters, deciders, and sinks are often shown with a particular, quasi-alchemical iconography: the upward-pointing triangle for sources, circles for stocks, a triangle with a line through it for

---

2. This is not a particularly ecologically responsible view in the real world, but in creating game systems, it can be useful to consider anything beyond the source or sink as being outside the system and to not worry about the dynamics of any larger system context.

converters, diamond for deciders, and downward-pointing triangles for sinks. The amount in a stock may be shown as individual resource tokens, by shading depicting how full the stock is, or by some other means. This particular iconography is adopted from Joris Dormans (Adams and Dormans 2012), the author of the online system-diagramming tool *Machinations*. The iconography and functionality in that tool is quite a bit more detailed than what is shown here, but it's not necessary to learn all of it to make use of these concepts in creating systems and system diagrams. These graphics are by no means universal or prescriptive (note that the "converter" icon used in Figure 2.4 is different from the one used here), but they are useful in many cases.

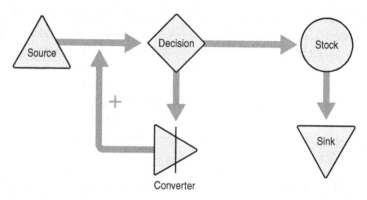

Figure 7.1 Common iconography for sources, stocks, converters, and sinks and flow between them. The functional meaning of diagrams like this is explored in this chapter

The Four Principal Loops

Building on the concepts of reinforcing and balancing loops, it's useful to keep in mind four principal kinds of conceptual loops that as game designers have to be concerned about:

- The game's model loop
- The player's mental loop
- The interactive loop
- The designer's loop

These have been discussed in earlier chapters, and we will reference them again here as a way of leading into a more specific discussion of loops within a game design.

The Game's Model Loop

As examined in Chapter 3—and also this chapter—a game has its own internal model of the world. This model is necessarily dynamic and looping so that the player can interact with it; if the model were static or linearly connected, there would be no interactivity and no gameplay. The game's dynamic model is what creates the game world as experienced by the player, and it is what creates the space for gameplay. If there are only a few viable paths through the game world, then the probability space for the game is narrow; the player has few if any meaningful decisions to make. When this happens, there is ultimately no gameplay, there is no engagement, and there is no fun. Developing the game's model via second-order design creates the space for player exploration, and thus sets up engagement and fun.

The game's model of the world is the combination of all the game systems as defined by the designer. We will examine different kinds of systems that create this model. Broadly speaking, they are represented by engines, economies, and ecologies. From these, we get many different kinds of common game systems, such as progression, combat, inventory, skill, quest, and other systems.

The Player's Mental Loop

In Chapter 4 we explored the player's mental model. This emerges from the mental looping structures that the player creates in building an understanding of the game's internal model. Like the game model, the player's mental model is also dynamic and looping, not static or linear.

This model has to be built by the player as they experience the game (while still keeping them engaged), and it needs to match closely with the game's internal model. If the player's actions in the game have unexpected—or worse, random—effects, the player will not be able to build or verify their mental model. In such a situation, their experience becomes nonsensical and not engaging.

In addition to the game's internal systems, the player's mental model includes both the explicit goals that the game sets before them, as well as the implicit goals that the player creates for themselves. The player's sense of progress in the game as they achieve these goals is often enabled by one or more progression systems in the game. This is an important part of the player's mental model and their sense of engagement and achievement.

The Interactive Loop

In Chapter 4, we also covered the interactive loop that exists between the game and the player. This give-and-take is how the player acts within the game and then learns about it based on the game's feedback. This loop involves and subsumes both the game's internal model and the player's mental model: each is a subsystem of (a part within) the system of the interactive loop.

The player's actions are inputs into the game's loop, and the subsequent change in state in the game model is communicated back to the player, acting as input to the player's own model and state.

It's important to note that until this loop exists, the game doesn't really exist in any functional sense. The game systems by themselves don't create the game experience; the player has to be able to successfully interact with the game first. When developing a game, "closing the loop" so that the player can fully interact with your game world is a highly satisfying, even magical experience for the designer. When this loop exists, the player is able to make a decision, take an action, and experience the feedback from the game based on its internal model, and the player thus improves their mental model. When this happens, it is the first time you have an indication that the game experience you are trying to build might actually exist as an overall system created by the game and the player (see the section "The Designer's Loop," later in this chapter).

While this interactive loop has been depicted as being solely between the player and the game (refer to Figures 4.2 and 4.4, for example), it may easily be extended to include multiple players all interacting with the game and (directly or indirectly) each other. The players use the game as the arbiter of the magic circle, and they use it (as well their own personal discussions) to communicate their current state and future goals in the game.

Within the game, players interact with each other using its tokens and rules. From the point of view of any one player, the full game incorporates both the game's internal model and the combined mental models of all other players involved, as expressed in the game itself. The game doesn't include each player's plans and intentions but does show how they are expressed via the game's structures. It is up to each player to build a predictive model not only of what the game itself will do but what the other players may do as they pursue their own goals.

Core Loops

As introduced in Chapter 4, a game's *core loops* are the interactions between the game and the player that form the player's primary focus—the activities that have the player's central attention (refer to Figures 4.4 and 4.11). As in any interactive loop, in a core loop, the player forms an intention and carries it out within the game, causing some change to occur in the game's internal model. This change is presented as feedback to the player, often with an increase in ability or information. This information allows the player to modify their mental model, including any learning (increase in understanding or skill within the game). This sets the stage for the player to form their next intent, starting the loop all over again.

A game must have at least one core loop to create engaging interactions with the player. It may have multiple core loops that take place at different times or on different time scales, as indicated by the different kinds of interactivity explored in Chapter 4 (see Figure 7.2, shown previously as Figure 4.6). For example, a role-playing game might have fast-paced combat as a primary core loop, with more strategic and long-term skill acquisition as an outer loop. In combat, the player uses action/feedback and short-term cognitive interactive loops in choosing how best to attack. The game provides feedback in terms of the player's opponent's state, as well as the opponent's actions to which the player must react. If the player is successful, the result of this core combat loop may be an increase in in-game resources, such as money, loot, or skill, as well as learning about how to better play the game, which provides the player with a sense of achievement and mastery. This enables the player to face greater challenges, such as fighting more combats against even tougher foes. As the player's attention changes from fast to slow (combat to skill selection, for example), the core loop of the game also changes.

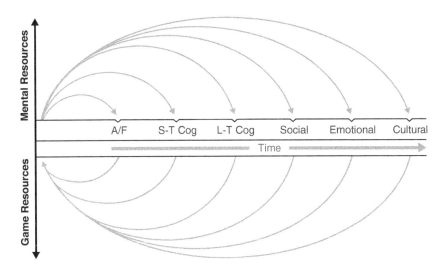

Figure 7.2 A review of the different kinds of interactive loops (refer to Chapter 4), each with its own time scale

In similar fashion, in many strategy games, the player moves between constructing buildings, making units, fighting with those units, and researching new buildings and units. This core loop is itself built out of smaller, shorter-term core loops. These are often referred to as "inner" (shorter, quicker) and "outer" (longer-term) loops. The "core" aspect isn't necessarily which loop is the fastest or innermost but which loop is most important to the player's experience at the time.[3]

Examples of Core Loops

For a real-world example, we can look at *Clash of Clans*, a highly successful action/strategy game. Figure 7.3 shows the core loops for this game. The gameplay consists of collecting resources, constructing (and later upgrading) buildings in your base/fortress to train units, and then sending those units to battle against other bases (typically owned by other players).

---

3. Or, in some cases, the core aspect may be where the player spends most of their time, or which part of the game the designer believes provides the greatest value. The usage of *core loop* as a term of art still isn't entirely consistent.

Together these player actions form the core loops of the game. There are important outer loops, too, such as those involving helping others in your clan and rising in levels. While those are important for the overall success and longevity of the game, the player actions "collect resources," "battle," and "build and train" are the core of this game. (Note that these names are used for convenience here but are not shown or referred to in the game.)

Either of the two loops formed by these actions can be seen as the innermost, or "most core," as the player spends significant time focusing on one or the other. Figure 7.3 shows the "collect" and "battle" loop as the innermost, as they have the shortest time-loop interactions.

Players click on the sources of resources to "collect" them and then put them in container buildings (stocks) for use now or storage (up to a limit) for later use. In the battling part of the game, there isn't a lot of actual interactivity (as in many mobile-platform games of this genre), but the player does have to decide when and where to deploy troops to attack, using a combination of fast action/feedback and short-term cognitive interactivity. (When defending, all the player can do is look on and hope their defenses hold; the player doesn't even have to be present when their base is attacked.)

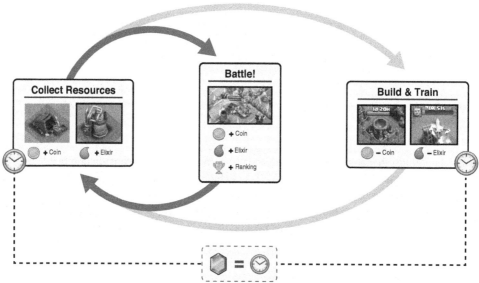

Gems are earned with achievements or bought with real money.
Gems are used to reduce production time.

Figure 7.3 The core loops for *Clash of Clans*. The player cycles between collecting, battling, and building as the three main activities in the game. They can take more time in collecting and building or speed this up with purchases. This same core loop diagram could be drawn more abstractly as a loop involving only battling and building or with greater specificity, showing the looping actions within each of these activities. The level of detail is not entirely arbitrary but should reflect what is most informative for the audience—whether developers, business stakeholders, or players

The battle loop is the more active, high-tension part of the game. In this loop, the player attacks another base with their troops and brings back coins and elixir, the primary in-game resources. The player may also increase their ranking (part of an outer loop). Of course, the player likely loses troops in battle that then need to be regenerated.

This takes us to the more restful, lower-tension, and generally longer-time period part of the game: "build and train." To train new troops and to defend their base, the player must collect and then spend gold and elixir to construct buildings. Some of these buildings are themselves sources (as described above) for gold and elixir—gold mines and elixir collectors. As resource sources, these buildings work automatically over time to create these resources. Other buildings use these resources to create (train) offensive and defensive units. Still others are containers (stock) for resources collected and troops trained.

There are limits to the functions of each of these buildings, of course: a source pumps out its resource at a certain rate; a storage building holds only so much gold or elixir; and only so many troops can be trained. To increase the speed of resource generation, the amount of resource that can be stored, or the number of troops that can be trained, the player must upgrade buildings, limited in this game by the upgrade level of the base's town hall.

In addition, the player is constrained by the fact that constructing buildings takes time, and so does training troops. This is the primary lever that *Clash of Clans*, a free-to-play (F2P) game, uses to induce players to pay money: players may use real-world currency to purchase gems as an intermediary in-game currency. As shown in Figure 7.3, these gems can be used to speed up construction or training time or to purchase additional gold or elixir. In effect, the player can trade money for time, fast-forwarding the game if they are willing to pay for it. This is a common trade-off in F2P games.

The description of the core loops at this level of hierarchical specificity hints at lower-level (or more specific) interaction loops within these. Inside the primary "build and train" core loop, the player must use collected resources to upgrade buildings or troops. Within the "battle" loop, the player must choose which units to train, upgrade, and use in battle. Each decision acts as part of a reinforcing loop (creating more or better units) and a balancing loop (forestalling other decisions once the resources have been used). This combination of reinforcing and balancing loops is common in the core loops of many games, providing the player multiple meaningful decisions as key parts of the gameplay.

Altogether these loops enable the player to create a robust, hierarchical mental model of both the structures in their base and their own goals. A player might have nested goals like, "I need to upgrade my gold storage so I can get enough to upgrade my town hall so I can upgrade my barracks.…" These interlocking structures (parts) and functions (behaviors) create a dynamic mental model that supports action/feedback, short-term cognitive, and long-term cognitive types of interactions. The outer loops of joining and being part of a clan (where players can help each other out) add a layer of social interactivity to the game. Altogether, this creates a highly engaging interactivity landscape that helps explain this game's enduring appeal.

Many other games use similar sets of core loops, often combining a high-tension, action-oriented battle, puzzle, or similar interaction loop with a lower-tension construction, crafting, trading, or similar loop. The former tend to employ faster action/feedback and short-term cognitive interactivity, while the latter tend toward slower long-term cognitive, emotional, and social interactions.[4]

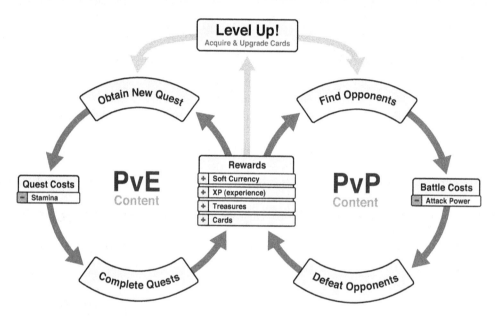

Figure 7.4 The core loops for *Marvel War of Heroes*. The player chooses between two reinforcing loops: PvE (player versus environment, or playing against the game) and PvP (player versus player, or playing against other human players). The loops are similar but have different internal parts (quests and opponents) and different internal balancing elements (stamina and attack power). These latter elements limit how many times the player can go through a loop without resting (or spending money to recharge). Typically players choose PvE exclusively early on, gradually moving to PvP over time. There are also significant outer loops to the game that are not shown here

As another example, we can look at the core loops for a game like *Marvel War of Heroes*, a mobile-based card-battling game in which players create decks of virtual cards containing

---

4. This division of loops may be so pervasive because it fits well with our own biological heritage: in humans and other mammals, the fast reaction-oriented sympathetic part of the nervous system covers "fight or flight" reactions, while the slower, longer-term-oriented parasympathetic part of the nervous system controls what has been called "rest and digest" functions. The first carries us through battle; the second helps us maintain and restore the balance to our bodily systems.

heroes from the Marvel universe to battle others. As shown in Figure 7.4, players can choose to take on new quests or missions against in-game groups like "The Masters of Evil," or they can go up against other players to fight directly (which is usually more challenging). In both cases, a player receives rewards that enhance their abilities to continue playing (experience, new cards, treasures, and so on), with the braking function of using up stamina or attack power that limit their ability to play indefinitely (at least without purchasing faster refills of these resources).

There is an important outer loop to this game, as with most games of this type, where players combine and enhance their heroes. These interactions typically use an interesting combination of action/feedback and long-term cognitive interaction: the player is rewarded for enhancing or combining two heroes (into a single, more powerful hero) with satisfying animations, special effects, and sounds, which act as effective instant feedback for their actions. They also have to make long-term strategic trade-offs about which heroes to enhance, which ones to use in battle, and so on that provide a longer time horizon to their gameplay; the game is about *both* battling in the moment and planning for how to battle the most effectively over the long term.

This outer loop drives the player's desire to continue battling in its own reinforcing loop: enhanced heroes mean better battle performance, and better battle performance leads to more rewards, some of which can be used to enhance their heroes further. While this outer loop is not core to the player's moment-by-moment experience, it is vital to the player's continued engagement with the game, as well as being the game's primary opportunity for commercial success.

Core Loops Summary

A game's core loops are its primary interactive systems. If the core loops support different time lengths of interactivity (as described here and in Chapter 4), they help create a game that is immediately engaging and remains so for long periods of time. It is via the core loops that the player creates a mental model of the game, including both their current actions and long-term goals with it, as well as improving their understanding and skill with the game over time. Simple games may have a single interactive core loop, but these tend to be shorter experiences overall. In the game *Boomshine*, for example, the player's core loop is to click one time (and one time only) per level and then witness the results of their action. This game lasts for a few minutes at most, though with each iteration, the player hones their mental model a little bit more, often increasing their skill with the game. As a result, players return to the game over and over again to test and improve their skill with it, in effect creating their own outer loop of replaying the game.

Game Mechanics

The understanding of interactive game loops provides the basis for a definition of *game mechanics*. This phrase is used a lot in game design to refer vaguely to recurring patterns and chunks of gameplay: platform-jumping is a common game mechanic, as are resource management, push your luck, and dice rolling. These game mechanics span the range from simple (draw a card) to long and complex (build an empire). It can therefore be difficult to nail down the essential characteristics of game mechanics; often they end up being "fuzzy chunks of gameplay" without further definition.

What these all have in common is their systemic nature: each game mechanic forms an interactive loop between the player(s) and the game. This loop is identifiable and, as its own system, is generally free of any particular game context; lots of games use draw a card or territory control as mechanics, for example. A game mechanic may be fast and simple with no subsystems within it, or it may contain many subsystems and take a long time to complete.

Game mechanics that the player encounters repeatedly throughout a game are sometimes referred to as the *core gameplay* or *core mechanic*, incorporating both the meaningful chunk of the game found in a particular mechanic and the idea of the core loop. When these mechanics are seen in many games in slightly different forms, this leads to the formation of *game genres*. For example, in the platformer genre, jumping is a core mechanic, often along with variations like double-jumps, jumping between moving platforms, wall jumping, and so on. In role-playing games, combat is a typical core mechanic, as are collecting loot and gaining power. Within each genre, games share identifiable mechanics that inform the player about the kinds of interactions they will have in the game. Each game differs from others of its genre, but the similarities in the systemic interactive loops created by their mechanics create a sense of familiarity that helps a player more easily create their mental model of the game.

Rather than create a list of common game mechanics, this chapter takes a more systemic approach in going over three primary kinds of gameplay loops (engines, economies, and ecologies) and how to combine them together into various mechanics.

The Designer's Loop

As mentioned throughout this book, what is in many ways the outermost loop of all is the designer's loop (see Figure 7.5, shown earlier as Figures I.3 and 4.3). The designer must view the game+player system as a unified whole from the outside, where both the game and the player are necessary subsystems. The designer interacts with this overarching system by watching players experience the game and adjusting the game's model to provide better engagement for the player. You can think of the game design process as a balancing loop, where the design as created by the designer is experienced by the player, who provides feedback to the designer. This feedback demonstrates the difference between the designer's intent and the player's experience. The designer then changes the design to (hopefully) reduce this difference, and the loop begins again.

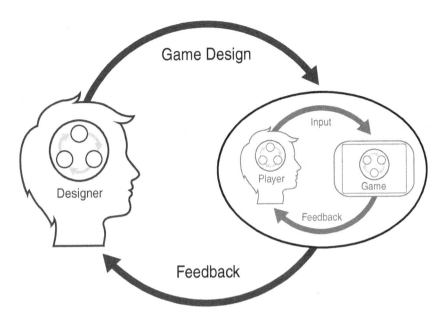

Figure 7.5 The designer's loop. As the game designer, you must construct the player's experience by making the game+player system

Creating, testing, and tweaking the game's internal model and systems is the essence of game design. Until you are able to see and interact with players interacting with your game, the game in many ways does not yet exist. A bunch of rules does not make a game. Even a simulation (a game model that runs on its own) is not yet a game. Having the game be "real" requires having the interactive game+player system in place. It is at this point that the designer's loop can also exist, and where you can make some of the best progress on your game design. We will see more of this loop in Chapter 12, "Making Your Game Real," in discussing the details of prototyping and playtesting.

Levels and Hierarchy

As shown in this brief recounting of the different principal loops in a game, systems necessarily involve hierarchical levels of organization. The interactive loop has as its parts the game and player loops; and the interactive loop is one part in the designer's loop (along with the designer's own plans and goals).

This principle is an important one to remember as we discuss game loops and systems: Systems typically contain other systems, with each being a part in a loop forming a higher-level system. Being able to construct systems of systems—loops within loops—while being able to keep track of what level you are currently working on in a hierarchical system *and* see the whole experience at the same time is a critical aspect of the game designer's skill set (refer to Figure 5.2). This is why being able to think in terms of systems is so vital for any game designer.

As an example, consider the ecology of wolves and deer first introduced in Chapter 2. As shown in Figure 7.6, the deer make up their own small system with a primarily reinforcing loop. Excluding external events, the deer population will increase as long as existing deer have sufficient food. However, the more deer there are, the less food is available. If the consumption of food outstrips the food coming in from the source, fewer deer will be born. For clarity, the effect of adults' starvation (running out of food) isn't explicitly shown here; instead, deer have another behavior (dying) that they sometimes do that takes them out of their system. The boundaries of this system are shown as the dashed circle in Figure 7.6. Food comes into the deer system from outside as a simple source, and death is a sink, taking deer out of the system.

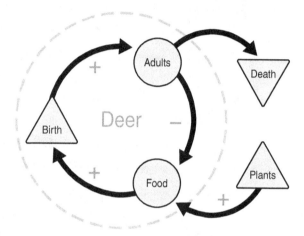

Figure 7.6 The mainly reinforcing loop (with a balancing component) of a deer population as a system diagram

A similarly detailed diagram could be drawn for wolves and plants, though the wolves' (and, in a sense, the plants') food source is deer, as shown in Figure 7.7. This figure is one organizational level up (one level more abstract) from the previous one. The circle (stock) labeled "Deer" in Figure 7.7 contains the entire system within the gray circle in Figure 7.6. That system is now shown as a part in the larger system.

In Figure 7.7 we see that the more deer there are, the larger the wolf population will become— at the expense of reducing the deer's numbers (the double arrows). This is its own little balancing loop, and an external effect from the point of view of the smaller deer-centric system (except for the deer having a "die" behavior, which the wolves may force). Deer have a similar balancing relationship with plants, their food, which are now part of the system rather than being an external simple source. And both deer and wolves, when they die, make for soil on which plants grow.

Note that the different rates of increase of plants, deer, and wolves balance this system. In addition to the mentioned balancing loops, here is a reinforcing loop between deer, soil, and plants that could indicate a runaway number of both deer and plants, except that it is balanced by the deer eating the plants (so they can't make new plants) and by the wolves eating the deer. Note too that this little ecology is also bounded by a dashed circle, indicating that it too may be a part in a still higher-level system.

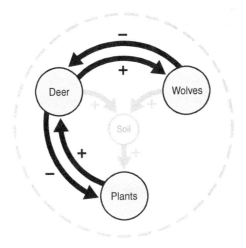

Figure 7.7 The higher-level deer/wolf ecology. The system from Figure 7.6 is a subsystem here, with the external source and sink replaced with stocks—parts that may be their own systems

Three Kinds of Gameplay Loops

As shown in the deer/wolf system in the preceding section, game systems are complex looping structures. (A game system would also include player interaction, which the deer/wolf system does not have.) These looping structures are what make the game go: they form the structural basis for the game's internal model of the world and, when running, they create the functional aspects of the game—the complex dynamic model with which the player interacts to create gameplay.

As discussed in Chapter 3, you can think of each of these functional systemic elements as "a machine that does X"—as in, "I want a machine that makes deer" or "I want an ecology between deer and wolves." Each game system "does something" by having its parts (often systems in their own right, as shown above) interact as part of systemic (complex, often hierarchical) looping structures.

These systems are a mix of reinforcing and balancing loops, depending on the overall purpose of the system. In most games, there is an overall predominance of reinforcing loops. This enables player gain and progression, where the player's in-game avatar or representation becomes more powerful over the course of the game.

Each system works with resources as described earlier: the parts' behaviors typically involve the increase, decrease, flow, and/or conversion or exchange of resources between parts; this is what creates the systemic loop. The loop may work with the same resource internally or may convert or exchange one for another resource as part of the loop. In a reinforcing system, these resources increase over time, and in a balancing system, they decrease to a predetermined level or to a dynamic balance. For this reason, reinforcing loops are sometimes thought of as "gaining," while balancing loops are thought of as "maintaining" a particular resource or set of resources.

These two sets of conditions—reinforcing or balancing and same or exchanged resources—give us three broad kinds of gameplay loops to examine. Each of these are important to game design in different ways, and all of them are discussed in greater detail in the following sections:

- **Engines:** Reinforcing or balancing with the same resource
- **Economies:** Reinforcing by exchanging resources
- **Ecologies:** Balancing by exchanging resources

Engines

The first type of systemic "machine" for us to consider is broadly called *engines*. This word has a number of meanings, of course, even within games—for example, a development engine makes the process of constructing a game easier by taking care of a number of tedious underlying tasks.

In game design terms, an engine may be either *boosting* (reinforcing) or *braking* (balancing). The first type adds resources to the game, and the second type drains them out.

Boosting Engines

A *boosting engine* is a system that adds resources to the game in a way that enables the player to choose between using them to act within the game in the moment or to invest them to gain a greater flow of resources in the future. (This is what Adams and Dormans [2012] call a *dynamic engine*, as opposed to a simple source acting as a *static engine*.) Boosting engines have a primary reinforcing loop that begins with a source creating a resource that flows out from it: this might be iron, action points, army units, magical power, or some other quantity of objects (see Figure 7.8). The player must decide whether to use these resources to act in the game right now or to invest in greater capabilities (greater resource flow) for the future.

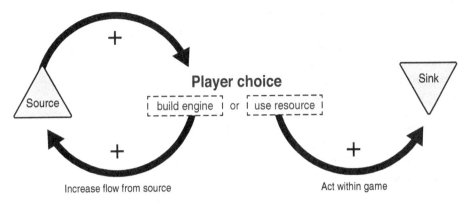

Figure 7.8 The primary reinforcing loop of a boosting engine system. Note that the diagram formed by the example iconography in Figure 7.1 is functionally equivalent to the loop shown here, though in this diagram, the player's choice is called out explicitly as the decision point

Games known as *engine-building* games use this system (or a more complex variation of it) as the primary way for the player to gain power and ability: as they build their engine, the player increases their capabilities within the game, or they can choose to use the resources to act within the game. Acting within the game typically brings its own short-term rewards, at the cost of spent resources, but building the engine invests for the future (and completes the reinforcing loop). Balancing the choice of when to invest versus when to act is a primary decision in these games. As a result, engine-building games tend toward long-term cognitive (strategic) interactivity when this is used as the game's core loop. If a player does not play strategically, they will lose—though if they play *too* strategically (investing more than acting), they can lose as well.

Examples

Many tabletop games use boosting engines as a primary driver of gameplay. An early example comes from the game *Monopoly*. Players begin with $1,500 and gain $200 from the bank (the "source") each time they go around the board. They can use that money to invest in properties that generate more money when people land on them. There is also a secondary engine-building loop in which players with all the properties of a given color can invest in houses and hotels, driving up the money-generating aspect of the property. The only reasons a player wouldn't want to invest money in a property in this game are so they can wait to buy a more preferred property and so they can defend against bankruptcy by having enough money to pay rent on other players' properties or pay other in-game costs.

More recent examples include games like *Dominion*, *Power Grid*, and *Splendor*. Some, like *Splendor*, combine the gain in resource flow with action: as a player, you use gems to purchase a card, and the card in turn adds to the number of "free" gems you have to use on each turn (increasing the resource flow from the source). In addition, this game also sets up a separate resource in the form of victory points. In such cases, the player's decision shifts slightly: they are going to gain capability (additional resource in the form of gems to use) with any action, but they must decide whether to spend their resources to increase only their future capabilities or spend more of them to also gain more victory points. This creates the same sort of balancing act described above, with the player choosing between immediate capability gain and potential gain in the future in the form of victory points.

Many computer-based strategy games also use engine-building systems: you can choose to spend resources to build fighting units, or you can invest those resources into constructing facilities that will build even better fighting units. As a form of outer reinforcing loop built on top of the primary engine system, in many such games, you can also send these fighting units out to bring back needed resources, albeit at the risk of losing some of those units in the process.

Engine Problems

Engine building can be a great core loop within a game, but boosting engines also are prone to certain issues. First, because they are based on reinforcing loops, they have the potential to run out of control in a rich-get-richer scenario unless there are balancing loops in place to prevent this. An old example of this is the 1990 arcade game *Rampart*. In this game, players built castles and then fired cannons at each other. After each round, the players would rebuild their castles, adding more walls and guns, based on their performance in the previous round. This created a strong reinforcing engine-building loop, with the problem being that once one player started winning, it was difficult or impossible for the other player to catch up. There were no in-game mechanisms for catching up, and the primary balancing loop was the fact that to keep playing, you had to keep putting more coins into the arcade machine. (When the game came to home TV-based game consoles that required no coins, this flaw became more obvious.)

On the other end, games based on boosting engines can stall if the player has insufficient resources to continue playing. Imagine if in *Monopoly* you started with only $500 instead of $1,500. Players would be able to purchase only a few properties and would run the risk of quickly being eliminated from the game due to bankruptcy. Or, in a fantasy game, if the only source of gold with which to buy magic weapons were a monster who can only be killed with a magic weapon, the player would be unable to progress in the game. This latter condition is sometimes known as a *deadlock*, a situation where a loop is done before it starts because the resource gained by running through the loop is also required to start it.

Overall, boosting engines require careful balancing of reinforcing and balancing loops: how much of a resource is produced, and how much the flow can be increased, along with other counterbalancing factors, such as how much the player has to spend on actions rather than investing in the game. For example, if in a strategy game constructing units is cheap and the units never die, then the player can quickly build up enough units that they don't need to worry about creating more. Then they can devote all their resources to investment and creating better units, which can lead to a runaway situation, such as one player dominating or, at minimum, all players quickly escalating the number and types of units they purchase with greater and greater investment. The latter situation can make for exciting escalating gameplay if players are balancing each other's progress; this is a staple of many strategy games on mobile platforms, for example. However, it can lead to players eventually becoming starved for new content when they have burned through all the existing units and can progress no further. Correcting for this with the balancing loop of exponentially increasing costs delays but ultimately does not prevent the content-exhaustion problem. (Progression balancing using exponential curves is discussed in detail in Chapter 10, "Game Balance Practice.")

A final problem with boosting engines can come from the act of balancing the game itself. Players will work to find an effective strategy to make the most powerful engine they can as quickly as possible so that they can win the game. Of course, this is set against their need to act in the game, which at least partially balances (and delays) their ability to invest and gain additional power in the game. If this set of loops is balanced too carefully, however, there is a risk that the game designer will unintentionally collapse the potential paths through the game-space, leaving only one strategy that makes sense. In game theory, this is known as a *dominant strategy*: one that is always preferable and has the highest probability of producing a win condition for the player who chooses it.

If, for example, in a fantasy game there is one combination of weapons and armor that beat all others, or if in a strategy game there is one kind of unit that can be purchased and beats all others, then the players will rush to exploit those and gain power quickly. However, in creating such a situation, the designer has left the players with few if any decisions to make: players will either rush to the preferred dominant strategy solution if they know it exists, or they will cast about until they find it, and then be frustrated that others knew of the secret optimal path before they did. In either case, the lack of meaningful decisions causes the player's engagement and sense of fun in the game to evaporate quickly.

Braking Engines

In contrast to boosting engines, *braking engines* have a predominant balancing loop. A braking engine is therefore in many ways the inverse of a boosting engine: a source in the loop generates a resource, but the action of the loop serves to *decrease* the amount of that resource and in some cases reduce the amount (or frequency) of gain of that resource in the future. A real-world example of this structure is the brakes on a car: when applied, they reduce the speed of the wheels either down to some level or to a complete stop. Another physical example is the mechanical governor we saw in Figure 1.7, where the motion of the spinning weights regulates the speed of the engine to which it is attached. These loops are also sometimes known as *friction* structures (Adams and Dormans 2012), as they slow the action or resource gain in gameplay.

This may seem like an odd structure for part of a game design, and unlike the other loop structures, these tend to be seen as parts within other loops rather than on their own. Referring back to earlier examples, however (refer to Figures 7.3 and 7.4), we can see how putting a regulator or a brake on a player's progress can be an important part of a game. In a card battling game like *Marvel War of Heroes*, players could continue to play without restriction if there were not some regulation and reduction of their abilities. In that game, both stamina and attack power serve this purpose. In other games, similar regulating or braking conditions include a variety of forms of friction, or conditions to which the players must attend and that divert resources from their overall progression. The "make repairs" Chance card in *Monopoly*, where players have to pay an amount proportional to the number of houses and hotels they own, is an example of this: a random event that drain's the player's resources as a way of regulating them. This card also exhibits the "rubberbanding" effect mentioned earlier, as it does not affect a lagging player nearly as much as it affects one who is winning and owns many properties.

Slowing to a Stop

Not surprisingly, braking engines must be used carefully within the context of a game. If the regulation of the player's resources is too severe, such that it overcomes the main reinforcing loop in a boosting engine or an economic system, the player will soon have insufficient resources to act in the game. As with a stagnating economy, the game will grind to a halt. For example, if the Chance card in *Monopoly* that requires the player to pay for repairs on all their properties appeared in the game more often, or if its costs were higher, it would have the effect of overly constraining the player's actions, leaving them unable to act in the game in other ways. Like a car with dragging brakes providing too much friction, this has the overall result of removing too much energy from the game's systems, and the game will slow to a stop.

Economies

The second type of systemic machine is the *economy*. Like the engine system, this is a commonly used word with different meanings. In the sense used here for game design, an *economy* is any system dominated by a reinforcing loop (or set of loops) where the increase in resources or value comes not from internal investment of a resource (as with boosting engines) but from exchanging one resource for another or converting one resource to another with a nonlinear gain in value. As game designer Brian Giaime (2015) said, "A game economy is the dynamic exchange of resources, time, and power between multiple systems and entities." These are exchanged "because players perceive a gain in value for the exchange."

Let's break that down. In a boosting engine, as described above, the player can choose whether to use a resource or invest it to increase the flow of that resource in the future. In an economy, the player can use a resource to perform a needed action in the game—for example, using wood as a resource to construct a building. Or the player can trade the wood for bread to feed their workers—who can then go chop down more wood. In this case, the player gains capability by trading one resource for another, enabling them to get even more of the resource they had in the first place, typically after a delay that keeps the player from creating a runaway reinforcing loop.

In the wood-for-bread example, the player could instead choose to convert their wood into lumber and exchange it for even more bread. Suppose that a worker controlled by the player requires one bread to cut down a tree and produce one wood. If the player can then trade one wood for two bread, they gain the ability to then chop down two more wood, so they have increased their capability (albeit after a delay, as on their next turn or similar). That is the core of the economic reinforcing loop. See Figure 7.9.

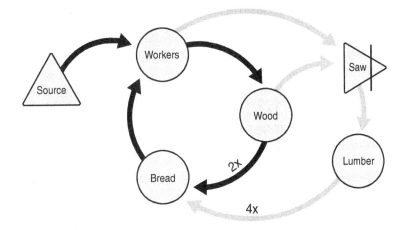

Figure 7.9 An economic system with an inner loop of trading wood for bread to allow the chopping of more wood, and an outer investment loop of building a sawmill to convert wood to lumber for a more valuable trade

Suppose further that if the player has a sawmill, a worker can convert one wood into one lumber—and one lumber can be exchanged for *four* bread. This creates a strongly nonlinear increase in ability and thus in economic value. The costs to the lumberjack player in this scenario for moving from trading wood for bread to lumber for bread are that the player has to do the following:

- Accumulate enough wood to construct the sawmill (boosting-engine investment)
- Devote a worker (a potentially scarce resource) to the saw to convert wood to lumber, so less wood is being chopped
- Take additional time to convert wood to lumber
- Pay back the investment of time and wood needed to create the sawmill and that they could have otherwise used to trade directly for bread

These scenarios, costs, and benefits provide the player with an interesting set of decisions of timing and investment that are at the heart of economic gameplay. The player is trying to gain ability and power within the context of the game by exchanging and/or converting one resource into another.

Unfolding Complexity

One other aspect of economic gameplay like this is the ability to introduce new objects and abilities, along with new resources and currencies (described shortly), as the game progresses. In the example above, a player may know only about bread and wood early in the game. Once they have mastered that limited economy, the game introduces the sawmill as a new object and lumber as a new resource. These allow for a new loop, expanding the player's mental model as well as the number of decisions they can make in the game (when to build the sawmill, how many workers to devote to it rather than to cutting down trees, and so on) since each object and resource opens up new possibilities.

Many games with economic loops use this concept by having production chains that are introduced over time. Converting wood to lumber is a short chain. In the same game, the player might have to have other workers who mine ore, convert it to iron, convert that to steel, and convert that to tools or weapons. Each one requires a new building, workers, and potentially knowledge or skills—so you might have to build an academy to train smiths (converted from undifferentiated workers) before you can make weapons with your steel (Figure 7.10).

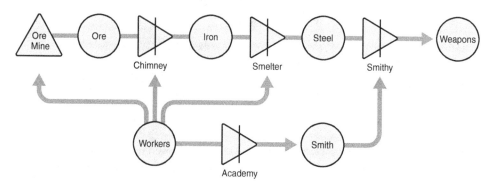

Figure 7.10 A production chain involving multiple conversions of resources and workers

For players who enjoy the cognitive challenges of building up and managing these chains, this creates engaging gameplay. While this can all be done by one player, one aspect of economic gameplay that makes it so interesting is that players can also take on specialized roles, creating some resources and trading for others: perhaps a player doesn't make their own weapons if they don't have a ready supply of ore, or they have to purchase the stone to make the chimney to refine the ore into iron. This purchase may be from another player or a computer-driven agent in the game; either way, it is another example of conversion and exchange of resources and currencies, which is the heart of economic-system gameplay.

Economic-system games can start simply and add new steps and loops, gradually unfolding into greater and greater systemic complexity as the player progresses. The player may start simply, with say an ore mine and selling the ore, then refining the ore to iron and finding that it sells for enough more to justify the expense and extra steps, and eventually working all the way up to having multiple resource paths that generate weapons and armor, among many other production-based goods.

This unfolding, additive system provides the player with a sense of exploration, mastery, and achievement as their mental model grows and he can do more in the game. As the game reveals increasing complexity, this provides the player with an experience of multiple interlocking systemic loops that create a broad play-space within which the player can make innumerable decisions. This creates long-term engagement and a deep sense of fun in the game.

Currencies

Economies often use currencies as a sort of catalytic resource, as described earlier. Strictly speaking, currencies are exchanged but not consumed as resources are, so they may be exchanged again. If the lumberjack player in the previous example could pay for bread using silver instead of wood, and if the baker player could then use that same silver to buy wheat to make bread, then the silver is a currency that is usable by both, and not just a resource that is converted in the transaction. Like a chemical catalyst, a currency enables the exchange but does not participate directly in it by being consumed during the exchange. However, in many game economies, currencies are effectively destroyed (drained out of the economy via a sink) when spent, even if they don't transform from one type of object into another, as a resource does.

Currencies have another important property as well: unlike resources that may have only one or a few direct uses, currencies can be used in almost any form of exchange. So if in a RPG a player finds 1,000 gold pieces, they may spend that currency on training, better weapons or armor, or information, or save them for spending later. This provides the player with a multitude of choices in addition to the feeling of having obtained a valuable reward.

However, currencies are also subject to the problems of inflation and stagnation, as described later in this chapter. In short, players must perceive a currency to have value as a means of exchange, or it just becomes an annoyance or something to be ignored. Keeping your in-game currencies in balance so that they retain some value without becoming overly precious can be a difficult design problem. This is something that must be viewed at the level of the whole economy as a system rather than by looking at only one part of it. It typically takes considerable iterative design and tweaking of economic values (resource creation rates, prices, and so on) to create a stable but still dynamic economy.

Economies with Engines

It is common for an economy to have engines built into it as subsidiary systemic loops. In the example above, the woodcutting player may have to decide whether to sell wood for bread or invest the wood in constructing a sawmill in order to get even more bread, as shown in Figure 7.9. Having sources that produce resources that can be used for internal investment or profitable exchange is the core of many engaging games: players must make economic trade-off decisions, balancing short-term needs with long-term desired gains.

Examples of Economies

Economies come in many different forms, some of which don't seem particularly "economic" at first glance. For example, in a typical role-playing game, the player's core loop likely is an economy. This loop can be bluntly described as "kill monster, get loot, buy stuff." There is more to it, of course, though the experience does often boil down to that. In particular, the resources that the player is exchanging for the "loot" are their time and (often) their character's health (also sometimes things like weapon and armor fatigue, as these become weaker with use). In economic terms, the player is essentially saying, "I will trade some of my time as a player and some of my character's health for the loot that this monster will provide to me." (Note, however, that combat itself is an ecology that exists as a subsystem of the overall economy, as discussed later in this chapter.)

In trading time and health for loot, the player is betting that their character will gain new abilities in the exchange, in the form of experience points (or new skills), the potential for better weapons and armor, and possibly gold with which they can buy new weapons and armor or repair the ones they have. None of these are assured in any given encounter with a monster. In that respect, each encounter provides a reward on a *variable schedule*—a powerful method for encouraging continued play. *Variable schedule* is a term from psychology used when someone is rewarded at various times for a particular behavior but doesn't know when the next reward will appear. You might think that being rewarded on a regular schedule would create the most engagement and best performance, but this isn't the case. A variable schedule reward creates strong engagement (persistent, focused behavior) and creates a spike of dopamine in the brain with each reward—making this particularly useful for fast action/feedback interactivity (Zald et al. 2004). This reward and resulting engagement is an important aspect of why we persist at playing games, gambling, purchasing stocks, and other similar behaviors.

Traditional trading economies also exist in many games. In these, resources of one type are exchanged for others, either by direct barter or mediated by the use of currencies. Each resource has to have value to the purchaser (as in the wood-for-bread example). In any working economy, purchasers either fulfill basic needs (food, shelter, and so on) with the things they buy, or they use them to create an increase in value—as with a smith who uses her time and skill to convert metal ingots into weapons, armor, or decorative objects. It is this increase in value that ultimately powers any economy, keeping the overall loop reinforcing itself.

Moving beyond single-resource economies to those using multiple resources, the systems become far more dynamic and unpredictable. If there are multiple buyers and sellers in the market (whether human players or NPCs), resources will have different relative values to different actors, depending on their needs and budget constraints. While the prices remain dynamic, over time and numerous transactions, the prices for a given resource will tend to settle into a fairly narrow range (assuming no external change). On the other hand, if there aren't many transactions for a given resource, its price may fluctuate wildly, given the relative value at any given time and lack of general history to act as a precedent for any particular price.

(At this point, we stand on the precipice of microeconomics, an entire subject on its own and an excellent analytic companion to the kind of system creation discussed here. However, that is beyond the scope of this book.)

In general, if more people are interested in a particular resource, its price goes up. The same is true if the amount of the resource available becomes reduced, assuming that there is still interest in it from potential purchasers. This is the classic economic law of *supply and demand*: if something is easily obtainable on the market, the price people are willing to pay for it drops; but if it becomes scarce and people still have a need for it, people will outbid each other trying to obtain the resource, and its price rises. The economy occurs if the sellers and buyers are able to come to an agreement where both are willing to make an exchange.

Contained in this is an argument against a few practices that are common in many games. Designers often want to set the prices for resources or goods in their games rather than let them float based on supply and demand. To some degree, this makes sense: players want a consistent experience and don't want to know that the lizard hides they just hauled back from the wilderness are suddenly worthless. At the same time, taking all variation—all the "float"— out of the market where the aggregate action of all sales sets the price, also takes the dynamics and life out of the economy. Among other things, this means fewer decisions players have to make since they don't have to look for the best place to sell, for example, since they know that their lizard hides will always sell for a certain amount in any location, as this has been centrally set by the game. This can work, but it reduces the economy to a mechanistic exercise. That may or may not be best for the game you're making. If you want players to have the opportunity to make economic decisions, you need to allow for some variability in prices. If, however, it's more important for the player's experience that they are just able to sell their goods than that they get the best price, introducing pricing variability may just be adding to the player's mental load and taxing their interactivity budget.

Similar to central price setting, many games provide vendors who have infinite cash (or resources to trade), infinite stock, and an infinite appetite for whatever the player is selling. If the NPC vendor buys 10 lizard skins for 1 gold piece each, he will buy the next 10—and the next 100 or 1,000—for the same amount. As with fixed prices, this creates a consistent experience for the player but also one that is relatively lifeless and presents no challenges or meaningful decisions to the player.

Player-to-player economies are far more dynamic in large part because the players themselves set the prices for all the resources they exchange. This can create terrific amounts of economic gameplay, but it also presents significant problems, as discussed in the following section.

Economic Issues

Economies can suffer from some of the same issues that can plague boosting engines. First among these is the problem where one player is able to harness the reinforcing loop to their advantage and the exclusion of others. By doing so, this player can quickly zoom ahead in an in-game rich-get-richer scenario. If unchecked, this capability can lead to one player (or a small number) gaining disproportionate benefit from the game—that is, winning based on forcing others to lose. This often comes at the cost of other players' enjoyment, or even at the cost of their presence in the game. Classic board games like *Monopoly* and *Risk* are based on the idea of eliminating players as the game progresses until there is only one remaining. This is a classic zero-sum view ("I win, you lose"), where in an economic sense all value is concentrated in one player. Unless your desire is to make a hyper-competitive game, most people will not end up enjoying themselves (unless they find the thrill of potential loss itself attractive), and allowing this kind of runaway economic scenario will not create a healthy, engaging game design.

There are a variety of ways to prevent or mitigate the runaway reinforcement loop. As discussed earlier in this chapter (and in the discussion of ecologies later in the chapter), balancing loops can be used to either help those lagging behind or slow those who are getting too far ahead. Collectively, these techniques are sometimes called "rubberbanding," from the image of forcibly hauling back a leading player or bringing forward a lagging one, as if they were connected by an elastic band that has reached its limit. (Sometimes this is also referred to as "forgive losers and punish winners" to keep the game going.)

Often a sharp, one-time balancing effect is sufficient as a corrective action, as when a losing player in *Mario Kart* is able to lob a spiny shell (commonly known as the "blue shell") at the player in first place, thereby stopping them for a few seconds while others catch up. Another similar device is the thief in the *Settlers of Catan* games. This isn't automatically used against the leading player, but players typically try to put it on land used by one or more of the leading players to prevent them from gaining valuable resources from that area until the thief can be moved. Finally, built-in effects, like the balancing loop used in *Power Grid* to determine turn order, helps prevent one player from running away with success in a game with a prominent economy, thus helping to preserve the engagement and fun for all players.

Inflation

There are two other main ways in which game economies experience issues and tend to fail. The first, as discussed earlier, is with a primary reinforcing loop that is too strong. This is also similar to a common problem seen in engines: if the exchange or conversion is too easy or too profitable, the player ends up with too much of a given resource and not enough meaningful ways to spend it. In the real world, this is a classic recipe for economic inflation, and the same is true in games. This problem is sometimes known as "more faucets than drains" because resources are pouring into the game and have too few ways to drain out of it.

However, handled carefully, this inflation can be used to increase the player's engagement at least for a time: if players are able to gain amounts of currency that they once thought unattainable and then use that currency to purchase meaningful items in the game, they can feel powerful. When a lowly character who initially barely had two coppers to rub together attains vast sums of wealth that allow them to buy castles or extra lives, they can feel a great sense of achievement. But this is true only as long as the amounts remain meaningful in that the player can use them in some way in the game. The idle game *Adventure Capitalist* starts players as entrepreneurs running lemonade stands making a few dollars, the in-game currency. Eventually, if a player persists, they can find themselves purchasing and upgrading movie studios, banks, and oil companies, in the process accruing over $1 novemnonagintillion—that is a 1 followed by 300 zeros.[5]

Whether that amount of money is in any way meaningful is a different question. Few players last anywhere near that long in the game, as the gameplay typically becomes repetitive and not meaningful long before that. One way this and many other idle games have partially solved this problem is by creating another external boosting engine loop called the *prestige loop*. As the player progresses in the game, they accrue a "prestige" resource, such as angel investors in *Adventure Capitalist*. As with any boosting engine, the player can choose to use this resource in the game or wait and "invest" it in their next iteration of it. When the player sees that their current rate of increase is too small to yield any meaningful benefit in a short period of time, they can restart the game and carry over only their prestige resources, and everything else gets wiped clean for a fresh start. The prestige resources then act as a multiplier to increase the rate of increase of the primary resource (cash in *Adventure Capitalist*). This enables the player to quickly get past the now-boring lower levels of the game and progress even further than the last time. Of course, they continue to accrue their prestige resource, so they have an incentive to cycle through the outer prestige loop once again when the game becomes boring. This prestige loop increases the life span of the game for the most dedicated players and is a great example of using a boosting engine structure to both make inflation work as part of the gameplay and extend the life of the game for the player.

Another example of economic inflation occurred in the economy surrounding *Diablo II*. In this fantasy RPG, every time you killed a monster, gold coins rained out of it, and often magic items did as well. While gold could be used as a currency to purchase some items in the game, players quickly found themselves awash in it with no use for it (more faucets than drains). Thus, in player-to-player transactions, it was worthless—a classic inflationary scenario. Players turned to various gems first as a new more valuable (if unofficial) currency, but due in large part to the amount of them given as loot (and to some degree to "dupes"—cheating players duplicating items themselves), these also quickly became worthless. In time, players settled on an item called the Stone of Jordan, or SOJ for short, as the preferred currency, as it was small, expensive, and useful in the game. However, eventually even that became nearly worthless, and players finally turned to "high runes" as their medium of exchange. These were also small (so easily transported), expensive, and useful, and unlike the SOJ, they had different statistics and so became seen as having different values, acting very much like different denominations of real-world paper currency.

---

5. Technically, the game goes up to just over $179 uncentillion, or about $1.79×10^{308} before there is an integer overflow and the dollar balance resets to zero.

This entire process occurred due to inflation, due to having a too-strong reinforcing loop pouring gold and other currencies into the economy and not enough content to keep the players satisfied: they no longer had meaningful decisions to make or goals to set for themselves within the economy. This is a problem that almost every game that features an economy has to face at some point, as it becomes increasingly difficult to add more and more content at the high end of the game without it becoming boring and repetitive to players.

Stagnation

Though it's less common, stagnation can also occur in an economy. Economic stagnation happens when the supply of resources or currency (money, loot, and so on) is too constrained or when the costs of remaining in the game are too high. In either case, players believe it is in their best interest to hang on to a dearly won coin or bit of loot rather than spend it and regret doing so later. Alternatively, they have to continue paying out currency for maintenance (a form of braking engine), and soon they simply do not have enough to keep their character, army, nation, and so on, going. One of the reasons stagnation is rare is because when it begins to happen, players simply stop playing the game. Nothing is keeping them there, especially when the game ceases to be fun, so they leave, and the game—and its economy—slowly grind to a painful halt.

In games economic stagnation happens when designers are so intent on balancing their in-game economy—refusing to let the reinforcing loop do its work and allow the economy to grow—that they take the life out of it. It's true that reducing the primary reinforcing loop will prevent inflationary problems, but doing so can also remove any useful economic gradient: when no one feels that a trade is in their favor, then no trades are made and ultimately there is no economy. Recall that a systemic loop requires interaction between parts. In an economic system, if there are no interactions that exchange or convert two resources, then there is no system, and thus, if this is a core loop, there is no game.

Ecologies

Like a braking engine, an *ecology* system has a predominant balancing loop, or set of loops, rather than a reinforcing one. In this balancing loop, resources are exchanged as they are in an economy, but they are exchanged such that each part ultimately balances rather than reinforces the others. Within the overall balancing loop, ecologies typically have reinforcing loops that exist within the parts as subsystems themselves (as shown in Figures 7.6 and 7.7), but these are not the primary driver of the system structure.

In an ecology, while the overall target is balance rather than unrestrained growth, this does not mean that the system approaches stagnation. As discussed in Chapters 1 and 2, a healthy ecology is in a state of metastability, also known as internal equilibrium or dynamic balance. The parts within the ecological system are constantly changing, but viewed as a whole, the system remains balanced. This can be seen in the deer/wolf example discussed earlier and in the discussion in Chapter 2 of the lynx and hare predator–prey relationship (refer to Figure 2.10) and the "trophic cascade" example of wolves being reintroduced to Yellowstone National Park (refer to Figure 2.22).

In principle, the kind of ecology shown in Figure 7.7 is fairly easy to understand: plants grow and deer eat them, making more deer (loosely speaking). Wolves eat the deer, making more wolves. And eventually deer and wolves die, decomposing and making more fertile soil for the plants. While each part in this loop—plants, deer, and wolves—is trying to maximize its growth (each is a subsystem with internal loops, as shown in Figure 7.6), overall they act by their behavior to counterbalance each other; in effect, together they act as braking engines against each other. The deer eat the plants, balancing their growth, and the wolves eat the deer, balancing theirs. Wolves are known as an "apex predator," meaning they typically have few or no direct competitors or predators. Such animals also tend to be few in number due to their enormous metabolic needs and slow growth—which also create balancing factors on their population. Their population growth is thus not constrained by predation but by the relative scarcity of their food sources.

Different Kinds of Ecologies

Not all ecologies are biological, even in terms of simulation. Most systems with a predominantly balancing loop and an exchange of resources can be analyzed as ecologies. For example, inventory systems in role-playing games can be seen as simple ecological systems. The more stuff you put into your character's inventory, the less space you have to carry more ("stuff" and "space" being the resource parts that are exchanged and that balance each other). In some games, like *Diablo II*, this is carried to an extreme, with each piece competing not just for space as an abstract resource but for a particular configuration of space.

Combat can also be considered an ecology: two or more sides (player character versus monster, for example) attempt to "balance" each other by their actions—a nice way of saying that they each try to kill the other. In doing so, assuming that the player character is the victor (the remaining subsystem that is not balanced out of existence), the rewards gained feed back into their overall economic loop.

Many games also have important social ecologies. The MMO *Dark Age of Camelot* had what it called "Realm vs. Realm" combat for different factions. There were three factions in the game, Albion, Hibernia, and Midgard. Members of each fought the others for dominance. The interesting thing about having three factions, or Realms, is that this kept the overall realm system in a metastable dynamic balance: if ever one of the Realms became too powerful, members of the other two would temporarily ally with each other to take down the leader. This led to a constantly changing balance that avoided stasis and was thus highly satisfying for the players. Had there been only two Realms in the game, the balancing loop would have been swamped by a reinforcing one: as soon as one side gained supremacy, players would begin to flock to the winning side, creating a runaway rich-get-richer scenario and making it impossible for the other realm to catch up. This is in fact what happened on many early *World of Warcraft* servers: for a variety of reasons (including just that the Alliance characters were more attractive), more players played on the Alliance side than on the Horde side. On servers that allowed player-versus-player combat, the Alliance was regularly dominant. It took a number of changes to the character types available and other incentives to begin to balance this, though it arguably has never been completely corrected—and certainly has never approached an organic, dynamic balance, as in *Dark Age of Camelot*.

Ecological Imbalances

With any system of exchange that is dominated by a balancing loop, the primary problems that can occur have to do with either balance that is too static and is therefore boring or balance that veers out of control and wrecks the overall system.

Balancing systems are sometimes described as being resilient or brittle: within a certain range of change, the ecology can rebalance itself. At some point, however, the system reaches a point of no return from which it cannot rebalance. Physiological systems are said to be in homeostasis when they are, as a sort of mini-ecology (in the terms we are using here), in dynamic balance internally despite outside influences. The outside air temperature may be hotter or colder than your body temperature, but your body will work hard to keep its temperature within a very narrow range. As long as your body can keep your temperature balanced, the system is resilient to outside changes. At some point, though, the body's ability to be resilient and rebalance breaks down: your body begins to freeze or overheat. If this continues, the body system itself will shut down, unable to recover. When this happens, the body as a system has gone from being resilient to brittle: there is a point of no return where the system cannot balance itself.

The problem in building game systems is that it can be very difficult to know when an ecological system has become brittle. If you had a lynx and hare ecology going and you saw the hare population nose-diving, you might think that the system had fallen over into being brittle and that soon everything would die off. Once you begin to see that such cycles are within normal historical parameters, you can better detect when the system is in a healthy dynamic balance and when it is about to veer off an edge with no chance of return. In large ecologies with sufficient historical data, it's possible to construct mathematical models to show when the overall system is "in control" or "out of control." These are terms used in statistical process control. Essentially, if a resource ever goes more than three standard deviations from its historical mean, the process is out of control, and the system is in severe danger of becoming brittle and collapsing. Unfortunately, in dynamic balancing systems, it can be too late when this lack of control is detected, and in games it is rare to have sufficient data on which to build a historical model of a resource's changing value.

While some amount of control of an ecological system is important, the danger in trying to control such a system too tightly is that you can either "oversteer," leading to a different brittle failure, or create an enforced static nature, rather than allowing the system's own dynamic balance to occur. For example, in a strategic game, if it becomes clear that one unit type is far stronger than is balanced with its cost, players will quickly detect this as a dominant strategy and build that type of unit as much as possible. This quickly unbalances the overall combat ecology, much like an invasive species taking over a biome in a real-world ecology. If this isn't corrected soon, players will build only that type of unit, collapsing the game-space (with no decisions left to make) and reducing their engagement and gameplay. One impulse in correcting this kind of situation can be to create a new kind of unit that specifically counters the first one. The problem here is that if the new unit is too powerful (often called "overpowered" for its cost, or OP), players begin to use that unit exclusively. Then the temptation to introduce *another* unit to counter the second one is very high, and soon the game begins to feel like the old song about a woman who swallowed a fly and her increasingly implausible attempts to get rid of it.[6]

Alternatively, some designers try to clamp down on all possible uncertainty to ensure that such a system is completely balanced, if in a completely static manner. This is often done for the purpose of ensuring a consistent experience for the player. In game terms, however, this becomes boring and un-engaging quickly, as there is no mental model for the players to construct and there are no decisions for them to make. In systemic terms, this also gives rise to a different form of brittleness: because the system is not dynamically balancing itself, it cannot react effectively to any significant outside influence, and so it will break down quickly if anything in the system of which it is a part affects it. To go back to the example of homeostasis and body temperature, if your temperature were locked to 37°C, your body would be unable to react effectively to a cool breeze or a warming ray of sunshine: either one would cause a disproportionate expenditure of energy to keep your body at the single locked temperature, and this would quickly be overwhelmed by even mild changes to external conditions. Your physiological systems would quickly become brittle and fail.

Combining Loops Together

Engines, economies, and ecologies are generally useful as primary system loop types; many more specific patterns—game mechanics—can be made from these. Many efforts have been made to create inventories or more detailed lists of patterns or mechanics, some of which you may find useful—in particular, Bjork and Holopainen (2004) and Adams and Dormans (2012). However, many game designers find such detailed lists to be of limited use and prefer instead to work with more general patterns like these as hierarchical building blocks for constructing specific gameplay systems.

It's rare for a game to have only one system or one game mechanic in it. Most games are combinations of systems operating at different hierarchical levels of organization, with one system being a part in the context of a larger system.

For example, in role-playing games there is typically a primary reinforcing economy centered on the player character's progression in the game: the player character is intended to become

---

6. This has real-world parallels in nonsystemic solutions to systemic problems, such as the 1962 *New York Times* article about the overuse of insecticides in Vietnam that began "American DDT spray killed the cats that ate the rats that devoured the crops that were the main props against Communist agitation in the central lowlands" (Bigart 1962).

more powerful over time by trading time (and hit points, and so on) for experience and loot, resulting in increased hit points, skill, better tools, and so on (see Figure 7.11). Within this high-level description, however, there may be many other systems: an experience- or skill-boosting engine, where the player has to choose when and how to invest points;[7] economic systems like item crafting or trading; or an ecological inventory system, as discussed earlier. There may also be a role-based economic system of different members of a party, each reinforcing the others' abilities by a form of exchange with their own (for example, tough "tank" characters absorb damage from opponents while ranged attack characters do damage from afar and while healer characters keep the tank in good health). There is typically some form of combat ecological system that exists within the overall player character economic system, and, as described earlier in this chapter, there may be one or more balancing systems (that is, braking engines) that prevent the player from progressing too quickly. These are often part of a larger system, as with the loss of energy or stamina (which must then regenerate over time) being part of an overall combat system in many free-to-play games. Altogether these systems illustrate why designing RPGs can be so complex and why playing them can be so engaging: there are many different systems operating at the same time, and the player is trying to maximize all of them at different levels of organizational hierarchy.

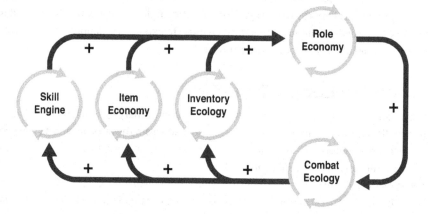

Figure 7.11 A typical role-playing game reinforcing/economic system for increasing character power in terms of skills and items. The overall system is made of engine, economy, and ecology subsystems. Note that for clarity, many interactions between subsystems are not shown (for example, the interactions between the inventory ecology and the item economy)

---

7. It's rare, but a few RPGs have situations where you can choose to spend experience points rather than use them for leveling up. For example, in *Advanced Dungeons and Dragons* version 3.5, you have to spend XP to cast some spells or create scrolls or magic items. I don't know of RPGs that allow you to sacrifice your experience points or skill points on a difficult action rather than investing them in a new level or skill (the *Deadlands* RPG comes close, as does *Torg*), but it could be an interesting twist to add to a game. It's the kind of mechanism that becomes apparent when you start seeing the skill-gain system as an engine.

As the subsystems shown in Figure 7.11 interact, they reinforce each other in an overall economy: the more the player has in skills and inventory, and the more characters they have in their party, the better able they will be to defeat monsters. The more monsters they defeat, the more experience and loot they gain. While the balancing nature of combat (balancing/reducing the character's abilities and regulating their overall progress) and inventory ecological system may force the character to make difficult decisions (for example, about what to keep or throw away), and thus potentially reduce the reinforcing loop of the character's progression, the predominant systemic effect is one of a loop reinforcing and increasing the character's overall power.

Bringing All the Systems Together

Viewing a role-playing game's systems as we've just looked at them shows you how designing a hierarchy of systems creates a broader and deeper play experience. The core loop can change as the player shifts focus from one subsystem to another or to the highest-level systemic loop. Having multiple systems working in parallel gives players more kinds of things to do, providing game breadth. Designing nested systems with the ability for the player to mentally zoom in on a lower-level subsystem or zoom out to a higher-level one (as in Figures 7.6, 7.7, and 7.11) provides comprehensible complexity in the game and thus game depth. This is how second-order design creates a space for play, as the player has goals and decisions within each system and subsystem. And, by revealing the complexities of these systems carefully over time, the game can help the player build a mental model of it in an engaging way: as each new system in a hierarchy is revealed, the player gains new knowledge, new decisions, and new ways to act within the world, along with a new sense of achievement based on these factors.

Examples of Game Systems

As discussed earlier in this chapter, engines, economies, and ecologies can form all sorts of systems, especially when combined together as hierarchical systems of systems. While an exhaustive list of all the possible ways these kinds of systems could be assembled isn't possible (such a list wouldn't be very systemic!), we can examine some well-known kinds systems in terms of their primary loops, what subsidiary systems they have inside them, and how they work with other systems to help create the unified whole of the desired game experience.

Progression Systems

Nearly all games present the player with some way to progress—to increase in ability, power, resources, or knowledge. In-game ability or power works hand-in-hand with a player's knowledge of the game. As they gain more knowledge of the game world (using knowledge as an in-game resource), a player is able to do more and perform better. Similarly, as they construct their mental model of the game, they gain the ability to navigate the game's systems more effectively, using their own internal tools and skills. Progression in the form of increasing the number of different kinds of things the player can do (due to being aware of more parallel systems and a deeper hierarchy of systems) is a good way to help the player build an effective mental model; this method introduces game concepts little by little and gives the player a feeling of increasing mastery at the same time.

Because progression loops are so pervasive and so easily rewarding to players, they often form the core loop of a game. They map closely to the interactive loop between player and game, where the player receives positive feedback and reward for their actions that then impel the player on to new choices and actions. Questions such as "What does the player do?" often reduce to "How does the player progress?" Because of the reinforcing nature of the loops, these systems are economies or engines and often have subsystems of either type built in.

Giving the player some way to progress, to increase their abilities in the game, can be a useful way to turn a toy into a game. As discussed in Chapter 3, games without explicit goals are often referred to as toys. It's often easy for some game designers (those who operate primarily as toymakers or inventors, as discussed in Chapter 5, "Working as a Systemic Game Designer") to come up with a small game system or mechanism that seems initially attractive but then fails to hold the player's interest for more than a few seconds or minutes. The reaction to these is often along the lines "that's neat…but what does the player do with it?" Some toys are fine as toys—but adding explicit goals, and therefore a progression system of some sort, can be a great way to turn a toy into a game and build in longer-term engagement.

Progression systems can be thought of in terms of reward or resource gain per unit time. This increase or reward might be experience points, gold, number of troops, or something else, depending on the game, or it might be less quantifiable, more in terms of the increase in the player's mental model and the cognitive tools they possess to manipulate the game's systems to their advantage. As we will discuss in Chapter 10, determining the dimensions for progression is an important aspect of tokenizing a game's design: the player may gain health, magic, knowledge, items, and/or other resources, each of which must be specified in the design as the state of different parts.

For each in-game dimension along which a player progresses, a rate of increase must be specified. In many cases, not only does the *amount* of a progressing resource increase but the *rate* itself increases over time. This both maintains the aspirational quality of the reward and prevents the reward from fading in significance as the player experiences what is known as *habituation* or *hedonic fatigue*.

Habituation and Utility

Increasing rewards give the player something to aspire to—a goal to shoot for. If today their reward is 10 points but they know that later they could do something that merits a reward of 50 or 100 points, this unmet goal will drive their behavior—as long as the goal remains meaningful and the reward feels significant. The heart of this is that for we humans, *wanting* rather than *having* drives attention and behavior—and thus engagement. Having a higher goal, even one that seems ridiculously out of reach initially, helps maintain players' engagement.

If, however, a player realizes they have achieved everything they can—they have beaten the biggest monster, obtained the most valuable treasure, and so on—then their engagement quickly drops off.

The loss of engagement due to a loss of perceived significance of rewards also happens when we get used to, or habituate to, an existing situation: no matter how good the current rewards are, we quickly tire of them; as mentioned earlier, this is called *hedonic fatigue* (or sometimes *hedonic adaptation* or *satiation*). In economics, this is known as *marginal utility*, and it has to do with how the value (or utility) of something changes as you get more of it. For example, the first bite of ice cream is great. The third is okay. By the twentieth bite, you may really not want any more at all: so 20 bites of ice cream is not 20 times the value of one bite! If you are forced to each too much ice cream, the utility can actually drop below zero; you really don't want any more.[8] (This has been tested empirically using ice cream, among other things, and you can try it yourself to see this effect [Mackenzie 2002].)

So being rewarded feels great—but the second time you get the same reward, it doesn't feel as good, and the third time it barely feels like a reward at all. We humans don't evaluate a reward objectively but see it in terms of its relative value, based on what we have already received. In a game, if a player feels that they are no longer being meaningfully rewarded, their engagement will suffer, and they will drop out of the "boring bottom" of the flow channel shown in Figure 4.11. As a result, rewards tend to get bigger over time, meaning that their rate of increase (again, whether in gold, experience, fame, or something else) also goes up over time. This results in an exponentially increasing curve for rewards as the rate of resources given increases over time.

Because the rate of increase goes up over time, as the player progresses, more resources are pumping into the game. Unless the in-game resource sinks also increase to match the sources, this results in an increase in resource supply and thus in inflation.

Realizing how habituation can ruin engagement, many games work hard to avoid it by using a variety of methods, including the following:

■ **Limiting sources:** Many games make resources scare by decreasing their sources—reducing the number of sources, decreasing the rate at which the resources are produced at each source, or increasing the cost or difficulty of obtaining the resources. This happens in role-playing games, for example, in the difficulty of obtaining a better weapon, obtaining the last piece of a set of armor that has nonlinear benefits as a set, or even obtaining the experience points needed for the next level, where the curve for this is nonlinear. (You'll learn more about this in Chapter 9, "Game Balance Methods," and Chapter 10.)

---

8. Note, however, that marginal utility can work the other way, too: in what are commonly known as *network effects*, some things—building blocks, telephones, networked computers, and so on—gain more utility slowly up to some point, after which having more of them makes each one have greater value, and the marginal value rises quickly. This continues up to a point of saturation, where the marginal utility increase slows again.

- **Limiting stock:** Games like *World of Warcraft* and those in the *Diablo* series put a cap on the inventory stock a player can keep, which creates a balancing ecology between "things I'm carrying" and "space I have left," as described earlier. Limiting how much the player can carry pushes off (but does not eliminate) inflation and also gives the player another progression path as he discovers how to increase the amount he can carry.

- **Increasing sinks:** Many games increase the outflow of resource items from the game. For example, in The *Legend of Zelda: Breath of the Wild* (as in many other games), weapons can be broken, meaning they are no longer useful and leave the game. As a result, the player almost never considers a good sword to be worthless (it retains its marginal utility) because you know you may need it when others break.

Inflation and accompanying habituation are common conditions, and they are difficult to avoid entirely. These conditions also highlights why taking a systemic approach to game design—including different kinds of hierarchical systems in a game—helps maintain player engagement. Games that depend on content and progression eventually come to an end. Added content becomes more and outlandish to support the exponential progression curves of challenge and reward, and it also becomes increasingly expensive to create and maintain. Games that rely more on systems that have a strong ecological, balancing component (for example, the "Realm vs. Realm" combat described earlier) are able to go on much longer with no clear limit on the player's engagement.

Combat Systems

Combat systems are typically ecologies, as described earlier: two or more opponents seek by their actions to balance each other and ultimately eliminate the other(s) from the game. In terms of time scale and interactivity, individual combat systems typically focus on action/feedback and short-term cognitive interactions. As a result, combat may be a significant part of the core loop of a game, but it is usually accompanied by other reinforcing loops—progression systems in particular—to provide longer-term goals and offset the inherent balancing nature of the combat system. Note that some games (especially mobile games) include combat systems in which the player has few if any decisions to make. While these games have the surrounding reinforcement loop as their core loop that keeps the player playing, the loss of the fast action/feedback interactivity in combat almost inevitably reduces the player's engagement and thus longevity in the game. Even with a strong core loop, compelling moment-to-moment decisions and interactivity remain vital to making a successful game.

Many games use combat as a primary balancing system that interacts with other systems. For example, the card game *Star Realms* has each player's individual core loop focused on engine building. Combat occurs between players as a way for each player to slow or balance an opponent's progress. This has the effect of heightening the need for effective decision making in the engine-building loop, as the player must choose to construct ships for immediate gain or long-term investment, knowing that the opponent will certainly provide a challenge to whatever choice the player makes.

Construction Systems

Many games include various kinds of "building" systems, where the player can add more to the world than was there before. This includes crafting, farming, breeding, and constructing and modifying vehicles, buildings, or (as in the case of role-playing games) an individual character. These systems typically involve both engines and economies (including long production chains), depending on whether the emphasis is on reinvesting past gains for future increases via an engine-based system (as many deck-building games do as their core loop) or exchanging resources to gain value. They tend to focus on short-term and long-term cognitive interactivity, though some very detailed construction systems include significant action/feedback components as well.

Construction systems are often supporting subsystems within a larger progression loop. In a role-playing game, the player builds up skills, weapons, armor, world knowledge, and often a social set (party and guild membership) as parts in a progression loop. Likewise, in strategy games, players pursue research to construct new buildings to train more powerful units to get greater fame and loot—a nicely nested series of engine and economic loops.

Skill and Technological Systems

Many games include long-term goals built around discovering new skills and technologies. These provide new abilities for the player (their character, empire, and so on) and are typically limited reinforcing loop engine systems. Often these are organized as "trees," where one skill or technology leads to two or three more, and the player navigates the skill or technology space to create a custom character or civilization. As discussed earlier, the player gains experience research points and then invests them in a particular new skill or technology to gain its abilities. Rarely does the player have the ability to use these points for a noninvesting action, though this is an area for exploration in game design.

Social and Political Systems

In games with social gameplay, interacting with others (especially other human players but sometimes also non-player characters), there may also be opportunities for systems of social or political play. These systems are social ecologies; it's not a huge leap from the negotiations between wolves and deer and those between various human factions.[9] Most cliques, competing gangs, political parties, and so on form an ecology, each balancing the other by striving for their own reinforcing dominance. The interactivity is long term and social, focusing on those types and time scales. As with any other ecology, if any "side" comes to a position where its actions are self-reinforcing and it has effectively won, outstripping its opponents in ways that can no longer be challenged, the system collapses, and there is no remaining gameplay.

---

9. Marvin Simkin wrote in 1992 that "Democracy is two wolves and a lamb voting on what to eat for lunch." He prefaced this with "Democracy is not freedom" and went on to write that "Freedom comes from the recognition of certain rights which may not be taken, not even by a 99% vote."

Defining a System's Loops—And Goals

Designing a system starts with the design goals you have for the system: what purpose does the system have within your game? To answer this you need to do the following:

- Construct the system's looping form to support the gameplay and player experience you want to create

- Consciously and carefully consider the kinds of player interactions, goals, and behaviors you want to enable by including this system in your game

- Clearly define the parts and their interactions you have to work with to create your system and other systems in the game with which this one will interact

Overall, the goals for any system can be expressed in terms of higher and lower hierarchical levels: First, consider goals in terms of the higher-level system that this one is a part of. The highest systemic level of this is the player's experience, which arises out of the game+player system. This includes the ways the player interacts with the game (fast or slow, perceptual, cognitive, emotional, or social), and the way they build their mental model to correspond with the systemic game model.

From there we descend into hierarchical subsystems. You may be building a system that exists within another higher-level system, such as the hierarchy of systems shown in Figures 7.6 and 7.7. In this case, you need to look at the system you're designing in its context—the larger system that this one is reinforcing or balancing and how it interacts with other peer-level systems (those that are other parts in the higher-level system).

Defining the Looping Structure

For the system you're designing, you need to consider what kind of looping structure it needs to have: is it a simple reinforcing or balancing loop, an engine, an economy, an ecology, or some hybrid of these? Does it also have subsystems within it? Sketching out the primary loops (see the discussion in the section "Tools," later in this chapter) will help you gain a quick understanding of the overall dynamic behavior of the system and how it supports the player's experience, as well as the subsystems and/or resources that interact to form the loop. Sketching the system's loops will also help you clarify where the system fits in the game and why it's needed. You will likely need to do this multiple times, defining and redefining the systems' structures and relationships. This iterative process will help you define the systems and the overall player experience more precisely, and it will also help you begin to define the game objects that become the parts of your system.

As you do this, you may find that a system you're designing really isn't needed after all—that it adds little to the player's experience. It's important that you not leave in a system that doesn't fit with the rest of the game. For example, a crafting system in a game about social relationships may be out of place. Don't keep it in the game just because you like it or worked hard on it. Set it aside, and either you'll find a place for it in the game later on, or you'll find a way to use it in another game.

In addition to the looping structures, you have to consider how the parts within the system, along with their interactions, support your gameplay goals for the system. This will lead you to confront issues of game balance and whether the system enables the player to make meaningful decisions. (The specifics of designing parts and balancing them are covered in Chapters 8, 9, and 10.)

By working at all these levels—parts, loops, and the whole—at the same time (or at least shifting your focus back and forth from one to another; refer to Figure 5.2), you can more clearly articulate your design goals not as static content, but as a set of dynamic machines that create the space within which the player can act.

Linking the Player Experience and System Design

In designing any game system, you need to think about how it fits into and supports the player experience. For example, in the case of a combat system, you should consider whether the gameplay you want is a grand sweeping army-to-army combat where the player sees the effects of their orders to different groups of units unfold over minutes or a more intense personal combat experience where the player determines every subtle movement or combination of moves on a subsecond basis. Each of these is overall a combat-ecology system, but the interactions the player has with the game differ greatly, as do the underlying game parts necessary to create the system and support the desired gameplay experience. Defining the goals for the system in terms of the player's interactions and experience, as well as the parts, attributes, and behaviors needed to support those will help you clarify the structure of the system itself.

Similarly, if you are designing a progression system, a natural consideration is how fast you should allow the player to progress. How can you give a player the feeling of early mastery in a fast interaction loop early on so you can build engagement but also continue to hold their interest over the long term? If the player has no positive feedback early in the game, they will be unable to construct their mental model and won't be engaged by the game. Creating a positive feedback "success experience" ("you did it!") in a core loop that occurs in the first minute or so of the game is a way to help the player begin building their model and become hooked by the game. Such positive feedback is important, but as discussed earlier, hedonic fatigue sets in if you keep giving the same rewards at the same rate. However, if the player is rewarded too much and progresses too fast, the game will be over—or become boring—quickly. On the other hand, if a player progresses too slowly, or if the progression itself is not intrinsically rewarding, then the game becomes a "grind,"[10] and the player persists only if they believe there is a sufficient reward waiting for them later; otherwise, they will simply drop the game as not being engaging.

Tools for Designing Game Systems

Designing game systems doesn't require any exotic tools. A great deal of work can be done with paper, whiteboards, and other simple tools. This work is highly iterative; you will end up sketching out looping structures over and over again to more accurately depict the kind of systems you want. Just the act of trying to draw out a looping diagram for a system helps you focus and clarify your thoughts on it and shows you how it works as part of the game. At some point, as these structures and diagrams begin to solidify, you need to move to making prototypes to see if your designs actually work and fulfill the goals you set for them.

Whiteboards and Fast Prototyping Tools

One of the most common tools for game designers is the whiteboard. This tool is completely "analog" (that is, it involves no electronics), and it allows you and those working with you to draw, erase, and redraw over and over in different colors. You can expect to spend a lot of time in front of whiteboards, puzzling out the systems diagrams you want to represent your gameplay.

There are a few digital tools as of this writing that can help with this stage of defining your systems. *Loopy*, a free online tool by Nicky Case (2017), allows you to easily draw reinforcing and balancing loops. While the functionality of this tool is limited, it enables you to create many kinds of looping diagrams with a clean and pleasing aesthetic and then to see them in action. A similar and far more detailed tool is Joris Dormans' *Machinations*, mentioned earlier. This tool provides a comprehensive toolset for creating working, functional looping diagrams and even full games (albeit without any game-like presentation—just the raw systems). Unfortunately, this tool is also aging quickly and appears to not be actively maintained. There are other tools, as well, including many intended for simulation rather than game design work, such as *NetLogo* (Wilensky 1999).

Beyond these tools for system or simulation creation, there are many other programming environments that can be used for rapid prototyping. Many designers like to use JavaScript, Python,

---

10. The "grind" is a familiar staple of many RPGs and MMOs. Players endure largely joyless quests or other explicit goals that the game has laid out for them as part of what has been called the *leveling treadmill*. This is the price the player pays for gaining greater levels and abilities so they can go on to grind more quests at a higher level. While grinding gameplay is not in itself engaging or fun, both players and designers have come to accept it as part of the landscape of these games. A more systemic approach to the player's experience and interactions may yield designs that do not rely on a mindless, repetitive grind but instead on systemic mastery.

and full game-development tools like *Unity* to create fast, ugly (the emphasis is not on art) prototypes to test their system designs. The key to using any of these is to use them as a means to an end: you want to test your ideas, moving from your conceptual looping system diagrams to fast working prototypes that you can examine, test, and refine as quickly as possible.

Challenges

Two major challenge with any of these tools are how complex or complete you can make an interactive system on one hand and the time it takes to learn and use them on the other.

A whiteboard is easy to use, and you can draw any system you like on it. On the other hand, you have to use your own brain as the computer to make it come to life—and humans are notoriously fallible when it comes to maintaining an accurate understanding of a dynamic system's behavior. *Machinations* includes more detailed operators, including user input ones, than does *Loopy*, but while both are relatively easy to learn and use, neither allows the creation of systems containing subsystems (at all in *Loopy*'s case, and in any modular, usable form with *Machinations*). *NetLogo* is more advanced in its capabilities and can be used to create full game systems for simple games, but it has a longer learning curve and is not as rapid in iterative prototyping as the simpler tools.

Whether this or a general language-based development system is best in terms of depth of expressivity and speed of prototyping depends on your design style and how willing you are to learn the language or tool. Ultimately, there is no one best solution; as has often been said, use what you consider to be the right tool for the job at the time.

Spreadsheets

A mainstay of any system design process is the electronic spreadsheet. Across the games industry, *Microsoft Excel* is the most popular, given its long history and many capabilities, but others, such as *Google Docs Spreadsheet* and *Apache OpenOffice*, have their own followings as well. In any case, you will need to be intimately familiar with using spreadsheets to enter, visualize, and compare the game data that define your lowest-level systems' parts and make your looping systems function. (We discuss how spreadsheets are used to this end in Chapters 8 and 10.)

Documenting Your System Designs

As with the game concept documents, it's vital when designing game systems to articulate them in a form that communicates well to others and that remains comprehensible to you during development. Anyone who works on your game (including you, months from when you start) needs to understand the following:

- Why the systems are designed as they are
- How the systems support the game concept and the desired player experience
- How the systems are embodied by the game's objects as the system parts

System Design Documents

The primary documentation for a system's design is an explanatory description of its goals and how it works. As the design is refined and becomes more settled, technical documentation is used primarily on the programming side—actually implementing the system in the game.

As with any other game design documentation, it is important to stay up-to-date on deliverables[11] like this as your design progresses. These are not write-once-and-forget documents but ones that should be updated and consulted often as you iterate on the system's design. Documentation is often dreaded or avoided, but failing to document a game can lead to making poor decisions in the future when you can no longer trace the thread of thinking that led you to a particular set of design decisions. This is especially true with system design, as there are often subtle design decisions that do not have obvious effects. Part of the job of documentation is to make these clear so that the essence of the system is not lost.

The System Design Document

The design document for a game system should include the following:

- The system name and a high-level description.
- The goals for this system, expressed in terms of the player's experience: how does this system help create the gameplay? This explanation is often qualitative and focused on the experiential nature of the system. Using words related to how the player feels when interacting with this system is entirely appropriate.
- A graphical depiction of the system, showing important subsystems and internal parts and behaviors. These typically take the form of the kinds of looping diagrams used throughout this book. A high-level diagram might look a lot like Figure 7.11.
- Any player interactions enabled or required by this system.
- A list of (or, ideally, live links to) the descriptions of subsystems, peer systems, and the system within which this one exists (the highest level of them being the game+player system).
- Any other details needed to fully understand the purpose of the system and its implementation.

Each system should have its own brief design document that incorporates these points. Just as it is important not to neglect this documentation, it is also important to make it as clear and brief as possible. Create a separate document for each system, not one huge document. Separate but linked documents (web pages, documents stored at Google Docs, wiki entries, and so on) are often ideal for this, as they enable you to edit each design document as needed without having to wade into a huge "design bible" that inevitably becomes out of date quickly.

---

11. A *deliverable* is anything that you're providing to others who have a stake in the game you're making. This may well be you in the future when you've long forgotten your own reasoning during the design process.

The System Technical Design Document

Along with creating a system design document, you need a more technical document that focuses more on how the system is to be implemented than why. These two documents should remain in step, but separating them this way allows the designers to focus on things like the player's experience and feelings while those more focused on the implementation can get right to how it is to be accomplished. In short, the design document is mainly for game designers, and the technical design document is mainly for game programmers. These two documents aren't always necessary, but it can be useful to separate them even if the same person is the designer and the programmer, as they provide two complementary but distinct points of view on the same system.

The technical document contains specific, implementable descriptions of the system's attributes and behaviors—that is, the code-like definitions for its parts and how they interact. As the design progresses and becomes more settled, the technical design document includes implementation-specific definitions for attributes by type (string, integer, and so on), valid ranges for each, formulas for how behaviors alter them to produce the effects described in the design document, and descriptions of tests and results to ensure that the system is working as expected. It likely includes format descriptions of and links to data files (spreadsheets or similar), and it may include software architectural elements such as class descriptions, depending on the level of specificity needed. (More is generally required on large teams and long-term projects.)

Mockups and Prototypes

In addition to—and often as part of—the documents described in the preceding sections, mockups and prototypes of your design help communicate the purpose and behavior of the system. They help ensure that you and others thoroughly understand your system's purpose, design, and function. They provide needed examples of how the system works and the kind of player experience it is designed to create or support. Note, however, that they do not provide examples of how the system should be implemented at a technical level; many shortcuts may be taken to get a prototype to work and would not be appropriate in the final game implementation.

Mockups are nonfunctional diagrams with supporting text. They may include player-facing drawings or storyboards and/or narrative descriptions (though more diagrams and less text is better!) of how the system works. For example, a mockup of a combat system includes a depiction of the choices the player has, as shown in the user interface, as well as a diagrammatic/narrative description of how a combat proceeds. This shows the effects of the player's choices and interactions with the system's internal functioning.

Whereas mockups are nonfunctional, prototypes for digital games have some actual working functionality. Prototypes are put together quickly to bring more life to the system description than a mockup, though this functionality may be highly limited and is likely to leave out important features that are not related to the system's function. They are also not meant to be indicative of final art and often use stand-in art that is as simple as possible; you want to keep the focus on the system being prototyped, not creating and refining art for the game. As a result, prototypes are often described as being fast and ugly—and in this case, these are positive qualities.

A prototype can be made in any tool, as described above, from a spreadsheet to a full programming environment. Prototypes should be considered off-limits for any transfer (other than of ideas) to a final working game: keep them fast, highly iterative, and ugly and then transfer the lessons you learned from them to the game's production code when you rewrite it completely. The temptation to copy and paste "just a little" of the system's code can be strong, but you will save yourself far more time and grief by not doing so than you will by giving in to this temptation.

Having a working system prototype referenced in your documentation helps you be more certain that your design meets the system's goals and makes the system's function (rather than its structure) more easily understood. This doesn't mean you need to prototype every system in the game, but the more important the systems—those that make up the game's core loops, for example—the more you want to create prototypes while it's still fast an inexpensive to do so. Discovering later during production of the game that the core loop or some major system doesn't work creates far larger and more expensive delays than does taking the time to iterate on prototypes early on.

More details on effective prototyping practices can be found in Chapter 12.

Questions to Consider About Your Game Loops

As with your description of the game's concept and the whole of the player's experience, there are useful questions to evaluate when reviewing the design of any game system as you develop it. The following are some of them:

- Is the system's purpose clear, especially to other people besides those who designed it (those on your team first and then players)? Note that this requires a working prototype and playtesting, as discussed in Chapter 12.

- Are the system's internal resources, currencies, and/or subsystems apparent and well understood?

- Is it clear where this system lives within the entire game? Is it a part in another higher-level system? Does it have peer subsystems within that higher-level system? Is it what forms one of the player's core loops in the game?

- Does the system have a readily definable primary loop of its own? Is there sufficient interaction and feedback between parts (whether atomic or subsystems) within the system? Does this loop act by reinforcing or balancing the resources within it to support the gameplay experience?

■ Is the system resilient to internal or external changes? Do you understand (and can you predict) in what situations the system will become brittle and fail? Are there any parts in the system that override the effects of all others, or are there choke points where if one part or subsystem fails, the entire system will fail?

■ Does the system provide for and even require meaningful decisions by the player? Does the system force the player into one dominant strategy or not provide interactions at an appropriate frequency (based on the type of interactivity to create the desired gameplay experience)? Alternatively, does the system require so many decisions from the player that the game is likely to be overwhelming?

■ Does the system provide sufficient feedback to the player about its internal operations that the player can build an effective mental model of how it works?

■ Can the system be progressively unfolded as the player's understanding of it increases? That is, can you represent a simple or high-level version of it to which increasing detail (and interaction) is added as the player learns how the system operates?

■ Does the system create emergent gameplay? Do the parts and subsystems within this system combine to create new effects that are not resident in any of them and, in particular, that surprise and delight the player?

■ Can you show how the system functions via a working prototype rather than just talking about it?

■ Is the system adequately and clearly documented, both in terms of its design goals and implementation-specific elements?

Summary

Looping systems are the beating, cycling heart of a game and the player's experience of it. As a systemic game designer, you need to be able to identify, analyze, and create game systems, breaking them down into their constituent loops.

Designing games systemically requires a knowledge of not only reinforcing and balancing loops but how resources and currencies move around between parts to create the system. Seeing things from a systemic point of view highlights the different principal loops involved in game design: the game's model, the player's mental model, the interactive loop (including the all-important core loops) and the game designer's loop surrounding all of these. This also allows us to look at different kinds of gameplay loops and how they combine together to create and support the gameplay desired for the player's experience. Finally, understanding and constructing game systems also requires the use of appropriate tools and communication of the designs via mockups, prototypes, and design documents.

CHAPTER 8

DEFINING GAME PARTS

As introduced in Chapter 2, "Designing Systems," systems are made of parts. In designing a game, defining the parts that make it up is where you encounter the most detail.

This chapter introduces different kinds of parts and dives into the details of how you go about defining and documenting these parts for your game, along with their attributes, values, and behaviors. The result is a set of known quantities that create the looping systems and the overall experience you want for your game.

Getting Down to Parts

Chapter 2 first introduced the idea of systems being made up of parts. These parts create loops between them by their actions. In game terms, parts are where we finally get really specific in the game's design by defining numbers and logical functions that determine how the game actually works.

As discussed in earlier chapters, the parts in a game work together to create a system by their looping interactions. From the point of view of any system, some or all of its parts may be subsystems, as described in Chapter 1, "Foundations of Systems," Chapters 2, and 7, "Creating Game Loops." In a game at least—where you do not have the luxury of defining hierarchical systems stretching all the way down to protons and quarks—at some point you have to create the parts that make up the foundation of the game. These parts are often called *simple* or *atomic* in that they are indivisible; it is at this level that we leave the notions of systemic looping behind in favor of more fundamental internal structures and behaviors.

These parts form the game's "nouns" and "verbs." Each part has its own internal attributes that determine its state (the "nouns") and behaviors that create its function (the "verbs"). Attributes have values and define resources, while behaviors define a part's interactions with other parts and the resource flows between them. These behaviors enable the creation of loops, which form systems.

Another way of saying this is that parts ultimately specify the interactions in the game as well as their effects—including feedback to the player—that enable the player to make meaningful decisions. These decisions and the interactive loop formed between the game and the player create the gameplay experience that you as the designer have in mind. As described in the section "The Designer's Loop" in Chapter 7, you need to be able to move between the levels of organization in the game as part of the design process. You need to be able to change your focus from atomic parts to systemic loops to overall experience so that you can be sure that what is defined at the lowest level creates the experience you want at the highest level.

This chapter examines in detail what goes into creating parts for your game—how to figure out what those parts should be, what they contain, and what they do. Compared to coming up with a concept and even designing the game's systems, this is the most grounded part of the game design process: it deals with bringing the more ethereal parts of the game down to Earth in the form of text strings, numbers, and mathematical and logical functions.

Defining Parts

To create parts for a game, you have to bring the conceptual ideas and dynamic processes from the whole and loop organizational levels down to the level of being what we have called being *spreadsheet specific*. This is where each part is fully defined, and its internal state is precisely specified such that there is no ambiguity about it. Ultimately, every part will be broken down into a series of structural tokens, as first described in Chapter 3, "Foundations of Games and Game Design" (and in Chapter 7, in the section "Parts as Loop Components"), along with behaviors that act on those structures to create the functional parts of the game and ultimately the loops that make the game's systems.

Types of Parts

Parts in a game represent all the *things* in the game's model of the universe and all the actions they can take. A part may denote a physical object such as a character, an army, a tree, and so on. Or a part may be a nonphysical concept, such as area of control, emotion, or even time. Finally, a part may be purely representational and related to the game's rules—for example, the maximum number of cards in a hand, displays or controls in the game's user interface, or the current turn order in a game. Each of these has state and behaviors, as described later in this chapter, created by internal attributes and their values at any given point in the game.

Your Game's Parts

If you have already begun sketching out some of the loops for your game (the game's internal model and any systems that are part of the interactive loop, as discussed in Chapter 7), you will likely begin to see in these loops the parts and their attributes—the resources, currencies, and values within the game world—that form the core parts of your game. These are a good place to start in defining the game's parts. Most games have a small number of parts that players focus on and with which they interact the most. These are usually found in the game's core loops: in a role-playing game, these are the player characters and their opponents; in a strategy game, they might be armies and the area controlled by the player.

Each of these primary parts leads you to others that the primary parts use and that are contained within them hierarchically: the player character has weapons, armor, spells, loot, and maybe pets or a horse. The army in a strategy game has different kinds of units within it, and the area controlled has nonphysical concerns such as adjacency and resource production. Listing these out will help you begin to see the number of parts and their hierarchical organization for your game. Using the systems defined at the loops level will help you see which parts are atomic and which are made from subsystems that need further specification.

As you work through the ever-lengthening list of parts, consider the different types of objects in your game: the physical, nonphysical, and representational—anything that needs internal data to define its state, has behaviors that affect other parts of the game, or with which the player interacts. So you might start with the player character, then the weapons that character carries, and then the representational user interface parts that form the inventory system for the game.

The list of parts will soon become long, unless your game is extremely narrowly focused. (This may be your first encounter with game scope; if so, consider that this list is a good proxy for how much work in the form of art, animation, and programming will go into your game.) It helps to keep your parts separate by type, often on different sheets of a spreadsheet. A good way to separate them is by grouping together those that share common attributes. This way, you don't have environmental objects mixed together with enemy NPCs and representational user interface objects like the cards currently in the player's hand. Keeping these separate will help you be sure your list isn't missing major parts needed for your game. You will also notice that objects of the same type (physical, nonphysical, or rules oriented) tend to have many attributes and behaviors in common.

There may also be background objects in your game world—decorations in the user interface, for example—that have no internal state or behaviors; these need to be included in an art list or user interface description, but they don't form parts that participate in any system in your game.

Internal State

As described earlier, every part within a system has internal state. In the case of simple, atomic parts, this is the current value of each attribute and (in computer terms) variable within the part. This state may include things like the current amount of health (hitPoints = 5), wealth (gold = 10), or any other resources the part contains. It also includes types (class = Ranger), strings (secretName = "Steve"), and any other definable trait that has a name and a value. These attributes are in effect stand-ins for the nearly infinite regress of real-world systems: instead of defining a whole set of metabolic systems that account for a character's health, for example, for convenience you can define a single attribute that says "this character has five hit points."

The concept of *name–value pairs* (also known as attribute–value pairs or key–value pairs) is a common one in computer programming and database construction. It allows for the creation of a name that can hold some amount of data that can change as the program runs. If this is numerical data of a particular kind (number of units in an army, dollars in an account, and so on), then this is the same as a stock in systems terms. In general, a part in a system has one or more attributes, each of which has a value at any given point in time. Together these attributes and their values create the state of the part.

In object-oriented programming terms, a part maps well to an instance of a class: it has data members (attributes with values) and methods or functions that carry out its behaviors. Object-oriented (and component-based) programming schemas often work well for creating parts, loops, and systemic wholes.

Determining Attributes

Creating the parts for your game requires defining the attributes that form each part's internal state and the functions that embody its behaviors. By doing this, you can then assemble the parts together to create systemic loops and thus create the gameplay experience you're looking for.

For each part you define, begin by adding the attributes it needs. You want to have as few attributes as possible, as each adds complexity to your rules and code and represents a new way to unbalance the game. Start with as few as possible and more as needed as you iterate through the design process. Whenever possible, combine two similar attributes on different parts; don't create two attributes for two different parts if one will do.

As with parts themselves, a good way to start here is to look for the attributes with which the player interacts the most or, alternatively, those that provide the most meaningful decisions for the player. If having two kinds of attack (slash versus pierce, for example) doesn't add much to the game, use just one attack attribute. Unless the game is about the highly specific and fine-tuned details of hand-to-hand fighting, one attribute for this is probably enough (and if not, you can add a second one later). Another way to look at this is to think about whether you can quickly communicate to the player how two attributes are different and why they are both important to the player in the game. If not, remove at least one of them or combine them into one.

You also want the attributes to be as broadly applicable across parts as possible. Avoid creating an attribute that is used on only one or two parts. If, for example, you want to put in a "visibility" attributes on a part that may be camouflaged or concealed, consider whether other parts may also be concealed in the game. If this is the only object in the game that has this ability, is it worth including, or is it better to make it available to other parts, too? Having a lot of one-use attributes will make the game more complicated (but not necessarily more engaging) and will make programming behaviors more difficult as well. That said, note that the player's representation within the game (the player's character, nation, and so on) may be an exception to this, potentially having multiple unique attributes, given the player's unique relationship to the rest of the game.

Finally, consider attributes related to both the amount and rate of a resource. For example, a bank account is likely to have an attribute describing the amount of money in it (for example, gold = 100); this describes the amount of the resource gold in the stock (the account). You might have additional attributes that determine the rate of change of that resource, such as income and debt. If income = 10 and debt = 3, then the balance would increase by 7 every time period (the time period might be another attribute on the account-part or, more likely, set to an attribute that is global to the game as a system, like per turn or per minute).

Attributes that describe an amount are sometimes called *first-order* attributes; those that affect the rate of change in a resource are *second-order* ones. It's possible to have *third-order* attributes and beyond as well: it might be that in the bank account example, income is slowly increasing (so the rate of resource change itself has a rate of change). Another way to look at third-order attributes includes applications like "how long to the next level" in RPGs. A character's experience points are a first-order attribute. The rate at which a character gains new ones (if there is an ongoing default rate, as in many idle games) is a second-order attribute. It's often the case that this rate changes with the character's level, going up with each level, as the number of experience points to the next level itself increases. The number of experience points to gain the next level and the new rate of change at that level are both examples of third-order attributes.

Whether to include these, especially second- and third-order values, as attributes or to encode them in behavioral functions on the part is itself a design decision. If you can represent the purpose of a potential attribute simply, then make it an attribute with a numeric value. If the value requires logic to determine, then it becomes the output of a behavior (and the part goes from being simple to being a system of its own).

Attribute Ranges

For every numeric attribute you define on a part, you need to determine the range of valid values as well. This range has several requirements. First, it needs to be something you as the designer can intuitively understand and—just as importantly—can communicate clearly to the player. It also needs to work well across all the parts that use it, and it needs to provide enough breadth for sufficient discrimination between values. At the same time, if the range is too large, there is a risk that you and/or the player will lose the feel for what the numbers mean.

For example, you may decide that the range for attack values on all parts that use that attribute is 0–10. You need to decide if you understand intuitively—and can communicate to the player—what a 5 versus a 6 on that range means and whether there is enough difference between a 5 and a 6 that you'll never need a 5.5 on that scale. If not, then you may want to change the range to be 0–100 instead. However, you probably won't need to use a range for an attack value of 0–1,000, as there's not likely to be any discernible difference between, say, 556 and 557. And, while for programming purposes a range of 0–128 or 0–255 is often useful due to byte representations, you will almost certainly end up transposing that back to a 0–100 or even 0–10 range for the player, as most people don't do well at thinking in binary or hexadecimal.

In most cases, numeric attributes are integers, as they are easy to understand, and integer-based mathematical operations are faster than those involving real (or floating-point) numbers. In some cases, as where multiple probability functions come into play, you may decide to define an attribute range of 0.0–1.0. This makes the math easier, but you still have the problem of making the values meaningful to the player and to yourself as the designer; many people have difficulty discerning a significant difference between numbers like 0.5 and 0.05. In cases like this, some designers like to define a large integer range such as 0–10,000 and then when it comes time to manipulate the values, they simply divide each by 10,000 to convert them to the range 0.0–1.0 (a mathematical manipulation known as *normalization*). For communication to the player, the number can be shown in whatever form makes the most sense in context, from integer numbers to text labels applied to those numbers (that is, ranging from "terrible" to "awesome," mapped to the underlying numbers).

Finally, while a full discussion of probability is beyond the scope of this book, it is important for you as a designer to understand the difference between linear ranges and ranges with different shapes (especially bell curves) and how they affect your design and gameplay. This is covered in more detail in Chapter 9, "Game Balance Methods." For now, understand that a percentile range is the numbers 1–100, where each number has an equal chance of appearing: 99 is as likely as 37 and 2. A range with differential probability is one like you get from rolling two six-sided dice. The range itself is 2 to 12, but each number does not have an equal chance of appearing (see Figure 9.1). When rolling two six-sided dice and adding the numbers shown, the chance of getting a 2 (two ones added together) is about 3%. The same is true for rolling a 12, since it happens only when each die rolls a 6. The most common number from rolling two six-sided dice is a 6, which has about a 17% chance of being rolled. The reason that this is so much more common is that the result of 6 can be gotten multiple ways (5+1, 4+2, 3+3, 2+4, and 1+5 when adding the two dice together).

When assigning ranges to attributes, you need to understand how that attribute will be determined as well as the appropriate overall range for it. A value of 10 means something very different in terms of probability in a linear scale from 1 to 10 than it does on a bell curve scale from 2 to 12, and it may well mean something different to you and to the player in your game in each case.

A Nautical Example

Going through a detailed example of finding the parts and attributes for a game may help you understand how this process works, as well as how it links together with the whole gameplay experience and the creation of looping systems.

Suppose you want to make a game about naval battles in the age of sail—cannon fire, sails snapping in the wind, crew boarding in the smoke after the ships crash together, all that. In hashing out the concept, you decide that because battles between sailing ships have times when there's not a lot of action, this game is more about strategic and tactical decisions than using fast-paced action. That decision helps you see the kinds of interactivity the game will have and how you will spend the player's interactivity budget.

During the concept process, you refine the concept: you might toy with ideas like including sea elves and sea dragons, but then you prudently decide to stay with the original core concept, steering clear of turning this into a fantasy game with a more sprawling scope. You're also more interested in big ships of the line engaging yardarm-to-yardarm than in sneak attacks by pirates on small sailboats. You eventually home in on the idea of players building up and fighting their naval ships against those of an enemy run by the game (as opposed to being played by another human player).

All these choices focus your game concept and help you decide on the systems you'll need: you decide that the player's overall goal is to build up their navy to defend their nation's shipping, so this implies a primary progression system that includes an economic loop: as the player successfully defends their ports and the trade that happens there, they are awarded more money to use to build and repair ships and hire men for crew. Another economic subsystem representing the merchant trading happens within the game model; the player doesn't directly interact with it, but you need to think about the parts for that system as well.

If enemy ships sink too many of the player's nation's merchants or, even worse, take a port city for their own, the player's ability to strike back will be limited due to the loss of funds. (Note that this indicates a potential rich-get-richer problem, where if a player begins to lose they may not have the ability to regain the upper hand, so you'll want to include some form of balancing loop to take care of that—maybe a one-time boon from the king of a lump sum for the player to use to take back the port.)

Given this, the game's core loop involves the player directing battles between the ships in their fleet and those in the enemy's fleet. There's an outer loop as well, where the player uses their income to build or repair ships and hire crew (and perhaps also gain intelligence or other activities).

Finding the Core Parts

Ships quickly emerge as the primary part within the game: they are key to the game's core loop and the player's overall progression system. Because the ships move around, you need some kind of navigation system, including representing how the ship is oriented to the wind to keep with the overall theme. And because ships fight other ships, you need a combat system (a balancing loop ecology with multiple ships acting against each other). Your navy will have multiple ships in it, and each needs to have its own attributes and behaviors defined so that it can take part in navigation and combat and also provide interesting decisions for the player to make. Each ship also needs to know which navy it belongs to, so ships don't fire on others from the same nation.

With all this information, there are innumerable ways to define a ship as a part in a game like this. The ship may be an atomic part containing only name–value pairs (including quantities of various resources), or it may have subsystems within it. For example, a ship has to have a crew. Is this just a numeric name–value pair, like "crew = 100," or is there a whole subsystem within the ship that governs crew training, morale, and so on?

This is the kind of game designer's decision you have to make in defining parts: you need to consider the experience you're trying to create and the player's interactivity budget, along with the looping systems you've begun to define. There is no one right answer except what is best for the game you are making. Is it better for *this* game if the crew is just a modifier on the ship that makes it sail faster and fight better, or do you want more detail, with officers defined individually and an overall crew having a certain level of training (that the player can pay to increase) and a level of morale that goes up and down during battle? Providing more detail generally provides more decisions for the player, but it's easy to go too far with this. If the player has 2 or 3 ships in their navy, this level of detail might be welcome; if they have 200, this is going to become an onerous chore for all but the most dedicated "age of sail" enthusiasts.

As a designer, you need to be open to these different possibilities, create an initial design, and playtest it to see if it works. (Chapter 12, "Making Your Game Real," provides more detail on playtesting.)

Defining Attributes

For now, you decide to create a few crew-related attributes within the ship: crewNumber, crewTraining, and crewMorale. Each of these has a value that is an integer number and will be used as inputs to the ship part's behaviors. Later, you might turn one or more of these into its own subsystem within the ship if the game experience needs it. This kind of change in the design process is common, but by starting simple, you can see if this is sufficient first. You also decide to add the nonnumeric attributes shipNation and shipName to provide the identifiers needed in the game for each ship, as mentioned earlier.

You need to go through a similar process with the ship's attributes that relate to navigation and combat. The ship might have a maxSpeed attribute, for example. What about how quickly the ship can turn, the maximum number of sails it can carry, and the number it currently has set? These all sound like candidates for additional integer attributes on the ship—though each could also easily lead to new subsystems, again depending on the amount of detail you want to have in the game—and to communicate to the player. These are all important design decisions you need to make.

For combat, the ship could have an attribute that describes how many working cannon it has in order to determine the strength of its attack. How fast and well those cannon fire will depend on the crew attributes mentioned earlier. While thinking about this, to give the game more texture, you decide that you will separate out the captain of each ship from its crew. This allows the player to allocate hero captains like Admiral Nelson, Lord Cochrane, or Lucky Jack Aubrey to each ship. Some captains sail or fight better than others, making the player's choice of who to put in command of each ship a meaningful decision in the game. This line of thinking makes it clear that these captains are parts themselves, with their own attributes that you need to define. Each ship now has an attribute called "captain" that is itself a part with its own internal attributes and behaviors that add to those of the ship.

The Detail Design Process

The preceding section doesn't present a complete list of the parts you need to define to create the tokens needed for your game, but it gives you an idea of how to begin and how detailed the process must be. Thinking up the concept for a game can be lots of fun for a designer, but to make the game become real, you have to get down to this level of specificity, defining each and every part and its attributes in the game. Some parts are simple and atomic, and others contain their own systems. As we will see, all parts have behaviors, and most contribute to player decisions in the game. All are part of systems needed to support the gameplay experience, whether in interacting with the player or interacting with other parts in the game's internal model.

You will typically want to limit the number of attributes, parts, and systems in the game that exist primarily as part of the game loop but that have little if any interaction with the player. The trade system mentioned above governs how much of a reward the player gets for protecting merchant shipping. This is an example of a system that exists without a lot of player visibility or interaction, but there will be few of these. Creating and balancing the parts in a system is a complex, iterative task (see Chapters 9 and 10, "Game Balance Practice"). If it's not going to result in interactions with and decisions for the player, it's often best to make these systems as simple as possible and put your efforts elsewhere. Otherwise, you can spend a great deal of time and effort on something the player will never see.

While this is just a start on the process of defining parts for a game, already you have a few parts that represent physical objects and hints at parts that are nonphysical and representational (the concept of nationality and ship name, for example), related more to the rules and user interface of the game. Looking at the different parts you have defined, some holes become obvious: wind should be an important part in the game, but it's not represented yet. It might have attributes for direction and intensity—and maybe how often it changes direction. Perhaps the wind is a complex part containing another subsystem that interacts with the ship. Should a ship with a better-trained crew sail faster? Probably, and because you already have the concept of training encoded in an attribute on the crew-part, it doesn't take a lot to add this.

This process of defining parts, attributes, and subsystems (recursively defining the parts within each) is not one you have to complete all at once. In fact, it's better to approach this iteratively as part of your designer's loop. First, define the parts and attributes that seem more clearly necessary for the game's core loops and the overall gameplay experience you want. Then move to defining the behaviors of the parts so you can link them into loops. Finally, iterate on this process, creating mockups and prototypes to test and refine your thinking as you go (see Chapter 12). Getting even an ugly prototype up and running with a full core loop will take you a long way toward understanding if the game itself is worth pursuing.

Specifying Behaviors for Parts

In addition to having state—attributes and their values—parts also have behaviors. These behaviors are the functional complement to the attributes' structure. They are the means by which parts interact to form looping systems and create gameplay: this is how engines, economies, escapements, and ecologies are made. These behaviors are also how the game's parts interact with and provide feedback to the player.

When specifying behaviors for parts, it's important to understand how the parts function and interact: what resources do they create, consume, or exchange? Remember that parts and resources may be physical, nonphysical, or representational, so their function may include creating or consuming resources such as movement, time, experience, sanity, and combos, in addition to more physical ones, such as health, money, and ore.

The player, too, is interacting with various parts and resources to play the game. They are trying to accumulate some resources and may be trying to get rid of or minimize others. Some parts with their attributes and resources use their behaviors to aid the player, and other parts use their behaviors to stand in the player's way, pushing back against the player's attempts to attain their goals. A player must make decisions as part of their mental loop that lead to interactions with the game as they choose which way to go and how to play the game.

Principles of Behavior Creation

The sum of all this is that for every change in a resource or an interaction between two parts or the player and the game, there must be a behavior. Defining behaviors can be difficult, especially as you try to keep in mind the systems and gameplay you are attempting to create. While the specifics of the process are different for every game, there are some overriding principles that will help guide your efforts.

Designing Behaviors with Local Action

It is important to create behaviors that can be said to act locally: that is, a behavior should interact with other parts that are at about the same level of organization and that are in the same operational context. Using the nautical example from above, we might create various behaviors on ship's cannon to be used in combat. It's reasonable that these functions might act on the ship's crew (making them more tired, for example) and on other ships (inflicting damage), as these are both at about the same level of organization and in the same operational context. Having cannon affect the amount of trade done in a particular port is decidedly nonlocal: the port is at a completely different level of organization in the game's model of the world, and operationally these two have little reasonable direct connection.

Another aspect of local action is that a part's behavior supplies an effect (for example, a change in resource) but does not determine for another part how that part responds. Using the cannon fire example, a ship might do 20 points of damage with its cannon to another ship, but it does not determine how that damage specifically affects its target. It might result in the loss of crew, cannon, sails, or even sinking, but the part that received that damage makes those determinations as part of its behavior. In the language of systems thinking, one part can *perturb* another part's state, but it cannot *determine* that part's state. In object-oriented programming, this principle is described as *encapsulation*—the idea that one object cannot "reach inside" another to set its attribute values.

Creating Generic, Modular Behaviors

Behaviors should be as general, modular, and generic or context-free as possible. Behaviors should be as simple as they can be, not incorporating more contextual information than necessary, and they should be generic enough to be useful in many situations. So, for example, when cannon on one ship fire at another ship, they inflict damage on that ship. That is local, simple, and modular, and it is free of any overarching context. The cannon do not need to know whether the other ship is an enemy or how much damage it has already taken; these are contextual cues that should be handled by other behaviors (for example, the player or an NPC captain deciding whether to fire the cannon).

This may seem like an obvious point, but extra context can easily creep into behaviors and limit their overall utility if you are not careful. This often happens as designers create elaborate scripted behaviors that become more dependent on context and thus more limited in the situations where they can be used. For example, if you have an NPC who can walk around a building, you might create an "open the door" behavior that they can use as part of going from one room to another. This behavior does not need to know why the NPC is going from one room to another or how to unlock a door or force it open: other behaviors take care of those contexts. In the same way, an "unlock door" function does only that. It does not open the door or need to know why the door is being opened. This level of modularity will help keep each behavior general in its purpose and within its sphere (unlocking a door, firing cannon, and so on), while tangling it up with additional information just makes it nonmodular and more narrow in how it can be applied. To continue the walking around example, compare the general "open door" behavior to one that has the purpose "move the NPC from their quarters to the command center." This behavior is complex and highly contextual: it can be used only when the NPC is already in their quarters and only when their destination is the command center; this is a lot of effort for very little usage, and it prevents any emergence from happening. Many scripted scenes and behaviors in games are made this way. They suffer from having only narrow utility and being brittle, in that they are not generally applicable to the NPC's function in the game.

Creating Emergence

The benefit of making behaviors that are local in scope, operate at a particular level of organization, and remain modular and general in their operation is that this is how emergent effects arise. These effects create endless variety, grab the player's attention, and enable better and longer player engagement for less content and lower development cost than attempting the same with heavily contextual scripting.

For example, in a flocking algorithm, each bird has three distinct behaviors that are local, modular, and generic. Recall from Chapter 1 that these are the three rules:

1. Fly in about the same direction and speed as other birds around you.
2. Don't collide with birds near you.
3. Try to move toward the center of mass of the birds around you.

Each of the rules is a behavior on each bird, and each bird exists as a part in the overall system. From the execution of these behaviors, dynamic and unpredictable flocks emerge.

Similarly, Conway's *Game of Life* (Gardner 1970) is a cellular automaton where each part—a cell in in a 2D grid—can be on (black) or off (white). The behavior of the cells encode simple, local, modular rules that determine whether a cell will be on or off on the next time tick:

1. If the cell has fewer than two neighbors that are on, this cell will be off.
2. If the cell is on and has two or three neighbors that are on, it remains on.
3. If the cell has more than three neighbors that are on, it will be off.
4. If a cell is off and has exactly three neighbors that are on, it turns on.

Note that these rules only look at the cell's operational context (the eight cells that are the "neighborhood" for a given cell), and they affect only the cell itself. There is no nonlocal effect or other context required for these behaviors to work. And yet, from these simple rules, magnificent and fascinating emergent effects appear.

Many other powerful examples of emergent properties arising from local, general-purpose rules exist in games and simulations. In Nicky Case's *Parable of the Polygons* (2014), there are two parts in the system with which players interact: triangles and squares. These polygons don't move on their own, but they do have a "happiness" behavior that changes their happiness attribute based on their local context:

1. A polygon is happy if exactly two of its neighbors are the same shape as it.
2. A polygon is "meh"—neither happy or unhappy—if all its neighbors are like it.
3. A polygon is unhappy if only one of its neighbors is like it. Only unhappy polygons may be moved.

The player's task in this game is to make as many polygons as happy as possible by moving them around, or at least to make sure that no polygon is unhappy. Movement is a player-interaction-based behavior and not one that the polygons can do for themselves.

This game is based on the work of economist Thomas Schelling, who showed that populations can become highly segregated even if no individual wants this to happen (Schelling 1969). The emergent segregation is the result of local, generic behaviors, as the *Parable of the Polygons* shows: just by moving squares and triangles around to be happy (based on the rules that affect them as parts in the overall game system), the player creates the emergent result of segregated areas that are mostly squares or mostly triangles, with little mixing between them (see Figure 8.1).

As a final example, the 2016 game *Slime Rancher* contains numerous examples of emergent gameplay based on parts (the cute little jelly-bean-like slimes) having specific, local, noncontextual behaviors (Popovich 2017). Two instances (of many) of this involve how different slimes act in the game.

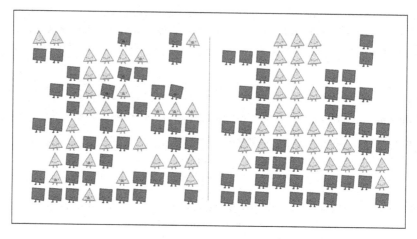

Figure 8.1 The *Parable of the Polygons*. Left, a population before the game is played, showing diverse placement but with unhappy polygons. Right, after the game is played, no polygons are unhappy, but their populations are more segregated

First, the slimes like to stack on top of each other when they're close together. It's just a behavior they have that has no greater purpose; it is local, generic, and not programmed to be part of anything bigger. Players often perceive it as the way the slimes play, or act together toward a common end, though neither of these are inherent in the actual behavior. Stacking up is local contextually and operationally, as it affects only nearby slimes and doesn't somehow change the character of the overall population. It's also remarkably effective as an enabler for other behaviors. For example, if the slimes are penned up but want to get to a nearby food source that they can detect, their natural affinity for stacking up will eventually enable some of them to get over the pen's barrier to get to the food. None of the slimes intend for this to happen; it's the emergent result of two local behaviors ("stack up" and "seek food"), though it is surprising and delightful to players.

Another more specific behavior is moving food. Some slimes, called "tabby slimes" (they look a bit like tabby cats), have a behavior where if they find food that they cannot eat, they pick it up and move it to another location that already has food. Again, this behavior is local and limited in its context (it requires the presence of food), but it results in the perception of either tabby slimes "stealing" food or, alternatively, bringing gifts of food to other slimes—depending on whether the player sees the tabby slime pick up the food and take it away or drop it off near some other slimes where there is already food. It also has the effect of redistributing food around the environment, which has the potential to perturb other slimes' behavior. This can cause emergent cascade effects that delight players but are not preprogrammed into the game.

Providing Feedback

A final important aspect of part-based behaviors is that parts provide feedback to the player about how the state of the game has changed. This is a vital point that enables the completion of the interactive loop between the player and the game: the player acts on the game, changing its internal state (perturbing but not determining, as mentioned above). The game then acts using behaviors on the parts within its model and provides feedback to the player to complete the loop. While there are always exceptions, it is not too strong to say that if you have a behavior—a verb—in your game, it *must* provide feedback to the player. If a part has no behavior or the behavior has no feedback, you need to question very carefully whether it's really needed in the game.

Getting feedback from the game is how the player goes about creating their mental model of it—learning, confirming or re-creating predictions, seeing what works effectively, and assessing their own increase in ability in the game. As part of their mental loop, the player compares the feedback provided by the game with what they expected, based on their existing model, and adjusts their model accordingly. This feedback is also what keeps the player engaged and playing the game.

Feedback and Player Expectations

If a game's feedback matches a player's expectations, that's a positive experience that reinforces the model and deepens their engagement with the game. If the feedback is surprising in that it doesn't match the player's model, but they are able to quickly adjust the model to match the feedback, that's a valid learning experience and is also experienced as positive. If, however, the feedback is missing, distorted, or so unexpected and incompatible with the player's mental model that they cannot quickly adjust their model to make sense of the feedback, this is most often a negative experience. That kind of off-putting experience reduces the player's engagement and their desire to continue with the game.

Feedback to the player informs them of the effects of their actions and the state changes that have occurred in the game. These changes may be due to the player's recent actions or to a process that has been in the works for some time. Think of this like turning on the stove to cook something: when you turn it on, you need to know immediately that a burner is heating up. And if you put some water on to boil, a little later you get feedback about the water's state (temperature) having changed as that process proceeds.

Kinds of Feedback

In a game, feedback to a player is most often visual and auditory, along with textual or symbolic information. Changes in an object's color, size, animation, or special effects (glow, fireworks, and so on) are all visual signals that something has changed that the player may need to attend to. These changes are often accompanied by auditory cues—tones, notes, changes in music, or other sound effects. Most games rely more on visual cues than auditory ones, in part because visual information is more specific about which part has changed than sound can easily convey. This does not mean that sound is unimportant, however; if anything, most games still make too little use (and too unimaginative use) of the palette of sound available to them.

As stated earlier, every such state change—the action of every behavior on a part in your game—should be accompanied by some feedback notification to the player. If a change is not relevant to the player and thus not worthy of feedback, you need to examine whether the change is necessary for the game. Does the player need to know about the state (and the change in state) of that part to improve their mental model of the game? Some feedback can be subtle, such as the slow filling of a thermometer bar to show change over time, but full state changes, such as when a building is finished being constructed and can now be used, requires more emphatic notification. If the player misses the fact that their army is ready or their water is boiling, they will be frustrated and move their attention from playing the game to focusing on its user interface to make sure they don't miss more notifications—and this may well result in a loss of engagement and enjoyment.

Amount, Timing, and Comprehension

If you question whether a player will be met with visual and auditory chaos because there is so much changing and so much feedback being offered at any given time, then you need to consider the amount of change in your game at any given time and how you are using the player's interactivity budget. If you are creating a fast-action game with lots going on and only fast action/feedback interactivity, then you can afford to be assaulting the player's senses with feedback. This is the appeal and challenge of many fast-action games. If, however, your game is more about strategy, relationships, or socialization, this may be a sign that you need to pare back the number of parts and behaviors in your game to allow the player to keep their interactivity and focus where you want it to be.

Timing of feedback is also important. In general, feedback needs to be immediate. As discussed in Chapter 4, "Interactivity and Fun," "immediate" means feedback needs to be presented to the player no more than 100 to 250 milliseconds after a change has occurred. Between about a quarter of a second and a second, the feedback will seem to have lagged annoyingly (again reducing the player's engagement), and if the feedback is delayed by more than about a second after an event or a change, the player may not associate it with the state change at all.

In addition to being immediate, feedback needs to be instantly understandable in its connection to the underlying state change. That is, you cannot expect the player to reason through obscure combinations of symbols that you provide to understand the feedback they are seeing. For example, you cannot expect that a player will understand that the appearance of a blue flame in the upper-left corner of their screen means that their water is boiling because people associate blue with water, and a flame looks like heat, so together that refers to boiling water. That's far too obscure and requires way too much thinking from the player. Remember that the player is trying to play the game, not play the user interface (or the game rules), and you want them to stay engaged with the game.

Generally, feedback that indicates "the state of this part has changed" is enough and should be instantly recognizable as such. Text is a poor medium for most feedback, again because the player's focus is on the game, not on the user interface. The short way that game designers sometimes put this is that "people don't read." While this is an overstatement, it's amazing how accurate it is: if someone is engaged in a game, they will often not read (and may not even consciously see) text feedback that you as the designer believe to be completely obvious. Even in situations where you include symbolic information—such as numbers floating off above the head of a character, indicating how much damage they're taking—it's more the color and motion than the specific quantity that is important. For feedback that requires more focus or reasoning, section it off (for example, in a dialog box or separate window) and let the player work through it at their own pace. Pause the game if at all possible until they have absorbed the complex tangle of information you have given them.

Finally, avoid at all costs providing misleading or nonsensical feedback. If fireworks go off in your game, make sure they mean something: do not have them go off randomly or to indicate different kinds of state changes in different situations. You can use this kind of feedback for almost any behavior that you want, as long as it's obvious, immediate, and used consistently. In the same way, sometimes you will want to use animations or sounds in your game to help bring the world to life, but you should be careful about doing so without tying these to some underlying state change, even if it's a trivial one. Players will interpret almost any visual and auditory feedback as meaning something, and they will try to find this meaning and add it to their mental models. If the changes aren't really feedback, if they don't mean something, then they are effectively noise that distracts players and reduces their engagement.

Back to the Nautical Example

Having earlier defined some of the attributes for parts like ships, crew, and captains in your age of sail naval game, you also need to design each part's behaviors. Ships move, attack, and presumably take damage from other ships. Are there other things a ship needs to do? You need to decide this in your early design, though you can (and will) revise such decisions during playtesting as you discover aspects of the game you didn't see before.

You decided earlier that captains and crew contribute to how the ship sails and fights. This forms the basis of some of the captain's and crew's behaviors; they are the functions for how they and ship interact as parts in the game and help construct the navigation and combat systems. (The crew may have more behaviors that you add as the design progresses, but you can start with these.)

Specifying each behavior ultimately comes down to a formula or logic that you will define and iterate on to get just right. This logic will become the rules for the game, whether expressed in ways that humans can compute for a tabletop game or in terms of code that the computer runs for a digital game.

For example, in defining the ship's attack behavior, specifying each behavior mainly comes down to the ship's attack attribute (defined for now as its number of usable cannons), as modified by the crew. You've also decided that you want the ship's captain to affect how well the ship fights—but maybe not directly. As a way to create interlocking systems, and to keep the captain part's behaviors more local, the captain has a behavior that adds a bonus (or minus!) to the crew's morale: this behavior is based on the Leadership attribute on the captain part. You can create a behavior called "fight" within the crew part that uses a combination of the crew's attribute values—how many crew members there are, their current morale (affected by the captain's leadership), and their training (affected by money the player has previously spent)—to create a modifier on the ship's attack behavior (see Figure 8.2). This sounds complex, but if communicated well, it will be easily incorporated into the player's mental model.

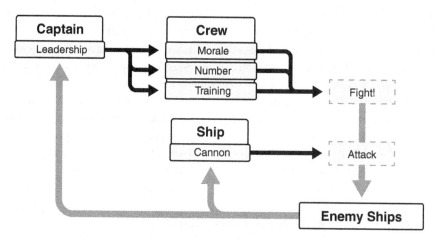

Figure 8.2 The effect the captain's leadership has on the crew, which affects their fighting ability on the ship. There is a tentative connection return for improving the captain's leadership, as explained in the text

For the ship's attack value, you need to create a weighted function such that if the ship has plenty of cannon but few crew members, the ship's attack modifier will be low (cannon cannot fire without crew). The same is true if the ship has lots of crew but they have poor morale or training, or if the ship has a great captain and a strong and happy crew but few cannon. However, if the ship has a strong captain, hearty and numerous crew, and lots of cannon, its attack will be strong. These conditions suggest a formula or set of logical functions that you can create to determine how each one affects the ship's fighting capability, how the player interacts with each, and the possible range of attack modifier values for the combat system. This may lead to subsidiary attributes on the ship part, such as the coefficient for weighting to determine how much the cannon, crew, and captain matter relative to each other. Iteratively adjusting this value as you play the game will help you find the balance you want, as discussed in Chapter 9.

A similar process goes into creating the ship's sailing system, but that also involves the external wind variable. The wind was added to the list of parts earlier, with attributes for direction and intensity. Is that enough detail for the sailing part of the game? That's a question for you to answer in terms of how it affects the gameplay experience.

At this stage of the process, you're off to a good start on effectively tokenizing the game concept you started with, nailing down the gameplay concepts with specific parts, attributes, and behaviors that create the systems you need. You need to test and tweak this whole design in early prototypes as quickly as you can, as you will certainly not get all the parts, attributes, and behaviors correct from the start. You also need to document your parts design, as discussed later in this chapter.

Creating Looping Systems

In the examples discussed here, each of the parts affects others via its own behaviors that are local in organization and effect and generic in how they connect to other parts and that provide ample feedback to the player. The final element that is needed for creating systemic effects is for the behaviors to form feedback loops between the parts rather than only operating linearly. This means that each part should both affect and be affected by other parts.

In our earlier nautical example, we discussed briefly the idea that ships would fight each other, with their attack strength being based on how many working cannons each ship has, the number and quality of their crew, and the captain's ability to lead. When ships take damage, they lose some crew and/or cannon, and the remaining crew lose morale. This reduces the ship's ability to attack back as strongly as before; the two ships form a balancing ecological loop (exchanging the "damage" resource with each other and reducing their own crew and cannon as needed).

However, the captain's contribution to how well the ship fights is a one-way connection. It works well but doesn't help build a dynamic system in the game. However, if the crew has some way—directly or indirectly—to affect the captain in return, then a loop has formed, and the game becomes more interesting for the player. Perhaps if the crew's morale remains high at the end of a combat, the captain gains additional leadership in an economic reinforcing loop (trading Morale for Leadership). Or maybe a longer-term loop makes more sense, such that captains gain Leadership only after winning a certain number of battles. The captain has to be successful to gain this benefit, and the benefit helps the captain be more successful in the future—a typical progression system.

There are many possibilities for loops like this in any game. You as the designer need to make sure that parts affect each other to form loops and that the parts' behaviors form interactive loops with the player. Of particular importance is that the key parts in the game help drive the game's core loops by their interactions with each other and the player. In this case, the player's moment-by-moment choices during a battle have an immediate effect on the captain, crew, and ship. In addition, the player's decisions about which captain to place on a ship, how many crew to have on the ship, and how much money to spend on cannons and maintenance all affect the outcomes of battles and the longer-term changes in the captain and crew.

As you look over the parts you have defined in your game, check to make sure that every part both affects some parts and is affected by them or others as well. Every part doesn't need to affect all others or be affected by them; the mental model for that would be very difficult to construct. But if every part affects a few others and is in turn affected by those or by others (locally and at about the same level of organization), you have the beginnings of looping systems in your game. Using the templates described in Chapter 7 for engines, economies, and ecologies will help you map out these loops. Remember, too, that every part in the game may be atomic, or it may have its own systemic loops within it. This is how you build hierarchy and depth in the game and, thus, increased engagement for the player.

Don't Get Lost in the Weeds or the Clouds

Having discussed parts, attributes, values, and behaviors, it's useful to take a step back and look at all this as a design process. Different kinds of designers—storytellers, inventors, and toymakers—feel at home in different stages of the design process. However, no matter which of those areas you prefer, you need to move up and down the organizational levels of your design from high concept to specific numerical values for attributes on parts without losing your overall view. It can be difficult to focus on one level without losing track of the others, and this can be especially difficult if one of these levels isn't your most comfortable place.

If you are more of a high-level storyteller designer, defining the attributes and behaviors for parts can sometimes feel daunting or like drudgery. It's important to come down to Earth and nail down your game design, as this is the only way it becomes real. On the other hand, if you're more at home in dealing with clear ideas for attributes and behaviors and how they fit together, working on the game concept can feel unnecessarily nebulous. It's necessary, however, to leave behind the world of precise detail and make sure that all the details actually combine to form something enjoyable. Your game needs to have a cohesive concept and not just be a bunch of parts flung together in the hopes that they make something fun. Not every game requires full realism or a wide variety of parts; one kind of catapult unit in a strategy game may be fine but not five, and three kinds of flowers or hairstyles or castle banners may be enough in other games. If defining parts is what you find enjoyable, don't overdo this as a way to hopefully create a coherent experience.

Another way to say this is to remember that every game has to have fully defined parts, attributes, and behaviors; no game functions without them. But those parts exist to construct loops and support the perceptual, cognitive, social, emotional, and cultural interactivity in the player that creates the game experience that you as a designer are trying to enable. The game isn't the same as the parts but is created by what emerges out of the interactions of the parts with each other and with the player. You don't get those interactions unless you have successfully created (and iteratively tested) spreadsheet-specific parts, but just having the parts won't make the game.

As with everything else that's systemic, you have to see the whole and the parts at the same time. You need to operate at the level of the parts while not losing the overall concept to make the whole thing work. As part of the designer's loop, you have to be able to move up and down the levels of abstraction and organization in your game design, making sure that the concept is clear, the systems support it, and the parts enable interesting, meaningful interactions and progression for the player.

Documenting Your Detailed Design

In earlier chapters, we discussed documenting your game's concept and system designs. It is with your game's detailed design—the description of the parts, attributes, values, and behaviors—that the specifics become crucial. This is what defines what your game is and why, as well as how it is to be implemented.

Getting Started and Overall Structure

When you begin figuring out the parts and attributes for your game, they may live on a whiteboard or in a text document, just so you have them recorded and exist in some order. As the list begins to take shape, and as you continue working with the parts, their attributes, and their values, you will want to transfer this information to textual design documents and spreadsheets.

The text documents preserve your intent for the parts in the game in a way that is precise enough to be implementable in programming or analog game rules. The spreadsheets are the home for all the specific, especially numeric, information about the attributes and values for parts in the game. In addition to capturing the particulars of your design, your spreadsheet documentation also enables you to rapidly test and iterate on your game, as described in the following sections.

Detailed Design Documents

To adequately describe the details of your game at the level of parts, attributes, values, and behaviors, write a set of design documents that specify everything about the details of your game. This includes the design rationale and a specific behavioral description that can be turned into code (or into game rules, if the player is acting as the computer). This preserves your intent (why each part is important) and provides a technical definition of how each is to be implemented.

While these documents necessarily contain textual descriptions of your game's parts, you should use pictures, diagrams, flow models, mockups, and so on wherever possible. Linking to external mockups and prototypes is also an excellent idea so that the reader can quickly under-stand how the game is supposed to operate at a detailed but functional level.

Being Assertive and Precise

In terms of specificity, treat your parts-level detailed design documents like the blueprints for a building. Be precise in describing all aspects of the design. Avoid being vague and state aspects of the design in present tense (the game behaves this way, not "the game will behave"). Avoid waffling words like "the game might." This documentation is where you stake out the game in no uncertain terms (that you can always come back and change as needed). Except when describing high-level aspects of the design, do not use qualitative phrases like "this enemy moves fast" or "this results in a big explosion" or "this turret turns left and right."

How fast? How big? How far? Whenever a quantity is called for (number of skills or levels, amount of damage, and so on), supply a number, a defined range, or a reference to an equation or another determining factor in this document or in the accompanying spreadsheet. If a decision on a specific number or range has not yet been made, say so and call it out as an issue to be resolved. Being precise in your writing forces you to eliminate the fuzziness that can accompany a design that is all in your head. It is far easier to discuss and find the holes in a proposal than an idea.

But Avoiding Overdoing It

All that said, creating too much design documentation can be as detrimental to your game as creating too little. If you know the details of a part of the game, document it using diagrams, mockups, text, and so on. If you're not sure, document what you're trying to create, your best ideas for how to do it, and what paths you've discarded—and then create prototypes (paper or electronic) to test the ideas. Don't waste time documenting a lot of different options, much less arguing about them: find the area of uncertainty and prototype it. Then once the path you want to take is clear, document that and why you chose it.

As with other design documents, it is best if these live online in a format that can be easily shared, linked to, commented on, and edited (with change tracking so you know who edited the docs when and so changes can be rolled back). The detailed design documents should link both to each other and to the systems and concept documents, as needed, to form a cohesive whole for your design. You should also consider having large, visible single-page design diagrams of particular systems so that different team members can see them and internalize them as part of the design. Overall, you want to avoid having a monolithic and impenetrable "design bible" and instead create a set of easily comprehended references that you and others on your team—artists, programmers, and so on—can reference during implementation and testing.

Keeping Your Documentation Up-to-Date

Any design documentation is only as good as it is current. Game designs are often referred to as "living" documents, in that they change as the game development progresses. As such, plan from the beginning to update your design as development proceeds. You will find new ideas, uncover new problems, and change the overall design as you make the game. If you let this slip, you will soon find that the game as implemented has drifted from the game as designed, and the documentation has become outdated, misleading, and eventually worse than useless.

Spreadsheet Details

In putting parts and their attribute values into a spreadsheet, typical usage is to list each part in a spreadsheet row and each attribute in a column (see Figure 8.3). Thus a part's state can be defined by supplying the appropriate values in each column on its row.

	A	B	C	D
1	Name	Attack	Damage	Speed
2	Dagger	0	2	5
3	Short sword	2	3	5
4	Cutlass	4	5	1
5	Broad sword	3	4	4
6	Rapier	3	3	5
7	Long sword	5	6	2
8	Great sword	8	8	0

Figure 8.3 A portion of a sample spreadsheet. Each part name is listed in column A, and the other attributes and values for each part are listed in columns B–D

If there are many different kinds of parts with disparate attributes (for example, weapons, flowers, cars, sports teams), they are listed in separate groups or (more often) on separate sheets, while parts of the same type are listed together. So, as shown in Figure 8.3, you might have a spreadsheet with each part in a list of "hand-to-hand weapons" listed with its name in the first column, row by row, with the attributes common to all of them listed in subsequent columns. Each weapon attribute—attack, damage, speed, and so on—is a value in a cell on that weapon's row in the sheet. Ranged weapons or magic spells might be listed on the same sheet if they shared most or all of the same attributes, or they could be listed on a separate sheet with their own attributes defining their internal state.

You may also have cells in your spreadsheet that describe the effect of each part's behavior in mathematical form. It's useful to include pointers in the spreadsheet to external text-and-diagram descriptions of the parts, attributes, and behaviors so that you and other stakeholders can easily access complementary descriptions of the details of your game.

Beyond Attributes and Values

A nonnumeric issue that can easily be taken care of in spreadsheets is the naming of parts. In many cases, a part in a game may have several names: an onscreen name, an internal handy reference name, and potentially a file or directory name for content (art, sound, and so on) files. A detailed spreadsheet is a great place to list each of these, and keeping this information in a spreadsheet will help with eventual localization, since the onscreen name can be replaced with its equivalent in other languages. In addition, assigning and maintaining internal naming schemes for files associated with parts that must be read in by a digital game's program can be handled here, too. While it isn't necessary to work this out right at the start, having a single defined standard for how you name various files that is followed scrupulously and shown in the spreadsheet will save immense headaches on a project of any size. Letting programmers, designers, and artists name the files whatever they want is a recipe for disaster, one that you're most likely to encounter when you have no time to untangle why a particular file is named as it is when no one can remember how that happened.

Another pointer for effective use of spreadsheets in detailed design involves using color formatting for enhancing readability. You can use cell-background color and similar means to differentiate part names, global coefficients, numbers that should not be changed, and so on. Anything that enhances the ability for someone to understand the organization of a large, complex spreadsheet is a big help.

Similarly, it's a good idea to use comments on cells to record why a name or value is as it is; is this a temporary value that you're testing, or is it one that has been thoroughly tested and now should not change? A quick comment in the cell will help you and others keep track of this. Of course, this means you have to keep your comments and other formatting up-to-date, as these can quickly become misleading if you let them slide into obsolescence.

Data-Driven Design

Finally, one of the most important uses of putting parts, attributes, and values into a spreadsheet is that you can use this data directly in your game (assuming a computer-based game[1]). It is well worth taking the time to create automatic exports to file formats such as CSV (comma-separated values), JSON, or XML so that the data can be read into your game directly. The game objects in code should have default initialization values that get overwritten by those in the data file, enabling you to use *data-driven design*. This enables you to keep your data and your code-based data structures separate. Then, if the spreadsheet and design documents are kept current such that the parts and attributes in the design (and spreadsheet) match up with those in the code, designers can try out new values without having to

---

1. Even in an analog game, this technique is useful: you can prepopulate the values of cards and import them automatically into a layout program to drastically reduce the time it takes to test and iterate the design.

change the code. This enables you to greatly increase the velocity of your iterative design and test cycles.

You can (and should) go one step further and have the game look for and check the timestamp on the data file exported from your spreadsheet and read it in again if it's changed. This enables you to change your game data while your game is running so you can test different part attribute values. This reduces your design-and-test cycle time still further, meaning you can try out many more options and get to a solid set of data much faster.

Questions to Consider About Your Detailed Design

Just as with the game's concept and systems, there are useful questions you can evaluate as you develop and review your detailed design of parts, attributes, values, and behaviors. The following are some examples:

- Are enough game parts defined to create the game's core loop? Do they each have attributes, values, value ranges, and behaviors?

- Do all the parts have significant interactions with each other and the player? Do all parts have effects on others while also being affected themselves?

- Have you defined different types of parts, including physical, nonphysical, and game-representational ones?

- What is the smallest number of states and behaviors you can use to build the loops and achieve the effects you want? Do these support the interactions and progression paths you want in the game?

- Are all the main parts specified enough to be implemented? Are they spreadsheet specific?

- Do the behaviors of the parts provide sufficient feedback to the player that they can understand when state changes occur and use this information to build their mental model?

- Does the player have enough interaction? Do the game's parts enable meaningful choices the players can make? Do the parts provide sufficient "knobs and dials" for the player to perturb the game's internal model?

- Are the behavioral effects of the parts local in scope and general in applicability? Are there any parts that have global effects, that have single-use or otherwise brittle behaviors, or that overtake all other part behaviors?

- Are all the parts, attributes, and behaviors adequately documented? Do you have text and diagram design documents that link to spreadsheets containing the part–attribute data? Can these spreadsheets be read into your game as you develop it to speed your iterative testing?

Summary

In specifying the parts, attributes, values, and behaviors for your game, you have reached the most detailed level of game design—and also the most grounded. By designing these parts effectively, you can set up the systems and support the player experience that you want to see in the game. By documenting them in both descriptive text and numerically in spreadsheets, you can ensure that your game is fully implementable and that the specific numbers support your overall design goals.

In Chapter 9, you will see how to make sure that the values and behavioral effects of the parts create a balanced play experience.

PART III

PRACTICE

GAME BALANCE METHODS

It is not enough to construct a working game with a strong concept and working systems. You must also make sure the game forms a cohesive whole with dynamic balance.

In this chapter we explore both intuition-based and quantitative methods you can use to make your game balanced and how they work with both transitive and intransitive game systems.

Finding Balance in Your Game

Game balance is a term often used by game designers to indicate how well a game plays. This balance is achieved based on the relationships between different parts in the game. As you saw in Chapter 8, "Defining Game Parts," those relationships ultimately come down to the attributes and values of different parts and the behaviors they use to affect each other, building up into parts and systems in the game.

Despite the fact that game balance is at its root about numbers (values on attributes), like many other concepts applied to gameplay (such as fun), balance is difficult to talk about with any precision. It includes aspects of the game's progression for each player and the game's progression as a whole: whether the player advances too quickly and easily or too slowly with too many impediments and whether all players progress at about the same rate without feeling as if they are in lockstep with each other. Balance is a property of the overall game+player system, so it incorporates the player's mental model and the game's model, involving psychology, the game's systems, and mathematical and other tools needed to evaluate them.

A game that is balanced avoids having one narrow dominant winning path or strategy or creating situations where one player has an inherent or insurmountable advantage. A balanced game presents the players with an explorable possibility space within which they can make meaningful decisions and build their mental model of the game by going in multiple viable directions. There is no single best dominant strategy, there is no constricting of the possibility space to make it obvious how to win, and there is not any one way of playing that in retrospect is obviously the easiest way to win.

Having an unbalanced game that narrows the player's decision space or allows for a dominant strategy reduces engagement and replay value; once you know the trick to winning, why keep playing? On the other hand, if each player has approximately the same opportunities, the game feels fair. One player or another may have more skill or better luck (depending on the game), but if the players feel that they *could* have won, and especially if they feel that another player did not seize on some imperfection in the game to their own advantage, even players who do not win may be encouraged to try again.

From the individual player's point of view, a balanced game is one in which the player can take risks and still recover and in which they don't feel as though the end of the game is determined long before it arrives. The player remains engaged with the game and in the "flow channel" described Chapter 4, "Interactivity and Fun," as their skill continues to be dynamically matched by the challenge presented by the game, without becoming either boringly easy or frustratingly hard.

In effect, a balanced game is like someone riding a bicycle: the balance is dynamic, not static, as the rider shifts position with course changes or to avoid obstacles. If the player or the game loses its balance (that is, if the player falls into an unrecoverable failure state, or if the game turns out to be balanced early on but not later), this is like the rider losing their balance and falling over. Losing balance and falling over is no better for a game than it is for a bicycle rider.

Few if any games start out balanced while they're being developed; this is something that you should achieve as part of the designer's loop. Iterative design and testing allow you to create a complex yet balanced and satisfying game. Creating your game out of hierarchical, interlocking systems helps these efforts, as you can balance each system on its own and then as part of a higher-level system rather than having to balance the whole game at one time as a single block.

While game balance is difficult to discuss precisely, the understanding you now have of systemic game design and how systems create games helps with this immensely. Approaching game balance in terms of how you manipulate parts and loops in a system helps create the effect—the balanced gameplay experience—that you want to see in your game.

Overview of Methods and Tools

Multiple methods can be used to balance a game. They primarily fall into two overall categories: qualitative and heuristic or intuition based and quantitative and mathematics based. Traditionally game designers have depended on the first category almost exclusively, but in recent years, the latter methods have seen increased use. Both have benefits and pitfalls, and you should see them as complementary rather than mutually exclusive.

Designer-Based Balancing

The first main method of game balancing is using your intuition as a game designer. For many people, this has long been a core part of what makes a good designer. Can you tell when a game "feels right?" As with other forms of creative media, such as books and movies, different game designers have different opinions about game design and balance. You may or may not enjoy a game, but that doesn't mean the game was poorly made or unbalanced; it just may not be your kind of game. There is some validity to this: some games, like *Dark Souls* and *Super Meat Boy*, are seen as being extremely difficult and not to everyone's taste. As a designer, you need to develop a set of design heuristics and an intuitive feel for what your players will enjoy. In many cases, you will have to rely on this form of judgment at least early in the design process, and you can return to it as you use other methods as well.

Cautions About Designer Intuition

While having a good feel for game design and balance issues is valuable, it can also lead you horribly wrong. Few if any game designers ever design a major system or a game that works right the first time without any significant changes. If (when) you create a game that looks beautiful to you and turns out to be entirely, unplayably broken, don't lose heart; this happens for every game and designer. And don't be too disappointed when you just can't get the values on some parts in your game to work; heuristic-based design can take you only so far.

Worse even than being led astray by personal intuition yourself is to have your design grind to a halt and see tensions rise within the team due to competing feelings about which way the design should go. It's unfortunately common to see people argue for hours or days, based on their intuition about a design question that could be resolved in much less time by building and testing a fast prototype. This arguing is an easy trap to fall into when you are hyperfocused on a part of your design; part of the discipline of being a game designer is to cut off such arguments by using other tools to resolve them.

All that said, game design heuristics and intuition are not worthless. The value of having a good feel for game design is that you can often see how a certain relationship between different attributes or parts helps create the gameplay experience you want to see. This can also help you decide when to continue down a particular path or know when to cut your losses and try going a different way. These designer heuristics and hunches are learned over years and while developing many games, but at the same time, no wise designer trusts them completely. This is why we have developed better methods and tools that take us beyond the designer's vision for what makes a good, balanced game.

Player-Based Balancing

The other kind of intuitive balancing moves beyond just the game designer and includes the players. This is a perfect instance of the designer's loop discussed earlier: the player interacts with the game, and then the designer interacts with the result of that interaction to change the game.

The heart of this method is playtesting: having players play your game while you are designing it and report back on their experience. This is one of the most important techniques for ensuring solid game design and effectively balanced gameplay, and one you should use liberally. (We discuss playtesting in more detail in Chapter 12, "Making Your Game Real.")

Cautions About Player Intuition

Playtesting is extremely valuable and should be part of every game designer's tool set, but it is not a cure-all. Some game designers (or game company executives who should know better) take playtesting to its seemingly logical extent and try to get players to *be* the designers. If you're asking the players what they think of a game, why not just ask them what they want in a game and have them design it?

The problem with this line of thinking is, of course, that game players aren't designers—any more than people who enjoy movies are directors or those who enjoy eating are chefs. It is important to get adequate and accurate feedback from your players, but it is vital to remember that it is feedback: players will often tell you about something they don't like, but in most cases they cannot tell you how to solve it. Finding those solutions remains the game designer's job.

Analytical Methods

Moving away from the internal, intuitive methods of game balancing takes us to methods that are more external and quantitative. These involve hard numbers rather than fuzzy feelings—at least to some degree. There is inevitably some amount of interpretation of analytical data, but nevertheless, using these methods can help you clear away a lot of opinion and replace it with unbiased data.

As the term implies, *analytical methods* involve analyzing—breaking down—existing data on how a game is played. This means that until you have enough people playing your game (and thus until your game is itself sufficiently playable), these methods likely won't be very useful. However, as your game progresses and especially once you have many hundreds or thousands of people playing, you can cull data from their play sessions and find extremely useful patterns within.

There are many forms of analytics you can track to assess the overall health of your game (see Chapter 10, "Game Balance Practice"). These include things like the number of people playing your game on any given day or over the course of a month. For balancing purposes, though, it's more useful to look at how players behave as they play the game. Do they follow some paths and not others, or do they do some quests over and over but avoid others? Anyplace the players have to make a major decision is an opportunity for you to learn more about how they play the game by recording their choices—and even how long it takes to make them.

For example, in a strategy game, you might want to look at which sides won how many battles; if one faction wins significantly more than another, there's clearly a balance problem hiding in there. Similarly, in a role-playing game, it's useful to understand which characters players choose to play, especially when they are first entering the game. Do they take time to read the descriptions you've made? Do they complete the tutorial or give up halfway through?

You can also look analytically at how much time it takes for different character types to progress to a certain point (for example, attain a given level). If thieves always level up the fastest, that might mean they have some inherent advantage that you want to even out with the other classes. On the other hand, it might mean that mainly advanced players who know the game well also play thieves and thus level faster than newer players. Looking not just at the initial data (which class levels are fastest) but also including other factors (such as how long the player has been playing) and even potential factors (like session length, how many other characters they have played, and so on) helps you find the most significant correlations. If it turns out that thieves do level up fastest, but they are typically played by players with a long history in the game, you may be able to add more challenges to this class to keep those players interested.

An Example: *Tumbleseed*

You can assess player behavior in terms of how players progress through the game. As a real-world example, the makers of the game *Tumbleseed* wrote a postmortem blog post about what went well and what went wrong with the game as a service to other developers (Wohlwend 2017). In the blog post, the developers talked about how many players and people in the media described the game as being "too hard," saying that it was "unfair and unforgiving." While being hard and unforgiving may not be a problem for all games, in their case, this perception severely limited the game's revenues and commercial success. As they note in their write-up, this may have been because of an apparent mismatch between the game's difficult gameplay and its bright, casual-seeming graphics. The team now says they doubt the game will ever fully recoup its development costs. In the postmortem, the internal data for how the players progressed through the game showed the following:

- 41% of players reached the Jungle
- 8.3% of players reached the Desert
- 1.8% of players reached the Snow
- 0.8% of players reached the Summit
- 0.2% of players beat the game

Without knowing anything about the game, you can tell a lot from these numbers. The fact that 59% of players who started the game didn't finish their first checkpoint (getting to the Jungle) and that the next two checkpoints each saw a loss of about 80% of the remaining players shows that there were big problems with the progress players made through the game. Those statistics should have raised huge alarms about difficulty ramping and balance (and probably should have been caught long before the game was released).

The team went on to identify the problems underlying these numbers and came to realize that to be successful in the game, players had to deal with all these factors at the same time:

- New control scheme to master
- New game system and rules to internalize
- New terrain to understand (randomly generated every time)
- New enemies (sometimes multiple) to learn
- New powers to utilize (some that are dangerous to the player)

Not surprisingly, the team concluded that players felt overwhelmed; in the terms we've been using in this book, the game design far exceeded the player's interactivity budget, tasking them hard on action/feedback, short-term cognitive, and long-term cognitive interactivity at the same time. The game required that the players rapidly build mental models while learning new interactions at multiple levels at the same time. No wonder most people just gave up!

While this may not seem like a game balance problem, it is clearly a common perception that the game was too hard, not sufficiently engaging, and ultimately not enough fun to continue playing. The solution here is not as simple as making one class stronger or weaker or making a particular level easier to get through. This is the kind of problem that you want to find early in your game's development, via playtesting if nothing else. (Clearly the game designer's intuition did not help here, as the game surely played well in the team's experience.) To the *Tumbleseed* team's credit, though, they did include in their game the ability to find out analytically how people progressed in the game; otherwise, they would have been completely in the dark about why the game was seen as being so difficult.[1]

As this example shows, being able to analyze player behavioral data like this requires some form of data collection from your game. This means the game has to be able to write the data you want to collect to memory or to a file and then send it to you at some frequency. Games that have a mobile or online component do this fairly easily, as they have to check the player's credentials on login anyway and can communicate in short bursts with a server to log information without too much trouble. With fully offline games, this can be more difficult, but even there, you can have the game write to a log file and then send it back to your server (with the player's permission). With analog (tabletop) games, your ability to collect analytics goes back to playtesting, including tracking quantitative measures such as the length of a game, the length of individual turns, different pieces or strategies played, and so on.

Cautions About Analytical Methods
With a sufficient focus on analytical game balancing, a potential pitfall is that you can start believing that with enough data, you can remove all the risk (and creativity) from game design. Some game developers have tried collecting massive amounts of data on player preferences related to genre, gameplay mechanics, art style, and so on and tried to smash it all together into a game that was, they thought, guaranteed to be successful. Unfortunately, these efforts don't work, in part because they don't take into account the systemic and emergent effects of what players want to see in a game—how genre, art style, gameplay, and other unaccounted factors all interact. The data also can't tell you what players can't tell you—what they would want if they saw it but they can't yet conceive of. (This is reminiscent of the statement attributed to Henry Ford that "if I had asked people what they wanted, they would have said faster horses.")

This does not mean that market-driven analytics are not useful in game design; they can help you understand what players might be interested in or where the market is already glutted. However, there is a big difference between what we might call analytics-*driven* design and analytics-*informed* design. As with any other kind of feedback, you as the game designer need to interpret it and put it in context. You cannot let the data (or the playtesters or your own feelings) overrule everything else.

Sample Size and Information Distortion
Another caution and form of interpretation needed here relates to sample size. If you can gather data from a large portion of your players and see that a significant percentage of

---

1. Unfortunately, faced with similar perceptions of difficulty in other games, some game designers have retreated behind the attitude "learn to play." This is not helpful for the players and shows that the designers do not understand their role in providing an engaging experience for others.

them never construct a certain building or play a certain type of character in your game, this is good information that should lead you to investigate to find out why this is the case. Unfortunately, sometimes this kind of information is difficult to get, and so developers rely on their friends, a small focus group, or a small portion of their community of players to tell them what is working or not working in the game. Each of these carries a significant risk that the small population is not representative of the whole. (The worst case is sometimes discussed as product changes that get made because your boss's nephew said he doesn't like something the way it is.)

Even with ample analytical information at hand, having an engaged community is a huge benefit, but it comes at a price. Players who love your game are often the most vocal about it—and the most resistant to change. You may have solid information that, say, a certain kind of vehicle is overpowered and needs to have its top speed reduced or that an item in the game simply needs to be removed so your team can rework it so that it doesn't break the game.

The result of making a change like this in your game is that some people will become very angry and very loud in voicing their displeasure. If you're not careful, this can cause you to override what you know to be solid design information taken from the behavior of all your players.

In one instance, I was leading a team that had to make significant changes to a game that was already deployed and being enjoyed by about 100,000 people every day. We planned the changes carefully, playtested them, and then deployed them into the game. Our forums blew up; many people were angry. Some on the team thought we had made a mistake and should roll back the changes, given the fury that was being directed our way. However, when we looked at the situation carefully and analytically, we discovered that several important measures of how people were playing the game were going up (a good thing), without any contraindications that something might be wrong. In addition, while the voices of those complaining were loud, when we looked closely, we found that there were maybe a few dozen people who were vocally against the changes we had made. Of course, in the echo chamber of our game community forums, this seemed like a lot, and those loud voices were sure they knew more about the game than we did (a common theme in game communities, unfortunately). But compared to everyone else who played the game each day, the angry vocal contingent represented a very small portion—less than 0.05% of all the players. They were some of the most committed players, it's true, but nevertheless we held to our analytical approach and improved the game for the other 99.95% of our players. Soon enough everyone became used to the change—and went on to complain about other things.

Now it is true that sometimes your most vocal players are also the "thought leaders" who can signal how the overall population will react. But it's just as often the case that the small vocal populations aren't representative of anyone else. Looking at the situation analytically with the data you have helps differentiate between these.

Mathematical Methods

The final set of quantitative methods for balancing a game fall loosely into the category of those involving mathematical modeling. While analytical methods use math as well, those methods are more backward-looking, using existing behavioral data, while these are more forward-looking, building models of how the game will work.

Mathematical models are most useful when creating a new game. They are particularly important to competitive games with lots of progression in one form or another. These methods help you define specific relationships between objects and ensure that none of them are unbalancing the game. Mathematical methods can become pretty complicated, requiring additional knowledge of math, probability, and statistics as they become more advanced. Some of the most generally applicable methods are discussed in Chapter 10, but this is a topic you might want to explore further based on the needs of your particular game.

Chapter 8 provides an introduction to using spreadsheets for storing game data—specifically the values for attributes on game objects that make up the parts of the game. This includes the use of rows for different objects and columns for their shared attributes, with the cells at the intersections holding the values for each object. Methods for keeping your spreadsheet more organized, including color formatting and comments, are also discussed. All these are necessary for keeping your game design data organized. Keep them in mind as you apply mathematical modeling techniques to your game design.

As discussed in Chapter 10, storing your design data in spreadsheets is key to visualizing the relationship between different objects and, in some cases, to creating mathematical models and formulas to set the values for computing additional values. Using your data this way, along with mathematical tools, helps you ensure the following:

- Costs and benefits for different objects are in balance.
- No single object becomes the one to beat all others or is beaten by all others.
- As objects, costs, and rewards progress in the game, they do so at approximately the same rate—and at a pace that fits both the player's sense of fairness and engagement and your designer sense of how fast or slow, easy or difficult, the game should be.

Cautions About Mathematical Modeling

While mathematical modeling is a vitally important tool for game balance, it is equally important to remember that it is a means to an end, not an end itself. You must avoid the illusion that by using mathematical tools you can get the balance for your game *just right*. In a game of any complexity, this is extremely unlikely, and it can be a distraction you end up chasing too long. Mathematical models will help you find the most unbalanced parts of your game, but they will not do so to an arbitrary standard of completeness or precision. (The time and effort it would take to do so, if it were possible, would be far greater than the time spent developing the rest of the game.)

These models also will not help you make aesthetic decisions. If you want a particular vehicle in your game to be a little faster or a little flashier and still not cost more, you will have to work out how to do this within the overall balance constraints you set. This might include creating other costs (maybe the fast, flashy car also has high maintenance costs or doesn't handle well), using either existing systems or attributes in your game or creating new ones.

Overall, while mathematical modeling methods are often highly useful, as with the other methods we have discussed, they are no substitute for the game designer's judgment. It is up to you as the designer to decide what kind of experience you want the player to have and to use tools appropriately to create the game to do so.

Using Probability in Game Balancing

Another important set of quantitative tools in balancing is those that employ probability to decide events. A full exploration of probability and statistics is beyond the scope of this book, but the following sections discuss some concepts you need to understand in designing and balancing games.

A Quick Primer on Probability in Games

Probability indicates the likelihood of something happening. If you're certain the Sun will come up tomorrow, you can say there is a 100% chance that it will happen. If you think it might rain, but you're not sure, you might say there is a 50% chance of rain. While we often speak of probabilities in percentage terms, an equivalent but slightly more useful way is to express them as a number between 0 and 1, where 100% = 1.0, and 50% = 0.5. Among other things, this allows us to do mathematical manipulations of probabilities more easily.

We use probability in games to simulate systems that we don't actually implement. As stated in Chapter 8, as a game designer, you have to choose where the hierarchy of the systems in your game bottoms out—the point at which you assign a name–value pair attribute to a part rather than creating a subsystem for it. In the same way, we assign probabilities to events whose internal compositions are too esoteric or finely detailed to create as systems in games. For example, if in your game a player character swings a sword at a monster or attempts to win someone over with their wit and charm, we often decide what happens next by using probability. The alternative is to dive deep into the details of the physics of the sword's blade and the monster's hide or the psychology and biochemistry of mutual attraction. At some point, the game design has to hit its simplest level. When that happens, we set a probability of success, create a random value, and see what happens.

Randomization

There are many devices for making a random selection in games. Polyhedral dice, cards, randomized counters, and other devices enable players of tabletop games to create random outcomes. In electronic games, random number generators in code can simulate these same kinds of random selections. If you play a digital game of solitaire, some part of the code is generating random numbers in a range of 1 to 52 and choosing which card comes next, based on the result.

It's important to note here that by using the word *random*, we aren't requiring anything more than apparent randomness. No extreme measures like the decay of atomic nuclei have to be used; as long as the shuffle of a deck of cards isn't intentionally incompetent or surreptitiously setting card order, and as long as the periodicity of a digital random number generator is below a discernable level, random number generators will work for almost all games. What matters in most cases is functionally acceptable randomness.

Separate and Linked Events

It's important to understand a few things about how probabilities and random events work. The first is how separate and linked events create probabilities. If you flip a coin, there is a 50% chance, or 0.5 probability, that it will come up either heads or tails. The coin has two sides, and only one can land face-up, so that's 1 out of 2, or 1/2 = 0.5. Note that the sum of the possible outcomes equals 1 (two outcomes, two sides, 2/2 = 1.0). This is always the case: all the possible outcomes added together have to add up to exactly 1.0.

Before you toss a coin, you don't know which side will come up; it's a random event. Suppose you flip it, and it comes up heads. Now suppose you toss it again. What's the probability that it will come up heads again? Does the previous result of heads change this at all? No; these are separate events. So if you flip a coin and somehow get a result of heads 100 times in a row, the probability of the next toss being heads is still 0.5. The coin-flip events are entirely separate.

On the other hand, if you choose to take a set of events together and say in advance that, for example, three coin tosses must all come up heads to achieve some result (either in sequence or with three different coins at the same time), then the events become linked: the overall condition isn't met unless it's met by every coin toss in the set. In this case, the probability of getting heads on three tosses in a row is not 0.5. Instead, you multiply the probability of each toss together to get the whole linked probability, so 0.5 × 0.5 × 0.5 = 1/2 × 1/2 × 1/2 = 1/8, or 12.5%. Notice that 12.5% is half of 25%, which is half of 50%. With each linked coin toss, you have two possible outcomes and so each time you are cutting the overall probability in half.

These same rules hold true for rolling dice or doing anything else to which you can attach probability. The probability of rolling a six on a six-sided die is 1/6, or about 0.167. But the probability of rolling two sixes at the same time—a linked set of events—is 1/6 × 1/6, or 0.028, or 2.8%.

Probability Distributions

Not all target numbers on two six-sided dice have the same probability of occurring. The probability is given by the number of different combinations that can create a target number, divided by the number of sides on the die (6), with that multiplied by itself for every die rolled.

So when rolling two six-sided dice together (often stated as 2d6), the denominator is always $6 \times 6 = 36$. To find the probability of getting a particular number when adding up both dice (which links the two rolls into one event), add together the number of combinations that will result in that number and divide that by 36. So if you want to find the probability of rolling a 5 on 2d6, add up the number of possible combinations: $1 + 4, 2 + 3, 3 + 2, 4 + 1$. There are 4 combinations, so you divide that by 36, which equals about an 11.1% chance of getting a 5 on the roll.

If you chart out the probabilities of the possible roll results on 2d6, ranging from 2 to 12 (two 1s to two 6s), you can see that the probabilities go up and down again, forming sort of a hill. This approximates what's known as a *bell curve* due to its shape (see Figure 9.1). This is also known as a *normal distribution*, or sometimes a *Gaussian distribution*. This characteristic shape often emerges when you have multiple events with independent probabilities (in this case, the result of each die roll) interacting together.

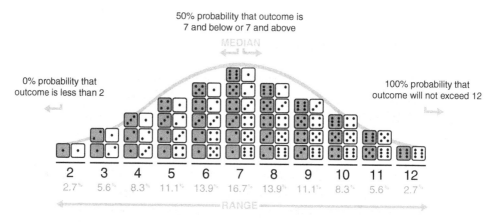

Figure 9.1 The probability of getting each result when rolling 2d6, as shown by the number of combinations that result in each number

As shown in Figure 9.1, the average of the values in the curve is called the *mean*; this is what you get if you add up all the data points under the curve and divide them by the number of data points. The peak, or top, of the curve is called the *mode*—this is the value that has the highest probability. In this case, the peak is in the middle, but it doesn't have to be. The number that is in the middle of the distribution, so that there are as many numbers above it as below it (regardless of their value), is called the *median*. Finally, the *range* is the span of values covered by the distribution. For 2d6, that's 2–12: you can't roll a 1 or a 13 on two six-sided dice, so they're out of the range.[2]

---

2. If you're not familiar with all these terms, a silly but effective way to remember them is this version of an old nursery rhyme: "Hey diddle diddle, the median's the middle; you add and divide for the mean. The mode is the one that appears the most, and the range is the difference between!"

In a symmetrical distribution, as shown in Figure 9.1, the mean, mode, and median are all the same. However, in other probability distributions, where the probabilities are not symmetric, they can all be different. If the median and mode are above the mean, then the "lump" in the distribution is pushed to the right. Similarly, if the mode and median are below the mean, then the distribution will look shifted to the left. For example, if you looked at the strength value for all characters in a role-playing game, you would likely discover that while some characters are stronger than others, the values do not form a symmetrical bell curve. If the scale is 1 to 100, the mean for this group is likely somewhere above 50, as players tend to like players who are stronger than what might be considered "average" for a large (non-adventuring) population.

Changing Probabilities

Another useful probability-related concept in game design is changing probabilities. If you are looking for a particular card in a regular playing card deck, say the queen of hearts, you could draw a card until you find the one you're looking for (without replacing the cards you've already drawn). On the first draw, if the deck has been shuffled, the probability that you'll get the queen of hearts is 1/52, or about 0.02. However, as you keep drawing cards without finding that card, the probability of finding it on the next draw continues to increase. If you've drawn 32 cards and still not found the target card, the probability on next draw is 1/20, as now there are only 20 cards left, and the queen of hearts is one of them. As you continue, the odds that the next draw will be your card go up. Eventually, when there's only one card left and you still haven't seen the queen of hearts, the probability is 1/1 = 1.0, or 100%.

This kind of changing probability is used in some games to give players the feeling that they're getting closer to some goal, even if the goal itself is entirely based on probability rather than skill. Some games include what are called "blind boxes," where you buy a box (physical or virtual) even though you don't know what prize you'll get. You know you have, say, a 1% chance of getting a really rare prize. If you open blind boxes, the events are separate, and so the probability of your getting the rare item in each one remains at 1%. However, in some digital games, the developers link the probabilities to keep the player engaged and playing. So if you don't get the rare item on the first blind box, it's like drawing a card out of a deck. If you want to try again, your probability has increased slightly. This is sometimes used to encourage players to keep trying, knowing that their probability of success is creeping up. However, games that do this typically have thousands or tens of thousands of potential digital items in their blind boxes, so the player's probability of getting the one item they want is very small. It requires many events—often many sequential purchases of blind boxes—for the player to finally get the prize they want.

Cognitive Biases and the Three-Door Problem

This use of blind boxes brings up a set of important points regarding the use of probabilities in games. The first is that people are, generally speaking, poor at understanding and estimating probabilities. A good demonstration of this is in how lottery ticket sales rise as the prize goes up in value—despite the fact that the probability of winning it is far less than that of being struck by lightning, hit by a meteor, or being attacked by a shark—possibly at the same time.

Another terrific illustration of how difficult it is to understand probabilities comes from what is known as the "three-door problem" (also known as the Monty Hall problem, after the former host of the game show *Let's Make a Deal*) (Selvin 1975). The problem goes like this: your host shows you three closed doors. Behind one of them is a valuable prize. Behind another is a mangy goat. And behind the third is nothing at all. You pick a door, say Door 1. Before opening the door you picked (#1), the host (who knows where the prize is and where the goat is—that's important to remember) instead opens a different door, #3, where you see the goat. The host then asks you, do you want to stay with your original choice, #1, or switch to #2? In terms of probabilities, the question is, which door now has the greatest probability of getting you the valuable prize?

On first hearing this, many people believe that it doesn't matter—the probabilities haven't really changed, so you have an equal probability of finding the prize behind either door. But that's not the case: it's actually very much in your favor to switch doors—you have a 1/3 chance if you stay with your original choice, but a 2/3 chance of being right if you change to the other door.

Before continuing, remember that this is about probabilities and cognitive biases—how we misunderstand probabilities. There is a sort of trick to this problem, but how people under-stand probabilities like this is relevant to game design. In this case, the trick is that the host knows where the prize is. He didn't open a door at random but chose the one that he knew had a goat behind it.

So, when you choose door 1, you have a 1/3 chance of being correct that it has the prize behind it. Your chance is 0.33 because you just don't know where the prize is; it's not moving around indeterminately but is sitting still behind one of the doors. Since you have a 0.33 probability of being right with the door you have chosen, that means that together, the other two doors have a 0.67 chance of having the prize behind one of them.

Now remember that the host knows where the prize is, so he's not going to open the door with the prize behind it by mistake. So when he opens door #3, he knows ahead of time that that's where the goat is. But the 0.33 and 0.67 probabilities haven't changed just because that door was opened, since it wasn't opened at random. This means that your original choice still has a 0.33 chance of being right (that's the chance that you really were right all along), but the other door now has all the remaining probability, or a 0.67 chance of being right. (Remember that the probability of all the possible outcomes has to add up to 1.0.) This means that while you could be right with your first choice, if you switch, you have doubled your chance of being correct and finding the prize.

You may have encountered this problem before, in which case this is all review. But if you haven't heard of this before, you might be thinking that this answer is wrong, and that the probabilities really are equal after the first door is opened. This is an important point you need to work through: understanding probabilities and our cognitive biases about how they work are important skills for a game designer.

Just in case, here's a modified version of the problem that may help: suppose that instead of 3 doors, there are 100 doors. Behind one is a prize, behind another is a goat, and all the rest are empty. To keep it simple, you choose door #1. You have a 1/100, or 0.01, chance of being correct. The probability that the prize is behind one of the other 99 doors is 99%, or 0.99. But once again, your host—who knows where the prize is and where the goat is—opens a bunch of doors. But this time he doesn't open just one door; instead, he opens 98 doors! So now you have door #1 that you chose, which remains closed. There's still a probability of 0.01 that the prize was there all along. You now see that door #10 had the goat behind it. All the other doors had nothing behind them—except door #58, which the host chose not to open. So you are down to two closed doors, #1 and #58, which your host left closed on purpose (not at random). There's a 0.01 probability that you were correct at the start, and the prize is behind door #1, and there is a 0.99 probability that the prize was behind one of the other doors, since the probability needs to add up to 1.0. But of all those other doors, the only one that the host left closed is #58. Do you switch to that door or keep the one you started with? If you switch, you have a 99% chance of being correct. In that case, you're guessing that the reason the host didn't open that particular door is because the prize is behind it. Of course, there is that 1% chance that you were right all along—but if you understand how the probabilities work, you'll switch and take the risk of the 1% chance that now you might be wrong.

Fairness

Closely aligned with players' cognitive biases about probabilities is their sense of whether a game is fair and how this affects game balance. If you played a game involving six-sided dice and discovered that one of them consistently rolled ones, you would think the die was unfair and so the game wasn't fair. But in games, especially digital games, players can come to see even pure probabilities as unfair. If there is a 1/3 (0.33, or 33%) chance of getting a prize for doing something in a game, and yet a player doesn't get the prize by the third or fourth attempt, some will begin to believe the game is broken or rigged against them. Naively, with a 0.33 probability, you would expect to be successful on *about* the third attempt—maybe sooner, maybe later. In fact, the probability for getting a win with a 33% chance of success within 3 trials is about 70%. But even after 10 trials, there's still about a 2% chance you might not have won. It's helpful for you to be able to understand how to figure out the percentage chance of success after a number of trials. This involves using what's called a *Bernoulli process*. In brief terms, you take the probability of success (0.33 in this example) and subtract that from 1.0 to show the chance of *failing*—that is, the chance that you will have zero successes in the trials. So that's $1.0 - 0.33 = 0.67$. Then you raise that to the power of the number of trials you're going to run, or how many chances the player has to succeed. So three trials is 0.67^3, which is the same as $0.67 \times 0.67 \times 0.67$. That equals 0.30. But remember, that's the chance of failure, of having no successes at all. So flip it back to the probability of success by subtracting it from 1.0 again, and you have a result of 0.70, or 70%.

While it is important for you as a game designer to understand how to calculate a probability like this, the problem is that players typically go by their intuition. As a result, if a player knows there's a 33% chance of success and still hasn't gotten the prize after the fifth try (about a 13.5% probability), they are likely to perceive the result as being unfair or even cheating on the game's part.

It's important when faced with situations like this that you remember that you are making a game for engagement and enjoyment, not for statistical rigor. You can sometimes tilt the probabilities in the player's favor—and sometimes against them in creative ways—without ruining the player's experience or the game's balance. For example, suppose you have an item in your game that is given out very rarely, say with a 1 in 100,000 chance (0.00001 probability), but the players have many opportunities to try for it—many die rolls, in effect. How many is *many*? With that probability, a player who tries 100 times has about a 1% chance of being successful. They would need to try nearly 70,000 times to have a 50% chance of success! That's a lot for a single player, but in a game with 1 million interested players, those virtual die rolls could happen very quickly.

If you want this item to be rare, do you need to be entirely fair and have the same probability on each attempt? Doing so is the easiest and often the most ethical thing to do. However, in thinking about the overall gameplay experience, you may want to adjust the odds. For example, in an online game where many players see each other and the items they have, getting a super-rare item brings with it a certain amount of notoriety. You may want to build up the tension of the players waiting for this item by tilting the odds against it being found, even to the point of making it impossible for the first few hours or days. Alternatively, you may want to *increase* the odds of the item appearing significantly—but only one time. If players see another player in the game with the super-rare Item of Awesomeness, they will often feel an incentive to try to get it themselves, thereby increasing their engagement with the game. But you don't want to flood the game with those items, as then they quickly lose their social value, so you need to readjust the probabilities instantly if you do allow for one of those items to appear in the game with higher odds.

The Likely Occurrence of Unlikely Events

As implied in the preceding section, with a large enough population, even very rare events are likely to occur on their own anyway, and so you may not need to tilt the scales. In an online game with 1 million people playing every day, say 100,000 of them make a single try for the Item of Awesomeness. The chance that an item with a 0.00001 probability will appear within 100,000 trials is about 63%—and that's in a single day. This is the flip side of "lottery logic." With enough people playing, *someone* is going to win, even though the chance of any given player winning is tiny. If you are running a game where you want to see improbable events happen, you can either tilt the scales slightly to encourage the players or rely on the large number of players you have to make the probabilities work for you.

One other form of tilting the probabilities needs to be mentioned here. In the case of many *social casino* games, the strict laws of fairness that are enforced on real casino gambling games do not apply. In social casino games, players put in virtual coins (often purchased with real money) but never get any real money out, so any legal issues of gambling are avoided. If you are making a social casino game, you are thus free to use all sorts of tricks to play on people's misunderstanding of probabilities and their cognitive biases. One of the most common of these is the *near miss*. Suppose you are making a slot machine–like game where you have to get, say, four pirate ships in a row on the display in order to win. Since this is all being done in software, the game may know even before the player bets or pulls the (virtual) lever whether their next spin will win. And since it's not actual gambling, you can mess around in the background to increase their engagement and keep them playing.

If the software has already determined that the player's next play does not win, you can cause it to show three pirate ships falling into line—one, two, three—with the fourth one looking like it's going to fall into place…and stopping one place short. Or going one place too far, so the four ships are not all in line. This is the near miss. It is entirely constructed by the software, but the player feels like he *almost won that time*. Even though the display is not random, and even though two sequential plays are independent events with their own probability, players nevertheless often feel that if they almost won once, they must have a higher probability of winning the next time. If I miss a basketball shot—and especially if I miss a bunch in a row—then I surely "have one coming." This is not how probability works, but it is often how players' minds work.

The question for you as a game designer is how to use this knowledge ethically. You can, for example, change the probabilities of the player making a basket (in virtual basketball), hitting a monster, and so on so that they don't become frustrated. If you monitor the number of misses and each time silently nudge upward the player's probability of being successful, the player is more likely to feel a sense of satisfaction and achievement (without ever knowing that the game made things easier for them behind the scenes). Alternatively, you can use this knowledge in a scenario like the one above: if a player can purchase more spins with real money to get a virtual prize in your game, you can use techniques like the near miss to encourage them to keep playing—and paying. If you take this too far, though, players will figure it out and drop your game in disgust and frustration, feeling that they never really had a chance to win (another cognitive error, just in the other direction). It is up to you to decide on the ethics of creating gameplay like this.

Transitive and Intransitive Systems

In addition to using quantitative, qualitative, and probabilistic methods for balancing a game, there are a few other important concepts to understand. One of them is what Ian Schreiber (2010) describes as *transitive* and *intransitive* relationships between game objects. These lead to balancing transitive and intransitive systems.

Transitive Balance

Systems made of parts with transitive relationships are those where every part within the system is better than one but inferior to another. The ancient game of *Rock-Paper-Scissors (RPS)* is a pervasive example of *transitive balance*: Rock crushes scissors, scissors cut paper, paper covers rock. Each part in the system both overcomes another and is beaten by a different one. No one part predominates or beats all the others.

Transitive systems are not limited to having three interrelated parts. There are many higher-number variants of *RPS*-like games, including those with up to 101 parts (Lovelace 1999). A more well-known variant of classic RPS is *"Rock-Paper-Scissors-Lizard-Spock,"* including new hand gestures for a lizard and the fictional Mr. Spock from *Star Trek* (Kass and Bryla 1995). In this variant, each part retains the quality of beating two parts and being beaten by two others: scissors cuts paper; paper covers rock; rock crushes lizard; lizard poisons Spock; Spock smashes scissors; scissors decapitates lizard; lizard eats paper; paper disproves Spock; Spock vaporizes rock; and rock crushes scissors. It's somewhat less confusing in graphical form, as shown in Figure 9.2. Trace the arrows, and you will see that each choice beats two and is beaten by two others.

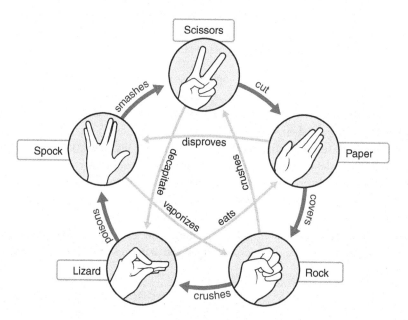

Figure 9.2 *Rock-Paper-Scissors-Lizard-Spock* as a system with transitive balance

There are many examples of systems with transitive relationships. For example, the five elements (sometimes called phases) in ancient Chinese philosophy are wood, fire, earth, metal, and water. Each gives rise to another and counteracts a different one. Wood feeds fire, for example, and controls earth (as tree roots prevent erosion). Earth in turn creates metal and counteracts (or dams) water (see Figure 9.3). Overall, *Wu Xing* ("five processes" or "five phases") is a highly systemic construction, focusing on the interdependent relationships between the dynamic parts rather than being reductionist like the ancient Greek collection of four elements. In Chinese thought, this system has been applied to everything from cosmology and alchemy to politics, society, martial arts, and individual health.

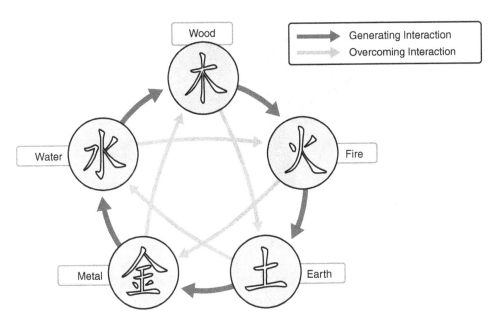

Figure 9.3 The transitive balance of the Chinese *Wu Xing* system

As an example from nature, some lizards use a transitive *RPS*-like set of relationships in competition for breeding: males with orange coloration beat those with blue, blue-colored males beat yellow, and yellow ones beat orange-colored ones. The evolutionary utility of this scheme is that "each [color] could invade another…when rare, but was itself invadable by another [color] when common" (Sinervo and Lively 1996).

This is directly analogous to popular gameplay pioneered in the MMO *Dark Age of Camelot* using an *RPS*-based system. This game used what the game designers termed *RvR*, or "Realm vs. Realm" combat, where characters of each of three factions, or realms, battled against each other for control of important areas in the game. Each of the factions was balanced to dominate another, if imperfectly. However, if any one of the factions grew too strong, the other two would combine to beat it, contributing to the balance of the overall system.

A final real-world example of transitive *RPS* relationships comes from a 1975 U.S. military training document (see Figure 9.4) (Army Training and Doctrine Command 1975). In this document, the U.S. Army explicitly invoked *Rock-Paper-Scissors*, applying it to the relationships between different kinds of military units. This same *RPS* pattern of combat ecology is common in games today. Many wargames consciously build in *RPS*-style combat because it's easy for players to understand and it's (relatively) easy to balance at a systemic level. Constructed correctly, transitive systems tend toward a dynamic balance, avoiding a devolution into an unbalanced rich-get-richer state.

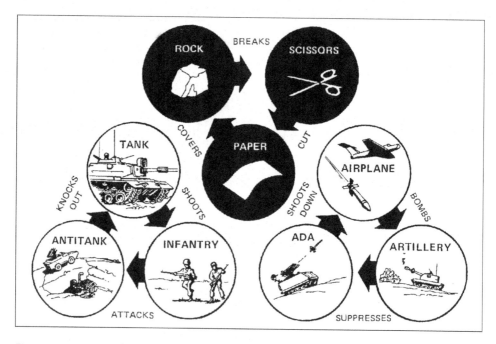

Figure 9.4 Transitive balance as applied in U.S. military training

Requirements for Transitive Balance

To transitively balance a system, the system must contain an odd number of parts—those that interact at the same level of organization (lizards, units, factions, and so on). This is the case because each part must satisfy the condition of beating or otherwise dominating exactly one-half of the remaining parts and being beaten by the other half. So in a transitive system with five parts, each one beats two parts and is beaten by the other two. This control of one part over another may be probabilistic in that one part may have a significant advantage (rather than an assured win) over half of the others, but the dominance must be clear for a transitive balance to emerge.

A system that has an equal number of parts cannot maintain a stable transitive balance because there is always the potential for one faction or unit type to develop an uneven advantage or disadvantage. This is the case with the Horde and Alliance factions in *World of Warcraft*, as discussed in Chapter 7, "Creating Game Loops," where the game has only two factions. This prevented a transitive balance from emerging and led to an ongoing ecological system collapse that the designers had to work hard to overcome.

In a transitively balanced system, each type of part may have multiple instances or subtypes, as long as they all aggregate into a distinct group in which the members all share the same transitive characteristics. That is, you can have multiple types of infantry units, cavalry units, and archery units, as long as the infantry as a group beat the cavalry as a group, the cavalry beat the archers, and all the archers beat the infantry. While it's possible to create transitive balance with systems containing more types (five, seven, or more), having this many makes defining the attribute values needed to ensure the transitive balance difficult to achieve. Even with only three, this can be challenging. This is one reason so few games go beyond three main unit types and rely instead on many subtypes.

Achieving Transitive Balance

Creating a transitive game system that is dynamically balance often requires working with multiple attributes shared by each part in the system. For example, we can assign relative values to each of four attributes—Attack, Defense, Range, and Speed—shared by the three unit types—Infantry, Cavalry, and Archers. By configuring the attribute values such that each has the same number of points overall, shown as + in Table 9.1, we achieve a first level of balance: none of the unit types has more overall capability than another (each has the same number of + overall). The different unit types have different distributions of these points: Infantry are best at attacking, Cavalry are fastest, and Archers are best at ranged attacks.

Table 9.1   Transitive Balance Across Unit Types

Unit Type	Attack	Defense	Range	Speed
Infantry	+++	++	+	+
Cavalry	++	+	+	+++
Archers	+	+	+++	++

Put into words, the table indicates that the following:

- **Infantry beats Cavalry:** Infantry's Attack of +++ beats cavalry's Defense of +. While the Cavalry can run away, they cannot win: if the Infantry closes with them, the Cavalry will lose.

- **Cavalry beats Archers:** Cavalry's Attack of ++ beats Archers' Defense of +, and the Cavalry's Speed of +++ means the Archers can't run away with Speed ++.

- **Archers beat Infantry:** Archers' Range of +++ beats the Infantry's Defense of +. While the Infantry has a higher Attack, the Archers move faster and so can stay out of range of the Infantry's attacks while raining arrows down on them.

This creates a transitively balanced combat ecology, with each part able to beat one and be beaten by another. It sets up an engaging decision-space for the player, who must decide how best to assign and deploy units to take advantage of the terrain, unit development, the opponent's potential weaknesses, and other factors that exist outside (or at a higher systemic level than) this transitive combat system and can perturb its behavior.

Understanding that the combat system exists as part of a larger system highlights why playtesting is still so important: if the system is too rigidly balanced and unresponsive to outside influences, no player will ever gain an advantage, and the game will grind back and forth without resolution. Alternatively, if players figure out that, for example, rocky terrain makes archers invincible, then this becomes the sole winning strategy. In such cases, the player's decision-space collapses to a single path, and the transitive balance no longer matters. By playtesting this under different conditions, you can make sure that the balance of the combat ecology is robust enough that it can remain resilient to outside conditions (terrain, weather, play styles, and so on) but without becoming static and unchangeable or reducible to a single strategy. The game must still be perturbable by the player's actions and other external influences, such that the player has meaningful decisions to make and multiple strategies to try in attempting to reach their goals.

Intransitive Balance

In systems like those described in the preceding section with transitive balance, no part is better than all the others; each is better than half and worse than half of the other parts. Note, however, that for any given pair of parts, one will be better than the other (always, or probabilistically). In the example given above, Infantry units beat Cavalry; within that one pair, one wins and the other loses. Taken alone, that is an instance of *intransitive balance*: some parts are just better than others.

While that may seem to be inherently unbalanced, it is just a different way of achieving overall balance in the system and in the game. Rather than balancing all the parts against each other, as with transitive balance (making all parts effectively equal at the system level), with intransitive balance, parts are balanced on the basis of their costs and benefits. Some parts necessarily have greater benefits, but they also have proportionately higher costs.

Systems with intransitive balance appear in most games that include some form of progression system. In such games, the play experience includes (typically as part of the core loop) some form of increase, achievement, or progress. This is the case when key parts of the game—the player's character, the objects they use, their armies, the number of crops, and so on—increase in effectiveness or, for lack of a better word, power.

This method of balancing objects or parts in the game makes intuitive sense: a player would expect a rusty dull dagger to cost less than an adamantium greatsword of eternal sharpness. How big the difference is between the costs of these two weapons, given their respective attributes, is the difficult question that needs to be answered in the game design. Making sure the costs and benefits across parts in the same system remain proportional typically requires a certain amount of work to define the mathematical relationship between types of parts, as well as a lot of iteration to make sure all the relationships remain balanced and make for engaging gameplay.

To balance intransitive systems, you need to define the necessary progression or power curve, which itself entails defining the costs and benefits it describes. This is the topic of Chapter 10.

Summary

Game balance can be an elusive quality to pursue, and yet it's one that every game needs. You need to be familiar with the various ways of balancing game systems: designer-based, player-based, analytical, and mathematical. Knowing when and how to use each of these methods is an important part of building your skill as a game designer.

Similarly, understanding how to build and balance both transitive and intransitive systems is necessary to achieve overall game balance. The specifics of creating progression curves and balancing systems with them are covered in Chapter 10.

CHAPTER 10

GAME BALANCE PRACTICE

A lot of practical game design involves balancing parts and systems using progression and power curves. This requires understanding the resources in your game systems as costs and benefits.

By using a variety of mathematical tools, you can create dynamic balance in a game without reducing the decision-space for the player. And by using analytical tools, you can assess and tune the game's balance based on the players' experiences.

Putting Methods into Practice

Balancing game systems requires a lot of nuts-and-bolts work with various forms of math, spreadsheets, and analytical models. You have to identify the core resources in each system and begin to balance around them. This enables you to identify both the costs and benefits in every part in the system and how the parts relate to each other on that basis. Armed with that and a deeper understanding of using different kinds of modeled curves, you can balance your game's systems more effectively.

Creating Progression and Power Curves

One of the most common mathematical modeling tools used to help balance game systems, especially intransitive ones, is curves describing increases of power and progression. These curves help ensure that objects in a game—both physical and nonphysical, such as weapons and experience point levels—remain balanced in relationship to each other.

The use of these curves is based on two ideas. First, there is a cost for every benefit in a game. As the costs rise, so too do the benefits, and vice versa; they are inextricably linked. The delay in the player being able to pay higher costs for additional benefits is what constrains the game's pace while still allowing the player to feel that they are improving.

Second, both the player's representation and the objects they use (or that oppose them) move ahead in the game by gaining benefits in the form of improved values on their attributes. By defining curves that regulate the progression of linked costs and benefits in a game, you can make sure that players improve in ability and challenge at the rate you intend for the pace of the game.

Defining Costs and Benefits

To create and use power and progression curves, you first have to define both the costs and benefits that are to be correlated and kept proportional by a curve. As long as costs and benefits remain achievable and in step with each other, this will help the player feel a sense of forward progress, and the game will remain engaging and enjoyable.

The relationship between the costs and benefits underlying any power or progression curve is an economic one (in the sense of the term *economic* introduced in Chapter 7, "Creating Game Loops"). The costs are exchanged by the player for the benefits desired. As a result of this exchange, the player must believe that they have meaningfully increased their power or ability in the game to their benefit. If the player feels that they are worse off after having advanced—gone up a level or gained additional units in their game—the resources (experience points, gold, and so on) that led to the exchange would lose their value, and the player's engagement would be weakened.

Both costs and benefits are typically expressed in terms of attributes relevant to the player and are thus resources. The costs may be based on experience points (such as for progression to a new level), in-game currency, commodities, battles won, animals raised, or anything else that represents an important resource in the game. Likewise, the benefits include changes like gaining more health, magic power, cards, provinces, action points, and so on—whatever is the resource that drives the player forward in the game.

Core Resources

The more important the progression or power curve, the more meaningful and important the resources involved must be. In most games, there is one or at most a few resources that a player is trying to maximize and/or not lose to keep playing. (These are not necessarily the same; think of trying to achieve high score and having a remaining number of lives in a classic arcade video game.) Because these resources are closely connected to the player's focus in playing the game, they are intimately related to the game's core loops as well. Therefore, we call these *core resources*. Examples of core resources include health and experience points in most role-playing games, money in tycoon games, and the amount of area controlled in strategy games.

To find your game's core resource(s), review the data in the spreadsheet you created for your game's parts, as discussed in Chapter 8, "Defining Game Parts." This data should describe all the attributes in the columns and have the named parts in the rows. You want to look for the attributes on which your players depend most. What are the resources (as represented by the part attributes) that the player needs to play the game and without which they cannot continue playing? These are core resources. There may be multiple core resources if there are multiple loops to the game, with the player focused on each one at different times. For progression and power in any given part of the game, though, you will typically be able to identify a particularly prominent core loop and the resource that goes with it.

If you identify multiple candidates for core resources, see if one of them actually overarches all the others. It may be that the core resource you want to use in balancing the parts is an emergent result of the synergy of several other attributes. Alternatively, see if the gameplay is such that the resources are sequential—for example, a game where all the players depend first on health, then on wealth, then on social standing during different phases of the game. While these are three entirely different resources, you may be able to define a single overarching *shadow resource* (one that you see but that is not overtly represented in the game) that contains each of these and then use that as the basis for your progression and power costs.

Alternatively, if the main resources really are incommensurate, you will need to create a progression curve for each one, paying special attention to how the player hands off from one to the next without losing their momentum or engagement with the game. As much as possible, however, you want to identify one core resource to be the mainstay of either the cost or benefit for your primary progression or power curve. This may take some time to do—even some reorganization of the attributes you're using on the game parts—but it will be worth doing if it enables you to create the intransitive, progressive balance you need for your game.

Subsidiary Resources

Identifying the game's core resources will help you identify and create the power and progression curves that are most central to your game and then create secondary curves based on them. Having identified your game's core resources, you can then look for other resources that support (maintain, improve, repair, and so on) the core ones. These are *subsidiary resources* to use in progression and power curves. For example, in a strategy game, the amount of area controlled is often the core resource. Gaining armies, fortifications, or technology supports the player's ability to gain and keep this resource, so benefits to those are indirectly benefits to the "area controlled" resource. In a romance-oriented game, the player might be trying to maximize their relationship with one particular person; if so, that relationship is the core resource. But to maximize that relationship, the player may need friends, money, information, and so on, which all constitute subsidiary resources.

Special Cases

In trying to create and catalog the costs and benefits you want to balance, in addition to core and subsidiary resources, you will sometimes find special case resources that primarily affect the other resources and have either a limited or periodic effects on their own. Suppose, for example, that the game is about piloting a spaceship through a dangerous asteroid field. The player's goal is to use the ship to gather ore and to use that ore to maximize the ship's speed and armor. The ore might be your core resource, with speed and armor subsidiary ones. But suppose further that the ship has an ability to do a speed boost. This boost can only be done once in a while, and when used, it damages the ship a little. This speed boost isn't a vital part of the core loop, but it is important from time to time. It mainly affects the subsidiary resources (speed and armor) but in a way that makes it difficult to determine exactly how important it is: this kind of ability isn't important at all until the player needs it, and then it's very important!

You can stack another special case on top of this: suppose the player can use some ore (a cost) to either increase the boost's duration or reduce its recharge time (both benefits). Making sure these are proportional to an increase in a straight numeric attribute (overall speed, armor, cargo space, and so on) is difficult to do. While in some cases designers who are particularly mathematically inclined can create an equation that algebraically reduces everything down to a single benefit—a single overarching shadow resource, as described earlier in this chapter—this can also be an infinitely receding goal that never quite works. Alternatively, you may be able to create such a resource equation, but in so doing you may have reduced the dimensionality of your game, making the trade-off relationships between different attributes too obvious to the player.

All of this points back to the reality that while mathematical tools can help you balance your game faster and more effectively, you will inevitably have to correlate some costs and benefits heuristically, by your own intuition and what you see as best for the game. Follow up any such changes with as much playtesting as you can in an iterative fashion. You will likely find that after doing so, the costs and benefits fall close to a particular curve but one that you may not have been able to predict in advance.

Defining Cost–Benefit Curves

Once you have an idea of the costs and benefits you want to map together based on the resources being balanced against each other, you can begin creating the curve that defines their relationship. There are several different kinds of mathematical curves that are useful to know about for creating balanced game systems. Each has uses and benefits, as well as limitations. Sometimes you will find a curve useful for mapping game attributes; in other cases, understanding how these curves work and the effects they produce can be a guide for how to create new game attributes that remain in balance with existing ones.

Linear Curves

It may sound strange to talk about a "linear curve." But *linear* in this case is a geometric term that refers to any graph that has a steady slope, which means the same rate of change throughout. The formula for this is $y = Ax + B$, so you can get any y value (for example, an in-game benefit) by multiplying an input (cost) value x by some number A and adding a constant, B, to it. Often $B = 0$, meaning that x and y are both equal at 0. The value of A determines the slope—how much y changes as x does.

The linear curve is the simplest of our curves, and in some ways it is the most limited for game uses. In power and progression curves, usually the slope is increasing, moving up and to the right. The A multiplier on x is positive, so values for y increase as x increases; that is, you get more powerful (or at least bigger numbers) as you go along. The relationship between the change in x and y is linear, so for every 1 change in x, y changes by an amount equal to A. This makes for a simple graph: if $A = 2$ (and $B = 0$), then when $x = 1$, $y = 2$. When $x = 3$, $y = 6$, and y goes up by 2 after that for every 1 change in x.

As x becomes larger, the change in y is the same—which means the change in y as a proportion of its overall value shrinks. Suppose again that the equation you are using is $y = 2x$. The change in y when x goes from 8 to 10 is significant (25% greater)—indicating a change of 16 to 20 in some in-game value, such as attack or defense. But when x goes from 98 to 100, y changes from 196 to 200. This is the same quantity of change in both cases (x increased by 2, so y increased by 4), but the functional change in the second case is far smaller—only 2% greater. In psychological terms, this allows hedonic fatigue to work against the player's experience: the latter change might get a "so what?" reaction and not feel like a big reward, even though it's of the same absolute magnitude change as the earlier one. As a result, while linear curves are easy to understand and implement, they aren't used a great deal on their own in power or progression curves.

Polynomial Curves

In linear curves, y is some multiple of x. In polynomial curves, y is x raised to some power: $y = x^n$, such as x^2 or x^3. Often there are one more additional numbers used as multipliers, so you may have an increase in y equal to $5x^2$ or similar. This use of an exponent on x causes the value of y to increase as x increases, and the rate of change—the amount between each value of y for two values of x—also increases. If $y = x^2$, then for $x = 1, 2, 3, 4, 5$ and $y = 1, 4, 9, 16, 25$. The y values are the squared values of x, and the difference between them gets larger each time. Looking at the difference between each y value and the one before, you can see the rate of change is increasing: 3, 5, 7, 9. (You may notice that this trend—the rate of change for the rate of change, also known as the *second difference*—is itself linear. This is a property of polynomial equations.)

The difference between values of y is what Bateman (2006) has called a *basic progression ratio*. In linear curves, this ratio remains constant. In polynomials, it continues to increase as the difference in y for every step in x increases. However, as x becomes large, the proportion of this change in y to the overall y value (the *total progression ratio*) becomes closer to 1.0—that is, closer to being linear. As we saw with linear equations, although the distance between y values continues to increase, as a proportion of the overall amount of y, the rate of that increase slows down. Another way to say this is that the curve flattens out, and so in game terms, curves based on polynomial equations often have the same issues as linear curves: at the high end, the rate of change seems to be about the same, reducing the impact of a change from one level (or y value) to another. On the other hand, this flattening of the curve also means that the next change in y is not astronomically far off for high values of x, as happens with exponential curves.

One other property of polynomial curves that can be useful to know is that a quadratic polynomial (which you may remember from high school in the form of $y = ax^2+bx+c$) is the product of two linear progressions (Achterman 2011). Suppose you have a role-playing game where the number of monsters the player has to kill on each level increases linearly: first 1, then 2, 3, 4, 5, and so on. This is nice and simple for the designer and the player. Suppose that the amount of gold you gain from each monster also increases linearly: 10, 20, 30, 40, and so on. Again, this is simple and easy to build as a mental model. What this means overall, though, is that the amount of gold you gain on each level goes up not linearly but quadratically because you are combining an increased number of monsters with an increased amount of gold. The gold you gain on each level thus rises faster—as 10, 40, 90, 160, 250, and so on. This is a good example of two systems interacting to create something that is more than the sum of them as parts.

Exponential Curves

With linear progressions, y equals some multiple of x. With polynomial progressions, y equals x to some exponential power. With exponential progressions, x is itself the exponent: y equals some number set to the power of x, as $y = A^x$ (or $y = B \times A^x$). As with polynomials, the rate of change—the difference in y-values for each succeeding x-value—increases as x increases; that is, the jumps get bigger. Unlike with polynomial equations, this rate does not flatten out but keeps increasing with every step.

Having the rate of increase continue to get larger can make future steps seem unreachably huge. However, if the base value A that is being raised to x is itself small, the curve doesn't increase too fast. For example, *RuneScape* uses a complex equation for experience point leveling requirements that includes an exponential equation of 1.1^x, so the steps increase relatively slowly, at least at first. This works well for players, as early levels seem attainable and players go through them fast (making players feel accomplished), while later ones seem at first to be so far off numerically as to almost require superhuman abilities to reach. By the time the players start reaching these levels, however, they are also gaining astronomical numbers of experience points, so they feel a continuing sense of achievement in both their individual victories (the numeric rewards do not seem paltry) and in their overall number of experience points gained.

While the increase in y for any value of x in an exponential equation always seems to zoom off as x increases, the total progression ratio with these equations is low compared to any current value of y. This means that no matter where the player is on the progression curve, "far away" level requirements (or similar) look unreasonably high, but nearby it looks easily attainable compared to the current total value. From the player's point of view, future progression values may look like the top of a high mountain, but nearby the slope never seems overly steep compared to how far the player has already come. This helps encourage the player to keep moving along the progression curve (the next step seems relatively easy with what they have already accomplished) without risking hedonic fatigue and the feeling that future rewards are not worth the effort.

Exponential curves are probably the most commonly used form of progression and power curves for games. The form of the equations makes it easy to adjust and fit progression or object values, and the combination of the appearance of local flatness and aspirational awesomeness in later high values works well at encouraging players to keep moving forward. On the other hand, the values in the higher reaches of these curves can be staggering—well into the billions, trillions, or higher. (As mentioned in Chapter 7, the exponential progression curves in *Adventure Capitalist* top out at 1 novemnonagintillion—a 1 followed by 300 zeros.) This can have the same sort of psychological effect that occurs with linear progressions: once the numbers become difficult to imagine just due to their size (for example, the difference between 1 quadrillion and 1 quintillion), they become less meaningful. While there is for many people a certain dopamine-fed pleasure in seeing numbers go up,[1] this by itself is subject to hedonic fatigue and, if pushed too far, eventually loses appeal.

For progression, using an exponential curve can help you set appropriate levels or other checkpoints where new benefits to the player are available. In such systems, typically the player has to build up a certain number of points (or other resource, but we will use points

---

1. As mentioned in Chapter 6, Michael Townsend, creator of the early (and highly engaging) ASCII-based idle game *A Dark Room*, said, "My target demographic was the intersection of People Who Like it When Numbers Go Up and People Who Like Exploring the Unknown" (Alexander 2014). These dual motivations amount to a potent combination of action/feedback, short-term, and long-term cognitive interactivity.

here as a general stand-in) that take them over the next threshold. As players progress in the game, they typically face more difficult challenges for which more points are awarded. As discussed earlier, this combination of increasing difficulty and reward helps avoid hedonic fatigue and provide the player with a sense of achievement. But if the player is getting more points, the thresholds for each level need to spread out, too, or the player will hit them faster and faster. Using an exponential equation can help you determine how many points are required for each threshold: each level or threshold is an *x* value, and the number of points required to attain that is the corresponding *y* value that comes from the exponential function you are using.

Because of the way these curves work, the base—the number you're raising to some power represented by *x*—gives you a good heuristic for how much power increases with each step. If you have a curve defined by an exponential equation like $y = 1.4^x$, you know that with each level, the values for *y* will be 1.4 times higher than they were at the last level. While the rise from level to level is not extreme, after four levels, the points required per level (or power awarded) has more than doubled.

Setting the equation components helps you set values for challenges and rewards that remain balanced with each other (that is, the points awarded for each challenge based on the number of points needed for the next level). By moving the base up and down (trying 1.2, 1.3, 1.5, and so on), you can balance challenges, power, and rewards to have the rise and perhaps the doubling time that you want for your game.

Table 10.1 shows sample values for the equation $XP = 1,000 \times 1.4^{level}$, as might be seen in a typical role-playing game. Note how the values increase slowly from level to level but nevertheless later become enormous. For any given level-to-level transition, the total progression ratio of about 1.4 (based on the equation, though not exact due to rounding) is not unreasonable; the number of points needed for any "next level" do not seem so huge, given the number of points the player has already achieved. Note also that in this example, the values have been rounded to the nearest 100 for clarity, and level 1 was arbitrarily set to 0 rather than 1,400, as would be mathematically correct.

Table 10.1 Examples of Experience Points (XP) Needed per Level,
Given $XP = 1,000 \times 1.4^{level}$

Level	XP Needed	Level	XP Needed
1	0	10	28,900
2	2,000	15	155,600
3	2,700	20	836,700
4	3,800	25	4,499,900
5	5,400	30	24,201,400

The process of setting the equation values isn't automatic: as the game designer, you need to decide how quickly (in terms of time, number of battles, and so on) the player should hit each threshold, how strong the challenges should be, and how big the rewards should be. Using an exponential (or similar) function helps you ensure that these are all balanced against each other. If, for example, you had a game where the challenges were going up at each level (or step or checkpoint) by a factor of 3 (3^x) but rewards in the form of the core resource—health, attack power, and so on—were going up only by a factor of 1.25 (1.25^x), the game would quickly become unplayable, as players would experience the challenges ramping up far faster than their ability to meet them.

Ultimately, the answers to questions of how many missions the player must complete or monsters they must kill before they get the next bump in abilities that will allow them to face even greater challenges are up to you as a game designer. While the math definitely helps, as with any other quantitative method, eventually you have to fall back on playtesting and your own judgment as a designer. Understanding the mathematics within your game will help you understand if the players are burning through the game too quickly or are frustrated because they feel like they cannot advance, but the math cannot tell you specifically to resolve these questions in your game.

Logistic Curves

Less often used for game balance but still useful to know about are a class of curves called *logistic functions*, also sometimes known as *sigmoid curves* for their s-shape. These curves are commonly used in simulations and artificial intelligence and have properties that are useful for creating power curves with a particular kind of dynamic balance. In particular, these curves mimic well many real-world processes, such as learning, and ecological processes with initially slow growth that then goes through rapid expansion that then slows down as resources are consumed.

The mathematical function for this curve is a bit more complicated than the math for the others:

$$y = \frac{L}{1 + e^{-k(x-x_0)}}$$

This may look kind of scary, but it's not too bad:

- L = the curve's maximum value—where you want it to top out
- e = Euler's number, which is a mathematical constant equal to about 2.718
- k = the steepness of the curve (You can make the increase in the middle shallow or steep.)
- x_0 = the x-value at the curve's midpoint (The lower half of the curve is less than this in x, and the upper half is greater than this.)

The shape of a curve provided by the logistic function is such that as x increases, the y-value increases slowly at first, then rapidly, then slowly again, then heading toward no change at all (see Figure 10.1). This kind of curve can be useful for creating different objects where the power increases slowly at first (requiring longer-term investment by players to move forward, for example), then rapidly as players quickly gain benefits for continuing in the middle range, and finally hitting diminishing returns on the upper end, where continued investment yields less and less benefit.

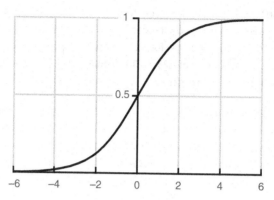

Figure 10.1 A typical curve from a logistic equation ($L = 6$, $k = 1.0$)

This type of curve creates an interesting nonlinear journey up the power curve for the player, and it does not suffer from the skyrocketing change in y values for each change in x that is seen in exponential curves. You can, for example, create interesting strategic decisions for a player by using "stacked" logistic curves, with each referring to an increase for a different resource. To effectively climb up this progression curve, the player needs to decide when to change from one to another as the first begins to hit diminishing returns. An example using four different resources with different logistic curve shapes is shown in Figure 10.2. This stacking arrangement can increase the breadth of values in an economy without unbalancing the whole thing, and it provides the fast-rise effects of an exponential curve divided among multiple logistic curves. In effect, if each resource or object represented in the economy is balanced along its curve, the whole economy is likely to be more easily balanced than if you tried to balance the same range along a single curve.

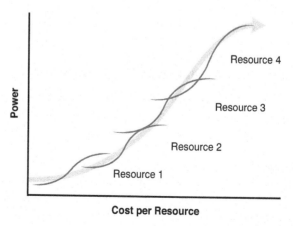

Figure 10.2 A power progression curve made from four stacked logistic curves, each corresponding to a separate in-game resource

Piecewise Linear Curves

Game designers often find themselves not wanting to fit progression or power to a pure equation or not wanting a smoothly changing equation underlying their game's progression. This smoothness can itself become kind of boring, especially if it's related to object power: the player knows the rate or the curve along which objects will grow in power, and there's no need to think about it or make decisions about it; the player knows that a $+n$ sword will always be a certain amount better than an $n - 1$ power sword. Even if the increase itself isn't linear, players will begin to intuitively think of it this way, especially if the power ratios involved in the progression curve are linear.

One solution to this is to hand-craft progression and power curves, either from nothing or by starting with and departing from an underlying equation. One way to do this is to approximate an exponential curve with a series of overlapping linear curves. This is known as a *piecewise-linear* curve and is made either by constructing the curve by addition or by *linear interpolation* (which, if you are not a math person, is not as scary as it may sound).

Suppose you want to award hit points (health) for characters in a RPG at a rate that's constant for a few levels and then increases. Say that characters gets 2 hit points per level in levels 1–10, 5 per level in levels 11–20, and 10 per level in levels 21–30. Given that you know those numbers, it's a simple matter to create a table in a spreadsheet starting with a base number of hit points for level 1, say 12. (For something like hit points, you want this to be more than 0, and in this example, 12 makes for a nicer graph.) Then with each level up to level 10, you add 2 to that, bringing the total to 30 at level 10. From there you add 5 with each level, taking the player to 80 hit points at level 20. Then you start adding 10 per level, taking the player to 180 hit points at level 30. This creates an easily understood piecewise linear curve, as shown in Figure 10.3.

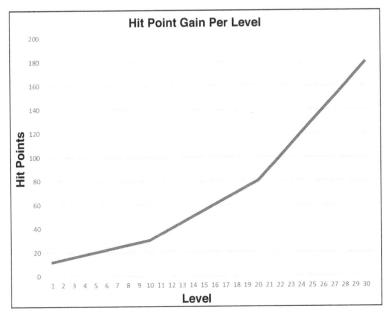

Figure 10.3 A piecewise hit point curve constructed from known rates of increase

However, sometimes you may not be able to simply count up the points by addition. Instead, you can use linear interpolation to create the graph, based on the kind of power increase and values you want to see.

Suppose in this case that you want to create a hit point curve that starts slow but then really takes off (so the player feels rewarded and can face tougher challenges). You know you want to start with a low number of hit points, such as 2, and you want to have awarded 20 points by level 10. But then you want the number to go up faster, so the player character has 100 by level 20. Given that, you can easily construct the linear curves between these points (levels 1, 10, and 20).

To interpolate the first segment, subtract the lower y-value (the number of hit points) from the higher: 20 − 2 = 18. Then get the higher x value (the level) minus the lower one: 10 − 1 = 9. Finally, divide the first (the y-values) by the second (the x-values): 18/9 = 2. In equation form, this is what you have:

$$hp\ per\ level = \frac{y_1 - y_0}{x_1 - x_0}$$

So you have a gain of 2 points per level (which is exactly the same as saying this line has a slope of 2). Then for the next segment you do the same thing. The larger y-value, y_1, is the maximum desired hit point value, 100, and the lower, y_0, is 20, the same as the upper value in the previous segment. The larger x value, x_1, is the top level specified, 20. The smaller x value, x_0, is the previous top level, 10. Using the equation above, you have 100 − 20 = 80 and 20 − 10 = 10, with 80/10 = 8, so you have the slope for the line, and a gain of hit points per level, of 8. Figure 10.4 shows the piecewise linear graph for this. This is a fairly simple demonstration of the process; if you create a table of these numbers in a spreadsheet yourself, you can easily play with the interpolation by changing the y (hit point) values at each segment endpoint (level) until you get the numbers and slope you want.

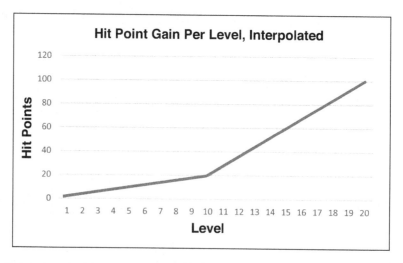

Figure 10.4 A piecewise hit point curve constructed with known endpoints and interpolating the increases

For any piecewise linear curve, each segment is linear, but the overall appearance is often curved or approximately exponential, as shown in Figure 10.3. Creating these segments is sometimes simpler than mapping to an exponential equation (especially if your math skills are a bit rusty), and in an interesting way, it can give players something to shoot for. In the graph in Figure 10.4, once players know there is a break at level 11 (where the number of new hit points jumps from 2 to 8 per level), they have an incentive to get there and treat that level as an interim goal.

Near-Arithmetic Progression Curves

In addition to piecewise linear curves, in some games, progression curves are hand-crafted to tune the player's experience. Bateman (2006) has called these *near-arithmetic progression* (*NAP*) curves, which are somewhat like linear (arithmetic) curves but without an underlying equation to describe them. NAP curves appear in role-playing games in particular, where progression and power curves are often made by feel or to preserve round numbers more than mathematics. For example, in the initial levels of *World of Warcraft*, the points needed for each additional level go up in round numbers: from level 1 to 2 requires 400 points. Then 500 additional from level 2 to 3 and level 3 to 4, then 700 from level 4 to 5 and level 5 to 6, and so on (WoWWiki n.d.) This pattern doesn't hold throughout all the levels, and the apparently hand-crafted NAP changes over as the levels progress.

Some games use hand-crafted curves like this to move away from the smooth and predictable equation-driven curves to more "bumpy" curves with varying areas of faster or slower benefit acceleration in order to "surprise and delight" players (Pecorella 2015). In addition to preventing players from becoming bored with predictable progression, this allows you as the designer to coordinate power curves such that one type of object or resource may provide more benefit for a given cost than another at various points in the curves. This allows the player to explore the power curve space by making decisions about how to spend resources to the best effect at different times in the game.

Making It Work for Gameplay, Not Math

As with the other curve types discussed here, NAP and similar hand-crafted curves reinforce two important points in making progression and power curves. First, while this is a mathematical exercise, it will never be perfect. You should try to make your progression and power curves work as well you can mathematically, as the more balanced you can make your game with them, the more iteration time you will save. Second, you will inevitably have to return to the qualitative techniques of playtesting and exercising your intuition as a designer to find the balance points you want in your game. This may mean you start with an exponential curve and end up with a more hand-crafted one for your game's progression, and that's fine. This is ultimately not a mathematical exercise but an exercise in making an effective, engaging, fun game.

Balancing Parts, Progression, and Systems

Once you have identified the core resources to use to begin balancing objects and systems in your game, you can begin to build the cost–benefit relationships between them. This often involves a combination of mathematical and intuitive techniques when creating a new game, including deciding what sort of balancing curve to use (for example, linear versus exponential), based on the needs of your game. If you have data about player behavior in an existing game, you can add analytical information to it to reduce (but not eliminate) the amount of iteration and playtesting needed.

Balancing Parts

One of the most common balancing tasks you will have to do is to make sure that parts used within a particular system are balanced against each other. This is typically a task of balancing intransitive objects: some are going to be better than others, but you want to make sure that they're also proportionate to their relative costs.

Balancing weapons in a combat system is a good example and will help illustrate the process. Each weapon shown in Figure 10.5 is a part in a role-playing game's combat system. (Note that this is the same data shown in Figure 8.3.) Each part has the attributes Attack, Damage, and Speed. The values for these attributes don't appear to be on the same scale (that is, all 1–10), which complicates matters a bit, but this is common. As shown in the spreadsheet, the dagger has the lowest Attack modifier, the great sword the highest. The same is true for Damage. For speed, the dagger, short sword, and rapier all share the fastest designation, and the great sword is by far the slowest.

	A	B	C	D
1	Name	Attack	Damage	Speed
2	Dagger	0	2	5
3	Short sword	2	3	5
4	Cutlass	4	5	1
5	Broad sword	3	4	4
6	Rapier	3	3	5
7	Long sword	5	6	2
8	Great sword	8	8	0

Figure 10.5 An example of a spreadsheet containing attribute data for various weapons to be balanced

Are these weapons balanced with respect to each other in terms of their abilities? They're clearly not the same, but *balanced* doesn't mean they have to be the same. To be balanced as intransitive parts in a system, they each have to have a valid place in the game. Each should be sufficiently different that there is a situation in which the player might choose to use the weapon. And, of course, they all have to feel to the player as if their benefits and costs offset each other.

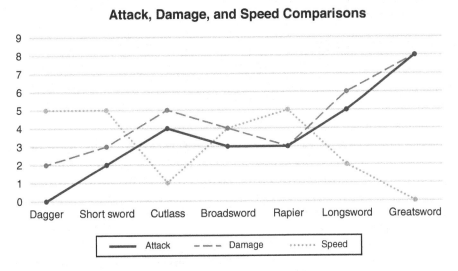

Figure 10.6 A comparison of weapon attributes in graphical form

Figure 10.6 is a graph that compares the weapon attributes. By looking at the attribute values as they are, you can see that there is some variance, but many of the values are clustered in a narrow midrange, with only the dagger and great sword really diverging from the group.[2] From just looking at this graph, it's not really clear whether these weapons are balanced against each other, but it seems likely that we may want to change these values to provide more variability—especially for the cutlass, broad sword, and rapier—and thus more choices for the player.

As discussed earlier, to balance these weapons, we need to consider both their costs and benefits—their abilities. However, in Figure 10.5, there are no costs shown. If the costs are equal, why would someone not use the most powerful weapon available? We need to determine the cost for each weapon, given its benefits, so that each feels viable in the game. It seems likely that a dagger should cost less than a great sword, but how much less? This ties in with the efficacy of each weapon in the game's combat system and the game's economic system. For this example,

---

2. Note that a line graph isn't technically appropriate here. Because the values graphed don't vary continuously from one weapon to another—there's nothing midway between the short sword and cutlass, for example—this data should really be shown in a bar chart. However, we're using this graph to visually assess how the various weapons relate to each other. In such cases, using a line graph like this can often give you a better feel for the data overall. Don't be afraid to explore different ways of visualizing your data: often the right graphic can provide important insights, even if the graph is technically "wrong" for the data.

we have to consider both of those as black boxes and need to focus on balancing the costs and benefits of the weapons.

To work out a viable cost for each weapon, we need to consult (and perhaps change) the attribute values related to the abilities as benefits to the player. Doing this is an iterative process that is different every time you do it, but this example can provide some guidelines.

The first thing to do is to find the core resource to balance around and consider the items' relative benefits in that light. As described earlier, most games have a core resource that drives a player's goals and actions. Understanding this is central to being able to balance intransitive objects in terms of their relative power or players in terms of their progression in the game.

In this example, we are designing a role-playing game, so we can use health (often expressed as hit points) as our core resource. In RPGs, if your character reduces an enemy's health to zero, your character wins and gains rewards (loot, experience points, and so on). On the other hand, if your character loses all health, they die, which is at minimum a setback that you as the player want to avoid. Given the central place of health in a role-playing game, it makes sense to have it be the core resource around which to balance weapons.

This gives us a starting place: which of the weapon attributes is most closely connected to reducing an opponent's health? The amount of health reduction done is based on the weapon's Damage attribute, so we can start there. However, to do damage with a weapon, a player first has to hit their opponent with it, which is governed by the Attack attribute—and the higher this number, the better the chance of hitting. But that's not the end of the story. In this combat system, weapon speed plays a role: slower weapons do not attack as often as fast ones. Once the player has a chance to bring their weapon to bear (based on its Speed), they can try to hit their opponent, using its Attack modifier. If they hit, they may do damage, which is the goal. So in terms of attributes that enable the player to reduce their opponent's health, Speed is the first gate, then Attack, then Damage.

With this knowledge (or at least a hypothesis…it may take several tries to get this right), we can start to combine the attribute values for each weapon to see if that leads us to a viable, balanced cost for each one. It would be simple if just adding these up gave us what look like usable cost values. However, adding up the Attack, Damage, and Speed for each shows us that the short sword and cutlass both end up with a cost of 10, only 3 more than the dagger and 1 less than the broad sword. Somehow that doesn't seem right.

Adjusting Attribute Weights

There are a couple things we can do from here. One is to assign weight coefficients to each of the attributes to give their values different weights in the overall cost. We will also want to look hard at the weapon attribute values to see if they make sense or should be moved around. By iterating on these (because they affect each other), we should be able to come up with a balanced and varied set of values for each weapon.

To set the multipliers on each attribute, we need to look at how the attributes work together in the combat systems. Because Damage is the attribute most directly related to our core resource, we can start by setting its coefficient to 1.0. We could leave the other attributes, Attack and Speed, also at a coefficient of 1.0, setting each of the attributes to be of equal importance, but as noted above, that doesn't give us satisfactory cost values. In addition, we know that if one weapon is faster than another, it has more chances to hit and actually do damage, so we probably want to bump up the Speed attribute's contribution to the overall value of the weapon. Let's start with a coefficient of 2. The attack attribute is also important, though in a system like this it's difficult to say exactly how important. Let's start with a value of 1.5, between the base value of Damage and the more heavily weighted Speed value.

By working with these data values in a spreadsheet, it's easy to fiddle around with the multipliers and see how they affect each weapon's cost. (You are encouraged to load the values shown in Figure 10.5 into a spreadsheet and follow along that way so you understand the process better.) With multipliers of 2x on Speed, 1.5x on Attack, and 1.0 on Damage, we can multiple each and add them up to get each weapon's total and tentative cost. These cost values start to look a little more reasonable. The range is 10 for the dagger to 20 for the great sword. This is maybe a little narrow (the great sword is only 2x as expensive as the least expensive weapon, the dagger) but not bad. However, now the cutlass costs even less than the short sword, which seems odd. Looking at the values for each, the cutlass is a much slower weapon, being a lot heavier, so it's losing out on "value" due its low Speed. It looks like it's time to move from the multipliers to playing with the weapon attribute values themselves.

While there will be cases where you cannot change the attribute values for parts (like these weapons) in a game, usually you will be able to do so. If not, you are stuck with manipulating the cost multipliers or, in some cases, adding situational balancing factors: if one item is less expensive than it should be, you might be able to make it difficult to purchase (for example, the player has to go into a dangerous area or significantly out of their way to do so). Such situational modifiers can make up for the inability to balance objects against each other directly but be aware that adding such indirect modifiers can make the overall balancing task much more difficult. For example, what if a player can't afford any other weapon and can't find where to purchase the one they want, or what if going there means certain death? In such a case, you've locked the player out of the game.

Adjusting Attribute Values

To start considering the weapon attributes as a whole, it can be helpful to choose one object as the base or midline, as we did in giving Damage a 1.0 modifier in the preceding section. In this case, the broad sword looks like a good candidate: we'll adjust its attributes to all be 5 so that it's in the middle of the range for each attribute. That's bumping it up a little bit, but doing so will help unclog the middle, where most of the weapons are congregating right now. A few other tweaks seem like they're probably good ideas—giving the dagger a little bit better Attack (going from 0 to 1), and moving the great sword from 8 Attack and 8 Damage to 10 in each. This helps open the range and try things out.

At about this time, it's a good idea to keep an eye on the graph of the weapons' attributes relative to each other to make sure they aren't clumping together and that nothing weird happens (like the cutlass becoming faster than the rapier, for example). It's also a good idea to keep tuning the attribute weights and watching how the combinations of these and the attribute changes affect each other.

Decoupling Cost from Value

Finally, when the values start looking not too strange, we can experiment with decoupling the number we have been using for cost and the actual in-game cost. Call the old cost value Mod Value for the utility value we get from the multiplier modifiers. Then we can move the in-game cost up or down independently by hand to get the effect we want. Graphing cost and Mod Value together again helps visually show the relationships between the weapons. The graph in Figure 10.7 doesn't directly show the individual weapon attributes balanced against each other, but it does show how they relate to each other after having been weighed and added together in the Mod Value. Note the logistic curve used in Figure 10.7 as well (tweaked to have a steepness value of 0.95 and a midpoint of 3.5). This acts as a guide and a confirmation that the weapons follow the kind of relationship we want.

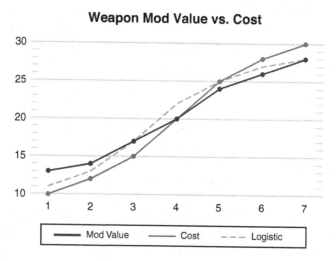

Figure 10.7 The weighted attribute value (Mod Value) graphed against hand-chosen cost figures, along with a logistic curve as a guide

In this case, after numerous iterative modifications of both the weapons' attributes and their multiplicative coefficients, we end up with the attribute values shown in the spreadsheet excerpt in Figure 10.8. Mod Value is the weighted sum of each weapon's Attack, Damage, and Speed values. Both the attribute values and the weight coefficients for Mod Value have now changed: in this spreadsheet, Damage retains a multiplier of 1.0, while Speed has a multiplier of 1.75, and Attack has a multiplier of 1.3. The precise values of these multipliers is not as important as whether they make sense for the game and the behavior of the weapons and whether they lead to both weapon benefits and costs that area balanced.

	A	B	C	D	E	F
1	Name	Attack	Damage	Speed	Mod value	Cost
2	Dagger	1	1	6	13	10
3	Short sword	2	1	6	14	12
4	Cutlass	4	7	3	17	15
5	Broad sword	5	5	5	20	20
6	Rapier	5	3	8	24	25
7	Long sword	7	6	6	26	28
8	Great sword	10	10	3	28	30

Figure 10.8 The revised weapon attribute values, including the Mod Value representing the weighted sum of Attack (1.3 weighted), Damage (1.0 weighted), and Speed (1.75 weighted) and the hand-selected cost values based on the Mod Value

We can also view these revised attribute values in graphical form to see more qualitatively how they differ from each other, as shown in Figure 10.9. The attributes all look reasonable, given the kinds of weapons being represented, and the attribute range is broad enough to apply to a lot of different situations. None of the weapons are too much alike, as each has different strengths and weaknesses. The cost–benefit curve shown in Figure 10.7 rises up and to the right, following most closely the logistic used. That the cost and benefit values follow this curve implies that their relationships are proportional, and players will be able to intuitively pick this up as they play.

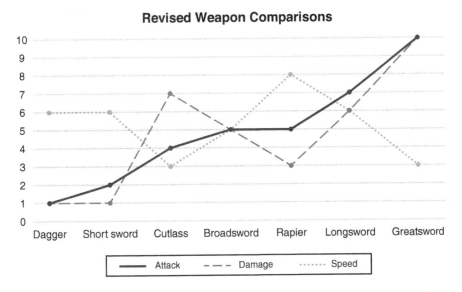

Figure 10.9 The revised weapon attribute values in line graph form. Note that while Attack values increase across weapons, each weapon has its own strengths and weaknesses, and the clog of similar values in the middle has been broken up

The cost–benefit graph in Figure 10.7 also shows that by hand-tuning the cost for each weapon after doing some mathematical modeling of the attribute weights, we can make the less effective weapons balanced slightly more in the player's favor: they cost less than their value might strictly indicate. This fits because they are less capable and are more likely to be the weapons new or poorer characters use. The more powerful high-end weapons show the opposite: they have a small premium attached, meaning that the graph of their cost slightly exceeds their inherent Mod Value. This keeps them somewhat aspirational; if you see someone with a great sword, you know it's a powerful weapon and that the character paid a significant price to get it. In addition, the cost and benefit lines cross right at the broad sword, keeping it solidly in the middle, as a kind of fixed point in the mental model for these weapons.

So far, this all looks good—but of course none of this has been playtested. We have thus far used a combination of mathematical and designer heuristic methods to balance these weapons as parts within the combat system. The next step is to use these with players in playtest situations to see which assumptions prove incorrect or whether the players can quickly and enjoyably build a mental model of the weapons' relative effectiveness and cost. In any real game situation, more iteration would almost certainly be called for to truly balance these items mathematically and from the designer's and players' points of view.

Balancing for Progression

Beyond balancing atomic parts within a system, as a game designer, you will often have to balance how the player or other objects improve during the game. Multiple kinds of progression are commonly found in games. First and foremost of these is how the player's representative in the game—their character, army, farm, or similar—improves in terms of attribute values during the course of the game. In addition, several aspects of economic progression need to be carefully balanced, including levels of currency and the availability and improvement in in-game objects that the player uses during the game.

In most games, the player (or at least their in-game representative) improves as the game is played. This gives the player a sense of achievement and meaning in the game. To create and balance a progression system for the player, you need to first decide on the attributes that are the primary carriers for their improvement. These are most often the core attributes discussed earlier. These attributes will lead you to the resources that represent the cost for advancing.

One of the most common examples of player progression is a player character improving by going up levels. The character accrues experience points and then spends them to gain additional health, improved powers, and often access to new content or abilities. Each of these benefits is an attribute that must be included in any progression curves and balancing (access to content being another example of a special-case attribute that may be difficult to quantify). This exchange is typically automatic, happening as soon as the character has sufficient experience points to cross the leveling threshold. Players don't typically think of this as "spending" these points, but functionally they are. Rather than reset the experience points balance to zero, however, most games make the next level increment higher than the current total; this allows for the use of exponential curves that describe the points needed for each level and provides the player with a sense of achievement at seeing these numbers always go up.

While you should have at least one core resource that governs the player's progression, it's possible to use more than one. Using more than one can increase the amount of work you have to do to assess the difficulty and the time it will take for the player to advance, as this has to be done for each resource separately. If, however, different resources offer different advancement rates, depending on where the player is in their progression, this gives them the opportunity to choose their path in the game strategically and creates many more meaningful decisions for them.

For example, you might have a game where the player's early progression is based on fighting and gaining health. The player can continue this path throughout the game, but they may also have the opportunity to switch to advancing based on their wealth and then again later based on the number of friends they have, as first health and then wealth deliver fewer additional benefits (that is, the rate of increase slows or the distance to the next level increases exponentially while points gained do not). Not all players will welcome such a multifaceted approach, so it's important that once a player begins advancing using a particular resource (and attendant activities) that they can continue doing so. Many players will want to take the most optimal course to advancement, however, so giving them the option to focus on a new resource, attribute, and activity for part of the game may increase their engagement.

In any event, it is important that a player always have the feeling that they are advancing. If a player ever feels that their progress has stopped—or that the next opportunity for advancement is effectively infinitely far away, given the rewards for their current level of challenge—then their engagement with the game will evaporate. (As noted in Chapter 7, the "prestige" outer loop in many idle games presents an additional way to advance once the primary method has begun to slow and become boring.) Whether the player has one or multiple resource dimensions along which they could be advancing, they must always see significant ways to progress along at least one of them.

Pacing

In most cases, progression is punctuated rather than being continuous. This means that any improvements appear at discrete intervals rather than dribbling out slowly as the player builds up more points. Getting the benefits of progression at set checkpoints is often more rewarding for players (and gives them something to look forward to), and it's also easier to balance because you can choose where to place the level-up points. However, there is no reason you could not create a continuous improvement curve, though it would likely be difficult to keep balanced.

To balance a progression system, you need to decide on the pace at which you want the player to advance. This pace can be defined in terms of number of monsters killed, number of provinces won, number of flowers gathered …whatever makes the most sense for your game and the resources around which you're building the progression path.

Part of determining the pace of player advancement is defining the shape of the curve that defines the relationship between the costs and benefits for advancement. If, for example, you want to award more and more points and yet have the players take longer to advance at each subsequent step, an exponential curve is likely your best choice. Many other choices are possible, too, as discussed earlier, and there are endless hybrids: you could create a hand-crafted piecewise linear curve for the start of your game to draw the player in and then transition to a series of stacked logistic curves, each relying on a different cost resource, that together approximate an exponential curve. There is no single formula for this, and you will need to spend some iterative design time finding what works best to the players engaged as they play and advance in your game.

Time and Attention

Underlying whatever other resources the player uses for progression, the ultimate resources that every player spends on your game are their attention and their time. These are almost but not quite the same. If a player is spending their attention on your game, then they are engaged and playing it actively—exploring, building, hunting, and so on. When balancing their progression, a major consideration is the number of these activities that they have to do to get the next installment of improvements. In many cases, you can (and should) map out to a high degree of specificity the activities the player is doing, the number of points or other rewards they get for doing these things, and how many times they need to do that to accrue the number of points needed to advance. In the simplest case, the activities provide a known number of points: so you can say, for example, that for every zoo animal a player feeds, they get 10 points. The player needs 100 points to get to the next level, so they need to feed 10 animals. If feeding an animal takes 2 minutes, it will take a player 20 minutes of full attention to advance to the next level.

In most games, the number of points awarded per activity isn't preset, or it's random within a range, and you may also have to account for the possibility of failure. So if in a game about being a gem merchant the player needs 1,000 points to get to the next level, and they get 50 to 200 points for every gem they successfully cut, then they need to cut 5 to 20 gems. However, the player may not always be successful. Given the difficulty of the task for their level of experience, you can estimate their success rate. If the gem-cutting success rate is estimated at 80% for the player's current level, then the player will need to cut about 7 to 25 gems, including failures. If each gem takes 1 to 3 minutes to cut, then that means at minimum, a player will need 7 to 75 minutes to get to the next level—and possibly more if you don't want to assume that they are working without pause the entire time. That's a very wide time range, so you may need to reconsider some of the aspects of this system to keep it balanced from the player's point of view, so that they feel like they are always making progress. Perhaps the longer they take to cut a gem (up to some maximum), the lower the chance of failure. Or maybe they can gain bonus points for cutting a gem really well. There are numerous ways like this to keep the time range reined in—but you have to know what the range of time to advancement is and whether it's going to be a problem from the player's point of view (or if it's just not the experience you are trying to create).

Closely linked to the player's attention is their time. These are often synonymous, but not always. If the player can start a process—growing crops, raising an army, and so on—and then go away and do something else while it's going on, then the game limits how rapidly they can advance but does not require their attention while they are getting there. Time is the ultimate resource any of us have, and as designers, we must be respectful of the player's time. If you include a component in the player progression system that regulates their advancement simply by clock time, you maintain greater control over the gameplay experience because you can say with assurance how rapidly they can progress in the game. On the other hand, this can lead to reduced engagement on the player's part because they may feel that all they have to do is start the next batch of crops growing or pies baking, and then they can leave. That gives them little to do in the game and greatly increases the probability that they will simply not be engaged enough to come back.

Secondary Progression

In addition to the player's progression via their core resources, it is likely in a game of significant complexity that you as the designer will have opportunities to create secondary progression paths. These can be more short term and help keep the player engaged, especially if their primary progression checkpoints are far apart.

An example of this kind of secondary advancement can be found in how *World of Warcraft* provides secondary advancement with the player character's inventory. Early on, characters are severely limited in how much they can carry with them. Players commonly have to make difficult decisions about which loot to keep or drop because they simply cannot carry everything.

However, as a character advances both in levels and in wealth, new inventory options open up to them: they can purchase (with their growing wealth) new, larger backpacks and bags that increase the amount they can carry. Some characters who also advance in crafting gain the ability to create these bags, which opens up yet another secondary progression path. The result is that as the character continues to advance, the limit on their inventory also rises. This isn't connected in a rigid way (such as the player gaining two more inventory slots at level 10) but rather as additional, secondary progression paths involving the character's level, wealth, and/or secondary skills. While these progression paths also need to remain balanced with the player's overall advancement, keeping these decoupled makes it easier for these progression systems to be largely self-balancing, as the player will attend to their need for increased inventory as it becomes an issue for their character.

Economic System Balance

Another major aspect of overall game balancing is systemic balance. Balancing economic systems is an important example of this. As introduced in Chapter 7, in-game economies create complex relationships between various resources as they are exchanged in a set of reinforcing loops to create greater value. Resources appear in the game from sources, are exchanged as part of the economy, and leave through sinks. These resources (and often the in-game objects that are made from them) can become a secondary progression path for the player, as wealth and possession of objects are common markers of both achievement and status. While balancing in-game economies and similar complex systems remains an inexact art at best (requiring all the types of methods outlined in Chapter 9, "Game Balance Methods"), there are some ways you can keep systems in your game from spiraling out of control.

Inflation, Stagnation, and Arbitrage

As discussed in Chapter 7, in-game economies often have some of the most difficult struggles with balance issues, particularly inflation. When there are too many sources pouring currency (or other resources) into an economy and not enough ways for the resources to leave it, more and more of these resources piles up within the economy, making it worth less and less to the player. This happens to virtually every game that has an in-game economy—at least in part because we simply have not yet discovered all the systemic economic principles to put into place to prevent rampant inflation from taking over.

Stagnation is another issue, albeit a less common one. With stagnation, there is not enough currency coming into the game via the sources to provide enough economic velocity—the rapidity with which resources flow from one location to another, very much like the rate at which water flows in a river. If the flow slows down, the "river" stagnates, and the economy dies. This typically happens in games when a designer is trying so hard to prevent inflation that they go too far the other way, making resources in the game overly precious, which eventually leads to frustration for most players.

A third issue with game balance is managing arbitrage. Simply put, arbitrage is the ability to buy a resource in one place for a given price and then (usually quickly) sell it for a higher price somewhere else. This is an extremely common real-world economic activity today, underlying everything from money markets to long-distance trade routes.

The Lesson Learned from Dolls and Crystal Balls

In games, if arbitrage is not managed carefully, massive inflation can occur. Probably the first known instance of arbitrage in an online game happened in *Habitat*, an online virtual world that launched in 1987, well before most people even knew about the Internet (Morningstar and Farmer 1990). This instance, like many of the lessons from *Habitat*, still provides useful information for game and online world designers today. In this case, Chip Morningstar and Randy Farmer, the guys running *Habitat*, were alarmed one morning to see that the supply of money in the game had quintupled overnight. This type of flood of money in a game is the kind of bug that can ruin an economy quickly. Strangely, though, there was no bug that they could find, and no players submitted reports. It took them a little while to reconstruct what had happened.

In *Habitat*, each player began the game with 2,000 tokens. Like most other in-game currencies, these tokens didn't come from anywhere; the game just created them as a source and gave them to each new player character. In addition, throughout the game world were vending machines called Vendroids, out of which the players could buy various items (the machines, acting as currency sinks, removed the money from the game). There were similar machines called Pawn Machines that would buy objects back from the players. Each Vendroid had its own prices, so there was some variability across them in order to make the economy more interesting to the players. It turned out that there were two Vendroids all the way across town from each other (a long way to walk in the game) that had particularly low prices on a couple of items. One had a price for selling dolls set to 75 tokens. This wouldn't be a problem, except that the players found a Pawn Machine that would buy them back for 100 tokens. This is an instant arbitrage opportunity, as the players could make a profit of 25 tokens per doll they bought and then sold, walking them across town each time to do so. This is exactly what some of the players did, taking all their money, buying as many dolls as they could carry, going across town, and selling each one for a profit.

That alone wouldn't have been so bad; you can make only so much money by selling dolls for a 25 token profit. However, the other Vendroid with unusually low pricing sold crystal balls for 18,000 tokens. That was a lot of money, meaning a lot of dolls to buy and sell to build up to be able to buy one crystal ball. The reason the players did so—taking most of the night, going back and forth, buying and selling dolls—is because they discovered a Pawn Machine that would buy the crystal balls back for *30,000 tokens*—an instant profit of 12,000 tokens. Keep in mind that each time a Pawn Machine purchased back a doll or a crystal ball, it became a source of tokens, creating them out of nothing, and thus contributing to flooding the money supply in the game. Once the players had the money to purchase two crystal balls (the second being far easier than the first), they were quickly able buy and sell more of them for much higher profits, building up massive bank balances over the course of the night.

When Randy and Chip found the enormous increase in money in the game the next morning, they tracked down some of the players who suddenly had huge bank balances. When asked about it, the players responded, "We got it fair and square! And we're not going to tell you how!" It took some time for them to be convinced that their new-found wealth wasn't going to be taken away—but the prices on the Vendroids did get fixed. Fortunately for the game and its economy, these players didn't hoard the money or flood it onto the market, which would have caused debilitating inflation across the game. Instead, they used it to buy items in the game and conduct the first player-run treasure hunts in an online game.

This example of economic arbitrage and the fast, dramatic increase in the amount of money in the game happened in the very earliest days of online games and in-game economies, and yet we are still learning these same lessons today. Games need sources to create money and other resources as rewards for the players. If these rewards are too stingy, the economy will stagnate, and the players will become frustrated and leave. If the rewards are about equal to what a player received last time, hedonic fatigue will quickly settle in, as old rewards fade in value quickly. As a result, most games with significant economies find that they have to continually add more money into the game as the players progress and then struggle to find enough sinks to pull the money back out again. For example, *World of Warcraft* has to pump more and more money into the game as rewards as player characters rise in levels, to the point that the in-game monetary value for each monster killed goes up more than 750 times from when the character is level 1 to when they're level 60 (Giaime 2015). If not paired up with similarly enormous sinks to drain the money out of the economy, this leads to a fundamentally unbalanced situation in which the designated currency (copper, silver, gold, and so on) ceases to have any meaning as a reward for the player.

Constructing a Game Economy

One way to create an in-game economy that is dynamic and yet guards against insufficient sinks and therefore inflation is to carefully construct the ranges for power and availability (rarity) for objects and the range of prices for those items that players are able to buy and sell. The massively multiplayer game *Albion Online* is an excellent example of this (Woodward 2017).

In this game, objects that can be found in the world are grouped into tiers indicating both rarity and approximate power or utility. (Dividing items among these tiers and balancing them on a per-attribute basis is a part-balancing task.) The first three tiers are for training resources, so they don't significantly affect the economy; Tiers 4 to 8 are the main parts in the player economy.

Each tier has a rarity—a probability that a given item from that tier will be found. *Albion Online* also separates the game world into areas where different tiered items can be found; this is a common technique in many games. There are innumerable ways to decide where items in your game world can be found, though it's typical to have the value or power of the items scale proportionately with the danger or difficulty involved in obtaining them.

The item power progression is described by an exponential curve using the equation 1.2^{tier}. This means that each tier is effectively 20% more advanced than the one before, so a Tier 8 item has about double the utility (attribute values, and so on) of a Tier 4 item. This is enough of a spread that the players feel like they are progressing as they use higher- and higher-tier items, but it is not so great that the distance between players at the top and bottom of the progression path is impossibly great. This is a good use for an exponential curve, as it compounds the difference level by level in a predictable way. If you wanted to have more of a difference between the top and bottom items, you could create more levels and/or use a larger base for the exponential equation. In the case of *Albion Online*, the designers arrived at this equation (overall power = 1.2^{tier}) empirically, after a great deal of playtesting. However, having found that this curve worked for the game, the team was able to save considerable time when adding new content because they didn't have to derive the curve over and over again.

In *Albion Online*, the rarity of each item on each tier also goes up exponentially but on a much steeper curve. Rarity describes the probability of finding an item at any given opportunity. It advances at a rate equal to 3^{tier}, meaning that each tier is 3x as rare (or 1/3 as likely to be found) as the one before it. A Tier 8 item in the game is thus 81x rarer than a Tier 4 item. This sets up a very steep gradient, meaning that items on the two highest tiers are extremely rare—and thus extremely valuable.

The decoupling of these two economic progression curves—one for item power and one for item rarity—is significant. It keeps the upward creep of power in check, as the rarity (and thus cost) per unit increase in power is high. This combined cost per unit power itself increases non-linearly (given the differences in the two exponential equations used).

In addition to keeping the power and rarity relationship in balance (proportional but increasing at different rates), this sets up the conditions for a robust player-driven economy. *Albion Online* has a complex crafting system that allows players to transmute lower-tier items into higher-tier ones and salvage items from a higher tier to a lower tier plus some money (thus providing a source for money to enter the game). Rather than tie this discussion to *Albion Online*'s design completely, we will consider the principles used there but in a more general form.

Price Boundaries

A key point that the *Albion Online* economy captures is what can be generally described as the need for price boundaries. These boundaries allow players ample room to create their own vibrant economy of prices floating up and down (creating lots of strategic and social interactivity), while keeping them from excluding others from the economy and making sure the prices in the economy stay in relatively noninflationary territory, given the money and items available in the game.

One way to set up these price boundaries is with a virtual import/export market—an independent set of economic sources and sinks. If you want to sell an item and can't find anyone who wants to buy it from you, you can always go down to the export market, which will buy it. It won't pay much, but you can always sell it there. In the same way, if you want to buy an item and can't find anyone who will sell it to you, you can go to the import market, where you can buy (almost) anything. With the exception of a few unique items that the game designer may set aside for special purposes, you can purchase anything on the import market—but it will cost you a lot.

This arrangement ensures that all items can be bought and sold, that no player is ever completely shut out of the market (provided they have enough in-game currency to purchase an item they want), and allows the designer to set the floor and ceiling on pricing in the in-game market. So long as there's sufficient distance between those bounds, players can create their own self-balancing market that is largely immune to the long-term effects of an excessive infusion of currency and thus has little inflation. There will from time to time be temporary price fluctuations if someone buys up all the horses or tries to sell many at once, but such changes do not structurally affect the economy's balance—and other players can always retreat to the import/export market, so no player can fully control it.

For example, if someone wants to sell a horse, they can put it up for any price that's greater than what they could sell it for on the export market and less than what someone else could buy a similar horse for on the import market. If they choose to sell the horse for less than what they could get on the export market, that's their decision, but the person who buys it from them could take the horse right over to the export market and sell it for an instant profit, so that's unlikely to happen. In the same way, if someone prices a horse higher than the price on the import market, no one is likely to buy it, as they can just go over to the import market instead and buy a horse for less there.

Creating the Market Channel

The key to creating and maintaining the market channel is linking the prices for the low and high end—the export and import pricing—to item rarity at each tier. (You can also substitute item power, though rarity is a commonly available value that serves as a core attribute here.) This ensures that rarer, more powerful items always have higher prices than those of lower rarity and power and, because of the way exponential equations rise, creates a broader market for the rarer items. For example, *Albion Online* is able to tie the low-end pricing to the value of those items in salvage and silver (the in-game currency), and the high-end pricing follows the rarity exponential curve. You could as easily peg the low-end export prices to any value that doesn't make the items completely worthless. For example, the export price could be set to 50% of the rarity value of an item's tier, or if you want to ground this more in the player's time, some portion of the average time value (expressed in in-game currency) of how long it would take a player to obtain an item of that rarity. Either can be expressed as a fraction of each item's rarity value. So if the rarity equation is 1.5^{tier}, the export (sale) value could be set to 50% of that. The high-end import value can also be tied to the rarity (or power, and so on) value but at a multiple of it, such as 200%. (Both of these multiplier values must be tuned during playtesting.)

This arrangement creates two curves based on the same exponential equation, meaning that as long as new items added to the game follow the same rarity scheme, their import and export prices will automatically fit in with this scheme. This also opens up a stable market channel that broadens with item value. Within this channel, the players can set whatever prices they like, and the game can set vendor prices that float up and down—for example, with supply and demand, based on aggregate player behavior. Figure 10.10 shows a graphic depiction of the market channel for a game with item rarity Tiers 1 to 10. Both import and export are using a rarity equation of 1.5^{tier}, with a 50% markdown on export and a 200% markup on import. Note that due to the way exponential equations work, increasing the base (here, 1.5) for the equation even a small amount increases the breadth of the market channel and thus potential price volatility within it.

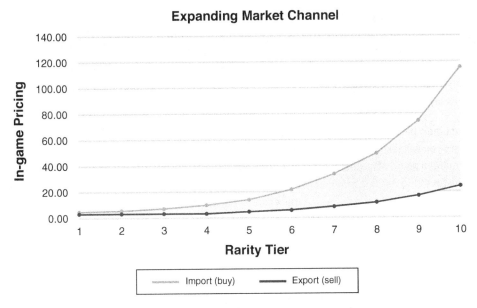

Figure 10.10 The market channel that defines and enables a balanced player-run economy. The shaded region is the channel—the area between the minimum sales price and the maximum purchase price, as defined by the game. There is little room for player price negotiation at lower rarity values, but as players advance in the game and begin trading in higher-tier items, their ability to participate in a broader market channel increases

Putting It All Together

Using the preceding examples, you could create a game with basic weapons, as shown in Figure 10.8, with their in-game costs based on their core resource values. If these are your lowest-tier or least-rare items, this establishes a set of lower bounds for item prices in the game. Then, you can determine each succeeding intransitive item's cost and benefits based on this same set of weights. For example, using the same formulas as above, you can easily determine how much more benefit a dagger with +2 Speed gains as opposed to a broad sword with +1 Damage. This in turn allows you to determine which tier each item occurs in, based on the pacing you want for the game and the overall cost–benefit groupings. (While not shown here, you could place these objects along a similar exponential "total benefit" curve, like the one shown in Figure 10.7.) From there you can create your market channel to allow players to buy and sell items in the game if you wish. Note that the channel is narrow for low-tier items, which means the market begins stable and nearly fixed, and it opens up as the items become more powerful and the players become more experienced. Of course, if the players can also craft items like weapons in your game, you need to ensure that the costs and rarities of the ingredients are somewhat lower than but rise proportionately to the cost of the items they produce. Being able to base the costs and rarities of crafting resources on the minimum and maximum prices of the items they produce helps you set them in a way that works within the game.

That's all easy to say in a few paragraphs; it's much more work in an actual game, where you might have dozens or hundreds of items to balance. If, however, you proceed from your parts and attribute design, determine the core resources, and find ways to create diverse intransitive objects that are balanced against each other, you can also create an economic progression curve that applies to each object and creates an engaging advancement-based experience for the player.

Creating a balanced in-game economy is one of the most complex and difficult system design tasks you will take on. As with the other types of balance discussed here, balancing an economy requires a blend of mathematical, analytical, and heuristic techniques. There is still no substitute for trying this out, building your own, playtesting it, and using these principles as you find your own balance points in your game economy or other complex game system.

Analytical Balance

As mentioned in Chapter 9, analytics is mathematical modeling's partner in quantitative methods for balancing your game. This use of balance goes far beyond determining transitive or intransitive item or even system balance. It centers more on the player's overall experience: is the game attractive and engaging and does it feel appropriately balanced to the player—and if so, for how long? The analytical measures of this are the output of (and thus often paired with) in-game metrics. The data you choose to collect may be certain measures, or metrics, and the results of that collection are your analytical data.

Three main types of metrics and resulting analytical data are important to game design and development:

- **Development process data:** Collecting data on your game's progress during development helps you know whether you are on track. See Chapter 12, "Making Your Game Real," for more on this.

- **Performance data:** Many games need to carefully watch their frame rate, use of memory, and so on. Software profiling and similar analytical techniques help programmers and technical artists make sure a game runs well on its target hardware.

- **User behavior data:** Looking at what your players do overall, as a group rather than as individuals, helps you understand the health and overall success of your game.

This section is focused on the third category: user behavior data. This is the type of analytics that's most related to ensuring that the player has a positive, balanced experience in your game. Unlike using math to build progression and power curves, using user behavior information isn't about setting up a structure for players to act within; it's based instead on recording and analyzing what they actually do. These techniques are therefore really only useful when you have a lot of players playing your game (often not until you're near a commercial launch) and only if you can retrieve this data on a regular (ideally near-real-time) basis.

Collecting Player Information

For analog tabletop games and offline games where you have no access to the player's behavioral data, user behavior data is difficult to obtain and often of little use. However, most games developed today have some form of online component or connection. Either the player is directly connecting to a game server or the game is able to send anonymous information back to a server for analysis. In addition, free-to-play (F2P) games yield and require a great deal more information about the players' behavior that helps you understand if the gameplay is balanced and the game overall is healthy.

If the game can report back to a central server, then you can place calls in the game software to record behavioral information. This information is recorded and typically sent back to the server as a short string that identifies a player's ID, where they are in the game when this information is collected, and any other information you may need (such as how far the player is into their current session).

It's tempting to put analytics calls on everything, but this can do more harm than good. Ultimately, you want to gather only the information that will help you create a more balanced, engaging experience. The metrics you collect are often called *key performance indicators* (*KPIs*). These are the numbers and metrics you watch to make sure your game is doing well, players are enjoying it, and nothing is horribly out of balance. Another way to say this is that if something is not a KPI, don't bother collecting it: it becomes data you have to spend time analyzing that has no real benefit.

When collecting user behavior data, you need to ensure that the information is recent and is regularly collected. Not being able to access recently collected information or having it be collected only sporadically does not help your understanding at all. If the information is more than an hour or so out of date, it is often stale and not very useful. If it's more than a day out of date, it may lead you to make poor decisions about the game (unless you're using it retrospectively or, for example, to compare to the same day in the previous week for trends in behavior). The ideal is continuous and near-real-time data collection: you should know what's going on in your game at any given moment. Realistically, this data may be collected only once every few minutes, but that's sufficient.

Grouping Players Together

The data you collect on a player is aggregated with data on other players into *cohorts* (or groups) so that you can get an overview of how most players interact with the game. (With only a few exceptions, individual player behavior information isn't useful and can even lead you astray.) One of the most common methods for creating player cohorts is to put all players who began playing on a certain day or week into one group. This group can then be tracked over time to see how their behavior changes. Looking at changes between cohorts can tell you a great deal about the health of your game; for example, by looking at the differences in advancement time, session length, or purchasing behavior between all players who started during the week of July 9 versus those who started during the week of July 16, you can see if your game is doing better or worse over time.

Analyzing Player Behavior

There are several categories of information you can gather related to player behavior. These can be loosely grouped into the following categories:

- Acquisition and first experience
- Retention
- Conversion
- Usage
- Community

Acquisition

You can learn a great deal about how attractive and engaging people perceive your game to be by looking at how you "acquire" players—bring them into the game—and how they react to their first time in the game—which is sometimes called the *first-time user experience* (FTUE) and is a critical element in gaining new players. Essentially, the player's FTUE is the game's first impression on them, kind of like a first date. If the game is confusing, off-putting, or frustrating, the player will drop it and not come back. If, however, it is attractive, engaging, and plays well with them, players are more likely to come back again.

In looking at early usage analytics, you may want to look at how many people come into your game—how many start up the game program at all—and how far they get into it in their first session. You may be able to push this back further, to look first at how many people download and install your game or click on the game on a web page. If you do, you will notice an extreme drop-off ratio at every step. Each game is different, but as a rough heuristic, you can count on losing about half of your players with every mouse click or tap from the time they first start your game until they are playing. This means that if you have three clicks to get through (say, selecting a nation, a character, and a gender) before someone can start playing, you have likely lost about 87% of your starting audience: 50% of 50% of 50%. Your game may see a somewhat different curve, but this heuristic should help you understand the necessity of getting players into the game as quickly as possible.

This progressive loss of players is an instance of what is called the *acquisition funnel*. You will never have more players than those who have heard of your game. By some counts, the drop-off rate of those who have heard of your game to those who go looking for it (on the web or in a store) is as much as 10x. The same goes for those who actually download the game, run it once, and then become regular users. Using the 10x drop-off ratio means that at each stage, you keep 1 in 10 players. So to get 1 regular, long-term player, you have to get 10 to start the game, 100 to download or install it, 1,000 to go looking for it, and 10,000 to know about it. Those are daunting numbers, and perhaps your game will do better—but don't count on it.

Getting Into the Game

Once players enter your game, you can record what they do next as they play the game. Recall the example of *Tumbleseed* from Chapter 9. The game creators measured their players' progress and determined that most of them never made it to the first major checkpoint and that about 80% of the players who made it that far didn't make it to the next milestone. Those are huge losses, indicating that in some way the game is not balanced or engaging. Either the players are finding the game boring or overwhelming. The remedies in each case are different, but the underlying issue is the same and can be addressed only when you figure out why players come in (clearly interested in the game) and the leave again soon after.

Measuring a player's FTUE often includes their response to the game's tutorial or opening moments. Tutorials are meant to teach players how to navigate the game, and yet they are often just frustrating and get in the player's way. On the other hand, having no tutorial can mean throwing the player into the game without their knowing what they're doing, which can be equally confusing and frustrating. Looking at how your players behave during the first few minutes of play can help you balance this part of the game so that you keep as many players as possible playing.

Retention

In addition to keeping players playing, you want to keep them coming back. Retention is often measured in terms of days. Day zero (D0) is the day someone first opens the game. D1 is the next day. D7 is a week after they first started playing, and D30 is one month later. You can group players into cohorts based on when they started playing and track their behavior from there. What percentage come back on D1, D7, and D30? How can you improve this by improving their FTUE and by making sure they have in-game incentives to come back? For example, many games (especially F2P games on mobile platforms) give the players bonuses or similar if they come back the next day after they start playing. The game is very clear about this and celebrates the player's return—as well it should. A game that can't bring players back the next day is going to have a very difficult time succeeding.

Another aspect of tracking players' playing behavior is to look at how the day-to-day numbers of players changes. The number of individual players who play on any given day is called the *daily active users* (DAU). This is sometimes referred to as a "heartbeat" number, as it can tell you at a glance if the game is doing okay right now. DAU varies considerably by day of the week, so seeing a drop-off on a Tuesday probably isn't significant, as this is often the lightest gameplay day for games. On the other hand, if on one Saturday you have half the DAU you had on the previous Saturday, that would be cause for alarm: something is going wrong, and you need to quickly find out what it is.

You can also look at *monthly active users* (MAU), the number of individuals who have played the game in the past 30 days. This is a retrospective number, trailing as it does 30 days into the past. However, by looking at the ratio of DAU divided by MAU—how many people played today compared to how many have played in the past month—you can get a strong indication of the game's overall health. This is often referred to as the game's *stickiness*—how likely people are to stick and to come back to play again. If this ratio goes up over time, your game is healthy. If it is going down—fewer people (as a ratio) are playing now than were playing earlier—that's a bad sign, and you should take quick action to find where the problems are.

You can also look at how long players keep playing not only in terms of an individual session but overall: this is what's called the player's *lifetime* within the game. Most players' lifetime is less than one day—they come in once and never come back. Improving your game's FTUE and early balance so that more players want to come back will increase the health of your game overall. On the other end, how long do regular players play the game? For a few weeks or a few months? Why do they stop? Behavioral analytics can help you understand why players stop playing your game—especially if they simply run out of things to do (which is more common in a content-driven game than a systemic game).

Conversion

In F2P games, the vast majority of players—often 98% to 99%—never buy anything in the game at all. In strict terms, these are players but not customers. Only people who actually make a purchase are customers. The act of changing a player to a customer is called *conversion*.

You can track when players in a given cohort make their first purchase, how much they spend per day on average, and how likely they are to make a second purchase after making a first one. There are lots of ways to look at this data to help you better understand your players' behavior. For example, it's often the case that on a cohort basis, players who have a better first-time experience are more likely to purchase sooner and more in a F2P game. Similarly, players who make one purchase are far more likely to make another; so if you can convince them that making one purchase is a good idea, they are more likely to buy things in the game again.

If you track how much players purchase in a free-to-play game and divide that across all players, you get the *average revenue per user* (ARPU). This is one of the key measures of revenue strength in a game. It may not seem to be related to balance, but if you have designed your game effectively for F2P monetization, players will respond with strong revenue on average.

There are numerous other metrics that are commonly tracked in F2P games, such as *average revenue per daily active user* (ARPDAU). For the discussion here, the most important remaining conversion metric is related both to how long the average player plays (their lifetime in the game) and how much they purchase during that time. As an average across all players, this is called *lifetime value* (LTV). This metric is probably the single most important one for assessing overall game and player experience balance and commercial success.

LTV is part of what is sometimes called the "iron equation" of F2P games. This equation says that the revenue received across all players for their entire time in the game must exceed the sum of the cost of acquiring the average player (including all marketing costs, for example) and the cost of operating the game on a per-player basis for their lifetime. This is the iron equation:

$$LTV > eCPU + Ops$$

eCPU is effective cost per user—how much it costs on average to bring in a new player. So if the average player plays your game for a year, and it costs $1 per month per player for the server, bandwidth, upkeep for the development team, and so on, AND you ended up having to pay $3 in marketing costs to acquire each player, on average, then the amount of revenue you get back, averaged across all players, had better be more than $3 + 1×12, or $15. This means that if, on average, across his or her entire lifetime, each player is paying you only $10, you're essentially going broke. This is a fate that befalls many F2P games that do not look at their player analytics in this light.

All this talk about revenue and monetization may not be what you think of as game balance or even game design. Monetization design is, however, increasingly part of game design. You as a game designer have to be aware of and open to both design and analytical solutions to creating a game that is commercially successful. This may mean selling a game online for a single price, which is a more traditional approach, or putting it up for free with the opportunity for players to choose to purchase in-game items if they want. Properly constructing the game experience so that players do not feel that they must make purchases but that they can if they wish and that they choose to do so enough to make the game successful is a key part of monetization design and analytical game balance.

Usage

Aside from issues of bringing in players, keeping them playing, and encouraging them to make purchases in the game, there are a variety of straightforward usage-based metrics you can collect and analyze.

For example, if you have quests in your game, do they all get completed about the same amount? If there is one that is done repeatedly, it might be unbalanced in the player's favor. Or if there is that almost no one completes, is it too difficult or tedious? You can also look at how people die in the game or how they lose; are there aspects of the game that you wouldn't see otherwise, but by looking at what leads to the player's demise or loss, you see an unbalanced portion of the game?

There are similar economic measures, too. In the example from *Habitat* recounted earlier in this chapter, the game's administrators were fortunate to have put in place measures of the change in the amount of money in the game overall and the balance of in-game money in each player's account on a daily basis. This enabled them to uncover a serious, potentially game-killing economic imbalance before it could get too far out of control.

Anything that affects the usage of your game, its sources and sinks, and how much of any core resource a player can build up is worth tracking analytically. While it is also important to not collect more analytical data than you can really use, if you are trying to figure out where to start, look at where you play sounds in the game: any event that provides auditory feedback to the player is likely an event you want to record as well. If this creates too much data that doesn't help, you can begin to filter these analytic calls down in number, but you will likely gain a better idea of the kinds of data you want to collect as you do so.

Community

Finally, by using analytics to better understand the players' social and community-oriented behavior, you can tell a great deal about the game's overall health and balance. You can, for example, track the amount of time players spend chatting in general and with particular people, along with the number of persistent social groups (for example, guilds) that form and their activity in the game. This enables you to build at least an approximate model of social contact in terms of who is connected to whom. This isn't needed for all games, of course, but being able to map out the social networks in your game can reveal a lot about who are the opinion-makers and early adopters whose behavior you might want to attend to. If, for example, a set of influential players begin reducing the amount of time they spend in the game, this could be an early sign of trouble (even just that they have run out of content).

You can also track the number and type of complaints you receive about different parts of the game. This can help reveal bugs, certainly, but it can also help you find parts of the game that the players feel are unbalanced—too difficult, tedious, or just not engaging. Correcting these makes the game better for everyone.

Summary

Balancing complex systems and gameplay experiences is a whole set of difficult, complex, often daunting tasks. This chapter provides an introduction to the practical elements and mental framework you need to create and balance everything from simple atomic parts to large complex hierarchical systems in a game.

Remember that balancing is necessarily an ongoing exercise. It's never perfect, and it's never really done. If the game seems basically fair to you and to the players, you're moving in the right direction. Remember, too, that every player who plays your game has the possibility of unbalancing it in new ways. If you have created resilient systems and worked to balance them as well as you can, however, you reduce the probability of the game breaking and of the player losing their sense of engagement with your game.

CHAPTER 11

WORKING AS A TEAM

In addition to any creative, system-building, or technical skills you have, to be successful as a game designer, you have to be able to work effectively as part of a team and help others do so as well.

Successful teams don't just happen; they're built intentionally, becoming systems of their own. Understanding the various roles in a development team and how they together form effective teams will help you work with others to build your game.

Teamwork

It's extremely rare for a game of any size to be made by one person on their own. Because of the wide variety of skills needed to create any game, almost all of them are products of multiple people coming together with a shared vision. This requires an immense amount of work in different disciplines—game design, programming, art, sound, writing, project management, marketing, and so on.

To make all this work, you have to move beyond the set of skills involved in conceiving and detailing a game design. In addition to being able to communicate your idea to others who aren't game designers, you have to be able to work effectively with them and make sure everyone's working together well. You have to be able to bring together the best people and use the best processes and tools to make your game real. Doing this is never simple and often takes game designers (and others) well out of their comfort zone. In many ways, designing a game is the easy part. Developing it with a team is much more difficult.

What Successful Teams Do

It's easy to underestimate how difficult it can be to assemble and maintain a successful team and how critically important this is for your game's success and your own long-term career success. Many management theories have speculated about what makes teams work well, and you can find lots of good books on this topic. Fortunately, we have actual data on what makes strong, successful teams—at least for game development.

In 2014, a group called the Game Outcomes Project, led by Paul Tozour, published some fascinating, detailed work on why games succeed or fail (Tozour et al. 2014). They created a detailed survey of about 120 questions and gathered nearly 300 responses from teams that had completed and released their games. This gave them, in their words, a "gold mine" of data.

With the results of this survey, Tozour's team was able to isolate multiple practices that correlate positively or negatively with successful games. They defined "success" broadly, relating to one or more factors:

- Return-on-investment (ROI)—that is, sufficient profitability of the game
- Critical or artistic success
- Meeting internal goals important to the team

Each of the effects the team identified is statistically significant. This means that if you follow the practices indicated, you clearly increase the chance that your game project will be successful.

Tozour's team made a list of their "top 40" items, in order of how much they affect a product's success. These are presented here in a somewhat abbreviated form and grouped thematically. (Reading the original posts on the study results is certainly recommended.)

The top items, if you boil them down, fall into these categories in terms of how much they contribute to creating a successful game:

- Creating and maintaining a clear, compelling vision of what your team is making
- Working effectively, staying focused, and avoiding unnecessary distractions and changes—but without extensive crunching
- Building cohesive teams that trust and respect each other, hold each other to high standards, but allow for mistakes too
- Communicating clearly and openly, resolving differences, and meeting regularly
- Treating each team member as an individual—professionally, personally, and financially

So what's not on this list of most important items? Two big things leap out immediately:

- Having a production methodology is important (#26 on their list), but whether you use Agile, Waterfall, or something else is less important.
- Having an experienced team is also important. It doesn't appear directly on the list, but if it did, it would be down around #36 out of 40 on this list of significant factors.

The above items may not be all that surprising, but neither are they necessarily obvious. They should be cardinal rules of game development, and yet far too many development teams ignore or violate one or more of them and then wonder why they aren't successful. They never quite get a clear vision of what they're doing, or they change course or technology platforms far too often. They have difficulty communicating openly and let disagreements fester and grow for months or years. Or they allow themselves to get into heartfelt arguments about one production method or another or one tool set or another. Each of these is a great way to make your game development project fail.

Developing a game is hard enough without your team being a source of stress and added difficulty. If you can discuss these principles with your team and get everyone to commit to following them (including helping each other when someone falls down on one of these—#5 and #35 on the list), then you will greatly increase the chance of your team and your game being successful.

Breaking down the above abbreviated list further, the following sections look at specific areas and where they appeared in terms of significance in the original results. Numbers in parentheses in these lists—such as (#1)—indicate where a particular item appeared on the original Game Outcomes Project list, which was grouped by degree of significance rather than theme.

Product Vision

Every game has a unifying vision that tells what the game is about. The vision is consistent with the whole of the player's experience. It includes the kinds of interactivity in the game, the emotions you want the player to feel, and the kinds of game mechanics you include.

As discussed in Chapter 6, "Designing the Whole Experience," this is something you should create early on in development.

As shown by the Game Outcomes Project results, various aspects of having a clear product vision are crucial to your success. Here they are, in order of importance:

- The vision is clear and understood by the team (#1).
    - This includes what will be delivered and what's expected of the team (#1).
    - The product vision is embodied in specs/design documents, complemented by ongoing design work (#36).
- The vision is compelling; it is viable and leads to clear action (#1).
- The vision is consistent and does not drift over time (#2).
    - The team is cautious about changes or deviations (#2).
    - All stakeholders are enlisted when changes are necessary (#21).
- The vision is shared: the team believes in and is enthusiastic about it (#3).

It's difficult to overstate the importance of having a clearly defined vision that is clearly documented and a team that is fully involved in executing on it. This is one reason the concept document described in Chapter 6 is so important. Not only does the vision need to be clearly defined, it needs to be well documented and understood by the team. A visitor to the team should be able to get consistent answers by stopping anyone in the hall and asking what doing, how it connects to the overall team vision, and where they see the project going. If you find yourself on a team where the vision isn't clear or isn't consistent with what's being done, drop everything else until you have these issues resolved. Anything else just leads to disaster.

All this is not to say that the vision can't change. As you design, prototype, and test ideas, you will discover new aspects of the game vision you didn't see before, and you should work to include them. However, that doesn't mean the vision should change every week or drift over time. As the Game Outcomes Project results indicate, having a clear, consistent, shared, and well-communicated vision is vital to having any sort of success in developing your game.

Sometimes, though, change will be forced on you from outside; maybe someone else releases a game too close to your own, or your budget or schedule realities change. When this happens, revise and re-create the game vision as quickly as possible, being sure to involve and get buy-in from all stakeholders (#21) and ensure that everyone understands (#1) and is enthusiastic about (#3) the product direction.

Finally, note that this clarity of vision isn't just for the team but includes each person's role and expectations. Working this out early and checking in periodically to make sure that no one's role or expectations have shifted is important.

Product Development

Developing a game as a product is difficult, to say the least. The result of this development has to be something that can be used by anyone with the appropriate hardware or who can open the box and read the rules. Typically, a game as a product is something that's sold commercially, though an increasing number of games are used in educational or similar contexts. In any case, moving from a concept to a fully realized, freestanding game as a product is difficult enough that many such efforts never make it.

Creating a successful game product requires adherence to the game vision and a unified team that, above all else, works together well. If those elements are in place, a surprising number of other aspects (technology, scope, budget, and so on) become much easier to manage.

These are the top-priority items for successful product development, according to the Game Outcomes Project:

- Development is focused and driven by the game vision (#1).
    - Team members understand and act on high-priority tasks driven by the product vision (#1).
    - Individuals don't go off on their own priorities (#1, #19).
- Leaders proactively identify and mitigate potential risks (#2).
- The team works effectively (#4).
    - The team removes distractions and avoids extended crunch time (#4).
    - The team is trained on and uses its chosen production methodology (#26).
    - The team ensures that tools work well and allow effective work (#29).
- The team estimates task durations frequently and as accurately as possible (#16).
    - Team members have the authority to determine their own day-to-day tasks and are involved in determining time allocations for tasks (#30).
    - The team carefully manages any necessary technology changes during development (#31).
    - The team determines priorities for each milestone, based on the current state of the project (#40).

It may seem obvious to say that a game's development should be driven by the vision for the game. Unfortunately, it's easy for a project to lurch off in a direction not really connected to the vision; maybe the team hasn't really bought in to the vision (or even just one person hasn't), or perhaps the team just slowly drifts away from it day by day. Making sure that everyone is working on the highest-priority tasks contributing to the design vision and not just working on shiny distractions or someone's personal priority will help keep the work being done from diverging from the agreed-upon vision.

Keeping a project on track also means that those leading it have to face difficult issues squarely and quickly, removing or mitigating risks as needed. This can be harder to do than it sounds: there are always issues arising that a producer or other team leader needs to handle (and keep from distracting the team). Doing so successfully allows team members to work more effectively and to take more control over their own work. This kind of local team control, including as much as possible determining individuals' own immediate priorities and task estimates (with feedback based on prior performance) is vital to keeping the team working well over the long haul—and thus to project success.

An important aspect of working well on a project for months or even years is significantly limiting the amount of *crunch time* (long hours for many days or weeks) that the team has to put in. Crunch time is an ongoing topic in the games industry, with some teams fully accepting it and others avoiding it entirely. The negative effects of working long hours are well documented (CDC 2017), but it remains a presence and an issue across the industry.

When working on any creative project, there will be unknowns that are difficult or impossible to schedule. When new priorities or problems arise suddenly, or when a task does not go as planned, it's easy for the whole team to fall behind schedule. Having this happen occasionally for short periods of time is not a significant issue if the team holds to the rest of the principles here (clear vision, working on high-priority items, and so on). However, when the vision isn't clear, production meanders, priorities change often, and tasks are poorly estimated, the team ends up having to put in many weeks of long hours to meet important (often immovable) production dates. Over time, this erodes team performance and morale, and it doesn't end up making for a better game in the long run.

Teams

Nearly all games are made by teams, and as a game designer, you will spend most of your career working as part of a team. What attributes do teams on successful game projects share in common? The Game Outcomes Project highlights several key characteristics:

- The team is cohesive, and its members believe in the game vision, team leaders, and each other. They share values and their sense of mission (#1, #8, #14, #17).
  - The team works to minimize turnover (#6) but also removes disruptive/disrespectful members swiftly (#12, #13).
  - The team maintains group and product priorities over individual priorities (#19).
  - The team is well organized, and the structure of the team is clearly understood (#25).
  - The team fosters an environment of mutual respect from management and the team (#12).
  - The team fosters an atmosphere of helpfulness (#35).

- The team is able to take risks (within the bounds of the product vision and priorities) and learn from mistakes (#5).

- Team members avoid wasteful design thrashing (#9).
- Team members celebrate novel ideas even if they don't work out (#10).
- Team members discuss failures openly (#18).

- Team members hold each other to high standards (#11, #17).
  - They invite respectful collaboration and review of work (#11, #39).
  - Team members reward those who ask for help or who support others (#35).
  - They call each other out when necessary on counterproductive behaviors (#17).
  - Individual responsibilities and roles match with their skills (#20).
  - Individuals have opportunities to learn and grow their skills (#28).
  - Team members hold each other accountable for meeting deadlines—but not to the point of eroding team morale (#34).

As discussed in this chapter, having an effective team dynamic is crucial to a project's progress. This is a lot of what makes a project something people want to be involved in rather than something they dread dealing with every day. An interesting part of this is that while team cohesion and lack of turnover are important, so is quickly removing those who are disruptive, put their own priorities first, or are otherwise socially or professionally toxic. While there is something of a mythology surrounding the "genius who's difficult to work with but is just too skilled to get rid of," long experience shows that such people are best removed from the team quickly. Letting them stay enables their behavior and creates a toxic environment for everyone else. While no one should be removed from a team without due consideration, giving yet another chance to someone who undermines the team's efforts or the other team members doesn't help build team cohesion; it just weakens the team in the long run.

This isn't to say that with one mistake someone should be out—team members should be able to try things and fail—but there's a difference between trying and failing and being a destructive influence on a team. People who do not act in the team's best interests, no matter how skilled they are or how important their role to the team, should be counseled quickly and then, if necessary, let go. Team members need to hold each other accountable for their work and for how they contribute to everyone's work and success. This includes getting their work done on time, balanced with the need to sometimes take risks, and maintaining high standards.

Communication

Working together with others—those with different skill sets, experiences, and goals—requires constant, effective communication. Everyone on a team needs to have these skills. As a game designer, you will often be called on to work with members of other parts of the team, and your ability to communicate will significantly affect the potential success of the product.

The following are some of the aspects of effective communication that successful game teams share:

- Everyone buys into decisions made by the team or team leaders (#3).
- The team resolves differences—product or personal—swiftly (#7, #12).
- Team members frequently receive feedback on their work (#9).
  - Team members receive ample praise on tasks that are well done (#22).
  - "No surprises management": If there's significant bad news, don't cover it up or hold it back; let the relevant people know (#9).
- The team is able and willing to speak openly, even on difficult subjects (#27).
  - Team members feel heard, even if a decision goes against their view (#15).
  - Politics are minimized by open, respectful communication (#17).
  - The team has an open-door policy, and everyone has access to senior leadership to raise concerns/offer feedback (#23).
- Team members are clear on the expectations for tasks and behaviors (#24).
- The team meets regularly to discuss topics of interest, ask questions, and identify bottlenecks (#33).

A team cannot be effective if its members don't communicate well. In systems terms, each team member is a part in the overall team system: if the team members don't interact constructively, the system falls apart. This includes informal and formal communication, both oral and written. It also includes some more difficult areas, like not hiding results when things go wrong ("no surprises management"), being able to criticize each other's work *constructively* (without reacting defensively in the face of this), and each team member fully committing to a decision even if they personally don't agree with it. This isn't to say that team members should be mindless drones, but there is great power in setting aside your own opinions once a decision has been made and supporting it with your actions. This means contributing wholeheartedly to the direction the group has decided on, even if you disagree. Those who cannot do so (in the worst case, saying the right things but not following that up with their actions) are very often the same ones who become toxic to the team when things become really difficult, deep into production.

The point above about meeting often, though low on the list, is nevertheless important: a team needs to communicate not just well but often. Having daily status meetings where everyone attends is a *minimum*. On large teams, this may turn into small quick meetings of functional teams followed by fast meetings of the team leads, but the principle is the same. Far better than just having daily meetings is when team members (as a whole or in smaller overlapping groups) get together to go over the game, improve their skills, work out problems, or just socialize. Not everyone on the team has to be friends, but they do have to respect each other and know how to communicate effectively for the team, and the project, to do well.

Individuals

Communication and teamwork are clearly vital aspects of success. But every team is made up of individuals. As individuals, we all have different needs. Successful teams manage to balance the needs of the entire team and product with the valid needs of each member of the team. The Game Outcomes Project found the following about successful teams:

- The team allows everyone to grow, even into new roles (#28).
- Team members genuinely care about each other as human beings (#37).
- The team uses individually tailored financial incentives, not royalties or bonuses tied to review scores or similar (#38).

Each person is on a unique journey. It sounds like a cliché, but it's true and worth keeping in mind. Most production teams spend a few months or maybe a few years together and then go their separate ways on your different paths. Seeing team members as individuals rather than just in terms of their functional role (game designer, lead programmer, art intern, and so on) will help you remember that each individual's personal and professional needs have to be balanced with those of the team.

Teams are much more effective when members have some level of genuine empathy for each other—celebrating, supporting, and mourning together, as needed. This is what forges the relationship bonds and allows teams to get through difficult times together. There's nothing quite like being part of a team where everyone trusts each other. That doesn't mean they enable each other's weaknesses or that they don't point out mistakes or have disagreements, but if these difficult tasks can be done in a context of real mutual esteem, even caring, it enables the team to do much more.

While it's true that each person has their own needs and goals and that production teams typically are together for only a short time, it's also true that if you are able to balance the team needs with each individual's needs, you will end up creating a stronger team. Moreover, this is how you create the connections that allow you to build better teams in the future. When putting together a team, there are few things better than what might be termed an *Ocean's Eleven* moment: you call up, tell them what you're putting together, and the response is "I'm in."

Summing Up

In my experience in starting and running many teams, I have boiled principles like those discussed so far in this chapter down to three main ones:

- *Integrity*
  - Do what you say when you say.
  - Admit your mistakes when you make them.
  - Don't point fingers.

- *Flexibility*
    - Be able to change direction quickly.
    - Allow others to grow.
    - Don't get stuck in the past.

- *Communication*
    - Keep others informed; don't hoard information.
    - Offer and ask for help.
    - Provide timely feedback.

These recommendations are from my experience. The items listed in previous sections, from the Game Outcomes Project, have the benefit of being based on quantitative data, but I believe these my suggestions still useful. If you can internalize and balance these three values, they will see you a long way in any profession—and in life.

Team Roles

On any team there are multiple roles that have to be filled—people with entirely different skills who have to come together to make a successful team and a successful product. Knowing something about these roles and what skills and responsibilities go into each will help you both find your way as a member of a team and understand what goes into making up a full development team.

To begin a discussion of team roles in game development, we're going to zoom out first to the level of the company. From there we'll go back to the studio and then finally down to the game development team. Not every company uses this model, but this kind of organization is common.

Company Architecture

Most game companies (and commercial companies in general) are led by an *executive team*. This includes what's often called the C-team or C-suite, which consists of the following:

- **Chief executive officer (CEO):** The CEO is responsible for overall company direction, fund-raising, and working with the board of directors.

- **Chief operating officer (COO)/president:** The COO is responsible for the day-to-day functioning of the company and works with the CEO. (In smaller companies, a single person may be both the CEO and COO.)

- **Chief financial officer (CFO):** The CFO is responsible for company budgets, overseeing employee compensation, accounting, taxes, and so on.

- **Chief creative officer (CCO):** The COO is responsible for the creative mix of the company's portfolio and creative direction across studios.
- **Chief technical officer (CTO):** The CTO is responsible for the company's technology platforms, examining and adopting new technologies, programming standards, and so on.

There are sometimes others, too, including a chief information officer (usually the same as the CTO in a game company) and a chief marketing officer (usually a vice president [VP] or similar who reports to the CEO). There are many infrastructural roles—human resources, sometimes marketing, facilities, vendor relations, and so on—that typically report to the COO or to a VP who reports to the COO.

The CEO is often considered "the big boss"; they are most responsible for making sure the company performs well and meets its overall objectives. But the CEO's boss is the board of directors. The CEO meets regularly with the board to discuss strategy and corporate direction and, when necessary, to raise more investment funding. The members of the board are not generally employees of the company but represent the interests of those who have invested money in the company (in particular, whether it is being used well and how, eventually, investors will get some multiple of their money back). Most small companies that have no investors also lack a board of directors, though they may have a board of advisors to help them. It is extremely rare for a large company to have no external investors or board of directors.

Studio Roles

Reporting to the CEO or COO are typically a group of vice presidents and/or general managers (VPs and GMs—the titles become highly varied), who in turn lead organizations referred to as *studios*. That term is commonly used but doesn't have a single agreed-upon meaning. Loosely, a studio is a group of development teams working on similar sorts of game products. Often their products are grouped by genre or franchise (a series of products with the same underlying brand).

The VP or GM leading a studio has what's called *P&L responsibility*—meaning that they are ultimately responsible for the profits and losses, the revenues and costs, of the groups under their management. This means they have broad authority over hiring, production direction, and team composition.

Reporting to the studio head (the VP or GM) are one or more executive producers (EPs), often a creative director (CD), and sometimes a group of shared services. Each EP heads up a single development or product team. The CD oversees all the game design in the studio and may also report to the company's CCO—or there may be a single CD who is also the CCO.

The shared services include the individuals and teams that work across all the product teams. Often this includes marketing and sometimes other groups, like business intelligence (BI) or analytics, quality assurance (QA), community management, art, and especially sound design, as fewer sound designers are needed across teams than any other functional role.

If any of the product teams has particular needs or requires more than a few people from these areas all the time, some individuals may move from a shared pool into an individual team. But generally people who work on these teams are seen as being less connected to any particular project and are thus able to move around more easily. This means the company also has to hire fewer people on these teams and that they don't become redundant when no longer needed by a particular team. The alternative is that companies "staff up" by hiring lots of people for a particular role, say QA, and then lay those people off again when they're no longer needed. Unfortunately, even with shared resource teams, this happens a lot in some companies.

Development Team Organization

Typically the executive producer leads and oversees a single game development team. Their focus is on making sure the right game gets made and that it's made correctly. Although the EP role is not, strictly speaking, a game design role, this individual often has the final authority for a game under development and is thus often the "vision holder" of the game. Often the EP will work closely with the team's lead designer or creative director, but the EP is the ultimate stop for any issue, creative or otherwise.

Reporting to the EP are a series of functional teams: game design, programming, and art, along with the production team and others (see Figure 11.1). The EP has to balance competing needs and issues from these teams to make sure the game is made well and (in postproduction) runs well. In some cases, the EP will have budgetary authority over their team; this depends on the EP's seniority and the size of the team as much as anything else.

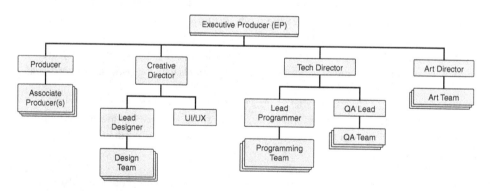

Figure 11.1 A typical game development team organization chart

Producers

Reporting to the executive producer are one or more producers and, on large teams, one or more associate producers (APs). A small team might have just one producer. A large team might have one or two senior producers with several producers (sometimes called line producers in that case) reporting to them and multiple APs assisting and reporting to the producers.

As a general rule, you typically see 1 producer for about every 10 other members of the game development team. If there are more, this might indicate problems on the team, or there just may be "too many cooks in the kitchen." If you have fewer than that, then either the functional teams are highly self-managing or there is chaos waiting to break lose when the team becomes stressed.

APs are a common entry-level position in game development; these individuals tend to work on the daily details of tasks and schedules with one of the other functional teams (game design, programming, and so on). As they gain more experience, an AP may be promoted to producer and from there to senior producer and eventually executive producer. (Each of these steps can take several years of experience.) At each stage, the individual's horizons and responsibilities become broader, with more issues to juggle.

Producers along with game designers often have vague job descriptions. Producers are the ones who make sure progress gets made well, issues get solved quickly, and teams work effectively without problems or distractions. Depending on the organization, the APs and producers manage the team's milestones, tasks, and schedules or help the functional teams manage their own. They don't typically add anything directly to the game, but they make everything else work. As a team, the producers need to always know what is going on in each functional team—who's doing what and, especially, where the big risk points are. It has been said that you should be able to shake a producer awake in the middle of the night, and they should be able to tell you the top three risks facing the team at the moment. That might be an exaggeration, but not by much.

Important skills for producers include being organized, being determined and persistent, and being a good leader. No team will really follow you because you force them to; team members will following you only if they want to and if they believe in your leadership. The producers are the ones often trying to get team members to do something (or finish something), and the team has to believe in their leadership, especially in hard times. As part of being a good leader, a producer also has to have a solid service mentality. A lot of thankless jobs that go into getting a game made, from scrubbing toilets to ordering snacks to making sure everyone has the right mice and keyboards—and if there is no one else to take care of these issues, they fall on the production team.

Finally, producers have to be good at listening and at being decisive. A producer has to be able to tell someone on their team no in a way that the individual will accept. Sometimes when everyone really wants something—a cool new feature, an afternoon to go see a newly released movie, or new chairs—it is the producer's job to keep everyone focused on the team's goals and gently but firmly keep them all working well, even if that means saying no—a lot.

Project Managers and Product Managers

In some game companies, there is an interesting split among producers: some are called *project managers* and others are called *product managers*. Both are subcategories of producers.

Project managers are focused on a game before its release. They work with the team on milestones and schedules, watch for trouble spots where the team may begin to lose some forward motion, and keep the team on task and safe from distractions. They also make sure that everyone is able to do their job—that no one is blocked in their progress—and often work with external teams.

By contrast, product managers are focused on a game that has launched and is currently being sold. They are more responsible for product marketing, managing community relations, in some cases working on in-game monetization, and tracking usage analytics. Not all teams need a live product manager, but this is becoming a more familiar role as more games have an online component.

Game Designers

The game designer role is the one that you may be the most familiar with by now. Game designers do all the things discussed in this book: think up new concepts, create systems, define parts, and almost endlessly pore over attribute values in spreadsheets.

Entry-level titles for game designers tend to be *junior* or *associate game designer* (these vary from company to company). When starting out, a new designer will, as with most early-career positions, work in a small and well-defined area. A typical activity for new designers is working on the detail design of specific items and levels in a game and, in some cases, on balancing them against each other.

After getting a few years' experience, and in particular after having been through the entire process of designing and releasing a game, a junior game designer becomes a game designer. The focus in this role tends to be on building subsystems (for example, the archery subsystem for a combat system), designing specific mechanics, and writing limited narrative or other text for the game. Most game designers spend five years or more doing this kind of work as they accrue experience.

At some point, a game designer, especially in a large organizations, is likely to advance to becoming a senior game designer or a lead game designer. In many cases, these are essentially the same, with the latter role entailing the management of other game designers and junior game designers. Senior and lead designers tend to be the ones creating entire systems and core loops, creating long narrative arcs, doing world creation, and overall overseeing the high-level structure of the game design.

Often the lead game designer will report directly to the executive producer; they have a peer relationship with the other functional team leaders. While all the team leaders must work together, each has a particular area of concentration. Occasionally there will be a creative director attached to the team as well, either in addition to or instead of a CD at the studio level. In this case, the lead designer reports to the creative director, who oversees the highest level of creative direction, making sure the whole game holds together in terms of its gameplay and that sufficient progress is being made on the highest-priority items related to gameplay.

UI/UX

The team members who create the game's *user interface* (*UI*) and define its *user interactions* (*UX*) are in a hybrid position. Many UI designers start off as artists because this area is most often characterized by how the user interface looks to the player. But they also have to understand perceptual and cognitive psychology—how people see and hear different cues, how they click or swipe effectively, and so on.

User interaction designers are often more concerned with the functional architecture of the user interface and the player's path through it. These may also be artists or game designers or, increasingly, people specifically trained in user interaction methods.

Where UI/UX sits in a game development organization varies across the games industry. Sometimes it's grouped with production, other places it's put it with art, and still other places it's put it with game design. Figure 11.1 shows UI/UX as being a sibling of game design, reporting to the creative director, but this is only one of many possible configurations.

Programmers

Technical roles on a game development team are filled by people generally known as *programmers*, though sometimes known a bit more formally as *software engineers*. These are people who typically have a university degree in computer science or a similar field and who are focused on making the game design actually work. Some programmers also do game design, but the two activities require distinctly different skills and ways of thinking, and they are often difficult to do well simultaneously. Focusing on one or the other is necessary in building a career, even if you have talent and experience in both.

As with producers and game designers, most programmers start out in junior roles that go by many different names, such as junior programmer or software engineer I. As they become more experienced, programmers eventually encounter a career split between becoming more of a managing or lead programmer and being more of a deeply knowledgeable architect. Being a lead programmer generally involves managing other technical people—something many programmers would just as soon avoid—but it also allows you to have more visibility and direction over the entire project. Architects do not manage other programmers but nevertheless have a significant effect on the technical construction of the game. The team's architect is the one who determines the overall structure of the game's software, determines tools that will be used, knows the "pipeline" or flow of files and data through the development team, creates important naming conventions, and so on. In doing so, the architect often works with the technical director or even the company CTO to keep decisions that have long-term impact consistent across teams.

Similar to game designers, either the lead programmer or a technical director may oversee all the technical aspects of the project, and they report to the executive producer. If the development team has its own quality assurance team, the QA people typically report to the technical director, who has the overall management authority and oversight for the technical members of the team and works with the other functional team leaders to keep the game's development moving forward.

Over time, as programmers become more experienced, they tend to specialize in one of many areas, including the following:

- **Client side:** Graphics, UI/UX programming, physics, animation, audio
- **Server side:** Game systems programming, game engines, scripting, networking
- **Database:** Broadly applicable and highly technical areas of storing and retrieving data efficiently
- **Tools:** Analytics, profiling, testing, automation
- **Artificial intelligence:** Creating effective opponents in the game
- **Prototyping:** Creating fast, usable prototypes quickly, over and over again

Some programmers span most or even all of these areas and are referred to as "full-stack" programmers. For example, several years ago, full-stack LAMP programmers were in high demand. LAMP stands for Linux/Apache/MySQL/PHP—the "stack" of tools from operating system to product development language that these programmers worked with daily.

While all members of a development team uses a variety of tools to do their work, programmers probably use the most. They must be familiar with integrated development environments (IDEs), source or version control systems, issue and task tracking systems, graphics engines, database tools, code profilers, parsers, and many more. Moreover, as the LAMP example above shows, the life span of any given tool set tends not to be more than a few years long. Programmers must be dedicated to continually learning new languages, tools, and new or updated methods to stay current and effective in their careers.

The number of programmers on a project varies widely. Early on, in the concept and prototyping phase, there may be only one or two programmers. On the other end of the scale, a large project in full development may have a technical director, an architect, a lead programmer, and several programmers each for the specialization areas listed above. Client-side programmers tend to be the most numerous on a team, and AI and tools programmers being the least numerous.

Quality Assurance

As mentioned earlier in this chapter, quality assurance (QA) can either be a shared resource across the studio (or even the company), moving from project to project as needed, or may reside within the development team. If QA is on the team, the QA lead typically reports to the technical director, though in some cases this individual is a peer with the other functional team leaders and report directly to the executive producer.

QA is a common entry point for careers in the games industry for those who go on to become game designers, producers, and even programmers. The focus of this group is to make sure the game functions as expected and in a way that will be satisfying to the players. QA team members are sometimes called *QA testers* or *QA engineers*, depending on their focus. The former spend more time testing gameplay, and the latter work on programming automated tests to make sure the game is working as desired. While QA testers do find bugs in the software, this is almost incidental to their purpose: their goal is to make sure the game creates the intended experience and that that experience is fun and balanced.

To work in QA, you must be technically and detail minded, thorough, and patient. You will often have to test the same piece of gameplay over and over again, looking for problems and documenting them clearly when they occur. You must therefore be able to communicate well, both informally and formally, orally or in writing. This requires a certain amount of diplomacy: you have to be able to tell a designer or programmer why the game doesn't work in a way that will be understood and not easily dismissed.

Art and Sound

Visual and audio artists add movement and life to games and make them far more engaging than they would otherwise be. It is their work as much as any other that spurs the player's imagination.

Visual artists tend to have degrees in studio art or similar fields; some now enter the games industry with various degrees in making games or game art. There are many specialized forms of game art that artists typically move into, such as concept art, 2D drawn art, 3D modeling, animation, special effects, technical art, and user interface art. As with programming, the skills needed for each kind of art are now so significant that it's rare to find someone who spans more than two or three of these areas, and many artists focus on just one as they move through their career.

The structure of the visual art team is similar to that of the programming team: there is often a lead artist who manages multiple artists, along with an art director (a peer to the creative director and technical director), and sometimes a senior artist who operates like the technical architect, overseeing the style and direction of the art made for the game without directly managing individual artists.

On many teams, there are as many artists as programmers—or even more. Typically a team will have only one or two concept, technical, and special effects artists, while the rest focus on modeling, animation, and other tasks, like creating textures for models and rigging them (creating internal "bones") so that they can be animated. It is also common for a producer to reduce the amount of art that has to be made by the internal team by outsourcing some of it to external groups that only produce art for other companies' games.

Sound design is no less necessary for a successful game than visual art. However, there tend to be far fewer sound designers in a studio than visual artists—each sound designer often working with several teams at the same time. This is due in part to the nature of sound for games, which requires less overall production than visual art on a minute-by-minute basis, and to some degree in part because game developers have traditionally not paid as much attention to sound and music as they might have. This is changing, and more players are paying attention to excellent sound and music and more games are releasing their music as freestanding soundtracks. Developers are increasingly understanding the positive effect that well-designed sound can have in their games and are devoting more time and attention to it. Generating sound and music for games is both highly technical and creative, requiring a good mix of both sets of skills.

Other Teams

In addition to these functional teams, there are often other teams working either as shared resources or as parts of the development team. These include community management, working with the game's player community, and analytics and business intelligence, winnowing the quantitative information about player behavior and the competitive landscape to improve future development. As mentioned earlier, these tend not to be part of the development team itself but closely allied groups with which you may find yourself working from time to time.

Who Do You Need and When?

If you are building a new team to work on a game, you may have the desire to quickly make the team as large as you can. This will only lead to frustration on the team's part, as you really don't have enough work for more than a few people at the beginning. Many of the best teams start with a small core exploratory team composed of senior people who can move quickly and try out new ideas until they're sure of the game's direction, its core loop, and overall gameplay. A single designer, programmer, and artist is often all you need to get started. Three people can work very closely together, trying out new ideas fast—designing, prototyping, testing, and refining or throwing away ideas as needed. Because the process is necessarily iterative, you need to make sure that everyone on this small team is willing and able to work this way—with a lot of work generated and then tossed out (even good work that just doesn't fit the game).

In addition to fast iteration, another benefit of this model is avoiding a bottleneck with deliverables from the design team. It's a fallacy to think that as the game designer (or eventually one of a team of designers), you can design the whole game and then just have it be implemented without iteration or revision. There is a lot of work for designers to do in refining the concept, finding the fun, creating the systems, defining the parts, and making sure the game works as a game. The more of this you can do early on, before more people join the team, the better off you and your game will be. If you have to make big game design direction decisions later, when there are several programmers, artists, producers and others all waiting to see what direction things go so they can do their work, you're going to waste a lot of their time—and probably create a suboptimal design under pressure.

The Team as a System

Any team works as a complex system: it has individual parts that interact with each other to create something larger than the parts themselves. Within a company, teams operate hierarchically, as they do in any system: the development teams, studios, and overall company each form systems at different levels of organization. This is something that is often difficult for those starting out in games, or any complex industry, to see at first. It is easy to fall into seeing the whole thing from just one point of view instead of understanding that there are many parts and, as a result, many points of view within the overall system.

Many years ago, when trying to explain to a young developer why his part of the process wasn't the only (or even the most important) part, and certainly didn't represent the whole, I wanted to come up with a way for him to understand the layers—the systemic hierarchy—that goes into making a game. I wrote the following (which has since been quoted in many places online):

An idea is not a design

A design is not a prototype

A prototype is not a program

A program is not a product

A product is not a business

A business is not profits

Profits are not an exit

And an exit is not happiness

The point here is to emphasize that many different areas of skill go into making every game, product, and business. At each level there are entirely new and different talents that need to be brought to bear to be successful. Every part in this hierarchical system needs to work well, and no part can assert itself over the others as being preeminent (except, perhaps, for happiness).

Summary

Working as part of an effective team is vital to your success as a game designer. As you begin active development, you have to know how to work as part of a team of people with diverse skills that will take you far outside game design. You also need to know what a successful team looks like so you can contribute more effectively. By understanding how the various functional, studio, and corporate roles fit together to create a hierarchical system of teams, you can better work in your role to the benefit of all the teams of which you are a part.

CHAPTER 12

MAKING YOUR GAME REAL

A lot of work goes into creating a game beyond designing it. This chapter discusses the real-world aspects of getting a game started and developed as you and your team bring it to life.

These practical elements build on the foundation created in the first section of the book and the principles discussed in the second section, adding tangible context to them both.

Getting Started

Making a game is a long, difficult, and complex process. Throughout most of this book, we have talked about how to design a game. But to make your game real, in addition to design, you have to know something about how to successfully develop a game. That's the purpose of this chapter.

In addition to being able to work as part of a team, to actually create your game, you need to know about the processes involved in doing so:

- Communicating your idea for a game
- Iteratively prototyping and playtesting your game
- Navigating the different phases of the game development process
- Not just starting but actually finishing your game

Making the Pitch

One of the first tasks that moves beyond quietly toiling on your game design is telling others about it—and trying to get them to believe in it. If you can't communicate your idea, you can't make the game actually work. This is where pitching your game comes in.

What does it mean to pitch a game? *Pitch* is an industry term that simply means to tell others about your game, with the purpose of persuading your audience and passing along your excitement about it. Pitching a game is how you communicate your vision. Early on in your process, you may have a few diagrams and documents, or maybe just an idea that you think could become something great. But you're not going to be able to make the game real on your own. Inevitably, you have to convince others of why your idea is valuable—why, with everything else that's pulling at them, they should give you their time, attention, money, and/or talents to help you make your game real.

Preparing to Pitch

Pitching happens in a wide variety of contexts. How you go about making your pitch depends a lot on your goals, your audience, and the context in which the pitch happens.

Knowing Your Goals

The first thing you need to be clear about in preparing and making a pitch is what you are trying to achieve. All pitching is intentionally persuasive—but the persuasion can happen in different ways and with different targets. The most common reason for pitching is probably to obtain funding so you can develop your game, whether you are pitching to external investors or to your company's management. There are other reasons to pitch, too, including validating your concept, working with the media as part of marketing your game, and building your team. Each requires different angles on the same ideas about your game to be effective.

Your concept remains the same no matter the reasons for your pitch, but the form of the pitch itself may change. If you are trying to validate your idea, you can focus on the concept itself and have others explore it with you. Often you will find new directions or hidden aspects of the game vision that you hadn't seen before just by talking about it. Or those you talk with will ask a question that sets up a twist in the game world or its narrative, indicating that they understand what you're describing well enough to see how that change might happen.

Working with the media to get your story told and trying to recruit new team members are similar: you want to sell the fantasy of the game. You want those with whom you are talking to be able to envision the game not even as it will actually look but in terms of how it will feel and be experienced by your eventual players. You want someone from the media to see how your game is new and fresh and something that their readers or viewers will want to hear about. And when recruiting, you want a potential team member to be persuaded to sign on, to see this project as the best use of their time and talents.

If you are pitching for funding, you want to provide enough of the concept that your audience understands and is excited by the idea. You also need to give them enough of your background and thinking about how to make the game that they don't see it as a risky project. And, of course, you need to be prepared with believable team size, schedule, and budgetary figures so that they can focus on the funding question. Many who are new to pitching spend too much time on the details of the game concept, which really isn't the point in this context; or they throw in too much detail on the exact composition of the development team and how the funding will be spent. It's important to be able to supply detail as it's needed, but too much can be as bad as too little in a funding pitch. You want to provide your audience with enough information that they see the appeal of the game, know that you understand how to make it, and believe that your figures for schedule and budget are plausible and viable. More than that just weighs down the conversation and adds the potential for confusion.

No matter what other goals you have for your pitch, every time to you talk with someone else about your game is an opportunity to refine and validate your concept. People will offer criticism, questions, and—if you're lucky—their growing interest and excitement about what you're describing. It's easy to miss this last part if you're not careful: when others become excited by your vision, they will often say things like, "Oh, it sounds like *Defense Grid* crossed with *Triple Town*," or they may begin to suggest their own ideas. These may sound like criticisms or distractions from where you want your game to go, but it's vital that you not shut down or ignore these comments; if nothing else, they indicate that the person you are talking with is forming a mental picture of the game, and the idea hangs together well enough for them to begin to associate it with other ideas. If you ignore such input, you risk becoming the lonely visionary who won't listen to anyone else and thus gets little done; this is a sad stereotype for a reason. It doesn't mean you should change your idea to fit every new comment that others make, but you do need to use their input to see how *they* see your game, based on your description, where your concept and pitch need improvement, or even where someone else simply has a better idea.

Knowing Your Audience

To engage successfully with your audience, you of course have to understand them. This often means doing some research prior to making a pitch. If you're talking to a potential investor or publisher, what else does that person invest in or that company make? What does a particular media outlet (whether it's an individual streamer or a major publication) typically cover? What is your audience looking for?

Seeing your pitch from your audience's perspective will help you hone your message and increase the probability of achieving the goals you have set out for the pitch. Investors are typically looking for a market opportunity. Game publishers are often looking for a game that fills a hole in their portfolio. Both investors and publishers have to look at every pitch as the potential beginning of a long-term relationship (you should, too) and in terms of the *opportunity cost* of investment. This means that, for example, that if you are asking for $1 million to complete your game, the investors need to ask themselves why your game is the best place to put that money and what else they won't be able to do once they commit those funds to you.

Media representatives are always looking for the next big story that they can deliver in an accessible way and within their (always tight) deadlines. They need to deliver stories that their readers or viewers will appreciate and ideally pass along to others. They are interested in what their audience is interested in, so you should know that before approaching media representatives or doing pitches with them.

Finally, if you're trying to recruit team members, they probably have other things they could be working on. (If they don't, do you really want your project to be their lifeboat?) You need to help them see why your game is ideal for their talents and worth their time.

Game developers often miss these points, being too focused on seeing their game from their own vantage point rather than their audience's point of view. When pitching, you need to consider your audience's goals and concerns, in addition to what they can offer you.

Knowing Your Material

Knowing your game and your audience are only part of what you need to make a successful pitch. You also need to be able to speak knowledgably about competing games, market trends, technology platforms, and any other potential risks to your proposal.

More than just knowing these things, you have to be able to discuss them easily and authoritatively, without stumbling over your words, appearing nervous, losing your train of thought, or, worse, trying to appear more knowledgeable than you are and making something up on the spot that you may later regret.

All of this points to the need for practicing your pitch. There is no substitute for practice, and there is no easy way around the time it takes. Even those who have pitched many times before continue to practice over and over. This is especially true of formal presentations to be given as part of a pitch meeting, but it's also true of informal happenstance pitches. You need to be ready when the opportunity arises, and you cannot stop to practice or often even gather your thoughts when the moment comes.

Another aspect of knowing your material is that you need to appear (and be!) sincere, excited, passionate, professional, and still somehow easygoing, all at the same time, while pitching your game. Being prepared and practicing your pitch many times will help with this. You don't want to rehearse so much that you appear wooden and insincere, but you should practice to the point where you diminish your own nervousness and get out of your own way and let your natural passion for the project shine through.

As part of practicing, don't just focus on the material itself. You need to learn to control your body language so that you appear at ease and in control. Don't fidget and learn to avoid repetitive stress-relief behaviors (wringing your hands, pushing your glasses up your nose, twisting your hair, and so on). Look your audience in the eye and smile—not so much that you appear to be aggressive but enough so that you can make sure they are tracking what you're saying. This can be a fine line; practicing with others will help. One helpful idea is to look at those to whom you're pitching closely enough that when you walk out of the meeting, you know their eye color. It's surprising how often most people don't pay even that much attention to those around them.

This highlights the point that in any pitch, there is also a certain amount of personal rapport and even charm that helps you build a connection with your audience. If you are too concerned about what to say next or are nervously fidgeting and staring into an empty corner of the room, then you cannot focus on your audience and how best to communicate with them. That will severely limit the amount that they actually hear and learn from you.

Contexts for Your Pitch

Pitches can happen almost anywhere. There are two extremes to this that you can easily prepare for. The first is the informal happenstance pitch, often called an *elevator pitch*. The second is the more formal presentation that happens in a pitch meeting.

The Elevator Pitch

Elevator pitches are more than just a metaphor—they really do happen in elevators sometimes. You might be at a conference and find yourself riding in an elevator with the vice president of a publisher you'd love to talk with. In that context, the VP is something of a captive audience—though you need to be careful not to treat them that way. If you can strike up a conversation, the question of "what are you working on?" is likely to come up. How you answer is the essence of your elevator pitch.

Of course, though, these pitches don't just happen in elevators. You could find yourself in the lobby of a building, waiting to board an airplane, or even in line at the grocery store, when a chance meeting can occur. In each case, you want to be ready: always be ready to pitch.

In an informal context like an elevator, the goal is not to explain everything about what you do—you're not going to pop open a full presentation—but instead to *briefly* state who you are, what you're working on, and what you're looking for. This has to be done in a way that piques the other's interest rather than coming off as aggressive or needy. "Hi, I'm <name> with <company>. I'm working on <one-sentence description> and interested in <goal>." That's about as information packed as you can make it without seeming socially aggressive. After assessing the other person's level of interest, you might simply move on to another topic if they're not interested; at minimum, you've had one more chance to practice your elevator pitch (plus, you never know who they might mention this to). If the person with whom you're talking appears somewhat interested but time is short, you could say something like, "Here, let me give you my card; I'd love to talk with you more about this later." Or if they appear actively intrigued, you might say, "Here's my card. Let's set up a time next week to talk about this in more detail."

That's it—that's a complete pitch. Resist the temptation to give the other person more details about what you're doing unless they specifically asks for them. More often than not, more detail is off-putting and reduces the chance that your audience will retain what you say or that you'll actually get an additional meeting.

The Pitch Meeting

The other end of the spectrum is the formal pitch meeting. This might happen where you work, if the creative director or general manager for your studio has invited you to pitch your idea for a new game, or at a potential publisher's or investor's office. Such pitches tend to last half an hour to an hour, including both a presentation from you and some questions from others in the room. Be careful to scale your presentation to the time you have available (practice!), being sure to leave at least 5 to 10 minutes for questions at the end.

The pitch presentation is typically made up of slides, video, and sometimes a demo, as discussed below. Be sure you are prepared with backups for your presentation on different media so that you can load it onto another computer or, in the worst case, even pass out paper copies.

In going through your presentation, watch your pacing. You want to keep the presentation moving along—but not so fast that you lose your audience's attention and not so slowly that you're boring them. Keeping an eye on whether the people in the meeting are tracking with you is important. Of course, you want to speak clearly and avoid fidgeting. Again, practice is invaluable.

When you're asked a question, either during the presentation or afterward, answer it briefly and as fully as you can. If you're fortunate, a question during the presentation will highlight a point you're about to make or that will come up later in the presentation. This indicates that the person who asked is paying attention and building a mental model of your presentation as you speak. In such cases, briefly answer the question and point out that you'll address it more fully in a moment (but be sure to do so!). Avoid technical details unless you're specifically asked about them, and don't veer off topic. It's okay to take a moment and collect your thoughts before answering a question, too; this is much better than trying to fill the silence with stammered words. You also want to be alert for what's sometimes called "the question behind the question"— the real concern that's being asked about. If someone brings up a game like the one you're proposing, are they really asking about competition or trying to validate their model of your concept? Or if they ask about who else is on the team, are they really asking about potential budget issues, or are they asking about your experience and ability to develop the game? Answer what's been asked but then see if you can dig deeper and try to address what's likely underlying that question.

Sometimes a question will be entirely unexpected, and you will find yourself wholly unprepared for it. If that's the case, don't be afraid to say "I don't know." Or, if it's applicable, say "I don't know, but I'll find out and get back to you." Either is far better than trying to bluster your way through an answer while covering your own ignorance; that just reduces your audience's regard for you and everything else you've said. In some cases, you can even ask those in your audience what they think, what their experience has been, or what they would recommend; just be careful to appear (sincerely) open to new information but not ill-informed. Of course, if you've practiced your presentation, you should be prepared for most questions. You can even add an appendix to the end of your presentation that you show to help answers questions. (This makes you look like you're on top of things, which is great.)

If you don't get any questions at the end, that's often a bad sign: it means what you said didn't have any impact or strike your audience as interesting. (Maybe they were so awed by your concept and presentation that they can't even form a critical question … but this is unlikely.) In effect, they didn't build a mental model of your game as you described it, so they have no gaps to be filled in. On the other hand, if the meeting goes over time with lots of questions and different points being made, then you know your audience is engaged and has internalized at least some of what you have been talking about.

Pitch Content

For both informal and formal pitches, the beginning is usually the same. After that, the two types of pitches diverge completely. You want to begin with quick introductions—yourself and any others who are with you. This should be quick because it's not really your audience's focus. At the same time, you want to briefly speak to your credibility and credentials that qualify you as knowing what you're talking about. Especially in a formal presentation, you can quickly mention what you have done in the past that puts you in a position to know what you're taking on and complete it well. This concise introduction also helps you establish yourself as friendly and open, and it helps your audience settle in to focus on your message.

After quick introductions, you should begin your presentation, starting with the concept for your game. You should already have worked out a high-level concept statement, as described in Chapter 6, "Designing the Whole Experience"; the whole discussion of the concept document feeds right into your pitch. To review, your concept statement is a polished, clear, and carefully worded sentence or two that describes your game, why it's unique (or at least fresh—why anyone should be interested in it), and, if possible, what kind of experience it provides the player. One metric is that if your concept statement uses more than one comma, it's too long. You can also think of this as "your game in a tweet"; if your concept goes on for more than about 140 characters, that's probably too long, too.

The following are examples of templates for concept statements:

- "<My game> is a game about <activity> that <is fresh for these few reasons>."
- "In <my game> you <face this challenge> with <this twist> that <gives you this feeling/experience>."
- "<My game> is <movie x> meets <book y>."
- "<My game> is <movie x> meets <TV show y> in a world like <thing z>."

The challenge here is that your concept statement needs to be short and pithy but also cover the entire game. It needs to be brief enough that someone hearing it for the first time can grasp the entire statement without being overloaded and having to hear it again. And the concept statement needs to communicate not only what your game is about but also what makes it different from other games. You want to make this statement as short and memorable as possible, which can be a surprisingly difficult task.

Arriving at a concept statement like this is not easy, and you should spend the time needed to refine and practice it with other people. What seems simple and understandable to you often won't sound that way to others. Be prepared to iterate on this a lot, right down to making tiny changes in wording to get the statement to the right place. Practicing this statement will also help you get it so clear in your head that you can say it well even when you're nervous—whether because you've just stepped into an elevator with someone you want to meet or because you find yourself at the front of a board room with the projector shining in your eyes.

If this pitch is a chance or brief meeting, that introduction and concept statement is probably all you have time for. You don't want to seem overly eager (much less desperate), just friendly and excited about what you're working on. In this kind of situation, the final thing you want to leave with is your "call to action," discussed later in this chapter. If, on the other hand, you have more time to go into detail, especially if this is a formal pitch, you need to expand on your concept statement. This includes the information commonly found in a concept document (see Chapter 6) such as the game's genre, target audience, and unique selling points.

Remember the Iceberg

From the concept statement to the additional information contained in the concept document and throughout the rest of the pitch, you want to follow the "iceberg" approach described in Chapter 6. Don't try to pack all the information about your game into your pitch and don't overwhelm your audience with detail. Start with the tip of the iceberg for the concept and design, help the audience build a mental model of your game, and then add more information as needed. Be prepared to drill down into the details of any particular areas as you're asked about them.

If you are giving a formal pitch, you should assume that you will use some form of presentation slides; this is common and generally assumed. However, you want to keep the information on these slides as clear and understandable as possible. Minimize text; slides with only images on them are perfectly acceptable and will help the audience listen to you rather than read ahead on the slides. (However, working with picture-only slides also requires more practice on your part, to avoid losing your place.) Definitely avoid showing anything that approaches a visual "wall of text"; more than about three to at most five bullet points or text that wraps across multiple lines is too much. Remember that you need to avoid the temptation to try to tell your audience everything all at once. You should generally plan to have no more than 10 slides in your presentation. Fewer slides is fine, as long as you're communicating everything you need to. If you have more slides than that, you may be trying to cram in too much. As mentioned earlier, it is a good idea to have appendix slides that aren't part of the main presentation but to which you can refer for more detail if asked.

After you have gone over your concept and related topics and said a little more about your team, you will want to give an outline, with examples, of the gameplay. Show the core loop graphically. (If you can't yet describe the core loop clearly, you aren't ready to be pitching.) Provide brief information about the world where the game takes place, along with examples of the art style for the game. Ideally, this includes early concept art your team has created, but reference/mood art taken from other sources is fine, as long as you label it as such.

Throughout your presentation, you want to be sure your slides appear professional and competent: no spelling errors or formatting mismatches, no surprises or glitches. Keep to one or two different fonts and lots of clear, professional graphics. If you make a core loop diagram in a graphics program, for example, make sure it looks polished, not like a quickly made first draft. The small rough edges that you might hope people will overlook are often the very things that their eyes snag on and that distract from and reduce the impact of your presentation.

In addition to discussing the concept, gameplay, and art style, you need to build the audience's confidence in both you and the game. To do this, there are a number of options you have for what to show as part of your pitch, in order of preference:

1. An already completed game that is being sold, including both recent and projected sales and marketing figures. Nothing instills confidence in an investor, a publisher, or a media outlet like actual sales.

2. A completed or nearly completed product, even if it's not yet being sold, along with a strong business case with marketing and sales projections.

3. An interactive demo of the game, including polished art and user interface. You may want to start with a video of a demo but have the actual live demo ready, too.

4. A working interactive prototype that highlights the core gameplay.

5. A video trailer of what you believe the game will look like when finished. Note that if you have a demo, prototype, or video, you should be sure it includes sound! To paraphrase George Lucas, "sound is half the picture" (Fantel 1992).

6. A set of static mockups, which is really the minimum you should use for a pitch.

Unless this is an informal or quick pitch, you want to avoid relying on vague verbal descriptions of how you see the game working in the future—this is often referred to as "hand waving" and is something best avoided. The only thing worse than this in a presentation would be a poorly constructed slide deck with a lot of text and few pictures of the game in progress.

Throughout your presentation, you want to build excitement and confidence in you and your game while also reducing the perception of risk. Publishers don't fund risky ideas, the media don't want to report on things that have little chance of becoming real, and new people often don't join projects that look like they might fail (unless they know and trust you personally already).

You want to be confident but not aggressive. Don't push back on questions that are asked; just roll with them and answer them the best you can. This is something else you can practice: you need to be able to answer questions without directly saying that the person who asked has no idea what they're talking about. You also don't want to appear nervous or scared—and definitely shouldn't apologize for being nervous or joke about it. Just get on with the presentation, remembering that you've practiced this dozens of times. Remain professional and courteous at all times. Be friendly but also understand that the pitch isn't about making friends; stick to your goals. Don't assume too much familiarity with those in the room but don't be stiffly formal either. (Easy, right?)

Issuing a Call to Action and Follow-up

Having gone through your presentation, whether one sentence or an hour-long presentation, the last thing to do is to issue a "call to action." This is what you want to have happen—and especially what you want others to do—as a result of this pitch. Go back to your goals. What do you want get from giving this pitch? Was this a brief meeting where you exchanged cards and set up the next meeting? Or was this a formal pitch that you hoped would end with a handshake on millions of dollars of funding? You have to say what you want; as the old saying goes, you don't get what you don't ask for. Don't press for more certainty than your audience can give but don't leave things any more ambiguous than they need to be, either. If at all possible, set a date for a follow-up call or meeting or, even better, a decision date.

After the Pitch

After the pitch is complete, you will want to follow up with whomever you pitched to. At minimum, send a brief email or similar thanking the individuals for their time. If questions are asked during the pitch that you can't answer immediately, write them down and use them as a vehicle for natural follow-up later on.

If your pitch meeting goes well, you should celebrate. It means you're past a big hurdle and can soon start the real work of developing your game. However, most of the time you pitch, you will fail. That's just how pitching works. You need to be prepared to not see a positive outcome and to get back up and pitch again and again. Persistence is a big part of pitching and developing any game.

When a meeting doesn't go well, review what was said for comments that don't fit with your own assumptions: is there something about the game, the market, or even your team that you're hearing that doesn't match what you see? This can be very difficult to admit to, but you can learn valuable lessons by being open to points of view that don't match—or that even actively undercut—your own.

While having a pitch meeting not go your way is never fun, getting a "fast no" is actually in your favor. It means you can move on, adjust what needs to be changed, and keep looking forward. Publishers, executives, investors, reporters, and potential team members all have more opportunities than they could possibly say yes to, if they are at all good at what they do. This means they have to say no a lot. Unfortunately, sometimes publishers and investors don't want to say no, even if they're not saying yes. They want to keep their options open as long as possible. This can lead to what one British game developer called "death by tea and crumpets." You're never going to get a yes or a no answer, and in the meantime the publisher or investor is happy to have meetings now and then to talk about what you're doing—without making any commitment. This can prevent you from moving on to better opportunities, and if you're a small developer, it can threaten your entire company. Thus when pitching to a publisher or an investor, push (in a professional, courteous manner) for a fast resolution—and be thankful for the fast no when it comes.

Whether a pitch meeting goes well or not, you should meet with your team, or, if you were pitching alone, take time in a quiet space to write down your thoughts about the meeting. Once you're out of the building (not in the elevator or the lobby, but back in your car or wherever, just to be safe), go over the meeting while it's still fresh. Critique your performance by acknowledging both what went well and what didn't. See what you can do next time to learn from this meeting and improve the pitch. No matter how this one went, there will always be another pitch.

Building the Game

Having discussed pitching your game, we now turn to what actually goes into building the game. This is necessarily a complex, iterative process that is never the same twice. However, there are regularities and heuristics that have evolved in the games industry to make for a more effective development process.

Designing, Building, and Testing

Designing, building, and testing your game are all activities that should go on throughout development. They form their own loop, with each leading to the next. They are not fully sequential, however, as each happens while the others are under way. As you begin working on the game concept, you can also start working on reference art and then concept art. As soon as you have some idea of the game's core loop, you should be building it out and testing it, while continuing to work on the design.

Initially, you and your team will be more focused on design than anything else. Over time, as the design solidifies, most of your attention will be on implementing the design. Finally, design changes will become smaller and smaller in scope, development will wind down, and most of the effort will be on testing and fixing any bugs found. However, while there are different points of emphasis, it is important to understand that these are not three distinct phases: when you are designing, you must also be building and testing to refine the design. As you continue to build the game, there will still be design changes, though they should be more and more circumscribed in scope and greater in detail and balancing. Testing the gameplay should happen throughout development and not be put off to the end.

Finding the Fun Fast

As you begin designing your game, your first major goal should be to test the game's primary concept to make sure it's a viable game. This is often called "find the fun fast," and you can't afford to put it off until later and risk wasting valuable time and resources in the meantime. Sometimes an idea sounds good and just doesn't quite come together. Or in starting to develop it, technical, interactivity, or gameplay issues that were invisible before become obvious. If this is the case, you want to know as quickly as possible. And if it's not, knowing that the game is fundamentally sound gives you more confidence as you develop it.

The way you find the fun is to get the interactive loop of the game working. It doesn't matter if there's no real art or if a lot of the gameplay is missing: you need to close the loop between the player and the game so that real interactivity is possible. This should be your first big milestone toward developing your game concept. Don't get trapped into thinking that you first need to build a map editor or decide on the game's iconography or write the backstory for the main character; all these may be important, but at first they are distractions.

The truth is that until you have closed the interactive loop and determined that in fact there is something in your design that's engaging and fun, you do not have a game. Until you know you have a game, it doesn't make sense to work too much on anything else.

Effective Game Prototyping

A key part of the design–build–test loop is building rapid prototypes. Early on, this is how you find the fun fast. As the project goes forward, you will find other ways to use prototypes to test other aspects of the game.

In game development, the definition of *prototype* (like so much else) is broad and not always clear. We can define *prototype* a little more specifically, however, based on years of evolving best practices. A game prototype is any working portion of a game that allows at least one interactive loop. A noninteractive image isn't a prototype; it's a mockup (even when it's animated). A video of gameplay (real or predetermined) isn't a prototype, either. A running simulation also isn't a game prototype if it's noninteractive (though there are sometimes reasons to make specialized technical tests like this). In essence, if someone can't play it, it's not a game prototype.

The reason game prototypes must include interaction is that otherwise, they are not really testing the game or helping you move toward its completion. A noninteractive program may test an algorithm or simulation, but it is not creating and testing a game. Brief excursions into nongame territory when making a game are often needed. But to keep the development moving forward and your confidence high in the game design, a prototype must at every step be interactive and move closer to the game you eventually want to see.

Analog and Digital Prototypes

Prototypes can take different forms and include different numbers and types of features. Prototypes for tabletop games may be made out of just about anything, from scraps of paper on up. For digital games, early prototypes are often made out of physical materials (paper, dice, a whiteboard), and they may contain just enough to create a single interactive loop, especially early on in development. Whether a prototype is digital or analog, though, the interactive aspect—with the player forming an intention, carrying it out via an action in the game, perturbing the internal game model, and having the game create feedback for the player—is a necessary part of any prototype.

You create prototypes to make your game ideas tangible and testable—to find out if what you think will make an engaging game actually does. Early in development, a digital prototype is a relatively simple standalone program designed to test one portion of the game, focusing first on the core loops. Later prototypes may be considerably more complex, incorporating more of the game itself.

Keeping Prototypes Separate

The freestanding nature of prototypes points to a vital aspect: prototypes are never part of the game product itself. They are always implemented separately. As development moves along, you may end up using portions of your digital game program as the basis for a prototype, but the code from the prototype never goes in the other direction: it does not ever become part of the game product, no matter how enticing it may be to make it so. This is an important lesson that can be tempting to ignore, but ignoring it only leads to more problems. Prototypes must remain free to be fast, ugly, and entirely unoptimized internally. If you find yourself ever slowing down when developing a prototype to "code something up the right way" or wondering if maybe you can copy and paste some prototype code into your game, you need to stop and reconsider. What you're making then is neither a prototype nor a viable part of your game but a horrible hybrid that will create trouble for you in the long run.

Getting Started with Prototyping

While a game prototype must show some form of interaction, there is very little else that should keep you from creating prototypes of your game as soon as you have the idea and form the concept for the game. Start simply. Don't feel like you need to have an entire economy or combat system created before you can make a prototype. Start with something like basic movement in the world or another simple in-game action. While prototypes are great for testing things like different art and animation styles, leave those for later: focus first on making an interactive loop and then using that to allow a player to enact even a very simple goal (for example, moving from here to over there) in a way that makes sense in your game. Over time, add more choices and more interactive loops—but not too quickly: make sure the basic, core loops in the game are engaging and fun. If they're not, no amount of dressing them up will make them fun later; they will always be lackluster, frustrating parts of your game.

Answering Questions

Prototypes allow you to ask and answer questions about your game. The first and biggest one is "Is this fun?" Even with a rudimentary prototype, you should be able to begin to answer this question about the basic core loops in your game.

Don't be surprised that the answer to this question is very often no. Many times a prototype will show that your design doesn't work. Your first prototypes in particular will often reveal that what you thought was going to be a great core loop for your game turns out to be tedious or boring. As a rule, especially until you learn to curate your own ideas better, your first ideas on a design will be *terrible*. At best, they might be mediocre and derivative of designs found in other game. But you likely won't see this until you have tried out the design in a prototype, freeing it from the confines of your brain and putting it out in the real world. That's when you get to see how thoroughly broken it is.

Seeing a design idea fall completely flat can be extremely disheartening, but don't let it slow you down. This is a large part of game design. Learn from what worked and didn't, get ready to try again, and take solace in the fact that you have just discovered a hard truth with very little investment; it's far better to find this out now than after six months of development. If one prototype doesn't work, learn from it and try another way of approaching your concept. You may have to adjust your thinking on the game; maybe it's better to make it faster paced or instead more strategic, or maybe there's an emotional core there that you hadn't seen before. Just because a particular way of approaching the game concept doesn't work doesn't mean the concept itself is worthless; you may just have to try different prototypes to see what works. This is why "finding the fun" is so important and why you need to do this as soon as possible. You will save yourself a lot of unnecessary work (and grief) later on by figuring this out now.

Clear Goals and Questions

Beyond the most basic (and most important) questions about your game, it's important when constructing a prototype to always have a clear goal and question in mind. This question should be unambiguous and lead to a significant change in your game and how you develop it. If you find members of the team uncertain or arguing about which direction to go, that's an excellent situation to turn into a prototype: stop arguing, figure out the question, build a prototype to test it, and see where it takes you. Questions like "Is one resource enough, or do we need more?" or "Does this style of combat feel fun to players?" are good places to start. The more precise you can make the question and the prototype, and especially if you can quickly try more than one option at a time (whether by tuning variables or trying entirely different modes in the game), the more you will learn and the better off you will be.

It's also important to be clear about your assumptions about the player: for a given prototype, what does the player know about the game? What are their goals? How much of a mental model of the game have they built? As stated before, the player's goal may be simple, like "move from here to there," or it may be more complex, like "complete this quest without being seen by an enemy." It really depends on where you are in the prototyping and game design process, but at each step of the way, your goals, and your player's goals, have to be clear for each prototype you build.

Knowing the Intended Audience

In addition to having clear questions and goals in mind when making a prototype, you also need to clearly understand who is the intended audience. Most prototypes will be made quickly and will be ugly, intended only to test a particular part of the design. These are meant only for use within the game team and are best kept within those safe confines. For these prototypes, you should spend as little time on "niceties" or polish as possible. Use whatever is easiest for graphics in a digital prototype—squares or Xs. Or don't even make it digital at all: create the game in analog form using paper, markers, dice, and whatever else you need to just to test a concept. The faster you make prototypes like this, often the uglier they are—but also the more effective they are at answering the questions you need clarified.

Other prototypes will have a broader audience and need a different emphasis. For example, in some organizations, it's required to create what's known as a *vertical slice* of your game. This is, in theory, like a slice through a cake, showing all the layers. In the case of a game, it means showing an instance of the different systems in the game all working together: a polished user interface, consistent interaction methods, engaging and polished art, interesting exploration, balanced combat, and so on, all the way down to a working database for the game. The general idea is that once you have built this, developing the rest of the game is just a matter of building the rest of the levels, weapons, costumes, and so on. Many people mistake a complex (looping) system for a complicated (linear) one. Game design and development are necessarily complex systems, and if you are creating anything innovative at all, the systems cannot be reduced to linear ones ("great, now just make more levels!") on the basis of something like a vertical slice.

That said, stakeholders from outside your team (investors, company management, and so on) sometimes do need to see what to them looks like viable progress on the game so that they can see where it's going and whether you're making sufficient progress. Unfortunately, those in such positions sometimes do not really understand how game development works, and (despite what they may say) often cannot see the engaging experience you are creating when a prototype consists of, for example, a small circle on the screen dodging squares. There is a tension where showing such stakeholders a fast, ugly, but engaging prototype may lead them to focus on the wrong parts of the prototype. If they are unable to look past the terrible graphics to the experience you are trying to design and test for, they may lose confidence in the project. This is an extremely common occurrence, unfortunately, especially for teams trying anything really new. In such cases, it often works better to create a completely noninteractive video "demo" of the game as it will eventually look. Even this can drain resources and distract your team from actually making the game, but it is nevertheless often an important thing to do. Such a video can also help the team stay connected and working toward the same vision, and that can be a big help on a large project.

Other Prototypes

Beyond testing game design ideas or showing progress to stakeholders, there are often other kinds of prototypes you will end up making of your game. Some of them are noninteractive, or nearly so, such as when you need to test whether a system deep inside the game's model of the world is working correctly. You may need to test a set of graphical effects in the game, or to test qualitative aspects of the game's user interface (its "juiciness"), such as brief animations on controls. Testing parts of the game like this is perfectly valid, and such testing can often be included along with another game prototype test. If it can't, take the same approach with these as with an interactive game prototype: know what you're testing and the questions you're asking and how the answers will change the game, and be prepared to iterate until it feels right.

Move Fast and Throw It Away

For a time, Facebook's motto was "Move fast and break things. Unless you are breaking stuff, you aren't moving fast enough" (Taplin 2017). That doesn't fit every situation or company, certainly, but it is a great way to look at prototyping. In prototyping, you need to move fast, and you need to not be afraid to break things. You need to feel free to try out things that may not work and that may even fail spectacularly.

This is why it's so important that, as mentioned earlier, your prototypes remain separate from your actual game. You can and should learn from what you make in your prototypes, but especially with digital prototypes, it's vitally important not to copy over any of the code from a prototype back to the game itself. Refactor the code (analyze it, see what works well, and then rewrite it) but do not copy it. You need to maintain the ability to move fast and try out new concepts on the one hand and maintain good code hygiene on the other. The point of a game prototype is not to create reusable, stable code but to answer a question about the game design.

Effective Playtesting

While you're building your game, you need to test the experience you're building, whether in prototype form or in more finished form in the actual game. Early on in the process, you will primarily be testing the game—or its prototypes—with members of the team. As development goes on, you will want to quickly test it with others who don't know anything about the game and who, preferably, don't know you. This is a crucial and rarely comfortable process, one where you will see things that were clear and easy to you be opaque and frustrating to others. And if you wait until you feel ready, you're certainly waiting too long.

The Importance of Playtesting

You need to test your gameplay—the game's experience—so you can see how others who know nothing about it react to it. You need to gather new points of view on the game and especially find areas that are obvious to you but not to others. You want to see how others experience the game. Is it engaging, enthralling, fun? Is it an experience players would want to continue?

You should not assume that you know what players will think of your game. You can, if you want, speculate on where new players will have trouble and what they will find obvious and easy. However, you are likely to be wrong more often than you are right. This is one of the most valuable parts about playtesting: it shows you what is completely clear to you but is utterly mysterious to others not familiar with the game.

While you are trying to see how others experience your game, and especially to see where it can be improved, you are not trying to get solutions to problems from playtests. Players can and will offer you their experiences and input, but you should not expect them to offer solutions. They may do so (this is common), but you need to look behind the solution they are offering to see what they believe the problem is. Your solution to the underlying problem may be entirely different than their suggestion.

When to Test

You should begin testing your game as soon as you can. Definitely do so before you think the game is ready to be tested. Most game designers find this to be a difficult process and seek refuge in "It's not ready yet!" You need to resist this impulse, set aside your fears and your pride, and get your game in front of players.

In general, more tests that are shorter are better than fewer tests that are longer. Whenever you make a significant change to the game, you should run a playtest on it. The same is true if you find an area where you're not sure the best direction to go, or if it's just been a few weeks since your last playtest. Early on this might amount to testing once every two weeks or so; later in development, testing every week or even every few days as you refine the game is worthwhile.

Goals for Your Playtests

Playtesting is not about finding bugs in your code (especially if you're working with fast and ugly prototypes, as described earlier). It's about testing the game design to see if players understand it, can make an effective mental model around it, and find the game engaging and fun. Early on you want to test basic concepts from the game design to see if they're valid and engaging. As you build up more systems in the game, you will want to test how easily the players comprehend the game and how effectively they can build mental models of it.

You also want to look for areas where the players go astray—where their mental models do not conform to your expectations and the game's internal model—or where they are confused, frustrated, or have no idea what to do next. These are incredibly important areas to uncover for making the game enjoyable and engaging.

Finally, playtesting at some point veers into usability testing. Can the player understand what's presented in the user interface, and is it easy or cumbersome to use? This isn't testing the overall experience itself, but testing the usability of the user interface inevitably makes up an important part of the game as experienced by the player.

Who Playtests Your Game?

The first thing to get out of the way in considering who playtests your game is that it's *not you*. You are the least qualified and most biased person there is with regard to getting any useful information about how playable your game is. You will inevitably test your game yourself many, many times—but this is in no way a substitute for having others play it. Ultimately your experience has no bearing at all on how engaging or fun the game is to others.

Your team members, friends, and family members are also poor test subjects. They cannot offer anything like objective thoughts on the game, and even unconsciously they will bend over backward to try to see the game as engaging and understandable, even if it is fundamentally broken.

At the same time, especially when working with early, rough, ugly prototypes, you probably want to keep them very close to your team. A few confidants who aren't on your team can help with early testing, if they are able to see past poor stand-in graphics and the like and are able to provide effective feedback about the underlying game. But keep in mind that once someone has played the game, they will never be able to approach it the same way again. You cannot "un-know" something. This means you can't, for example, run the same person through testing the early part of your game as a naive player more than once.

Having repeat players can be helpful, as they can tell you what they like better or worse and whether something makes more sense to them after having played before. Just don't mistake that for the experience of someone who has never seen your game before—they might have a completely different opinion.

As your game develops and your prototypes become more polished (more built on the existing game), you will want to broaden the number and types of people who are testing it. In particular, you will want to match more closely those playing it with those whom you think will be your target audience. However, you want to be careful not to limit the testing pool too much, as you can miss out on important insights and opportunities for your game. You may, for example, miss potential players who would enjoy your game if it happens that you have set your target market too narrowly or off-center from those who truly enjoy it. You will also want to be careful about enthusiastic hardcore gamers. They can be useful in testing, but their knowledge of games and their firm opinions about what makes a "good" game may introduce more noise than signal into your test results.

Preparing Your Playtest

Before you begin a playtest, you need to clearly understand your goals for the test and how you will conduct it. There are logistical concerns, such as where to hold your playtest. Any quiet area where the players won't be distracted is fine. In some cases, it doesn't even need to be very quiet; games have been tested successfully in busy university commons, for example.

Some developers advocate using special facilities with one-way glass for observing the players and/or video of their faces, as well as the keyboard and screen. These are useful but are often far more than you need to effectively playtest your game and obtain good data from it. Don't let this kind of requirement stop you from testing early and often. Especially early in development, just make a prototype and test it. This is far more useful than waiting for the right facilities to become available.

In a similar vein, some developers like to pay their testers. This is often not necessary, but if you have any ethical concerns, find a way to do what's fair. When using university students for playtesting, offering a free slice of pizza has been extremely effective. In other cases, offering a low-value gift card is appropriate. The more involved the test and follow-up survey, the more you should consider offering some sort of compensation.

Writing a Script

Before playtesting, write out a script for every part of it. This includes everything from greeting the player to running the test, asking any posttest questions, and letting the player go. This script should be detailed down to the level of what you say at each step. This will help you a lot especially as you get started on playtesting, so that you're saying only what you intend without being nervous or distracting to the players. This also helps you be certain that you're giving them the same context and instructions each time.

Start your playtest script with a greeting and a brief warm-up discussion with the player. Make sure they're comfortable. Get whatever information you need from them, such as their name and contact information and, if they're willing, age and gender (but gather only the information you really need). You might want to ask about other games they play both as a way to calibrate their experience and to help them get into the mindset of testing your game.

As a matter of professional ethics, it's important that before you begin the playtest, you inform the player that this is a test of the game, not of them, and that whatever they do is perfectly acceptable. It's a good idea (and may be required in some places) to give them a short statement to this effect and read it aloud at the same time. State clearly that they can stop playing and leave whenever they like and that answering any questions about the game is entirely voluntary. It helps to get them to initial a form to this effect or at least get verbal acknowledgment of these points so that you know the player has heard (and/or read) them.

It's rare that a player wants to stop a test in the middle, but it does happen. If a player wants to stop playing at any moment during the test, simply stop the test: do not encourage the them to keep playing. Asking them to continue can involve ethical issues. In addition, their desire to stop provides important information for you about your game.

In advance of the playtest, prepare to record the player's behavior. This may include simple forms for you to take notes on, or if you are able (and if your tester agrees), video recording of both the screen and the their face while testing. Many developers like to gather video of playtests for later review, but keep in mind that this will significantly increase the time needed for analysis of the test, and it will not necessarily yield more informative results, especially early in development.

Creating a Survey

You will want to create a brief posttest survey for the players to fill out. Survey design is an area that requires some expertise, so be careful about how you construct your survey and the individual questions. It is important to create balanced questions, with as many negative as positive responses. This helps you avoid asking leading questions and keeps the questions as unbiased as possible so the players don't feel nudged into giving a particular opinion. If you can, use digital/online surveys that allow you to present the questions in random order, as this helps reduce bias in the players' answers as well and makes analysis easier.

Your survey should ask just a few questions that all relate directly to your goal for the playtest and to the player's experience with the game, including their comprehension and mental model of the game. While it's tempting to ask about every aspect of the game every time—did they like the graphics, was the music too loud, were the opponents too easy or too tough, and so on—don't ask about areas of the game that don't match with your current goals for the test. Doing so just bogs down the player with more questions to answer and gives you data you're not really going to use. At the same time, if a player spontaneously says something about the game, that's important information to note and add to your list of issues to examine.

You can quantify individual opinions by using questions with a numeric scale, typically with five to seven alternatives. These can range from "disagree strongly" to "agree strongly," with neutral in the middle, or you can create a similar range of possible answers that allow players to state their opinions in a way that is easy for you to assess and score later. Be sure that the statements associated with each option make strong statements with which the player can agree or disagree. The following are some examples of statements and answer scales:

1. **It was easy for me to move around in the game.**

   Disagree Strongly—Disagree—Neutral—Agree—Agree Strongly

2. **I understood what was going on in the game at all times.**

   Disagree Strongly—Disagree—Neutral—Agree—Agree Strongly

3. **I had clear goals in mind that I was trying to accomplish.**

   Disagree Strongly—Disagree—Neutral—Agree—Agree Strongly

4. **I could play this again easily without reviewing the rules.**

   Disagree Strongly—Disagree—Neutral—Agree—Agree Strongly

You can also create open-ended questions that are still quantifiable by providing the player with a number of choices, any or all of which are acceptable. Here is an example:

Check the words that apply to your experience in the game

Exciting   Fast   Confusing   Boring   Overwhelming   Thoughtful

Strategic   Broken   Engaging

Be sure to provide equal numbers of positive, negative, and neutral traits among the choices and not to put them in any particular order (such as best to worst).

In some cases (depending on the purpose of a particular playtest), you can ask questions about how well the player understands the game or the user interface and how well they have been able to build their mental model of the game. You might ask comprehension questions—for example, by showing the player a few symbols or icons from the game and asking what the symbols mean. You can also ask more process-oriented questions, whose answers reveal their mental model, such as asking "Suppose you wanted to find how many soldiers are available. Describe the steps you would go through to do this." Or "Here is a screenshot of a common moment from the game. Describe what you would do next in this situation, using your finger as your mouse pointer." Questions like these are often best presented in oral form and recorded on audio or video, as this allows the player to respond more freely than in writing.

Finally, you can ask a few short-answer questions that the player answers either verbally or in written form, including an open-ended question for any remaining comments. Examples include:

Briefly explain the rules to this game as you understand them.

What surprised you in this game?

What did you think you were supposed to accomplish in the game?

What games did this remind you of?

Some developers like to ask the question "How much would you pay for this game?" This can be useful for assessing the player's positive or negative experience with the game and to get a vague estimate of the value they place on it. However, don't treat this as a viable way to establish pricing. People's actual behavior often varies significantly from what they say they would pay when it really comes down to doing so.

Final Checks

Be sure to test your script before you test your game! That is, run through a mock playtest with someone else, even a team member, just to make sure that everything makes sense and flows together well. Then, when you're ready to conduct your first playtest, you'll be able to focus on the player and the game and won't be stumbling or thinking of things you need to fix in the test or script.

Running a Playtest

Playtests do not need to be long; most last just a few minutes, and they generally don't last more than 10 to 20 minutes. They only need long enough for you to gather the information you're looking for.

As you begin, you should tell the testers as little as possible about your game. In some cases, you may want to vary this by test: tell the player the name of the game or show them potential cover artwork; in other cases, give them a broad overview or even your elevator pitch for the game to see how this affects their comprehension and enjoyment of the game. In still other cases, you will want to give them no information at all—though it helps to tell the player that you're going to proceed without further information so they aren't confused about it. Whatever you tell them, follow your script so you don't inadvertently say too much or tell some players more than others. Remember that you won't be there to explain the game or the in-joke in its title, and so on, after it's released, so limit the information you give players before the test begins.

During the playtest, stay out of the player's line of sight, do not hover over them, and speak as little as possible. Let them concentrate on the game. The player may have questions; you should answer as few of them as possible and as briefly as possible. You need to let them play the game—and you need to witness their confusion and even their frustration. Encourage them to keep going (unless they clearly want to stop) without giving them any hints or specific information. Do not ever point something out on the screen or say anything like "Try clicking in the upper-left corner" or "Go back one menu and read it again." Do not explain the game and especially do not respond to any criticism they may offer. Explaining some part of the game or, worse, being defensive about it ruins the playtest and wastes your time and the player's as well.

Write down what the player does, what they say, and places where they seem confused and especially anything that indicates some sort of emotional reaction—sudden understanding, delight, confusion, frustration, and so on. If the player asks for reassurance, just tell them they're doing fine and to keep going. Keep your reactions bland and general; players will look for signs about whether they're doing okay (even unconsciously) and whether voicing criticism is really all right. You need to set aside your fears, pride, and any defensiveness and simply take whatever they give you.

If the player completes what you want out of the test, or if they simply grind to a halt and can't see how to proceed, consider the playtest over. You can then ask a few questions about what they were trying to do and what they expected to happen—again, these can be useful for understanding their mental model. But from there, you need to move into the posttest phase.

Finishing Up the Playtest

As you wrap up the playtest, ask the players for their general thoughts. Pay close attention to what they say first; their top-of-mind reaction can be very important. Also look at the structure of what they say; they may try to say something nice first to soften the blow of the real criticism they want to offer. You need to be open to hearing all of it and not shut down any criticism or become defensive of the game.

After giving the player a moment to offer any first impressions, give them the survey you prepared earlier. Again, do not say anything that might bias their answers; stick to your script. Offer them the survey, thank them for their time and honesty, and ask them to fill out the survey if they're willing to do so. When they're done (or if they decline to fill out the survey), ask them for any final thoughts they have on the game, thank them again, and let them go.

Testing Methods

There are several methods you can apply during a playtest, depending on your goals for the test and your confidence in your own abilities.

Observation

Many playtests consist mainly of observing the player's behavior while playing the game. This can create valuable insights into how they see and experiences the game. It can be instructive to watch (and, if desired, record) where the players go first, what options they focus on or ignore, and at any given moment whether they do what you as the designer expected. You should watch for signs of engagement (closely watching the screen, pursed lips, blinking more slowly, and so on) and for emotional reactions of any type. These may include looks or expressions of surprise, delight, or frustration. Recording where the player becomes confused, gets stuck, or goes back and forth over the same content (or the same part of the user interface) several times can also illuminate where they are trying and failing to do so something.

Directed Experience and Exploration

In addition to observing a player's behavior as they play your game, there are other methods you can add to find out more about their experience. You can give them a particular goal to accomplish as part of the script (*not* to just get them out of being confused), especially if the player has tested the game before and already has some idea of how to play. Or you can tell them to simply explore and see where they go—and, just as importantly, what they ignore or avoid.

Wizard of Oz

If the playtest is an early one, especially one that is being done with analog materials (paper, dice, and so on), you can do what's called a "Wizard of Oz" protocol, where you play the part of the computer running the game (you are the wizard behind the curtain) to see how the player reacts. These tests are low-fidelity, meaning that you can't accurately judge the behavior of someone playing a later digital version from an early version like this, but this type of test can give you insights into the player's expectations and mental model, which can help you as you develop the game.

Thinking Aloud

In some tests, it can be helpful to ask the player to speak aloud the entire time about what they are thinking, intending, wondering about, and so on. This can be difficult for them, and they may often need to be reminded as they subside into silence, especially when they're trying to figure something out. A short prompt ("please keep talking") can help them start back up again. While the player's performance in the game will be lower than if they were silent (especially in games that tax their interactivity budget), thinking aloud can yield useful insights for you as to their internal goals and mental model. This method can be especially helpful if in other tests you're seeing players become confused or lose their way, and you're not certain why.

You can try out different methods like this, as long as they relate to the your goals for the playtest. Again, don't waste your time with tests that aren't going to have a direct effect on how you develop your game.

Analyzing Feedback

As soon as a playtest is complete, immediately take a moment to write down any impressions you had from it. This can include player reactions you saw, bugs that need to be fixed, or ideas for how to make the gameplay better. In addition, set aside time to analyze the data you've obtained. Review your notes from each player's test, looking for common experiences, themes, what was most important to them, and so on. Review the quantitative data from your survey to look for trends there, too. Don't worry about—and certainly don't reject—negative comments. Just as a playtest isn't a test of the player's ability, negative comments aren't comments on your ability as a game designer; a playtest is all about how well the game creates the experience you are trying to create. Learn from what the players say, especially from the negative comments, to make the game better.

One player may love the game, while another finds it incomprehensible. Those tend to be outliers: you need to look carefully for events and experiences that are common between players. At the same time, don't strain too much for patterns, much less try to look for statistically significant findings (unless you have a whole team to set up, run, and analyze your playtests for you, with dozens of players each time). You should be looking for directional experiences that can help you refine your design and answer questions you have about what's working and what's not.

These directional experiences take place not only across players but across time. Watch players' experiences and responses as the game develop. Do they find the same parts consistently engaging? Are there some areas that are confusing that after changes and more development are now enjoyable? Or, alternatively, do changes you make to the game make some parts more difficult and less enjoyable for the players?

Finally, remember that those playing your game have a valid point of view, but they are not designers. You should take their feedback seriously but look at it more as identifying problems than as offering solutions. As you see what your players are seeing, this may reveal important aspects of the game to you, sometimes even causing you to change the design of the game significantly. With a recent pirate-themed game, in early playtests, players found the exploration portions boring and said they felt like filler between combats. The combat was the fun part for them. So the designer reconsidered the game and ended up focusing on just ship-to-ship battles, making a more engaging (and more easily implementable) game as a result. This happens with large developers, too; for example, early in the development of *The Sims*, the team thought of the game mostly as a life simulator like an old-style *Tamagotchi*. However, players consistently reported being more interested in the interactions between the Sims and the stories that emerged for them as they played the game. As a result, both the development and marketing of the game changed and made it far more successful than it would have been otherwise.

Phases of Production

As you are designing and testing your game, you must, of course, also be building it. There are many ways to actually construct a game, including just jumping in and getting to it. However, long experience (and the Game Outcomes Project, discussed in Chapter 11, "Working as a Team") shows that building a game iteratively using a design–build–test loop works well, and as a result, this is the norm in game development today. Noniterative methods (for example, "waterfall" development, where you move from specification to implementation to test to release, like water dropping down a waterfall) rarely work well in game development, especially if the game requires any degree of innovation—and almost all do. Innovating effectively in developing a game requires significant iteration.

Iteration in a Linear World

Iterative design is uncomfortable for some development teams (and company executives) because it seems like it could never end: you just keep iterating over and over and never really get anywhere. This is a valid concern, as the process of iterating can feel like you're doing something when you're really getting nowhere. (As Benjamin Franklin is said to have quipped, "Never confuse motion with action.") Sometimes those not directly involved with the development process wonder why all this iterating and trying of different approaches around is necessary; why not just go ahead and build the game in a straightforward, linear fashion? Of course, because game development is necessarily complex and looping, not complicated and linear, this doesn't work.

Iteration through the design–build–test cycle is vital for games and for any other project where you are trying to create something new. No matter how amazing your game concept is, there is simply no way to know in advance if it's actually engaging or where it needs to be changed. The only way to know this is to design the game and start building and testing it as quickly as possible. In situations like this, it's not possible to specify and design the game in one pass, then implement it, and then test it and release it. You need significant iteration across the whole process.

Stage Gating

Developing your game iteratively does not, however, mean that once you start, you are wholly committed to it, wherever the iteration might lead; every concept needs to be reviewed at different stages to see if it works (prototyped and playtested with positive results) and is viable in the market. One effective method for doing this is called *stage gating*. With this method, multiple projects are started (and/or multiple designs based on the same overall concept). Each is then evaluated at regular intervals to see if it is still viable, is progressing well, and shows sufficient promise. Early in the process, this may happen rapidly, once every two weeks, for example, when the design and early prototypes should be iterating rapidly based on playtesting feedback.

Projects that do not make sufficient progress and/or that appear to have too much risk are either sent back for significant revision or simply cut from further development. This is never an easy thing to do, but it is essential: it allows you to put more resources on projects that are more viable but without eliminating the exploration of new ideas that is necessary in game development. The work that's done on projects that are culled out isn't lost. As game designer Daniel Cook explains, these are put into a *concept bank* for possible use later: "You never know when the remnants of an old idea will nourish a strong new project" (Cook 2007).

Iterative Production

Within the concept of iterative development, there are numerous methods you can use to make a game. A wide number of variants on Agile with scrum have become common across the games industry, as they (at least mostly) fit well with iterative game development.

Some of the important features of Agile and scrum are regular design–build–test loops that happen on a two- to four-week schedule (each of which is a *sprint*, in Agile terms), within which there are smaller daily loops (punctuated by scrum meetings) to keep everyone on the team together and knowledgeable about what the rest of the team is doing. It isn't a big stretch to call these the core loops for game development.

The two- to four-week sprint loops are consistent with the designer's loop discussed in Chapter 4, "Interactivity and Fun," and Chapter 7 "Creating Game Loops." Early in the development process, most of the effort should be on mapping out the game design and beginning to build small prototypes of the gameplay. As the project moves along, this balance should shift to include more implementation beyond prototypes (along with continued testing) and then move to more testing than anything else. Throughout, it helps to keep the project on track by maintaining relatively short (two- to four-week) loops, each with an iteration of planning (based on evaluation of the previous tests), design, development, and testing. As this happens, the project goes through multiple phases. They have different names in different parts of the games industry, but the basic concepts are pretty consistent.

The Concept Phase

The concept phase is where the game is just getting started. In this phase, you create the concept document (refer to Chapter 6), begin putting together an art and sound style, and develop a few small, fast, ugly prototypes to prove the basic concept and validate the core loops. You may also start on some of the primary systems documents.

The concept phase tends to last one to three months, depending on the clarity of the concept for what you're trying to build. During and at the end of this phase, you should have a gate: at that gate, if the concept can't be shown to work in a prototype, start over or go on to something else but don't put any more resources into the game as it stands. It doesn't make sense to keep developing a concept until the concept and core loops are clearly understood and fun (even if in limited form).

The Preproduction Phase

Once the basic concept seems sound, you should fill out as many details as possible based on the concept document and what you learned from your early prototypes. Your need to make sure the game is one that you can produce with the resources you have.

The primary purpose of the preproduction phase is to make certain that you and your (still small) team understand what the game is, what it will cost, and how long it will take to develop it. You will be taking what you learned in putting together the game concept and turning that into additional documents—some related directly to game design, some more about how long it will take to create the game you have envisioned.

You need detailed documents about the game's starting features and all art assets, sound assets, and anything else that is made as part of production that will be needed to launch the game. These lists will be wrong, no question, in that what's actually needed will have changed by the time the game is actually done. You still need these to be as complete an inventory as possible of what's needed, or you can't even begin to size up the next stage of development.

Features and Assets

The outline of features in your game comes from your concept document and early system descriptions and prototypes. This determines what will be available to the player when the game launches. You should be careful not to make this list too long to avoid increasing the scope and risk of the game's development (and thus increasing the chance of not passing a stage gate). However, if the list is too short, you may be leaving out vital aspects of the game that keep it from being a fully engaging experience. In recent years, the concept of a *minimum viable product* (*MVP*) has been used to indicate the number and mix of features that a game absolutely cannot launch without. The MVP concept is now changing in some areas to be more process oriented rather than being about a specific set of feature deliverables. Nevertheless, knowing what is core to your game, what cannot be added later, is an important milestone to reach. Fortunately, if you have constructed your concept, core loops, and primary systems, you should be able to tell fairly quickly what the game must have to launch and what can come in a later version or later release of the game.

Based on your base feature list or MVP, you also need to construct a master list of all assets to be made for the game. The asset list must have within it the name, description, and any special notes (size, animations, and so on) for every piece of art, sound, animation, and so on for every portion of the game—from the user interface to every monster, character, forest creature, or whatever else is in your game. Creating this list is a daunting task, but if you consider it in terms of the parts you need to create to implement the systems in your game, it becomes more manageable.

The Project Plan

As you consider every system and every bit of content you need for your game, you will come to a better understanding of the personnel and technology you will need to implement it. This is where you need to start bringing in help from senior producers and programmers—for example, as part of the lead-up to a stage gate meeting. Get their input on the feasibility of the game and see where it needs to be trimmed back or which areas look the riskiest from their points of view. With this information and their help, you can put together a budget and a project plan for the game.

The project plan is a roadmap of sorts, which shows what needs to be built when. When preparing a project plan, some producers like to plan an entire project, day by day or week by week. This is almost always wasted effort, as the game's development path will change radically along the way. Instead, focus on creating detailed schedules on a daily level (day by day, task by task, for each person on the team) for about the next four weeks and then schedule the following four weeks at a slightly lower level of detail (major tasks that need to be accomplished). These schedules should include sufficient time for full sprints or similar iterative patterns involving time for design, implementation, playtesting, and evaluation and planning, leading back to the next phase of design.

After this initial detailed period, plan out what the development priorities (programming, art generation, new design documents) will be on a weekly level for the next four to eight weeks so you have a schedule that covers three months. Then create month-by-month lists of what will be accomplished for the next three months (giving you six months total so far), and finally make lists of what is expected to be done on a quarter-by-quarter basis thereafter. As you go forward, the schedule should be maintained in this same way, rolling forward week by week and month by month. As a result, you always know in great detail what is expected over the next month or two and then in less and less detail for the months and quarters beyond that. This will help you review your progress on a monthly or sprint basis as your project moves forward and through additional stage gates.

Keep Moving Through Pre-production

Preproduction typically lasts at least two to three months, sometimes as long as six. That's a long time, but it's worth spending the time here as long as you are working effectively. All this is preparation for the next difficult stage. You want to be careful that preproduction doesn't become a period of iterating but not moving forward—of not being willing to commit to the game or cancel it. As a result, you should consider having a stage gate meeting at least once in the middle of preproduction and once at the end. This will help keep you from drifting off track while also allowing the team sufficient time to iterate on the game in between these meetings. As you conclude preproduction with the schedule and budget, your concept and system documents, and the completed asset lists, you can be sure (and demonstrate to others) that you know what you're building and what resources and time it will take to do so.

Of course, during this time, while you are putting together budgets and art lists and the like, you are also continuing with iterative development: writing systems documents that refer to the concept document, building prototypes and testing these ideas, and laying the very beginnings of the software architecture for the game overall. When you have confidence in your concept, system architecture, initial features, schedule, and budget, you are ready to move through a stage gate (to make sure all is well and the project is worth doing) and from there into production.

The Production Phase

When you know what to build, it's time to build it. That sounds highly noniterative, but that is (mostly) not true. By this point, your design is mostly known and somewhat tested via prototypes and early playtesting. There is a lot that you know that works. But there is a lot that is necessarily still unknown and won't become known until the game features can be tested. It is important that you maintain your iterative design–build–test loops throughout production, relying less and less on prototypes and more and more on the game itself for testing as time goes on. You will undoubtedly discover new ideas, new ways of presenting features, and potentially new systems that you want to have in your game but that you didn't know about before.

New features are to be expected, but it's important to avoid the classic problem *scope creep*. Adding "just one more" cool new system or feature can be very tempting, but you must remember that every time you do this, you add time and risk to the game. Each new addition should be fully and carefully evaluated in light of the rest of the game and in terms of what it brings to the game. Each has to undergo its own miniature concept and preproduction phases before it can be admitted into production—and if there's not time for that, there's not time to add it to the game.

It should often be the case that concept and system designs for new features or systems may be completed, possibly along with a fast early prototype, only for you (or the team) to decide to leave them aside for now. That doesn't mean the feature is gone forever; it goes in the concept bank to be used later, but it is in effect stage-gated out of the initial version of the game. It may be that adding it back in later will make sense. But it isn't worth weighing down your game with every new idea that comes along until you simply can't complete it. It's far better to keep the game design clean, focused, and to the point of the original concept, with a treasure trove of ideas that can be added later—after the game is a worldwide success.

Production Analytics

As mentioned in Chapter 10, "Game Balance Practice," during production, it can be important to identify metrics that you can analyze to help you know if your project is on track. Metrics can be tracked at the level of tasks, individuals, and iterative milestones.

Individual tasks should be tracked in terms of their initial completion estimate and how long they actually take to complete. So if the team decides that a particular design or development task should take two days to complete, and after four it's still not complete, there's a problem. It may seem small, but this is how projects go wrong. To quote software architect Fred Brooks, "How does a project get to be a year late? … One day at a time" (Brooks 1995).

Just as completion time for tasks can be tracked, so can team members' estimates of their own tasks. This must be done carefully to encourage individuals to better performance not make them feel stigmatized if their project estimates are inconsistent. There are numerous ways to track this, including keeping a history of initial estimates versus actual delivery times, to see what kind of ratio emerges. After enough time has elapsed to gain sufficient data, this ratio can act both as a multiplier on an individual's estimates and as a way for them to learn better task-estimation skills. For example, suppose someone's tasks are often delivered late, and after tallying the initial estimates and actual delivery dates, you find that their average is to be about 20% late. In the future, this ratio can be applied to their estimates, multiplying whatever completion time they give by 1.2 to get a more accurate picture of how long the work will take. If, however, they see this result and begin to make more effective estimates, soon delivery time will be closer to their estimate and well below the 1.2x time—meaning that their ratio will be revised downward. When a team members are more effective in task estimation and completion, the project has a better chance of staying on schedule.

Finally, at each project milestone—for example, at the end of each sprint or other iteration—the team members should take stock of what they have accomplished as opposed to what they had planned to accomplish in that time. This level of reflection on the process—a very small postmortem on the past iteration—helps the team remain aware of their project's status without glossing over any significant problems or risks that arise. The use of *burndown charts* and similar ways of visualizing the progress and remaining work on all relevant tasks for a given sprint are helpful in this regard, as they allow the team to see their performance both while the work is being done and after the iteration is complete.

The Alpha Milestone

During production, games eventually approach what is known as an alpha milestone. In some ways, this is a holdover from old methods of developing games; traditionally, alpha marked the border between the implementation and test phases of development, when all the features were supposed to be in place. This milestone still carries some of that definition (and again, definitions differ across the games industry), though now a great deal of testing is assumed to be going on throughout development. From another point of view, this milestone is somewhat consistent with an "early access" release on Steam, where players gain exposure to a game in development, and developers begin to get far more data about how players actually play their game.

The main point of the alpha milestone is to have a checkpoint where the game is demonstrated to be largely playable: all the major systems, features, and assets are in place, and the game can be assessed based on that. There are almost certainly still major bugs in the game, but the core loops and secondary gameplay are all in place and have been tested with people outside the team. If the game meets these criteria, it passes successfully through the gate. Otherwise, it may require more iterative work—or may need to be canceled.

Prior to the alpha milestone, the team is focused mainly on building systems and features and validating their gameplay via playtests. After this milestone is passed, the team changes to focus primarily on testing the game and fixing bugs, not adding or implementing new features or systems. Some small amount of ongoing design work may be happening, but this should be confined to balancing systems for enjoyable gameplay and tweaking low-level attribute values.

As the game approaches a stable state (albeit still with bugs), the review inherent in achieving the alpha milestone is a great place for another stage gate. You once again need to ask "Is the game worth continuing forward?" It's easy to say yes, given all the work that has gone into it. But even with as much work as has been done, in many ways the really difficult and expensive parts are still to come. Killing a game late in production means there are major issues that likely should have been identified earlier, but that shouldn't dissuade you or your team from doing so if the game just isn't engaging or fun. If you do cancel it at a late stage, you should look back and evaluate not only what went wrong with the game but what went wrong with your process to prevent the debilitating issues from being found and addressed much earlier.

Beta/First Release Milestone

Once the game's features, systems, and assets are in place, the team's focus turns almost entirely to balancing, bug fixing, and polishing the game. Some aspects of this polishing include small changes to attribute values deep in different game systems' parts. For example, one creature may run just slightly faster than another, altering the balance in that part of the game. Another major aspect of polishing is fixing up art, animations, and especially portions of the user interface. Giving the UI more juice doesn't affect the gameplay directly, but it does make the game more attractive and engaging.

As fewer and fewer major bugs are found and the game is stable, testing with players continues to ensure that the game remains fun and engaging. As this state is reached, the game comes to the beta milestone.

The beta milestone used to be when a game or another product was judged internally to be usable and stable enough to be shown to the general public. These days, we often expose games to players much earlier in the process. Beta now often has more to do with testing monetization (for free-to-play games), deployment infrastructure, content delivery networks, and other ancillary aspects of releasing the game. In free-to-play games in particular, this is also when the first significant metrics for the game are looked at, in terms of how many people play the game and especially how many return to it after the first day, week, and month. If these metrics don't show that the game can be commercially successful, then it may be canceled even at this late stage (which happens at large studios more than you might expect).

The Commercial Release

After all the work that has gone into designing, developing, and testing your game, you finally come to the day when it is to be fully released to the public. Reaching this milestone takes a long time and a lot of difficult work. You now have a game up and running and available in the world. This is a moment to savor. This is also when the game in some ways ceases to be only yours, as the players will quickly begin to see it as theirs, too. You now need to turn your attention more to what the players think and what your analytics tell you so that you can prioritize what to add or fix next.

Finishing Your Game

A surprising number of people who start making a game never complete it. From the moment you start musing about your game and throughout all the time you're designing, developing, and testing it, you must make and keep a personal commitment to finishing it—or, if necessary, canceling it and starting over. A long time ago I heard a saying that has stuck with me: "Anything finished is better than *everything* unfinished." This includes your unfinished game.

Any game that's for sale or that can be played for free on a website, no matter how limited and terribly made, is better than the super-amazing idea you have in your head—*just because that game exists and your idea does not*. If you want your game to be awesome, you have to make it real. And the only way to make it real is to design it, develop it, and ultimately *finish it.*

The most difficult parts of game development are not in the early conceptual stages. Ideas are easy, numerous, and (much to the dismay of many inexperienced designers) not worth anything on their own. Coming up with a full game concept may tax your creativity, but this part of the process is in many ways the most free and fun. The difficult times arise late in development, when you might think you're almost done. Then you do your first big playtest of the full game with people who have never seen it (or you) before…and you end up with pages and pages of bugs, criticism, points of confusion, and broken and unbalanced systems. This can be extremely disheartening. You need to push through these times and keep your eye on the goal of finishing the game. This is where having a cohesive concept and team really pay off. You will need to work long hours at fixing seemingly small problems, and these fixes all add up to making the game fully playable by others.

Now, "finish" does not mean "make perfect." No game—or any other creative work—will ever be truly complete in its creator's eyes, much less perfect! But as difficult as it is to do, you need to do the work of designing, developing, and letting others playtest your game. You need to go through the difficult times of developing it, seeing it fail playtests and stage gates, and being refined again and again until you finally have something real.

As soon as you possibly can—as soon as your game is playable and engaging and exciting to players—you need to release it and let it go. You will almost certainly think the game is not ready to be released yet. You may fear finally seeing the game go into the wild. And you might wonder how it can just be over now, after you have worked so hard for so long on it. Once you are into the long haul of development, it can seem strange that the game could be finished. Surely there must be a few more bugs to work on first? When you get to this point, when the playtests are going well, even though you're sure there's more to do, it's time to let it go.

Fortunately, today's technology makes it possible in many cases to continue working on the game after you release it. But to be able to really learn what needs to be refined, you still have to finish the game first—and then let it go to truly see what others beyond a small group of playtesters think of it.

Consider this to be the outermost designer's loop: you will learn lessons from releasing a game and seeing it perform in the market that you could not learn any other way. Once you have gone through the entire process, from the early exciting concept through the valley of the difficulties of development, and finally to the point where your game is "out there," you will finally, truly be a game designer.

Summary

Making your game real requires a great deal of work beyond game design. To start, you must be able to communicate your idea effectively, in settings ranging from an elevator to a board room. You need to be able to pass along your excitement to potential funders, media contacts, and team members. You also need to be able to listen for criticism of your game design as you validate the concept.

You have to appreciate the importance of iterative development, including fast prototyping, frequent playtesting, and stringent stage-gating. This plus an understanding of the phases of game development—the early concept stage, preproduction, production, alpha, and beta—will help you develop your game at a rapid but sustainable pace.

Finally, you need to recognize the difficulty and essential nature of actually finishing your game. The vast majority of good ideas for games never get prototyped. Of those that do, most never actually get finished. The work to getting over that line where other players now have access to your game in final, polished form is extremely difficult and should not be underestimated. At the same time, doing the work is how you advance your experience, skill, understanding, and career as a game designer.

BIBLIOGRAPHY

Achterman, D. 2011. *The Craft of Game Systems*. November 12. Accessed March 1, 2017.
    https://craftofgamesystems.wordpress.com/2011/12/30/system-design-general-guidelines/.

Adams, E., and J. Dormans. 2012. *Game Mechanics: Advanced Game Design*. New Riders Publishing.

Alexander, C. 1979. *The Timeless Way of Building*. Oxford University Press.

Alexander, C., S. Ishikawa, and M. Silverstein. 1977. *A Pattern Language: Towns, Buildings, Construction*.
    Oxford University Press.

Alexander, L. 2014. *A Dark Room's Unique Journey from the Web to iOS*. Accessed March 25, 2017.
    http://www.gamasutra.com/view/news/212230/A_Dark_Rooms_unique_journey_from_the_web_
    to_iOS.php.

—. 2012. *GDC 2012: Sid Meier on How to See Games as Sets of Interesting Decisions*. Accessed 2016.
    http://www.gamasutra.com/view/news/164869/GDC_2012_Sid_Meier_on_how_to_see_games_
    as_sets_of_interesting_decisions.php.

Animal Control Technologies. n.d. *Rabbit Problems in Australia*. Accessed 2016.
    http://www.animalcontrol.com.au/rabbit.htm.

Aristotle. 350 BCE. *Metaphysics*. Accessed September 3, 2017. http://classics.mit.edu/Aristotle/
    metaphysics.8.viii.html.

Armson, R. 2011. *Growing Wings on the Way: Systems Thinking for Messy Situations*. Triarchy Press.

Army Training and Doctrine Command. 1975. *TRADOC Bulletin 2. Soviet ATGMs: Capabilities and
    Countermeasures (Declassified)*. U.S. Army.

Bartle, R. 1996. *Hearts, Clubs, Diamonds, Spades: Players Who Suit MUDs*. Accessed March 20, 2017.
    http://mud.co.uk/richard/hcds.htm.

Bateman, C. 2006. *Mathematics of XP*. August 8. Accessed June 15, 2017. http://onlyagame.typepad.com/
    only_a_game/2006/08/mathematics_of_.html.

Berry, N. 2011. *What Is Your Body Worth?* Accessed September 3, 2017. http://www.datagenetics.com/
    blog/april12011/.

Bertalnaffy, L. 1968. *General System Theory: Foundations, Development, Applications*. Braziller.

Bertalnaffy, L. 1949. "Zu Einer Allgemeinen Systemlehre, Blätter für Deutsche Philosophie, 3/4,"
    Biologia Generalis, 19, 139–164.

Bigart, H. 1962. "A DDT Tale Aids Reds in Vietnam," *New York Times*, February 2, 3.

Birk, M., I. Iacovides, D. Johnson, and R. Mandryk. 2015. "The False Dichotomy Between Positive and
    Negative Affect in Game Play," *Proceedings of CHIPlay*. London.

Bjork, S., and J. Holopainen. 2004. *Patterns in Game Design*. New York: Charles River Media.

Bogost, Ian. 2009. "Persuasive Games: Familiarity, Habituation, and Catchiness." Accessed November
    24, 2016. http://www.gamasutra.com/view/feature/3977/persuasive_games_familiarity_.php.

Booth, J. 2011 *GDC Vault 2011—Prototype Through Production: Pro Guitar in ROCK BAND 3*.
    Accessed September 11, 2017. http://www.gdcvault.com/play/1014382/
    Prototype-Through-Production-Pro-Guitar.

Box, G., and N. Draper. 1987. *Empirical Model-Building and Response Surfaces*. Wiley.

Bretz, R. 1983. *Media for Interactive Communication*. Sage.

Brooks, F. 1995. *The Mythical Man-Month: Essays on Software Engineering*. Addison-Wesley.

Bruins, M. 2009. "The Evolution and Contribution of Plant Breeding to Global Agriculture," *Proceedings
    of the Second World Seed Conference*. Accessed September 3, 2017. http://www.fao.org/
    docrep/014/am490e/am490e01.pdf.

Bura, S. 2008. *Emotion Engineering in Videogames.* Accessed July 28, 2017. http://www.stephanebura.com/emotion/.

Caillois, R, and M. Barash. 1961. *Man, Play, and Games.* University of Illinois Press.

Capra, F. 2014. *The Systems View of Life: A Unifying Vision.* Cambridge University Press.

—. 1975. *The Tao of Physics.* Shambala Press.

Card, S., T. Moran, and A. Newell. 1983. *The Psychology of Human-Computer Interaction.* Erlbaum.

Case, N. 2017. *Loopy.* Accessed June 6, 2017. ncase.me/loopy.

—. 2014. *Parable of the Polygons.* Accessed March 15, 2017. http://ncase.me/polygons/.

CDC. 2017. *Work Schedules: Shift Work and Long Hours.* Accessed July 10, 2017. https://www.cdc.gov/niosh/topics/workschedules/.

Cheshire, T. 2011. "In Depth: How Rovio Made *Angry Birds* a Winner (and What's Next)," *Wired,* March 7. Accessed February 2, 2017. http://www.wired.co.uk/article/how-rovio-made-angry-birds-a-winner.

Cook, D. 2012. *Loops and Arcs.* Accessed February 24, 2017. http://www.lostgarden.com/2012/04/loops-and-arcs.html.

—. 2011a. *Shadow Emotions and Primary Emotions.* Accessed July 28, 2017. http://www.lostgarden.com/2011/07/shadow-emotions-and-primary-emotions.html.

—. 2011b. *Game Design Logs.* Accessed September 10, 2017. http://www.lostgarden.com/2011/05/game-design-logs.html

—. 2010. *Steambirds: Survival: Goodbye Handcrafted Levels.* Accessed July 27, 2017. http://www.lostgarden.com/2010/12/steambirds-survival-goodbye-handcrafted.html.

—. 2007. *Rockets, Cars, and Gardens: Visualizing Waterfall, Agile, and Stage Gate.* Accessed July 13, 2017. http://www.lostgarden.com/2007/02/rockets-cars-and-gardens-visualizing.html.

Cooke, B. 1988. "The Effects of Rabbit Grazing on Regeneration of Sheoaks, Allocasuarina, Verticilliata, and Saltwater TJ-Trees, Melaleuca Halmaturorum, in the Coorong National Park, South Australia," *Australian Journal of Ecology, 13,* 11–20.

Cookson, B. 2006. *Crossing the River: The History of London's Thames River Bridges from Richmond to the Tower.* Mainstream Publishing.

Costikyan, G. 1994. *I Have No Words and I Must Design.* Accessed 2016. http://www.costik.com/nowords.html.

Crawford, C. 1984. *The Art of Computer Game Design.* McGraw-Hill/Osborne Media.

—. 2010. *The Computer Game Developer's Conference.* Accessed December 24, 2016. http://www.erasmatazz.com/personal/experiences/the-computer-game-developer.html.

Csikszentmihalyi, M. 1990. *Flow: The Psychology of Optimal Experience.* Harper & Row.

Damasio, A. 2003. *Looking for Spinoza: Joy, Sorrow, and the Feeling Brain.* Harcourt.

Dennet, D. 1995. *Darwin's Dangerous Idea.* Simon & Schuster.

Descartes, R. 1637/2001. *Discourses on Method, Volume V, The Harvard Classics.* Accessed June 10, 2016. http://www.bartleby.com/34/1/5.html.

Dewey, J. 1934. *Art as Experience.* Perigee Books.

Dinar, M., C. Maclellan, A. Danielescu, J. Shah, and P. Langley. 2012. "Beyond Function–Behavior–Structure," *Design Computing and Cognition,* 511–527.

Dmytryshyn, Y. 2014. *App Stickiness and Its Metrics.* Accessed July 28, 2017. https://stanfy.com/blog/app-stickiness-and-its-metrics/.

Dormans, J. n.d. *Machinations.* Accessed June 6, 2017. www.jorisdormans.nl/machinations.

Einstein, A., M. Born, and H. Born. 1971. *The Born-Einstein Letters: Correspondence Between Albert Einstein and Max and Hedwig Born from 1916–1955, with Commentary by Max Born.* Accessed June 10, 2016. https://archive.org/stream/TheBornEinsteinLetters/Born-TheBornEinsteinLetter_djvu.txt.

Ekman, P. 1992. "Facial Expressions of Emotions: New Findings, New Questions," *Psychological Science, 3,* 34–38.

Eldridge, C. 1940. *Eyewitness Account of Tacoma Narrows Bridge.* Accessed September 3, 2017. http://www.wsdot.wa.gov/tnbhistory/people/eyewitness.htm.

Ellenor, G. 2014. *Understanding "Systemic" in Video Game Development.* Accessed December 15, 2017. https://medium.com/@gellenor/understanding-systemic-in-video-game-development-59df3fe1868e.

Fantel, H. 1992. "In the Action with Star Wars Sound," *New York Times,* May 3. Accessed July 9, 2017. http://www.nytimes.com/1992/05/03/arts/home-entertainment-in-the-action-with-star-wars-sound.html.

Fitts, P., and J. Peterson. 1964. "Information Capacity of Discrete Motor Responses," *Journal of Experimental Psychology,* 67(2), 103–112.

Forrester, J. 1971. "Counterintuitive Behavior of Social Systems," *Technology Review, 73*(3), 52–68.

Fuller, B. 1975. *Synergetics: Explorations in the Geometry of Thinking.* Macmillan Publishing Co.

Gabler, K., K. Gray, M. Kucic, and S. Shodhan. 2005. *How to Prototype a Game in Under 7 Days.* Accessed March 10, 2017. http://www.gamasutra.com/view/feature/130848/how_to_prototype_a_game_in_under_7_.php?page=3.

Gambetti, R., and G. Graffigna. 2010. "The Concept of Engagement," *International Journal of Market Research,* 52(6), 801–826.

Game of War—Fire Age. 2017. Accessed March 12, 2017. https://thinkgaming.com/app-sales-data/3352/game-of-war-fire-age/.

Gardner, M. 1970. "Mathematical Games—The Fantastic Combinations of John Conway's New Solitaire Game *Life,*" *Scientific American, 223*, 120–123.

Garneau, P. 2001. *Fourteen Forms of Fun.* Accessed 2017. http://www.gamasutra.com/view/feature/227531/fourteen_forms_of_fun.php.

Gell-Mann, M. 1995. *The Quark and the Jaguar: Adventures in the Simple and the Complex.* Henry Holt and Co.

Gero, J. 1990. "Design Prototypes: A Knowledge Representation Schema for Design," *AI Magazine, 11*(4), 26–36.

Giaime, B. 2015. "Let's Build a Game Economy!" *PAXDev.* Seattle.

Gilbert, M. 2017. *Terrence Mann Shares Industry Wisdom and Vision for Nutmeg Summer Series.* Accessed March 15, 2017. http://dailycampus.com/stories/2017/2/6/terrance-mann-shares-industry-wisdom-and-vision-for-nutmeg-summer-series.

Goel, A., S. Rugaber, and S. Vattam. 2009. "Structure, Behavior, and Function of Complex Systems: The Structure, Behavior, and Function Modeling Language," *Artificial Intelligence for Engineering Design, Analysis and Manufacturing, 23*(1), 23–35.

Greenspan, A. 1996. *Remarks by Chairman Alan Greenspan.* Accessed August 8, 2017. https://www.federalreserve.gov/boarddocs/speeches/1996/19961205.htm.

Grodal, T. 2000. "Video Games and the Pleasure of Control." In D. Zillman and P. Vorderer (eds.), *Media Entertainment: The Psychology of Its Appeal* (pp. 197–213). Lawrence Erlbaum Associates.

Gwiazda, J., E. Ong, R. Held, and F. Thorn. 2000. *Vision: Myopia and Ambient Night-Time Lighting.*

History of CYOA. n.d. Accessed November 24, 2016. http://www.cyoa.com/pages/history-of-cyoa.

Heider, G. 1977. "More about Hull and Koffka. *American Psychologist, 32*(5), 383.

Holland, J. 1998. *Emergence: From Chaos to Order.* Perseus Books .

—. 1995. *Hidden Order: How Adaptation Builds Complexity.* Perseus Books.

Howe, C. 2017. "The Design of Time: Understanding Human Attention and Economies of Engagement," *Game Developer's Conference.* San Francisco.

Huizinga, Johan. 1955. *Homo Ludens, a Study of the Play-Element in Culture.* Perseus Books.

Hunicke, R., M. LeBlanc, and R. Zubek. 2004. *MDA: A Formal Approach to Game Design and Game Research*. Accessed December 20, 2016. http://www.cs.northwestern.edu/~hunicke/pubs/MDA.pdf.

Iberg. 2015. *WaTor—An OpenGL Based Screensaver*. Accessed September 3, 2017. http://www.codeproject.com/Articles/11214/WaTor-An-OpenGL-based-screensaver.

Ioannidis, G. 2008. *Double Pendulum*. http://en.wikipedia.org/wiki/File:DPLE.jpg.

Jobs, S. 1997. *Apple World Wide Developer's Conference Closing Keynote*. Accessed March 23, 2017. https://www.youtube.com/watch?v=GnO7D5UaDig.

Juul, J. 2003. *The Game, the Player, the World: Looking for a Heart of Gameness*. Accessed September 3, 2017. http://ocw.metu.edu.tr/pluginfile.php/4471/mod_resource/content/0/ceit706/week3_new/JesperJuul_GamePlayerWorld.pdf.

Juul, J., and J. Begy. 2016. "Good Feedback for Bad Players? A Preliminary Study of 'Juicy' Interface Feedback," *Proceedings of First Joint FDG/DiGRA Conference*. Dundee.

Kass, S., and K. Bryla. 1995. *Rock Paper Scissors Spock Lizard*. Accessed July 5, 2017. http://www.samkass.com/theories/RPSSL.html.

Kellerman, J., J. Lewis, and J. Laird. 1989. "Looking and Loving: The Effects of Mutual Gaze on Feelings of Romantic Love," *Journal of Research in Personality, 23*(2), 145–161.

Kietzmann, L. 2011. *Half-Minute Halo: An Interview with Jaime Griesemer*. Accessed March 12, 2017. https://www.engadget.com/2011/07/14/half-minute-halo-an-interview-with-jaime-griesemer/.

Koster, R. 2004. *A Theory of Fun for Game Design*. O'Reilly Media.

—. 2012. *Narrative Is Not a Game Mechanic*. Accessed February 24, 2017. http://www.raphkoster.com/2012/01/20/narrative-is-not-a-game-mechanic/.

Krugman, P. 2013. "Reinhart-Rogoff Continued," *New York Times*.

Kuhn, T. 1962. *The Structure of Scientific Revolutions*. University of Chicago Press.

Lane, R. 2015. *Disney/Pixar President Tells BYU How 5 Films Originally "Sucked."* Accessed March 17, 2017. http://utahvalley360.com/2015/01/27/disneypixar-president-tells-byu-4-films-originally-sucked/.

Lantz, F. 2015. *Game Design Advance*. Accessed January 5, 2017. http://gamedesignadvance.com/?p=2995.

Lau, E. 2016. *What Are the Things Required to Become a Hardcore Programmer?* Accessed September 3, 2017. https://www.quora.com/What-are-the-things-required-to-become-a-hardcore-programmer/answer/Edmond-Lau.

Lawrence, D. H. 1915. *The Rainbow*. Modern Library.

Lawrence, D. H., V. de Sola Pinto, and W. Roberts. 1972. *The Complete Poems of D.H. Lawrence*, vol 1. Heinemann Ltd.

Lawrence, D. H. 1928. *The Collected Poems of D.H. Lawrence*. Martin Seeker.

Lazzaro, N. 2004. *The 4 Keys 2 Fun*. Accessed July 28, 2017. http://www.nicolelazzaro.com/the4-keys-to-fun/.

Liddel, H., and Scott R. 1940. *A Greek-English Lexicon*. Oxford University Press.

Lloyd, W. 1833. *Two Lectures on the Checks to Population*. Oxford University Press.

Lotka, A. 1910. "Contribution to the Theory of Periodic Reaction," *Journal of Physical Chemistry, 14*(3), 271–274.

Lovelace, D. 1999. *RPS-101*. Accessed July 4, 2017. http://www.umop.com/rps.htm.

Luhmann, N. 2002, 2013. *Introduction to Systems Theory*. Polity Press.

Luhmann, N. 1997. *Die Gesellschaft der Gesellschaft*. Suhrkamp.

Mackenzie, J. 2002. *Utility and Indifference*. Accessed August 3, 2017. http://www1.udel.edu/johnmack/ncs/utility.html.

MacLulich, D. 1937. "Fluctuations in the Numbers of the Varying Hare (*Lepus americanus*)," *University of Toronto Studies Biological Series, 43*.

Maslow, A. 1968. *Toward a Psychology of Being*. D. Van Nostrand Company.

Master, PDF urist. 2015. *Mysterious Cat Deaths [Online forum comment]*. Accessed 2016.
http://www.bay12forums.com/smf/index.php?topic=154425.0.

Matsalla, R. 2016. *What Are the Hidden Motivations of Gamers?* Accessed March 20, 2017.
https://blog.fyber.com/hidden-motivations-gamers/.

Maturana, H. 1975. "The Organization of the Living: A Theory of the Living Organization," *International Journal of Man–Machine Studies, 7*, 313–332.

Maturana, H., and F. Varela. 1972. *Autopoiesis and Cognition*. Reidek Publishing Company.

—. 1987. *The Tree of Knowledge: The Biological Roots of Human Understanding*. Shambhala/New Science Press.

Mayer, A., J. Dorflinger, S. Rao, and M. Seidenberg. 2004. "Neural Networks Underlying Endogenous and Exogenous Visual–Spatial Orienting," *NeuroImage, 23*(2), 534–541.

McCrae, R., and O. John. 1992. "An Introduction to the Five-Factor Model and Its Applications," *Journal of Personality, 60*(2), 175–215.

McGonigal, J. 2011. *Reality is Broken: Why Games Make Us Better and How They Can Change the World*. London: Penguin Press.

Meadows, D. H., D. L. Meadows, J. Randers, and W. Behrens. 1972. *Limits to Growth: A Report for the Club of Rome's Project on the Predicament of Mankind*. Universe Books.

Meadows, D. 2008. *Thinking in Systems: A Primer*. Chelsea Green Publishing Company.

Mintz, J. 1993. "Fallout from Fire: Chip Prices Soar." *The Washington Post*, July 22.

Mollenkopf, S. 2017. *CES 2017: Steve Mollenkopf and Qualcomm Are Not Just Talking About 5G—They're Making It Happen*. Accessed January 10, 2017. https://www.qualcomm.com/news/onq/2017/01/05/ces-2017-steve-mollenkopf-keynote.

Monbiot, G. 2013. *For More Wonder, Rewild the World*. Accessed September 3, 2017.
https://www.ted.com/talks/george_monbiot_for_more_wonder_rewild_the_world

Morningstar, C., and R. Farmer. 1990. *The Lessons of Lucasfilm's Habitat*. Accessed July 7, 2017.
http://www.fudco.com/chip/lessons.html.

Nagasawa, M., S. Mitsui, S. En, N. Ohtani, M. Ohta, Y. Sakuma, et al. 2015. "Oxytocin-Gaze Positive Loop and the Coevolution of Human–Dog Bonds," *Science, 348*, 333–336.

Newhagen, J. 2004. "Interactivity, Dynamic Symbol Processing, and the Emergence of Content in Human Communication," *The Information Society, 20*, 395–400.

Newton, I. 1687/c1846. *The Mathematical Principles of Natural Philosophy*. Accessed June 10, 2016.
https://archive.org/details/newtonspmathema00newtrich.

Newton, Isaac. c.1687/1974. *Mathematical Papers of Isaac Newton*, vol. 6 (1684–1691). D. Whiteside (ed.). Cambridge University Press.

Nieoullon, A. 2002. "Dopamine and the Regulation of Cognition and Attention," *Progress in Neurobiology, 67*(1), 53–83.

Nisbett, R. 2003. *The Geography of Thought: How Asians and Westerners Think Differently…and Why*. Free Press.

Noda, K. 2008. *Go Strategy*. Accessed 2016. https://www.wikiwand.com/en/Go_strategy.

Norman, D. 1988. *The Design of Everyday Things*. Doubleday.

Norman, D., and S. Draper. 1986. *User-Centered System Design: New Perspectives on Human–Computer Interaction*. L. Erlbaum Associates, Inc.

Novikoff, A. 1945. "The Concept of Integrative Levels and Biology," *Science, 101*, 209–215.

NPS.gov. 2017. *Synchronous Fireflies—Great Smoky Mountains National Park*. Accessed July 24, 2017.
https://www.nps.gov/grsm/learn/nature/fireflies.htm.

Olff, M., J. Frijling, L. Kubzansky, B. Bradley, M. Ellenbogen, C. Cardoso, et al. 2013. "The Role of Oxytocin in Social Bonding, Stress Regulation and Mental Health: An Update on the Moderating Effects of Context and Interindividual Differences," *Psychoneuroendocrinology, 38*, 1883–1984.

Pearson, D. 2013. *Where I'm @: A Brief Look at the Resurgence of Roguelikes.* Accessed March 25, 2017. http://www.gamesindustry.biz/articles/2013-01-30-where-im-a-brief-look-at-the-resurgence-of-roguelikes.

Pecorella, A. 2015. *GDC Vault 2015—Idle Game Mechanics and Monetization of Self-Playing Games.* Accessed June 29, 2017. http://www.gdcvault.com/play/1022065/Idle-Games-The-Mechanics-and.

Piccione, P. 1980. "In Search of the Meaning of Senet," *Archeology,* July–August, 55–58.

Poincare, H. 1901. *La Science et l'Hypothese.* E. Flamarion.

Polansky, L. 2015. *Sufficiently Human.* Accessed December 29, 2016. http://sufficientlyhuman.com/archives/1008.

Popovich, N. 2017. *A Thousand Tiny Tales: Emergent Storytelling in Slime Rancher.* Accessed June 1, 2017. http://www.gdcvault.com/play/1024296/A-Thousand-Tiny-Tales-Emergent.

Quinn, G., C. Maguire, M. Shin, and R. Stone. 1999. "Myopia and Ambient Light at Night," *Nature, 399,* 113–114.

Rafaeli, S. 1988. "Interactivity: From New Media to Communication." In R. P. Hawkins, J. M. Weimann and S. Pingree (eds.), *Advancing Communication Science: Merging Mass and Interpersonal Process* (pp. 110–134). Sage.

Raleigh, M., M. McGuire, G. Brammer, D. Pollack, and A. Yuwiler. 1991. "Serotonergic Mechanisms Promote Dominance Acquisition in Adult Male Vervet Monkeys," *Brain Research, 559*(2): 181–190.

Reilly, C. 2017. *Qualcomm Says 5G Is the Biggest Thing Since Electricity.* Accessed January 10, 2017. https://www.cnet.com/news/qualcomm-ces-2017-keynote-5g-is-the-biggest-thing-since-electricity/?ftag=COS-05-10-aa0a&linkId=33111098.

Reinhart, C., and K. Rogoff. 2010. "Growth in a Time of Debt," *American Economic Review: Papers & Proceedings, 100,* 110–134. Accessed 2016. http://online.wsj.com/public/resources/documents/AER0413.pdf.

Reynolds, C. 1987. "Flocks, Herds, and Schools: A Distributed Behavioral Model." *Computer Graphics, 21*(4), 25–34.

Rollings, A., and D. Morris. 2000. *Game Architecture and Design.* Coriolis.

Routledge, R. 1881. *Discoveries & Inventions of the Nineteenth Century,* 5th ed. George Routledge and Sons.

Russell, J. 1980. "A Circumplex Model of Affect," *Journal of Personality and Social Psychology, 39,* 1161–1178.

Russell, J., M. Lewicka, and T. Nitt. 1989. "A Cross-Cultural Study of a Circumplex Model of Affect," *Journal of Personality and Social Psychology, 57,* 848–856.

Salen, K., and E. Zimmerman. 2003. *Rules of Play—Game Design Fundamentals.* MIT Press.

Schaufeli, W., M. Salanova, V. Gonzales-Roma, and A. Bakker. 2002. "The Measurement of Engagement and Burnout: A Two Sample Confirmatory Factor Analytical Approach," *Journal of Happiness Studies, 3*(1), 71–92.

Schelling, T. 1969. "Models of Segregation," *American Economic Review, 59*(2), 488–493.

Scheytt, P. 2012. *Boids 3D.* Accessed 12 7, 2016. https://vvvv.org/contribution/boids-3d.

Schreiber, I. 2010. *Game Balance Concepts.* Accessed July 4, 2017. https://gamebalanceconcepts.wordpress.com/2010/07/21/level-3-transitive-mechanics-and-cost-curves/.

Sellers, M. 2013. "Toward a Comprehensive Theory of Emotion for Biological and Artificial Agents," *Biologically Inspired Cognitive Architectures, 4,* 3–26.

Sellers, M. 2012. *What Are Some of the Most Interesting or Shocking Things Americans Believe About Themselves or Their Country?"* Accessed 2016. https://www.quora.com/What-are-some-of-the-most-interesting-or-shocking-things-Americans-believe-about-themselves-or-their-country/answer/Mike-Sellers.

Selvin, S. 1975. "A Problem in Probability [letter to the editor]," *American Statistician, 29*(1), 67.

Sempercon. 2014. *What Key Catalyst Is Driving Growth of the Internet of Everything?* Accessed September 3, 2017. http://www.sempercon.com/news/key-catalyst-driving-growth-internet-everything/.

Senge, P. 1990. *The Fifth Discipline.* Doubleday/Currency.

Seong, M. 2000. *Diamond Sutra: Transforming the Way We Perceive the World.* Wisdom Publications.

Sicart, M. 2008. "Defining Game Mechanics," *Game Studies, 8*(2).

Siebert, H. 2001. *Der Kobra-Effekt, Wie Man Irrwege der Wirtschaftspolitik Vermeidet.* Deutsche Verlags-Anstalt.

Simkin, M. 1992. *Individual Rights* Accessed May 5, 2017. http://articles.latimes.com/1992-01-12/local/me-358_1_jail-tax-individual-rights-san-diego.

Simler, K. 2014. *Your Oddly Shaped Mind.* Accessed September 3, 2017. http://www.meltingasphalt.com/the-aesthetics-of-personal-identity-mind/.

Simpson, Z. n.d. *The In-game Economics of Ultima Online.* Accessed September 3, 2017. http://www.mine-control.com/zack/uoecon/slides.html.

Sinervo, B., and C. Lively. 1996. "The Rock-Paper-Scissors Game and the Evolution of Alternative Male Strategies," *Nature, 340,* 240-243. Accessed July 3, 2017. http://bio.research.ucsc.edu/~barrylab/lizardland/male_lizards.overview.html.

Smuts, J. 1927. *Holism and Evolution,* 2nd ed. Macmillan and Co.

The State Barrier Fence of Western Australia. n.d. Accessed 2016. http://pandora.nla.gov.au/pan/43156/20040709-0000/agspsrv34.agric.wa.gov.au/programs/app/barrier/history.htm.

Sundar, S. 2004. "Theorizing Interactivity's Effects," *The Information Society, 20,* 385–389.

Sweller, J. 1988. "Cognitive Load During Problem Solving: Effects on Learning," *Cognitive Science, 12*(2), 257–285.

Swink, S. 2009. *Game Feel.* Morgan Kaufmann.

Taplin, J. 2017. *Move Fast and Break Things: How Facebook, Google, and Amazon Cornered Culture and Undermined Democracy.* Little, Brown and Company.

Teknibas, K., M. Gresalfi, K. Peppler, and R. Santo. 2014. *Gaming the System: Designing with the Gamestar Mechanic.* MIT Press.

Thoren, V. 1989. "Tycho Brahe." In C. Wilson and R. Taton (eds.), *Planetary Astronomy from the Renaissance to the Rise of Astrophysics* (pp. 3–21). Cambridge University Press.

Todd, D. 2007. *Game Design: From Blue Sky to Green Light.* AK Peters, Ltd.

Totilo, S. 2011. *Kotaku.* Accessed January 3, 2017. http://kotaku.com/5780082/the-maker-of-mario-kart-justifies-the-blue-shell.

Tozour, P., et al. 2014. *The Game Outcomes Project.* Accessed July 8, 2017. http://www.gamasutra.com/blogs/PaulTozour/20141216/232023/The_Game_Outcomes_Project_Part_1_The_Best_and_the_Rest.php.

Turner, M. 2016. *This Is the Best Research We've Seen on the State of the US Consumer, and It Makes for Grim Reading.* Accessed September 3, 2017. http://businessinsider.com/ubs-credit-note-us-consumer-2016-6.

U.S. Department of Education and U.S. Department of Labor. 1991. *What Work Requires of Schools: Secretary's Commission on Achieving Necessary Skills Report for America 2000.* U.S. Department of Labor.

Van Der Post, L. 1977. *Jung and the Story of Our Time.* Vintage Books.

Vigen, T. 2015. *Spurious Correlations.* Accessed September 3, 2017. http://www.tylervigen.com/spurious-correlations.

Volterra, V. 1926. "Fluctuations in the Abundance of a Species Considered Mathematically," *Nature, 188,* 558–560.

Wallace, D. 2014. *This Is Water*. Accessed September 3, 2017. https://vimeo.com/188418265.

Walum, H., L. Westberg, S. Henningsson, J. Neiderhiser, D. Reiss, W. Igl, J. Ganiban, et al. 2008. "Genetic Variation in the Vasopressin Receptor 1a Gene (AVPR1A) Associates with Pair-Bonding Behavior in Humans," *Proceedings of the National Academy of Sciences of the United States of America, 105*(37), 14153–14156.

Waters, H. 2010. "Now in 3-D: The Shape of Krill and Fish Schools," *Scientific American*. Accessed December 7, 2016. https://blogs.scientificamerican.com/guest-blog/now-in-3-d-the-shape-of-krill-and-fish-schools/.

Weinberger, D. 2002. *Small Pieces Loosely Joined: A Unified Theory of the Web*. Perseus Publishing.

Wertheimer, M. 1923. "Laws of Organization of Perceptual Forms (*Unterschungen zur Lehre von der Gestalt*)." In W. Ellis (ed.), *A Sourcebook of Gestalt Psychology* (pp. 310–350). Routledge.

White, C. 2008. *Anne Conway: Reverberations from a Mystical Naturalism*. State University of New York Press.

Wiener, N. 1948. *Cybernetics: Or the Control and Communication in the Animal and the Machine*. MIT Press.

Wikipedia. 2009. *Double Pendulum*. Accessed September 3, 2017. https://en.wikipedia.org/wiki/Double_pendulum.

Wilensky, U. 1999. *NetLogo*. Accessed June 1, 2017. http://ccl.northwestern.edu/netlogo.

Wilensky, U., and M. Resnick. 1999. "Thinking in Levels: A Dynamic Systems Approach to Making Sense of the World," *Journal of Science Education and Technology, 8*, 3–19.

Winter, J. 2010. *21 Types of Fun—What's Yours?* Accessed 2017. http://www.managementexchange.com/hack/21-types-fun-whats-yours.

Wittgenstein, L. 1958. *Philosophical Investigations*. Basil Blackwell.

Wohlwend, G. 2017. *Tumbleseed Postmortem*. Accessed June 29, 2017. http://aeiowu.com/writing/tumbleseed/.

Wolf, M., and B. Perron. 2003. *The Video Game Theory Reader*. Routledge.

Woodward, M. 2017. *Balancing the Economy for Albion Online*. Accessed July 7, 2017. http://www.gdcvault.com/play/1024070/Balancing-the-Economy-for-Albion.

WoWWiki. n.d. Accessed July 6, 2017. http://wowwiki.wikia.com/wiki/Formulas:XP_To_Level.

Yantis, S., and J. Jonides. 1990. "Abrupt Visual Onsets and Selective Attention: Voluntary Versus Automatic Allocation," *Journal of Experimental Psychology: Human Perception and Performance, 16*, 121–134.

Yee, N. 2016a. *7 Things We Learned About Primary Gaming Motivations from over 250,000 Gamers*. Accessed March 10, 2017. http://quanticfoundry.com/2016/12/15/primary-motivations/.

—. 2016b. *Gaming Motivations Align with Personality Traits*. Accessed March 20, 2017. http://quanticfoundry.com/2016/01/05/personality-correlates/.

—. 2017. *GDC 2017 Talk Slides*. Accessed March 20, 2017. http://quanticfoundry.com/gdc2017/.

Yerkes, R., and Dodson, J. 1908. "The Relation of Strength of Stimulus to Rapidity of Habit-Formation," *Journal of Comparative Neurology and Psychology, 18*, 459–482.

Zald, D., I. Boileau, W. El-Dearedy, R. Gunn, F. McGlone, G. Dichter, and A. Dagher. 2004. "Dopamine Transmission in the Human Striatum During Monetary Reward Tasks," *Journal of Neuroscience, 24*(17), 4105–4112.

INDEX

Numbers

3-door problem, 307–309
5G networking, 34

A

absorption, 134
acquisition funnel, 350–351
acquisition of players, 350–351
action games, 197
action/feedback interactivity, 138–139
    moment-to-moment gameplay, 141
    present-tense action, 139
    reflexive attention, 139
    stress and reward of fast action, 139–141
action-social motivations, 201
active opponents, 109
adaptability, 51, 82
ad-supported games, 211
Adventure Capitalist, 247, 325
adventure games, 197
aesthetics, MDA (Mechanics-Dynamics-
    Aesthetics) framework, 92–93
affordance, 131
agency (player), 100
Agile, 400–401
agon games, 91
agreeableness, 202
Albion Online, 344–345
alea games, 91
Alexander, Christopher, 32, 46–47, 60, 81
alpha milestone, 405–406
analog prototypes, 387
analytical balance, 299, 348
    analytics-driven design, 301
    analytics-informed design, 301
    cautions about, 301
    player behavior data
        acquisition and first experience, 350–351
        community, 354
        conversion, 352–353
        retention, 351–352
        usage, 353–354
    player cohorts, 349–350
    player information, collecting, 349
    sample size and information distortion,
        301–302
    Tumbleseed example, 299–301
analytics
    analysis from systems view, 182–184
    analytical balance, 299, 348
        analytics-driven design, 301
        analytics-informed design, 301
        cautions about, 301
        player behavior data, 350–354
        player cohorts, 349–350
        player information, collecting, 349
        *sample size and information distortion,
            301–302*
        Tumbleseed example, 299–301
    hypothesis-driven analysis, 17
    production analytics, 404–405
analytics-driven design, 301
analytics-informed design, 301
Angry Birds, 172, 188
Antichamber, 100
Apache OpenOffice, 261
APs (associate producers), 366–367
arbitrage, 342–344
architectural game elements, 111–112
    autotelic experience, 114–115
    content and systems, 112
        balancing, 114
        content-driven games, 112–113
        systemic games, 113–114
    meaning, 116–117
    narrative, 115–116
    themes, 116–117
architecture of companies, 364–365
Aristotle, 22, 46, 60, 96
arousal, 129–130, 132–133, 148